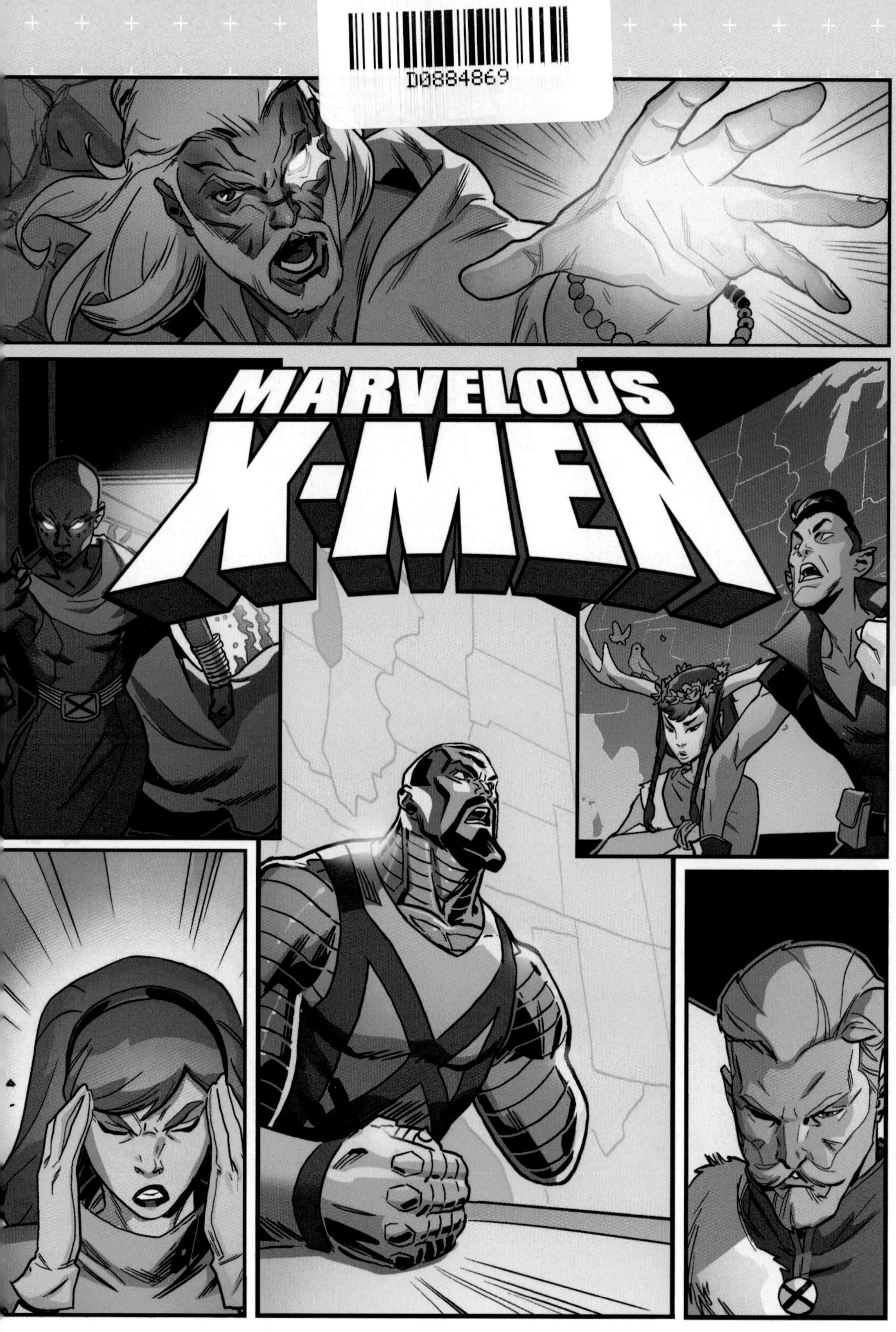
MARVELOUS
X-MEN

Welcome to a perfect world.
Everyone is a mutant — special, powerful, individual.
No more strife, oppression or dependence.
The Age of X-Man: a dream made real.
A dream that must be protected...at any cost.

The Marvelous X-Men — Colossus, Storm, Magneto, Nature Girl, X-23, Nightcrawler, Jean Grey and X-Man — are the planet's first line of defense. Using their unique abilities to keep the world safe, they are adored...as they should be.

MARVELOUS X-MEN

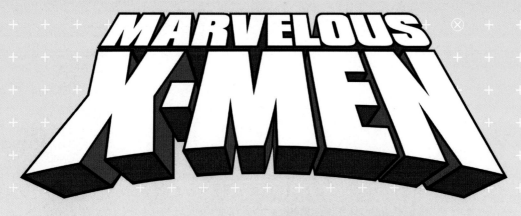

WRITERS **ZAC THOMPSON**
& **LONNIE NADLER**

AGE OF X-MAN ALPHA #1

ARTIST **RAMON ROSANAS**
COLOR ARTIST **TRÍONA FARRELL**
LETTERER **VC's CLAYTON COWLES**

THE MARVELOUS X-MEN #1-5

ARTIST **MARCO FAILLA**
COLOR ARTIST **MATT MILLA**
LETTERER **VC's JOE CARAMAGNA**

AGE OF X-MAN OMEGA #1

ARTIST **SIMONE BUONFANTINO**
COLOR ARTIST **TRÍONA FARRELL**
LETTERER **VC's CLAYTON COWLES**

COVER ART **PHIL NOTO**
ASSISTANT EDITOR **ANNALISE BISSA**
EDITOR **JORDAN D. WHITE**

COLLECTION EDITOR **JENNIFER GRÜNWALD**
ASSOCIATE MANAGING EDITOR **KATERI WOODY**
VP PRODUCTION & SPECIAL PROJECTS **JEFF YOUNGQUIST**
CAITLIN O'CONNELL ASSISTANT EDITOR
MARK D. BEAZLEY EDITOR, SPECIAL PROJECTS
JAY BOWEN BOOK DESIGNER

SVP PRINT, SALES & MARKETING **DAVID GABRIEL**
EDITOR IN CHIEF **C.B. CEBULSKI**
PRESIDENT **DAN BUCKLEY**
SVEN LARSEN DIRECTOR, LICENSED PUBLISHING
JOE QUESADA CHIEF CREATIVE OFFICER
ALAN FINE EXECUTIVE PRODUCER

AGE OF X-MAN: THE MARVELOUS X-MEN. Contains material originally published in magazine form as AGE OF X-MAN ALPHA #1, AGE OF X-MAN: THE MARVELOUS X-MEN #1-5 and AGE OF X-MAN OMEGA #1. First printing 2019. ISBN 978-1-302-91575-9. Published by MARVEL WORLDWIDE, INC., a subsidiary of MARVEL ENTERTAINMENT, LLC. OFFICE OF PUBLICATION: 135 West 50th Street, New York, NY 10020. **Printed in the U.S.A.** DAN BUCKLEY, President, Marvel Entertainment; JOHN NEE, Publisher; JOE QUESADA, Chief Creative Officer; TOM BREVOORT, SVP of Publishing; DAVID BOGART, Associate Publisher & SVP of Talent Affairs; DAVID GABRIEL, SVP of Sales & Marketing, Publishing; JEFF YOUNGQUIST, VP of Production & Special Projects; DAN CARR, Executive Director of Publishing Technology; ALEX MORALES, Director of Publishing Operations; DAN EDINGTON, Managing Editor; SUSAN CRESPI, Production Manager; STAN LEE, Chairman Emeritus. For information regarding advertising in Marvel Comics or on Marvel.com, please contact Vit DeBellis, Custom Solutions & Integrated Advertising Manager, at vdebellis@marvel.com. For Marvel subscription inquiries, please call 888-511-5480. **Manufactured between 6/28/2019 and 7/30/2019 by LSC COMMUNICATIONS INC., KENDALLVILLE, IN, USA.**

10 9 8 7 6 5 4 3 2 1

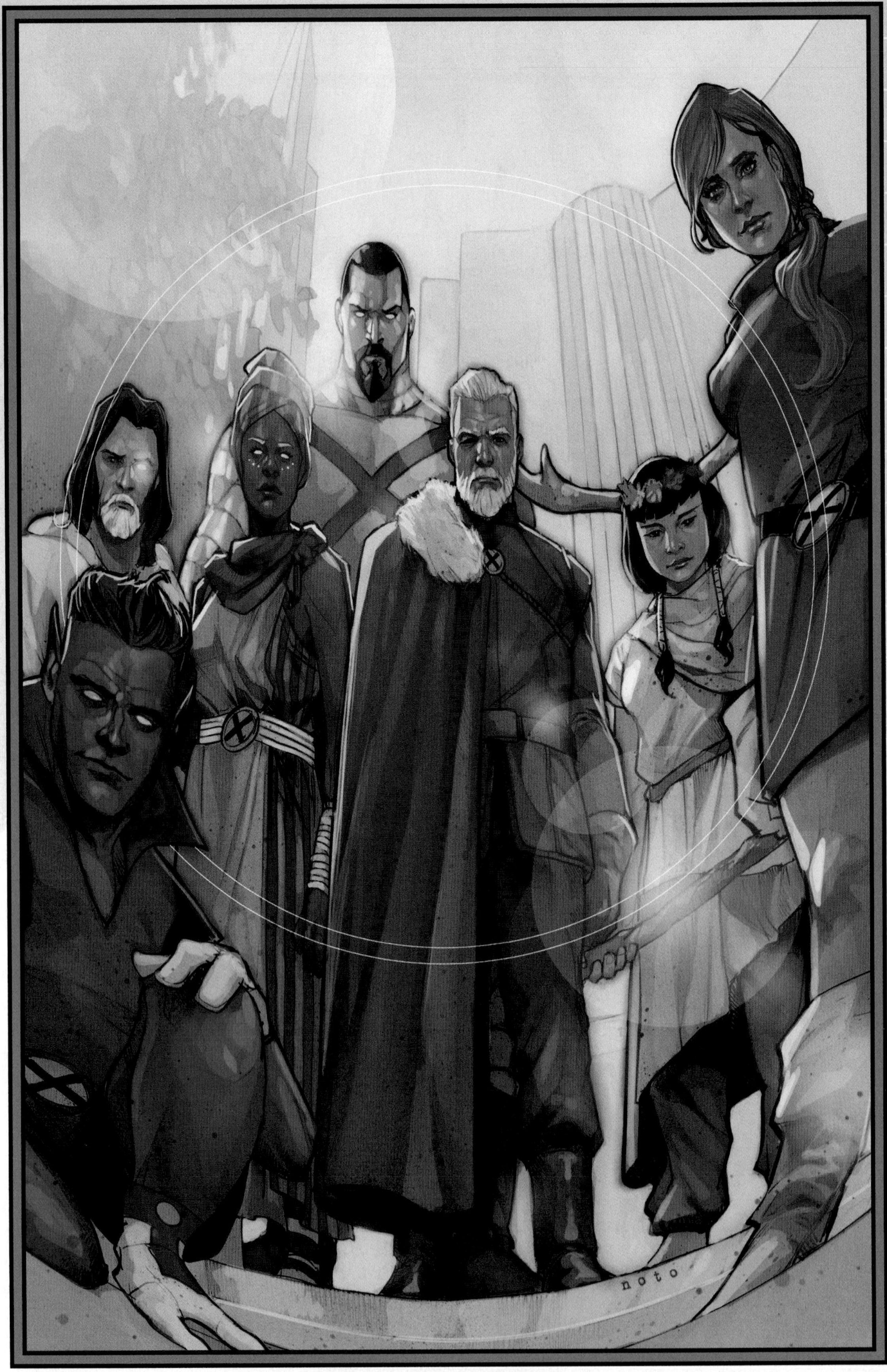
noto

AGE OF X-MAN ALPHA #1

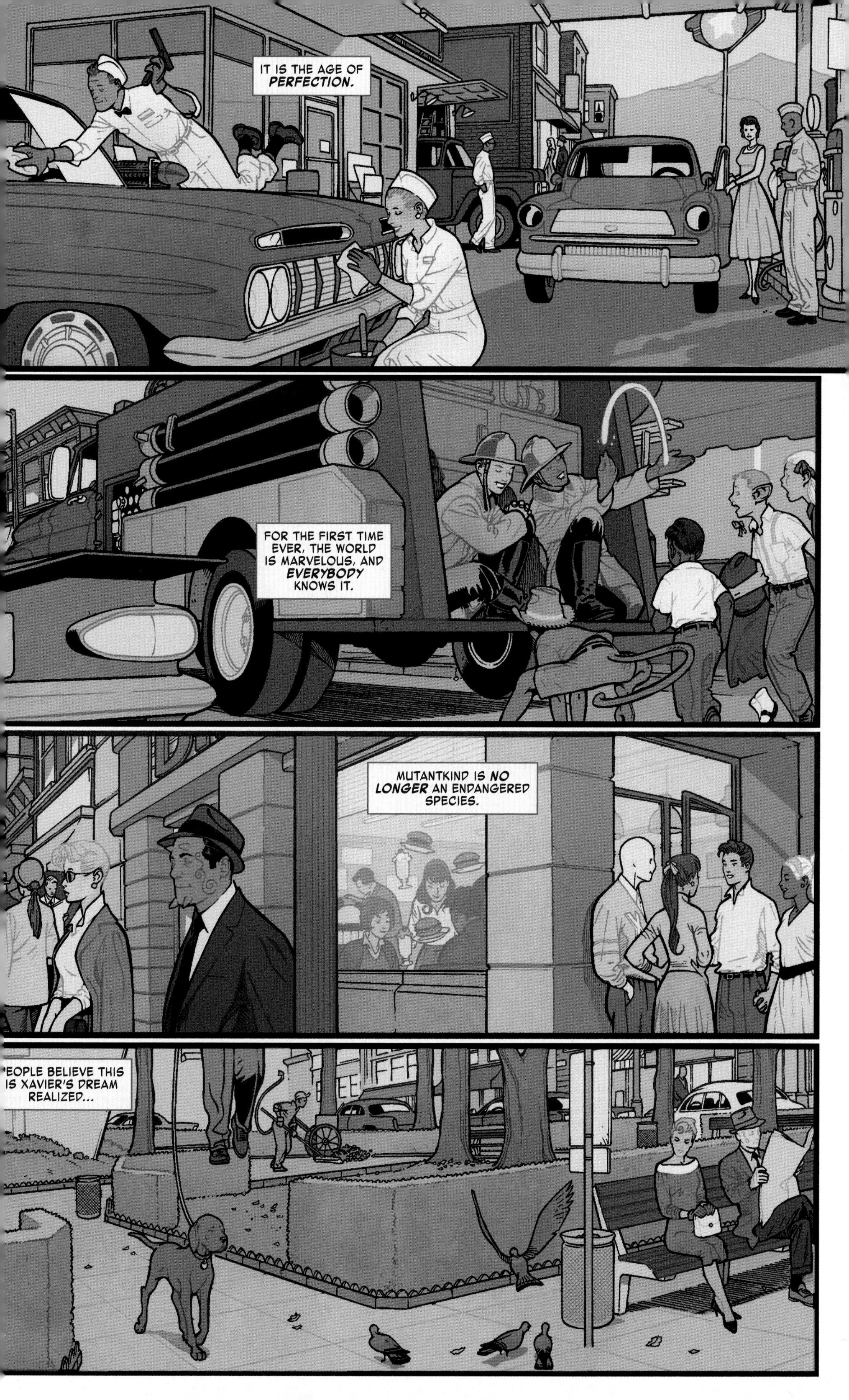
IT IS THE AGE OF PERFECTION.
FOR THE FIRST TIME EVER, THE WORLD IS MARVELOUS, AND EVERYBODY KNOWS IT.
MUTANTKIND IS NO LONGER AN ENDANGERED SPECIES.
PEOPLE BELIEVE THIS IS XAVIER'S DREAM REALIZED...

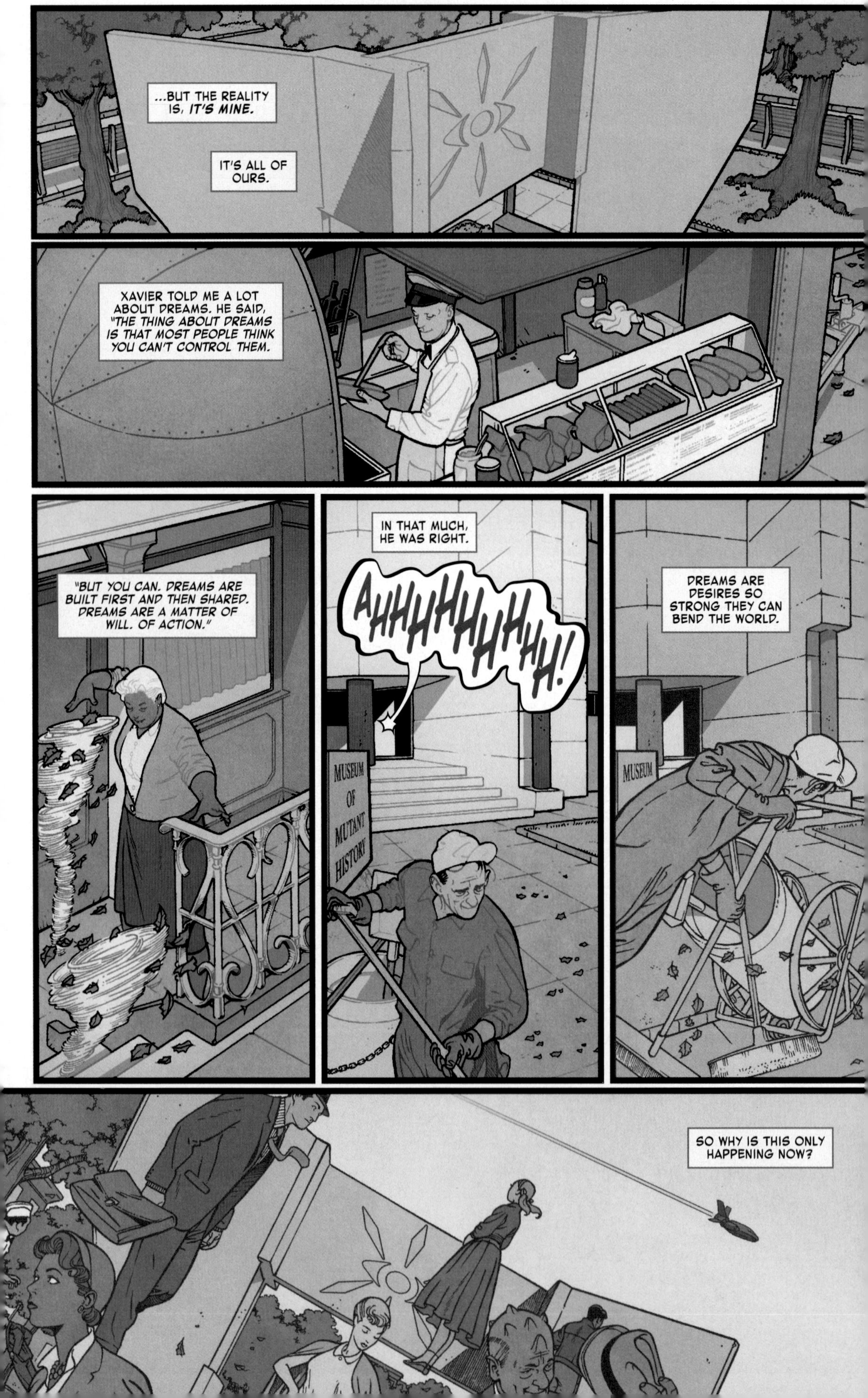
...BUT THE REALITY IS, *IT'S MINE.*
IT'S ALL OF OURS.
XAVIER TOLD ME A LOT ABOUT DREAMS. HE SAID, "THE THING ABOUT DREAMS IS THAT MOST PEOPLE THINK YOU CAN'T CONTROL THEM.
"BUT YOU CAN. DREAMS ARE BUILT FIRST AND THEN SHARED. DREAMS ARE A MATTER OF WILL. OF ACTION."
IN THAT MUCH, HE WAS RIGHT.
AHHHHHHHHHH!
MUSEUM OF MUTANT HISTORY
DREAMS ARE DESIRES SO STRONG THEY CAN BEND THE WORLD.
MUSEUM
SO WHY IS THIS ONLY HAPPENING NOW?

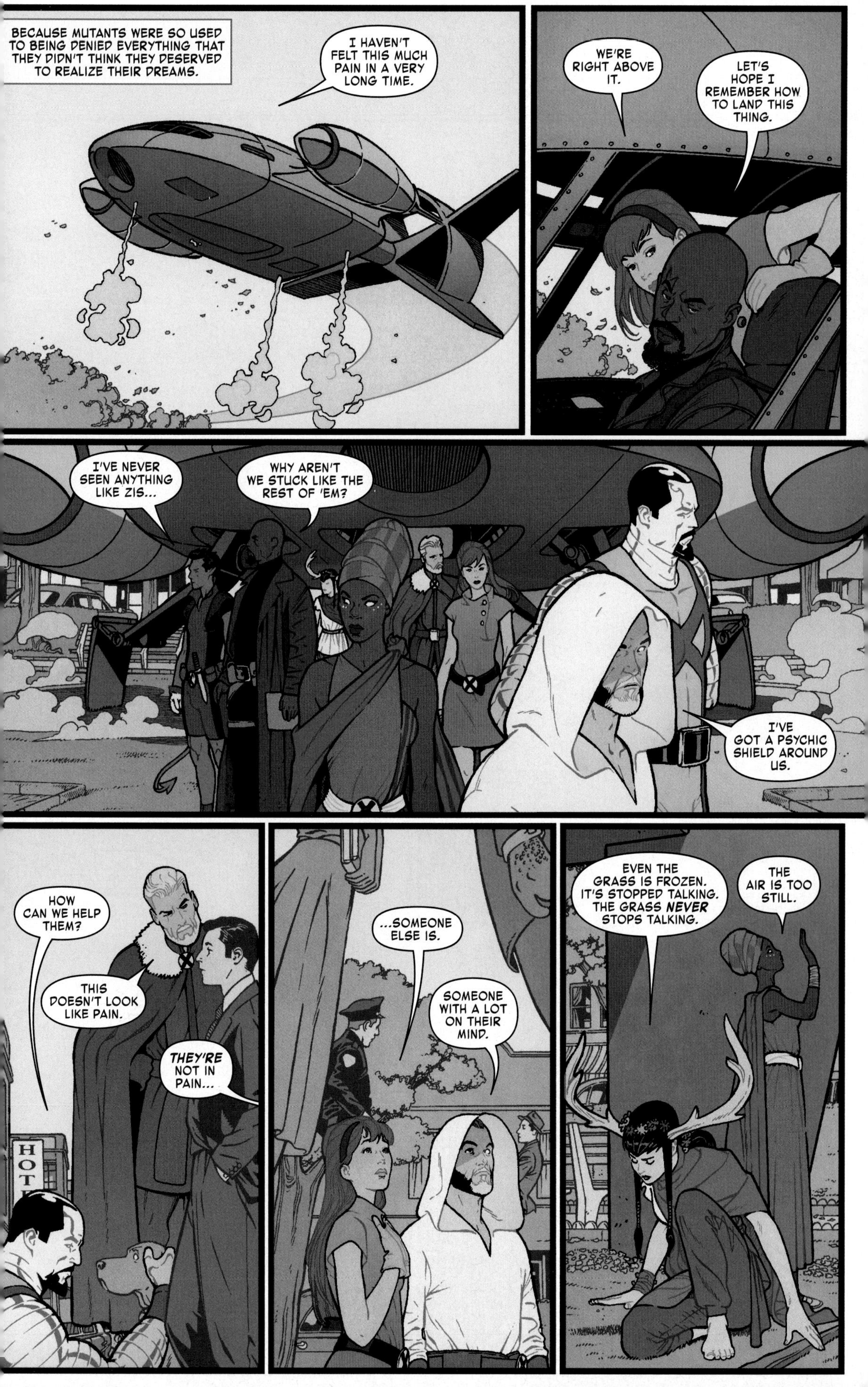
BECAUSE MUTANTS WERE SO USED TO BEING DENIED EVERYTHING THAT THEY DIDN'T THINK THEY DESERVED TO REALIZE THEIR DREAMS.
I HAVEN'T FELT THIS MUCH PAIN IN A VERY LONG TIME.
WE'RE RIGHT ABOVE IT.
LET'S HOPE I REMEMBER HOW TO LAND THIS THING.
I'VE NEVER SEEN ANYTHING LIKE ZIS...
WHY AREN'T WE STUCK LIKE THE REST OF 'EM?
I'VE GOT A PSYCHIC SHIELD AROUND US.
HOW CAN WE HELP THEM?
THIS DOESN'T LOOK LIKE PAIN.
THEY'RE NOT IN PAIN...
...SOMEONE ELSE IS.
SOMEONE WITH A LOT ON THEIR MIND.
EVEN THE GRASS IS FROZEN. IT'S STOPPED TALKING. THE GRASS *NEVER* STOPS TALKING.
THE AIR IS TOO STILL.
HOT

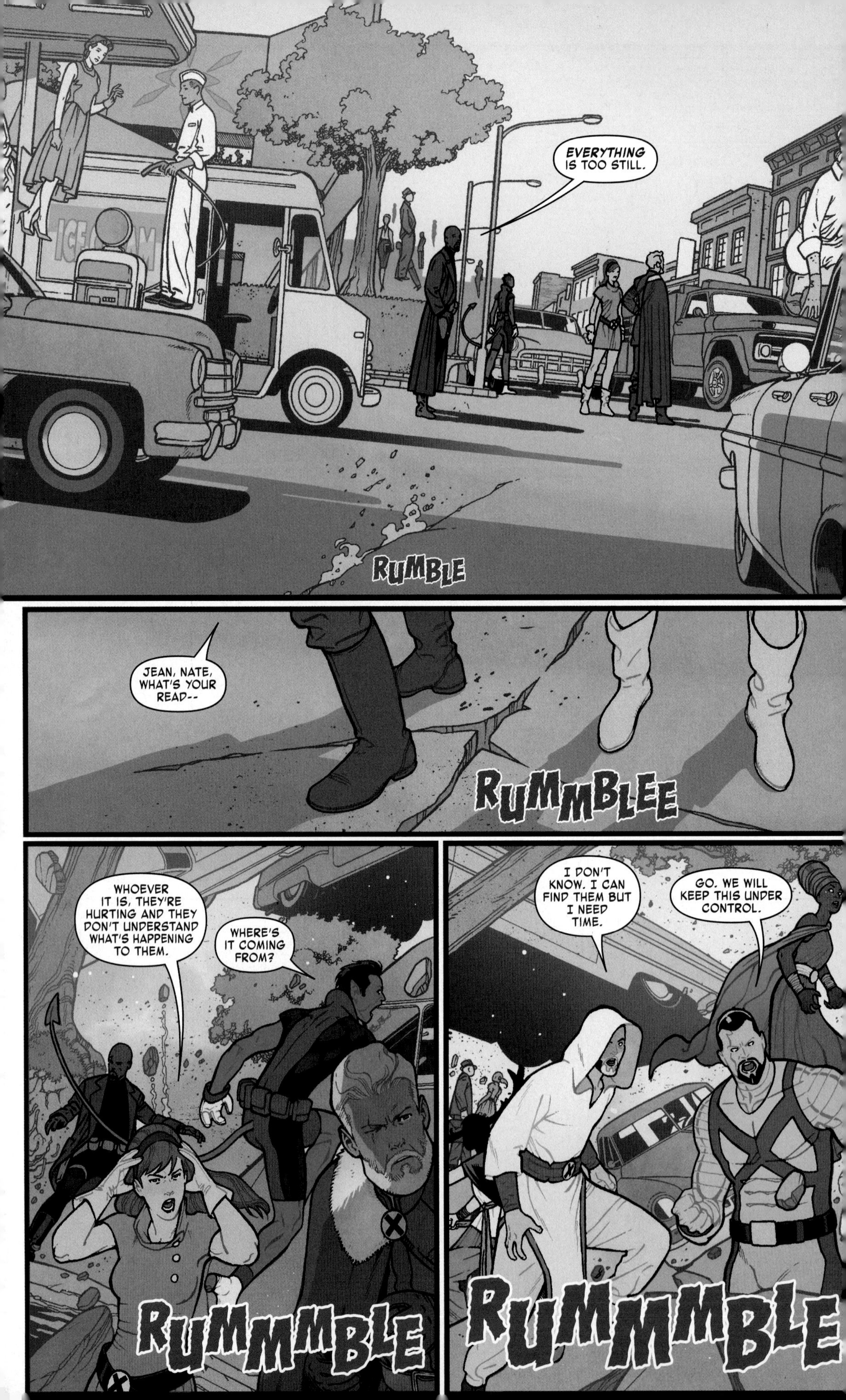
ICE CREAM
EVERYTHING IS TOO STILL.
RUMBLE
JEAN, NATE, WHAT'S YOUR READ--
RUMMBLEE
WHOEVER IT IS, THEY'RE HURTING AND THEY DON'T UNDERSTAND WHAT'S HAPPENING TO THEM.
WHERE'S IT COMING FROM?
RUMMMBLE
I DON'T KNOW. I CAN FIND THEM BUT I NEED TIME.
GO. WE WILL KEEP THIS UNDER CONTROL.
RUMMMBLE

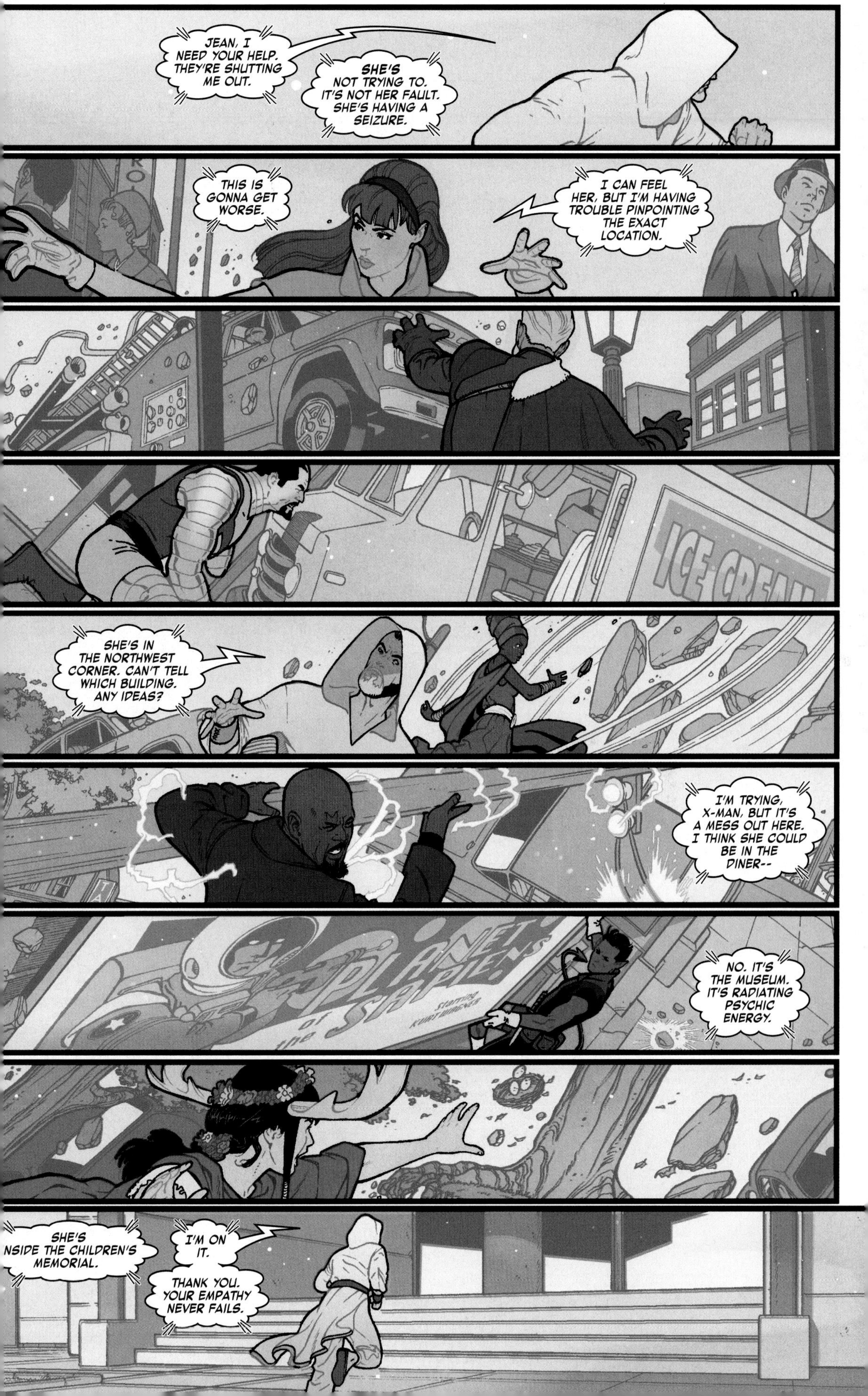
JEAN, I NEED YOUR HELP. THEY'RE SHUTTING ME OUT.
SHE'S NOT TRYING TO. IT'S NOT HER FAULT. SHE'S HAVING A SEIZURE.
THIS IS GONNA GET WORSE.
I CAN FEEL HER, BUT I'M HAVING TROUBLE PINPOINTING THE EXACT LOCATION.
ICE CREAM
SHE'S IN THE NORTHWEST CORNER. CAN'T TELL WHICH BUILDING. ANY IDEAS?
I'M TRYING, X-MAN, BUT IT'S A MESS OUT HERE. I THINK SHE COULD BE IN THE DINER--
NO. IT'S THE MUSEUM. IT'S RADIATING PSYCHIC ENERGY.
SHE'S NSIDE THE CHILDREN'S MEMORIAL.
I'M ON IT.
THANK YOU. YOUR EMPATHY NEVER FAILS.

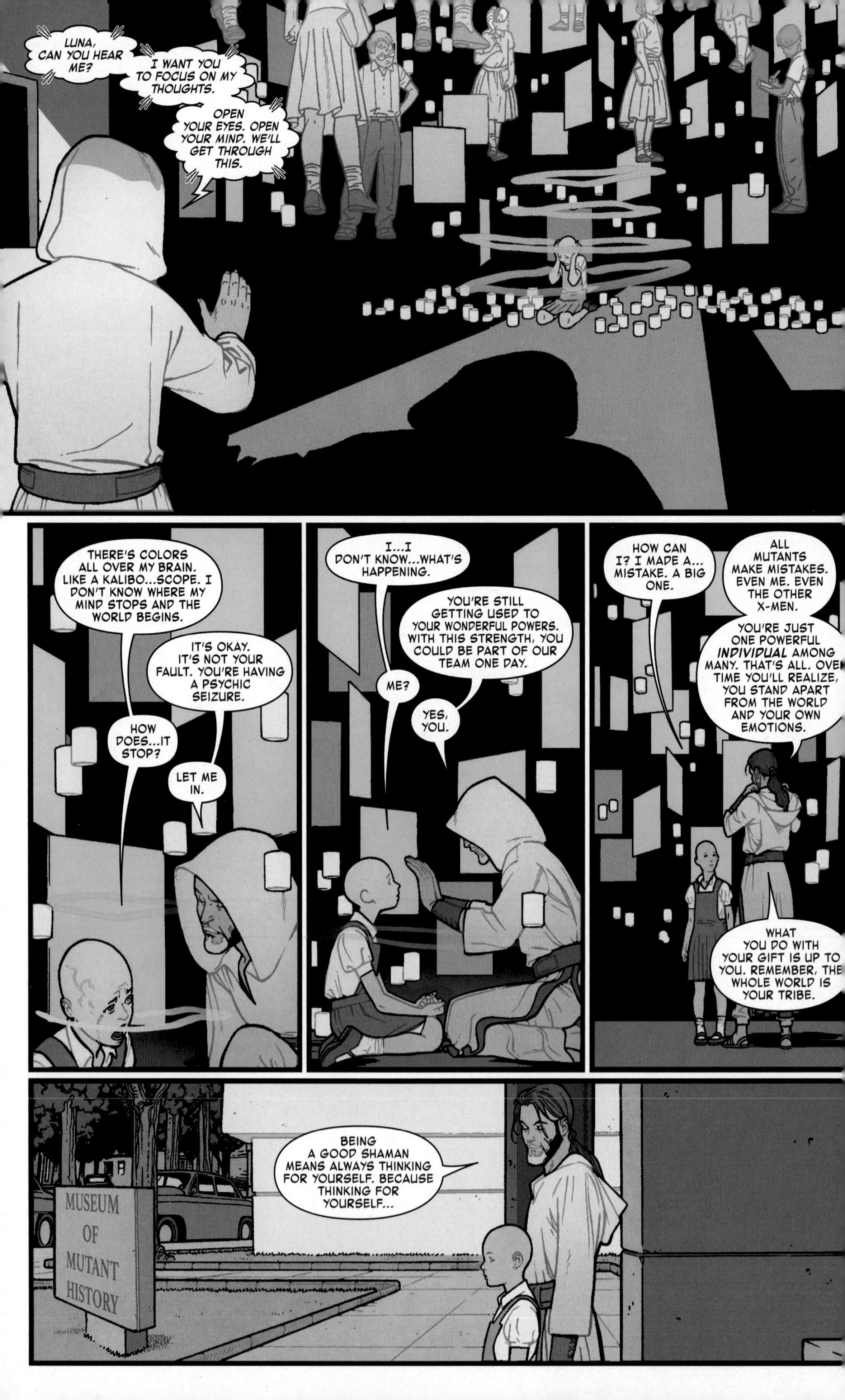
LUNA, CAN YOU HEAR ME?
I WANT YOU TO FOCUS ON MY THOUGHTS.
OPEN YOUR EYES. OPEN YOUR MIND. WE'LL GET THROUGH THIS.
THERE'S COLORS ALL OVER MY BRAIN. LIKE A KALIBO...SCOPE. I DON'T KNOW WHERE MY MIND STOPS AND THE WORLD BEGINS.
IT'S OKAY. IT'S NOT YOUR FAULT. YOU'RE HAVING A PSYCHIC SEIZURE.
HOW DOES...IT STOP?
LET ME IN.
I...I DON'T KNOW...WHAT'S HAPPENING.
YOU'RE STILL GETTING USED TO YOUR WONDERFUL POWERS. WITH THIS STRENGTH, YOU COULD BE PART OF OUR TEAM ONE DAY.
ME?
YES, YOU.
HOW CAN I? I MADE A... MISTAKE. A BIG ONE.
ALL MUTANTS MAKE MISTAKES. EVEN ME. EVEN THE OTHER X-MEN.
YOU'RE JUST ONE POWERFUL *INDIVIDUAL* AMONG MANY. THAT'S ALL. OVE TIME YOU'LL REALIZE, YOU STAND APART FROM THE WORLD AND YOUR OWN EMOTIONS.
WHAT YOU DO WITH YOUR GIFT IS UP TO YOU. REMEMBER, THE WHOLE WORLD IS YOUR TRIBE.
MUSEUM OF MUTANT HISTORY
BEING A GOOD SHAMAN MEANS ALWAYS THINKING FOR YOURSELF. BECAUSE THINKING FOR YOURSELF...

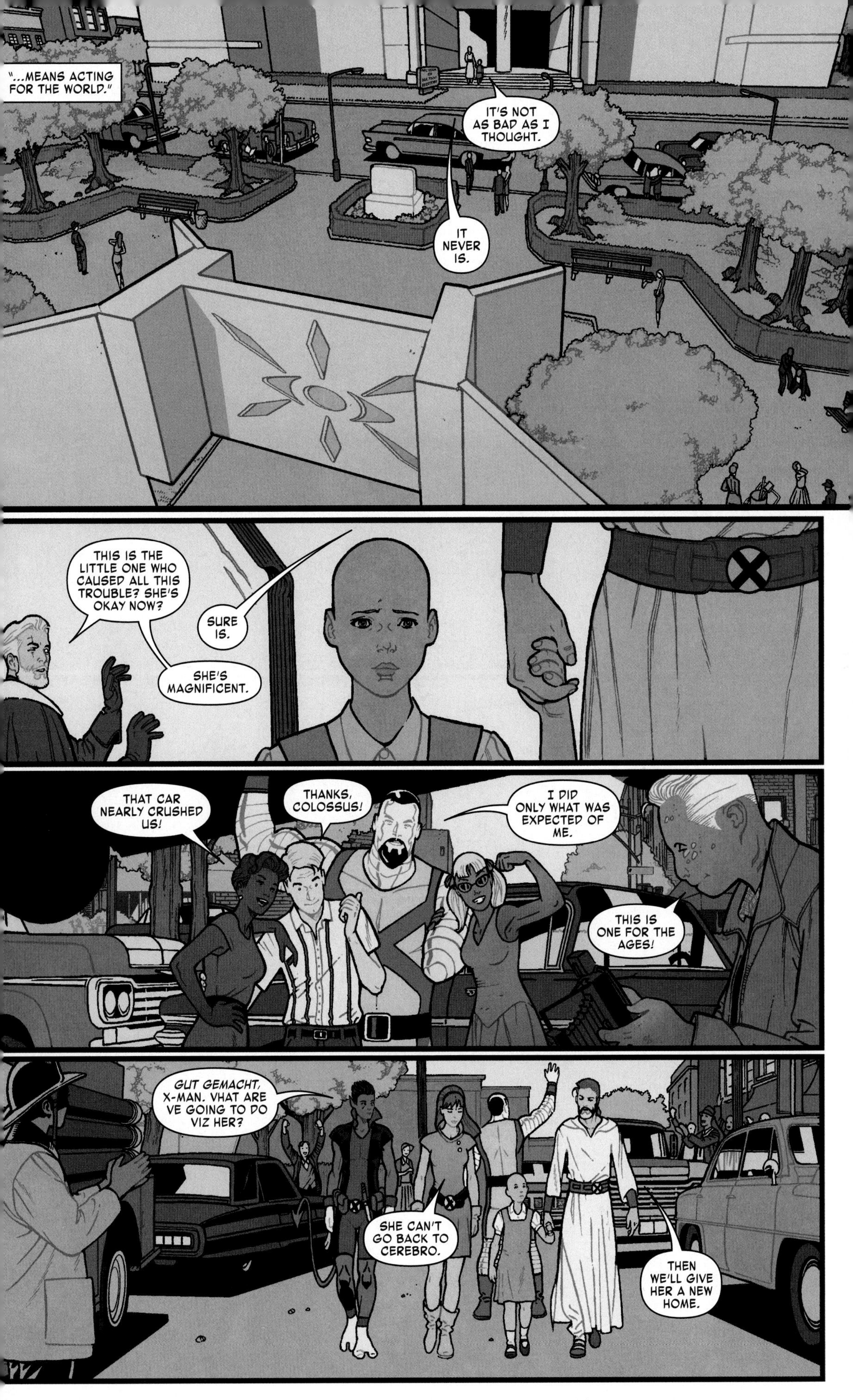
"...MEANS ACTING FOR THE WORLD."
IT'S NOT AS BAD AS I THOUGHT.
IT NEVER IS.
THIS IS THE LITTLE ONE WHO CAUSED ALL THIS TROUBLE? SHE'S OKAY NOW?
SURE IS.
SHE'S MAGNIFICENT.
THAT CAR NEARLY CRUSHED US!
THANKS, COLOSSUS!
I DID ONLY WHAT WAS EXPECTED OF ME.
THIS IS ONE FOR THE AGES!
GUT GEMACHT, X-MAN. VHAT ARE VE GOING TO DO VIZ HER?
SHE CAN'T GO BACK TO CEREBRO.
THEN WE'LL GIVE HER A NEW HOME.

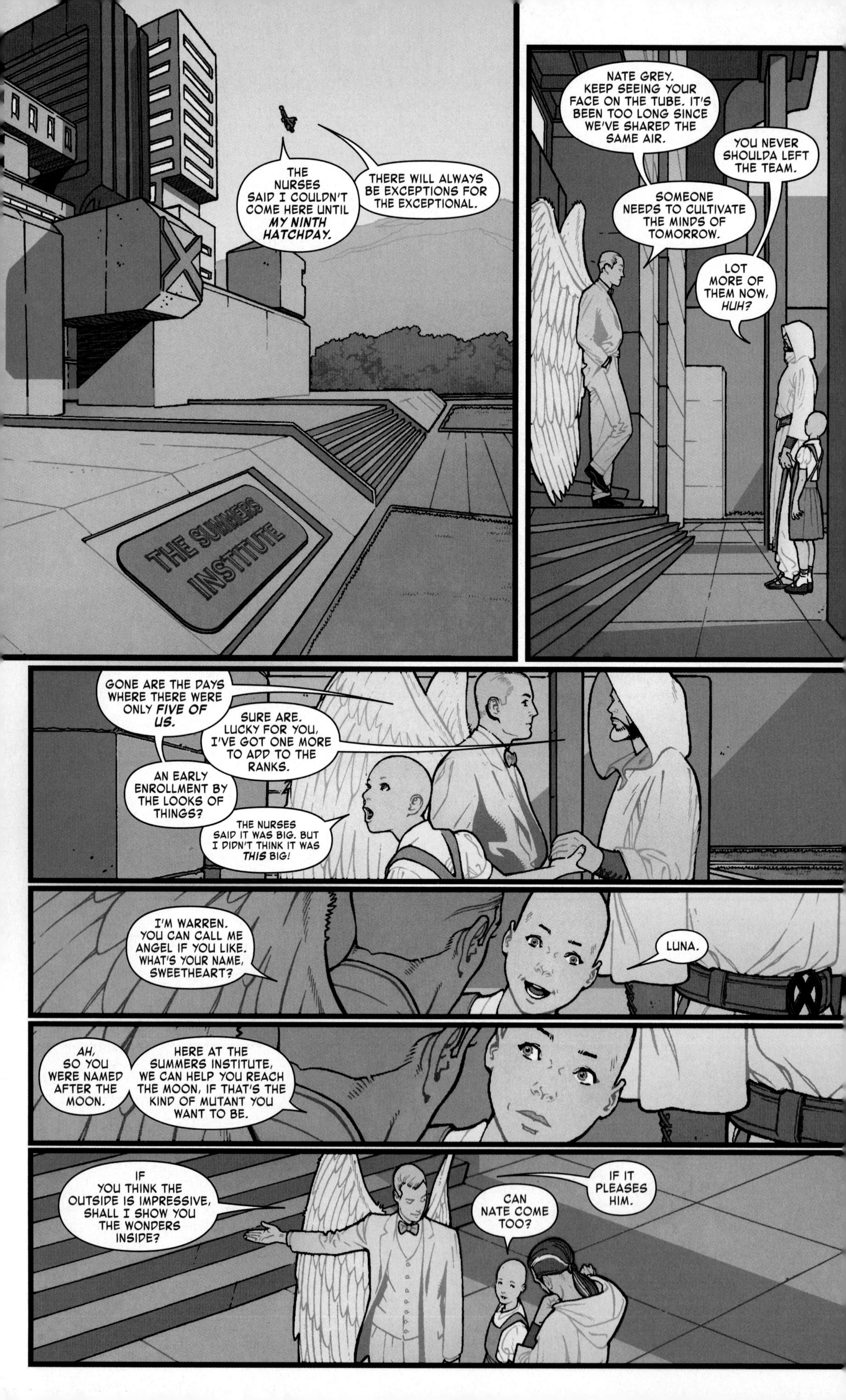
THE SUMMERS INSTITUTE
THE NURSES SAID I COULDN'T COME HERE UNTIL *MY NINTH HATCHDAY.*
THERE WILL ALWAYS BE EXCEPTIONS FOR THE EXCEPTIONAL.
NATE GREY. KEEP SEEING YOUR FACE ON THE TUBE. IT'S BEEN TOO LONG SINCE WE'VE SHARED THE SAME AIR.
YOU NEVER SHOULDA LEFT THE TEAM.
SOMEONE NEEDS TO CULTIVATE THE MINDS OF TOMORROW.
LOT MORE OF THEM NOW, *HUH?*
GONE ARE THE DAYS WHERE THERE WERE ONLY *FIVE OF US.*
SURE ARE. LUCKY FOR YOU, I'VE GOT ONE MORE TO ADD TO THE RANKS.
AN EARLY ENROLLMENT BY THE LOOKS OF THINGS?
THE NURSES SAID IT WAS BIG. BUT I DIDN'T THINK IT WAS *THIS* BIG!
I'M WARREN. YOU CAN CALL ME ANGEL IF YOU LIKE. WHAT'S YOUR NAME, SWEETHEART?
LUNA.
AH, SO YOU WERE NAMED AFTER THE MOON.
HERE AT THE SUMMERS INSTITUTE, WE CAN HELP YOU REACH THE MOON, IF THAT'S THE KIND OF MUTANT YOU WANT TO BE.
IF YOU THINK THE OUTSIDE IS IMPRESSIVE, SHALL I SHOW YOU THE WONDERS INSIDE?
CAN NATE COME TOO?
IF IT PLEASES HIM.

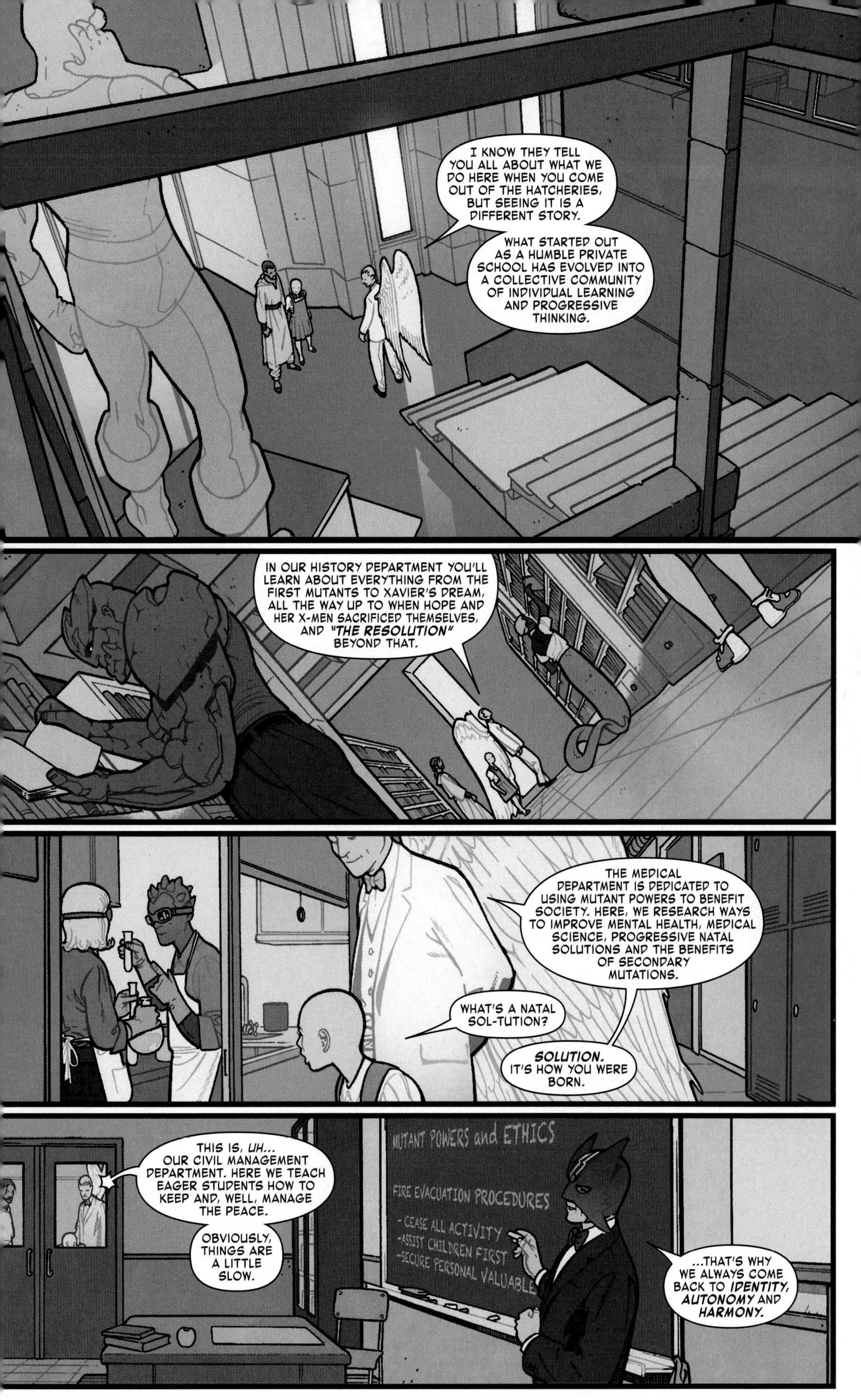
I KNOW THEY TELL YOU ALL ABOUT WHAT WE DO HERE WHEN YOU COME OUT OF THE HATCHERIES, BUT SEEING IT IS A DIFFERENT STORY.
WHAT STARTED OUT AS A HUMBLE PRIVATE SCHOOL HAS EVOLVED INTO A COLLECTIVE COMMUNITY OF INDIVIDUAL LEARNING AND PROGRESSIVE THINKING.
IN OUR HISTORY DEPARTMENT YOU'LL LEARN ABOUT EVERYTHING FROM THE FIRST MUTANTS TO XAVIER'S DREAM, ALL THE WAY UP TO WHEN HOPE AND HER X-MEN SACRIFICED THEMSELVES, AND *"THE RESOLUTION"* BEYOND THAT.
THE MEDICAL DEPARTMENT IS DEDICATED TO USING MUTANT POWERS TO BENEFIT SOCIETY. HERE, WE RESEARCH WAYS TO IMPROVE MENTAL HEALTH, MEDICAL SCIENCE, PROGRESSIVE NATAL SOLUTIONS AND THE BENEFITS OF SECONDARY MUTATIONS.
WHAT'S A NATAL SOL-TUTION?
SOLUTION. IT'S HOW YOU WERE BORN.
THIS IS, *UH...* OUR CIVIL MANAGEMENT DEPARTMENT. HERE WE TEACH EAGER STUDENTS HOW TO KEEP AND, WELL, MANAGE THE PEACE.
OBVIOUSLY, THINGS ARE A LITTLE SLOW.
MUTANT POWERS and ETHICS
FIRE EVACUATION PROCEDURES
- CEASE ALL ACTIVITY
-ASSIST CHILDREN FIRST
-SECURE PERSONAL VALUABLE
...THAT'S WHY WE ALWAYS COME BACK TO *IDENTITY, AUTONOMY* AND *HARMONY.*

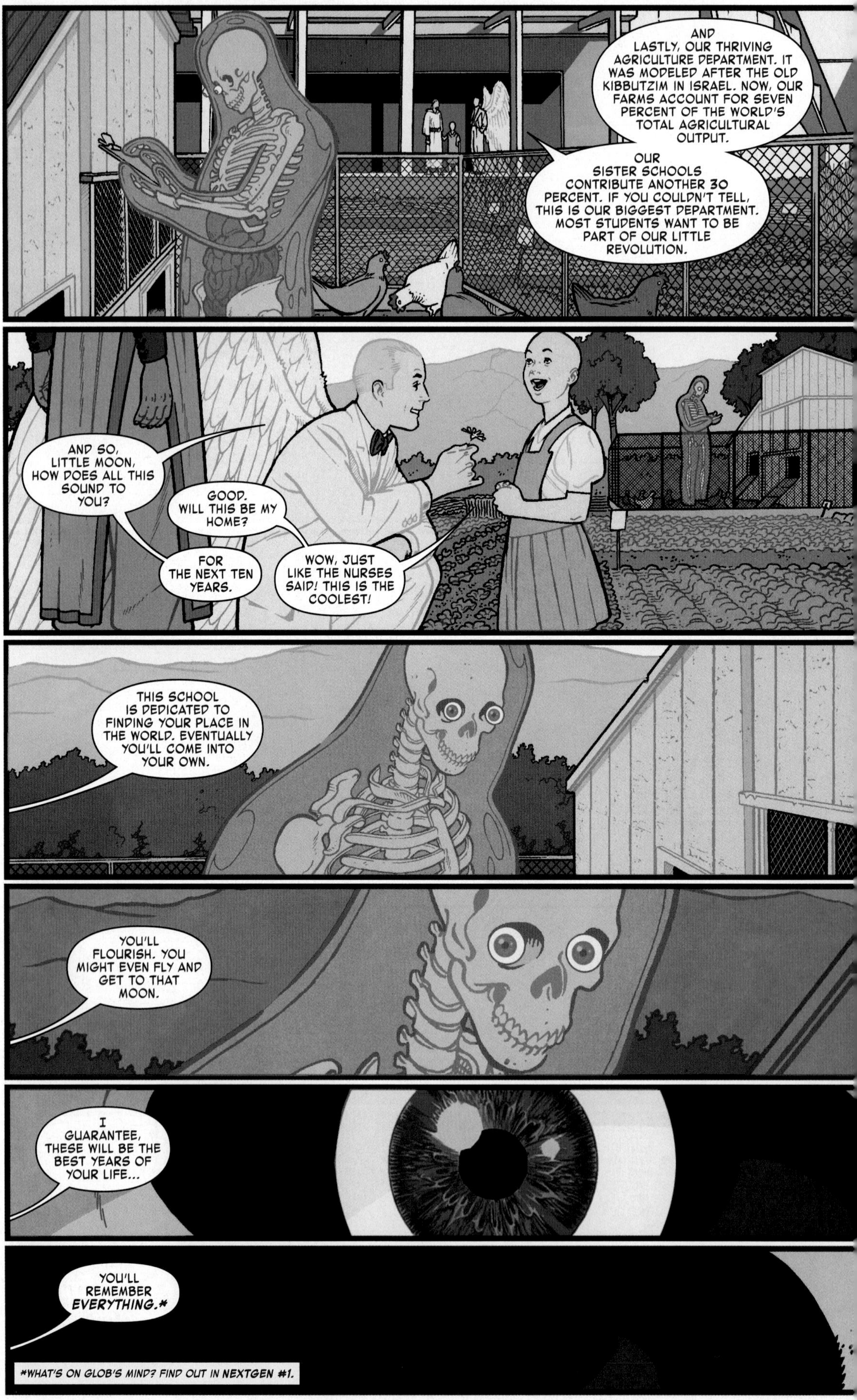
AND LASTLY, OUR THRIVING AGRICULTURE DEPARTMENT. IT WAS MODELED AFTER THE OLD KIBBUTZIM IN ISRAEL. NOW, OUR FARMS ACCOUNT FOR SEVEN PERCENT OF THE WORLD'S TOTAL AGRICULTURAL OUTPUT.
OUR SISTER SCHOOLS CONTRIBUTE ANOTHER 30 PERCENT. IF YOU COULDN'T TELL, THIS IS OUR BIGGEST DEPARTMENT. MOST STUDENTS WANT TO BE PART OF OUR LITTLE REVOLUTION.
AND SO, LITTLE MOON, HOW DOES ALL THIS SOUND TO YOU?
GOOD. WILL THIS BE MY HOME?
FOR THE NEXT TEN YEARS.
WOW, JUST LIKE THE NURSES SAID! THIS IS THE COOLEST!
THIS SCHOOL IS DEDICATED TO FINDING YOUR PLACE IN THE WORLD. EVENTUALLY YOU'LL COME INTO YOUR OWN.
YOU'LL FLOURISH. YOU MIGHT EVEN FLY AND GET TO THAT MOON.
I GUARANTEE, THESE WILL BE THE BEST YEARS OF YOUR LIFE...
YOU'LL REMEMBER EVERYTHING.*
*WHAT'S ON GLOB'S MIND? FIND OUT IN NEXTGEN #1.

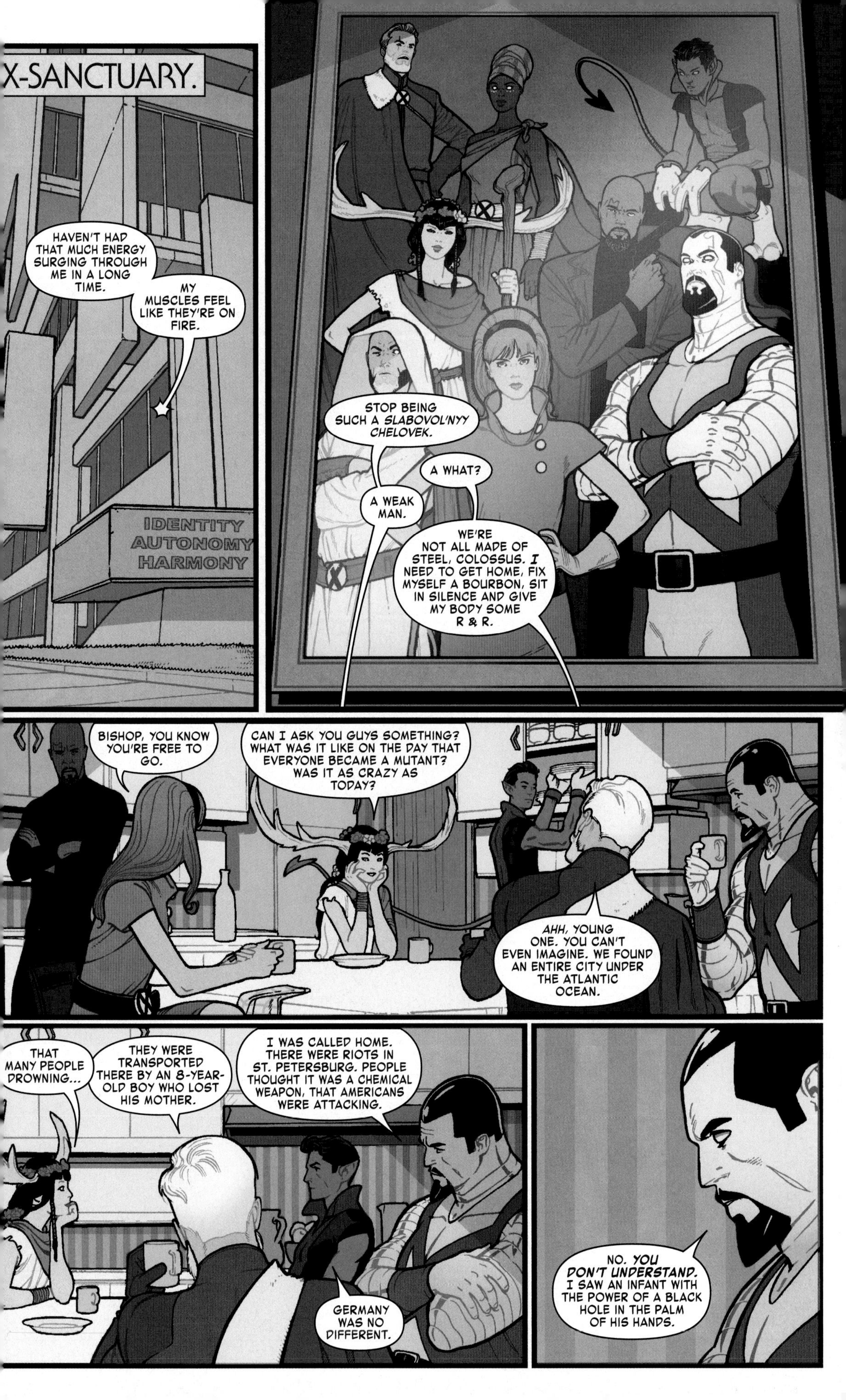
X-SANCTUARY.
HAVEN'T HAD THAT MUCH ENERGY SURGING THROUGH ME IN A LONG TIME.
MY MUSCLES FEEL LIKE THEY'RE ON FIRE.
IDENTITY AUTONOMY HARMONY
STOP BEING SUCH A *SLABOVOL'NYY CHELOVEK.*
A WHAT?
A WEAK MAN.
WE'RE NOT ALL MADE OF STEEL, COLOSSUS. *I* NEED TO GET HOME, FIX MYSELF A BOURBON, SIT IN SILENCE AND GIVE MY BODY SOME R & R.
BISHOP, YOU KNOW YOU'RE FREE TO GO.
CAN I ASK YOU GUYS SOMETHING? WHAT WAS IT LIKE ON THE DAY THAT EVERYONE BECAME A MUTANT? WAS IT AS CRAZY AS TODAY?
AHH, YOUNG ONE. YOU CAN'T EVEN IMAGINE. WE FOUND AN ENTIRE CITY UNDER THE ATLANTIC OCEAN.
THAT MANY PEOPLE DROWNING...
THEY WERE TRANSPORTED THERE BY AN 8-YEAR-OLD BOY WHO LOST HIS MOTHER.
I WAS CALLED HOME. THERE WERE RIOTS IN ST. PETERSBURG. PEOPLE THOUGHT IT WAS A CHEMICAL WEAPON, THAT AMERICANS WERE ATTACKING.
GERMANY WAS NO DIFFERENT.
NO. *YOU DON'T UNDERSTAND.* I SAW AN INFANT WITH THE POWER OF A BLACK HOLE IN THE PALM OF HIS HANDS.

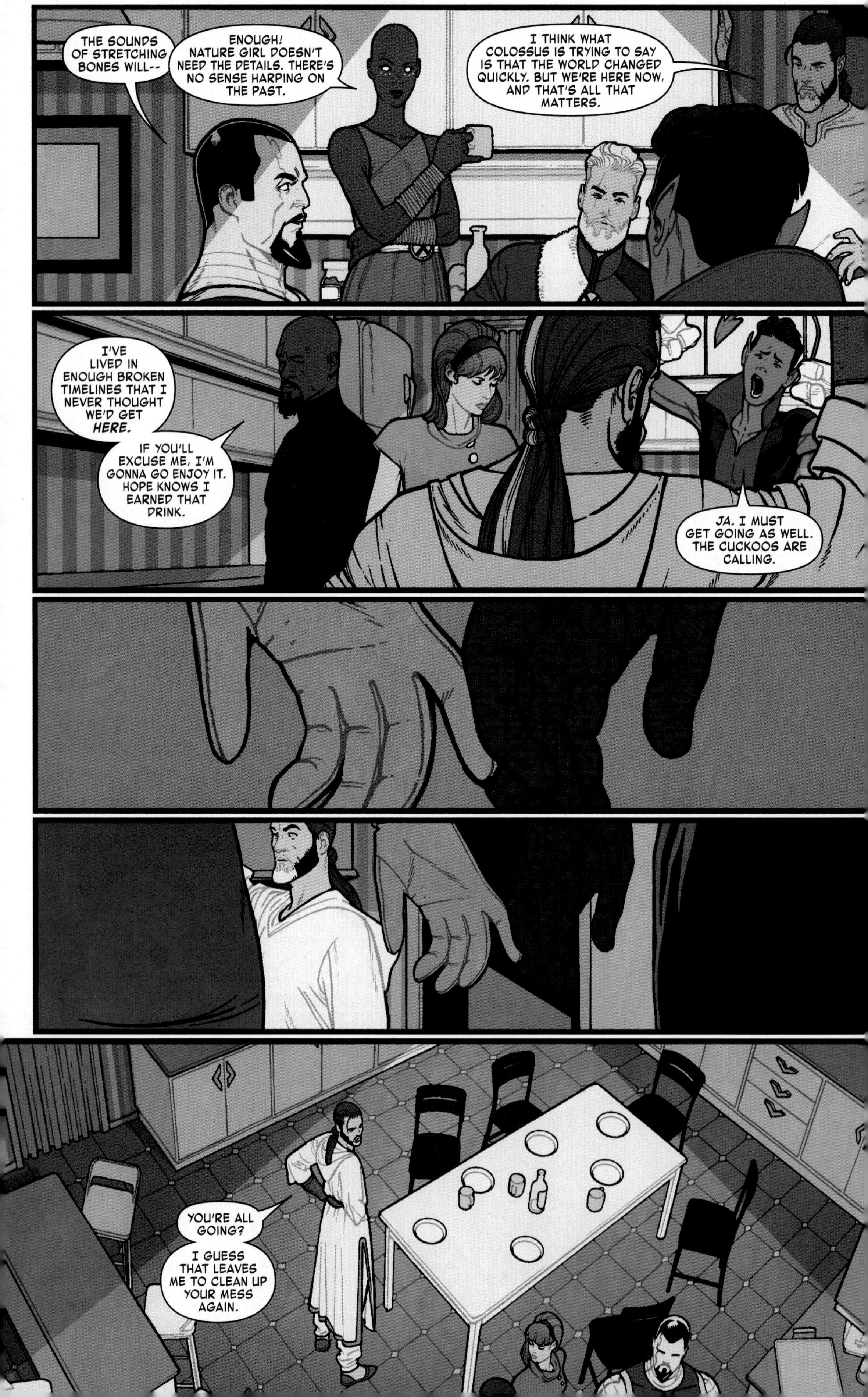
THE SOUNDS OF STRETCHING BONES WILL--
ENOUGH! NATURE GIRL DOESN'T NEED THE DETAILS. THERE'S NO SENSE HARPING ON THE PAST.
I THINK WHAT COLOSSUS IS TRYING TO SAY IS THAT THE WORLD CHANGED QUICKLY. BUT WE'RE HERE NOW, AND THAT'S ALL THAT MATTERS.
I'VE LIVED IN ENOUGH BROKEN TIMELINES THAT I NEVER THOUGHT WE'D GET *HERE.*
IF YOU'LL EXCUSE ME, I'M GONNA GO ENJOY IT. HOPE KNOWS I EARNED THAT DRINK.
JA. I MUST GET GOING AS WELL. THE CUCKOOS ARE CALLING.
YOU'RE ALL GOING?
I GUESS THAT LEAVES ME TO CLEAN UP YOUR MESS AGAIN.

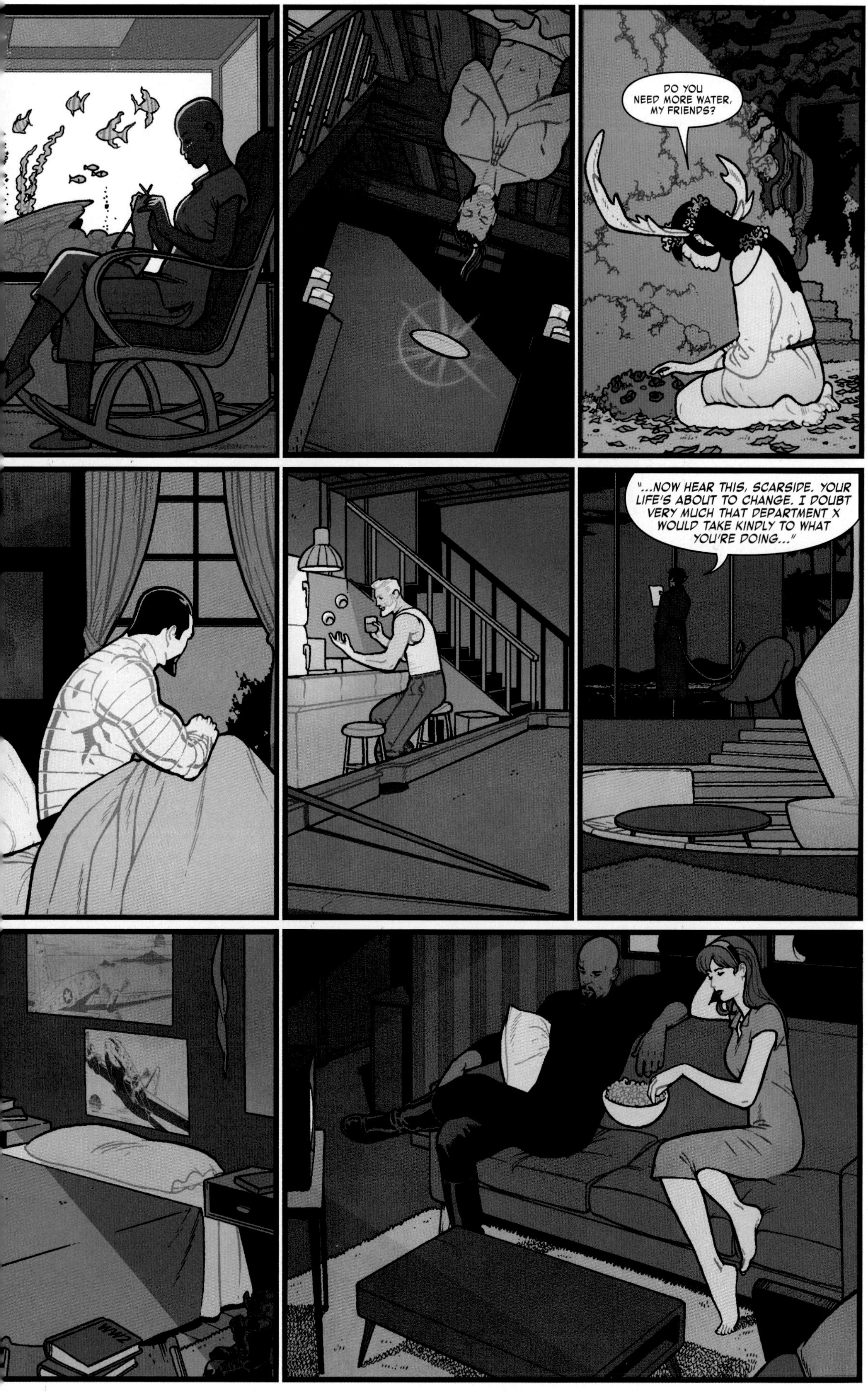
DO YOU NEED MORE WATER, MY FRIENDS?
"...NOW HEAR THIS, SCARSIDE. YOUR LIFE'S ABOUT TO CHANGE. I DOUBT VERY MUCH THAT DEPARTMENT X WOULD TAKE KINDLY TO WHAT YOU'RE DOING..."

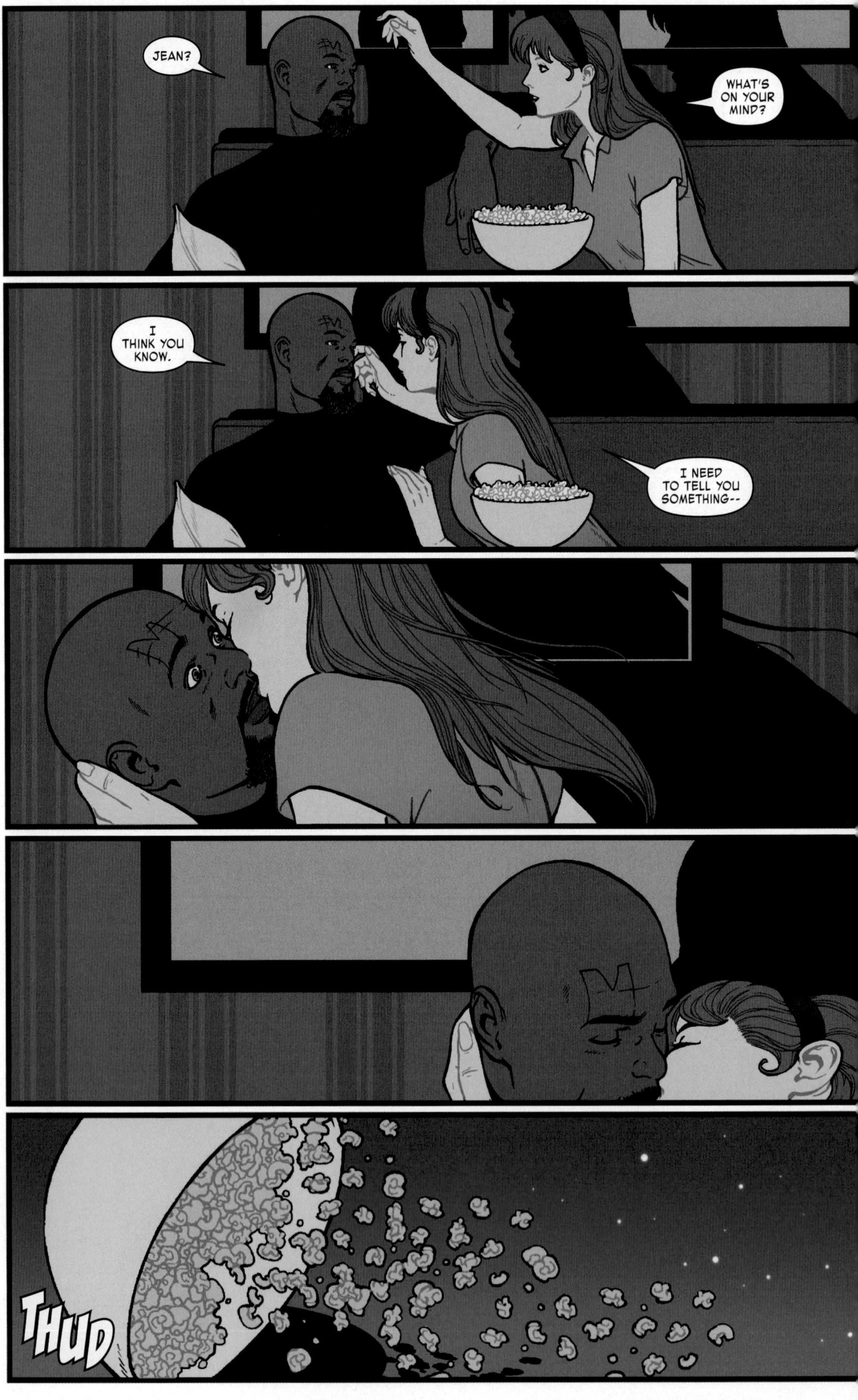
JEAN?
WHAT'S ON YOUR MIND?
I THINK YOU KNOW.
I NEED TO TELL YOU SOMETHING--
THUD

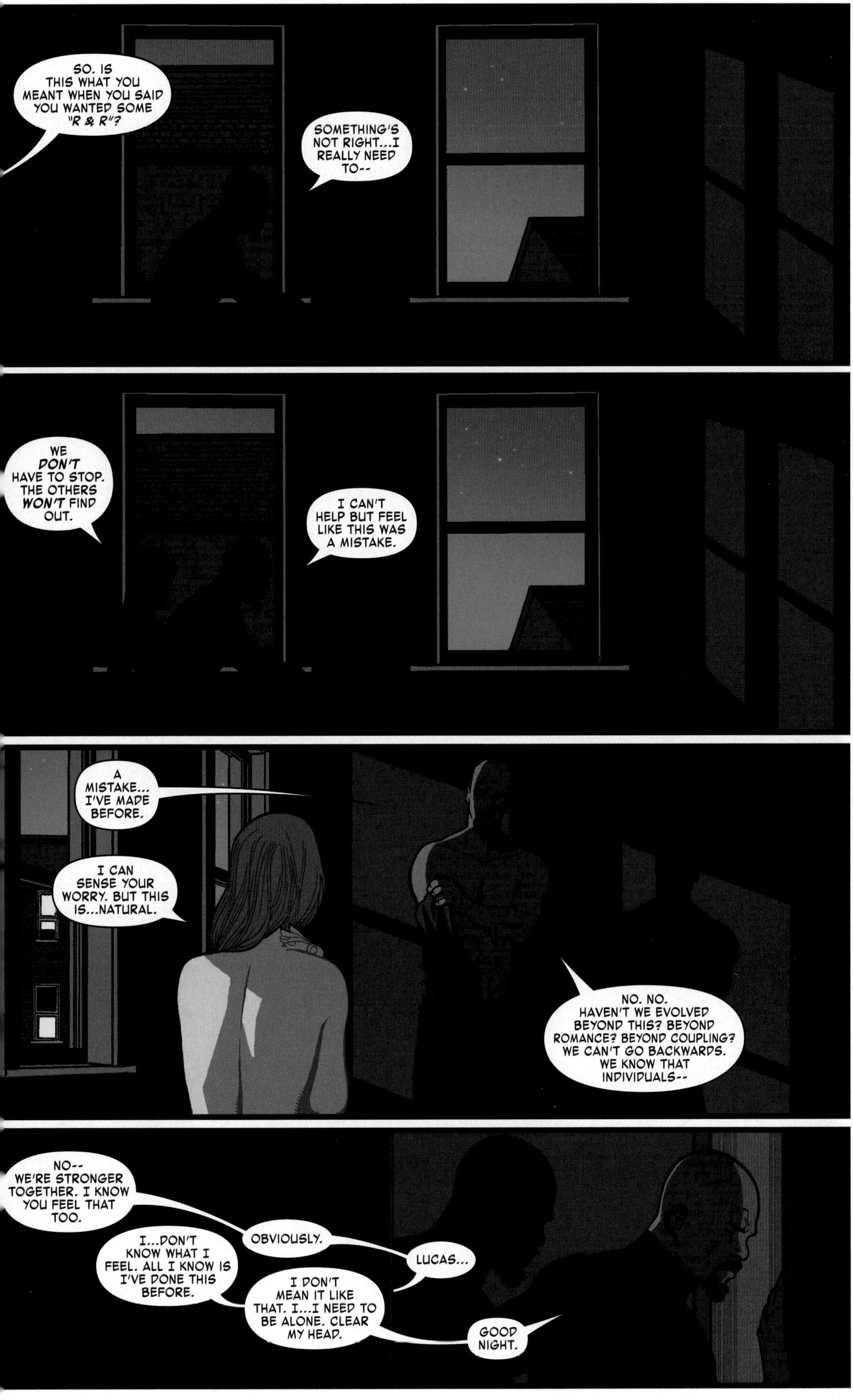
SO. IS THIS WHAT YOU MEANT WHEN YOU SAID YOU WANTED SOME "R & R"?
SOMETHING'S NOT RIGHT...I REALLY NEED TO--
WE DON'T HAVE TO STOP. THE OTHERS WON'T FIND OUT.
I CAN'T HELP BUT FEEL LIKE THIS WAS A MISTAKE.
A MISTAKE... I'VE MADE BEFORE.
I CAN SENSE YOUR WORRY. BUT THIS IS...NATURAL.
NO. NO. HAVEN'T WE EVOLVED BEYOND THIS? BEYOND ROMANCE? BEYOND COUPLING? WE CAN'T GO BACKWARDS. WE KNOW THAT INDIVIDUALS--
NO-- WE'RE STRONGER TOGETHER. I KNOW YOU FEEL THAT TOO.
OBVIOUSLY.
I...DON'T KNOW WHAT I FEEL. ALL I KNOW IS I'VE DONE THIS BEFORE.
LUCAS...
I DON'T MEAN IT LIKE THAT. I...I NEED TO BE ALONE. CLEAR MY HEAD.
GOOD NIGHT.

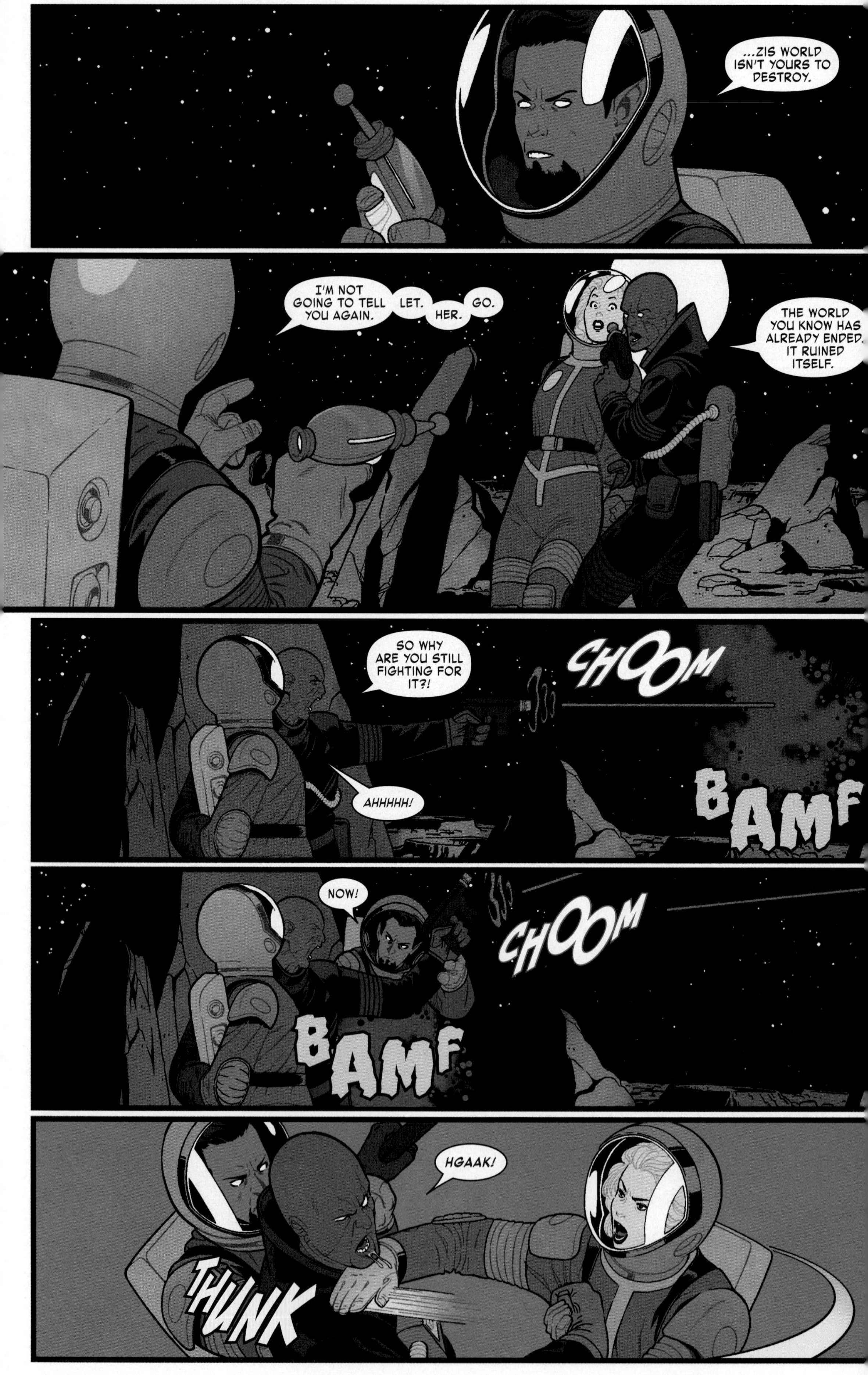
...ZIS WORLD ISN'T YOURS TO DESTROY.
I'M NOT GOING TO TELL YOU AGAIN.
LET.
HER.
GO.
THE WORLD YOU KNOW HAS ALREADY ENDED. IT RUINED ITSELF.
SO WHY ARE YOU STILL FIGHTING FOR IT?!
CHOOM
AHHHHH!
BAMF
NOW!
CHOOM
BAMF
HGAAK!
THUNK

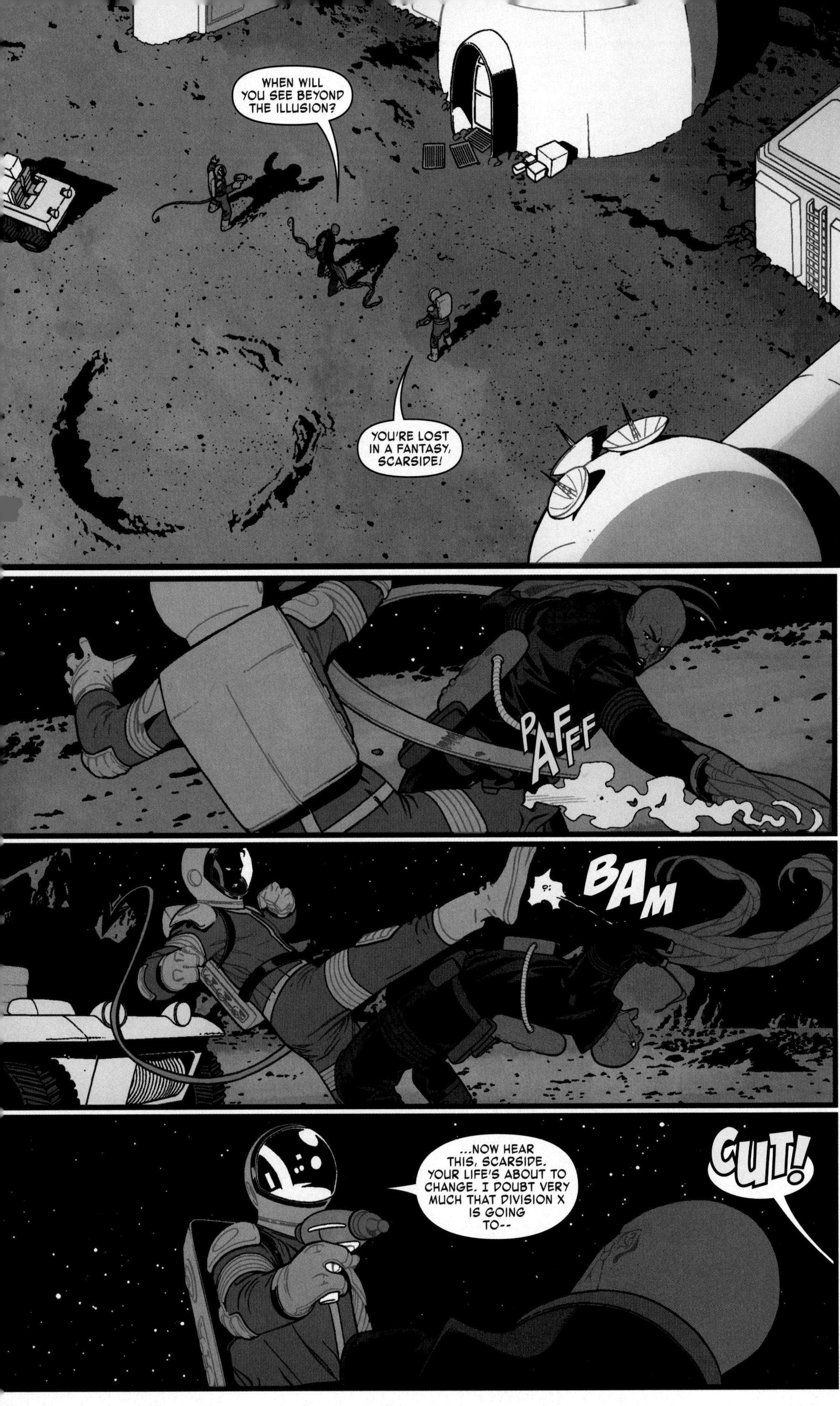
WHEN WILL YOU SEE BEYOND THE ILLUSION?
YOU'RE LOST IN A FANTASY, SCARSIDE!
PAFFF
BAM
...NOW HEAR THIS, SCARSIDE. YOUR LIFE'S ABOUT TO CHANGE. I DOUBT VERY MUCH THAT DIVISION X IS GOING TO--
CUT!

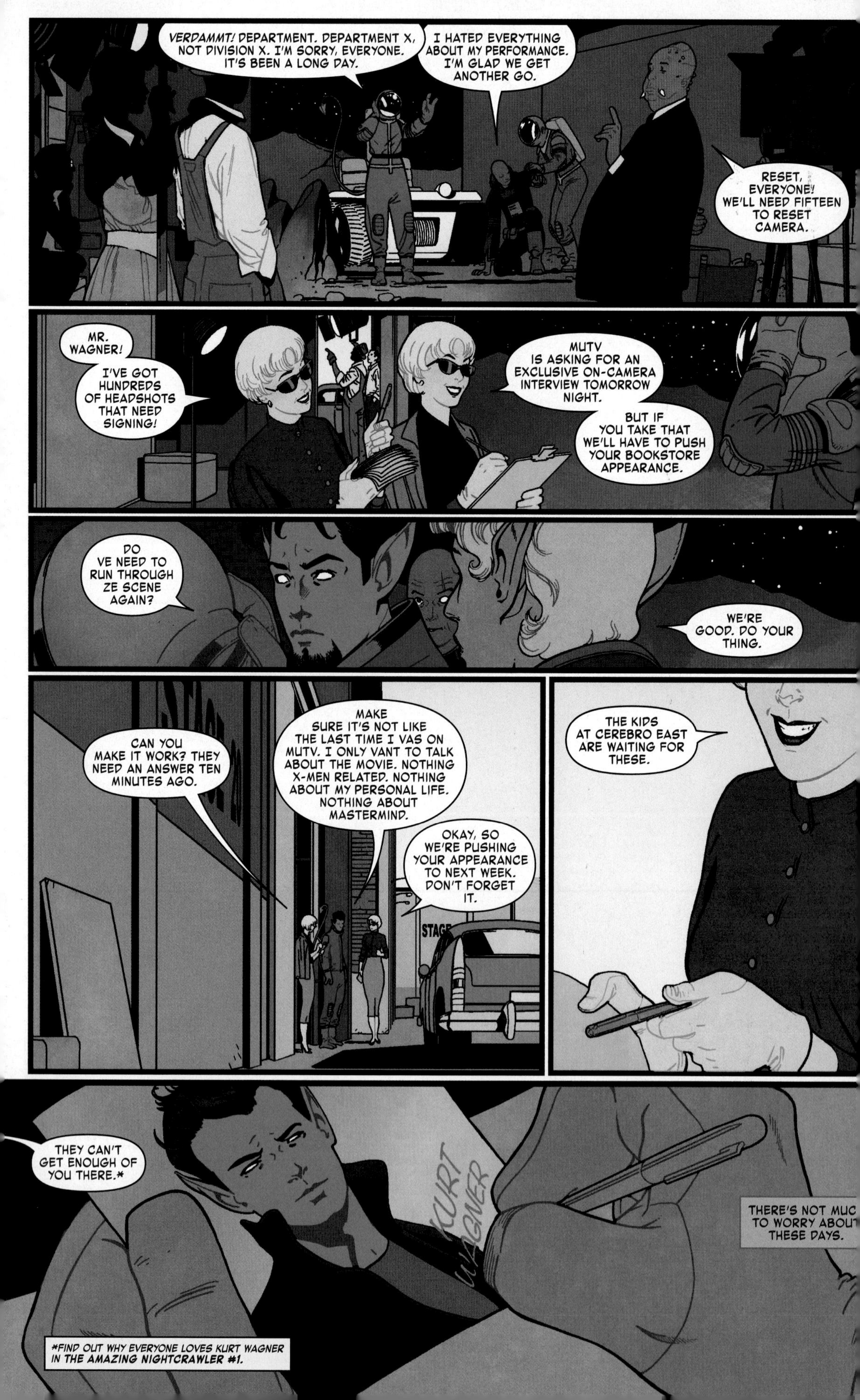

VERDAMMT! DEPARTMENT. DEPARTMENT X, NOT DIVISION X. I'M SORRY, EVERYONE. IT'S BEEN A LONG DAY.
I HATED EVERYTHING ABOUT MY PERFORMANCE. I'M GLAD WE GET ANOTHER GO.
RESET, EVERYONE! WE'LL NEED FIFTEEN TO RESET CAMERA.
MR. WAGNER!
I'VE GOT HUNDREDS OF HEADSHOTS THAT NEED SIGNING!
MUTV IS ASKING FOR AN EXCLUSIVE ON-CAMERA INTERVIEW TOMORROW NIGHT.
BUT IF YOU TAKE THAT WE'LL HAVE TO PUSH YOUR BOOKSTORE APPEARANCE.
DO VE NEED TO RUN THROUGH ZE SCENE AGAIN?
WE'RE GOOD. DO YOUR THING.
CAN YOU MAKE IT WORK? THEY NEED AN ANSWER TEN MINUTES AGO.
MAKE SURE IT'S NOT LIKE THE LAST TIME I VAS ON MUTV. I ONLY VANT TO TALK ABOUT THE MOVIE. NOTHING X-MEN RELATED. NOTHING ABOUT MY PERSONAL LIFE. NOTHING ABOUT MASTERMIND.
OKAY, SO WE'RE PUSHING YOUR APPEARANCE TO NEXT WEEK. DON'T FORGET IT.
STAGE
THE KIDS AT CEREBRO EAST ARE WAITING FOR THESE.
THEY CAN'T GET ENOUGH OF YOU THERE.*
KURT WAGNER
THERE'S NOT MUC TO WORRY ABOUT THESE DAYS.
*FIND OUT WHY EVERYONE LOVES KURT WAGNER IN THE AMAZING NIGHTCRAWLER #1.

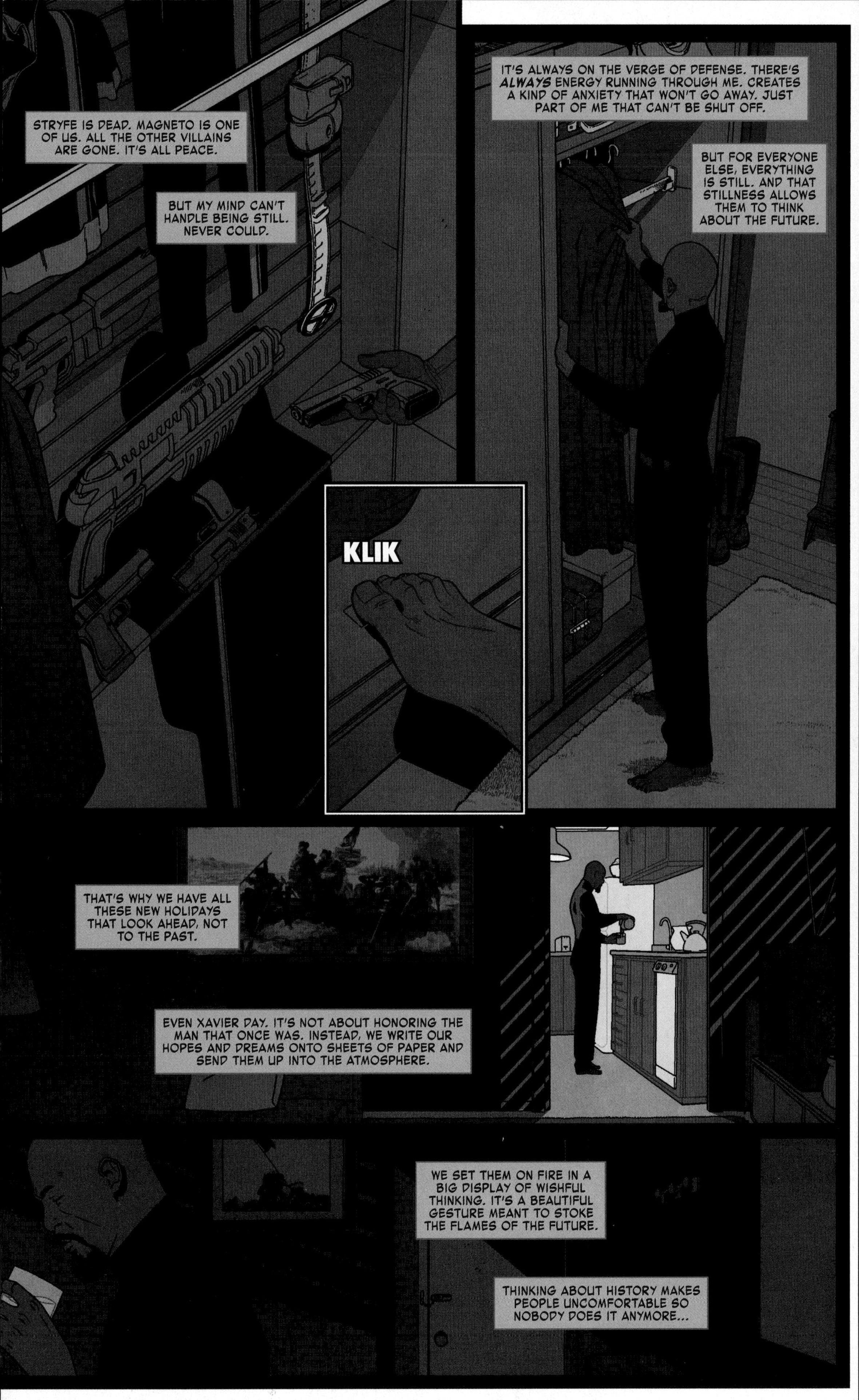
STRYFE IS DEAD. MAGNETO IS ONE OF US. ALL THE OTHER VILLAINS ARE GONE. IT'S ALL PEACE.
BUT MY MIND CAN'T HANDLE BEING STILL. NEVER COULD.
IT'S ALWAYS ON THE VERGE OF DEFENSE. THERE'S *ALWAYS* ENERGY RUNNING THROUGH ME. CREATES A KIND OF ANXIETY THAT WON'T GO AWAY. JUST PART OF ME THAT CAN'T BE SHUT OFF.
BUT FOR EVERYONE ELSE, EVERYTHING IS STILL. AND THAT STILLNESS ALLOWS THEM TO THINK ABOUT THE FUTURE.
KLIK
THAT'S WHY WE HAVE ALL THESE NEW HOLIDAYS THAT LOOK AHEAD, NOT TO THE PAST.
EVEN XAVIER DAY. IT'S NOT ABOUT HONORING THE MAN THAT ONCE WAS. INSTEAD, WE WRITE OUR HOPES AND DREAMS ONTO SHEETS OF PAPER AND SEND THEM UP INTO THE ATMOSPHERE.
WE SET THEM ON FIRE IN A BIG DISPLAY OF WISHFUL THINKING. IT'S A BEAUTIFUL GESTURE MEANT TO STOKE THE FLAMES OF THE FUTURE.
THINKING ABOUT HISTORY MAKES PEOPLE UNCOMFORTABLE SO NOBODY DOES IT ANYMORE...

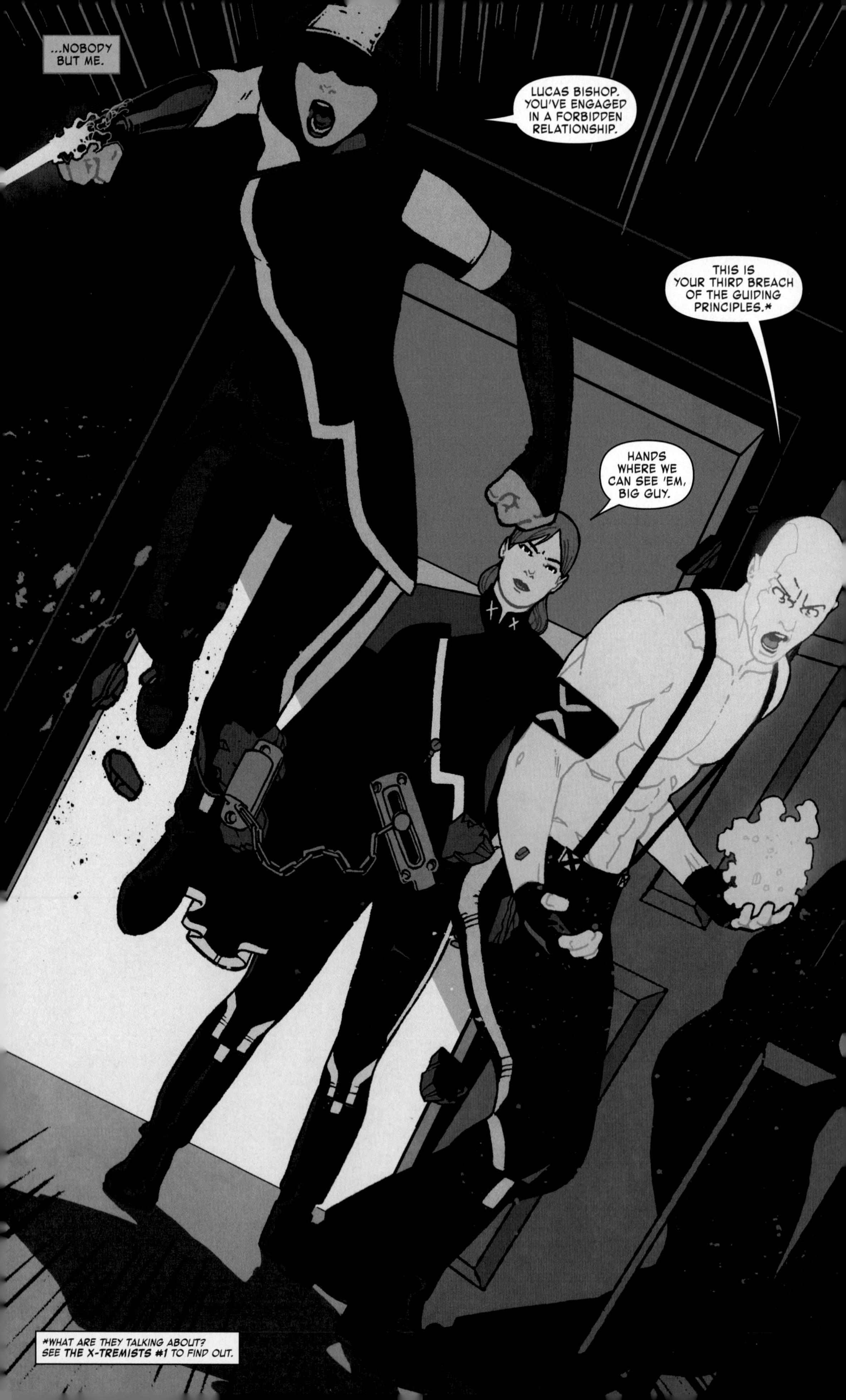
...NOBODY BUT ME.
LUCAS BISHOP. YOU'VE ENGAGED IN A FORBIDDEN RELATIONSHIP.
THIS IS YOUR THIRD BREACH OF THE GUIDING PRINCIPLES.*
HANDS WHERE WE CAN SEE 'EM, BIG GUY.
*WHAT ARE THEY TALKING ABOUT? SEE THE X-TREMISTS #1 TO FIND OUT.

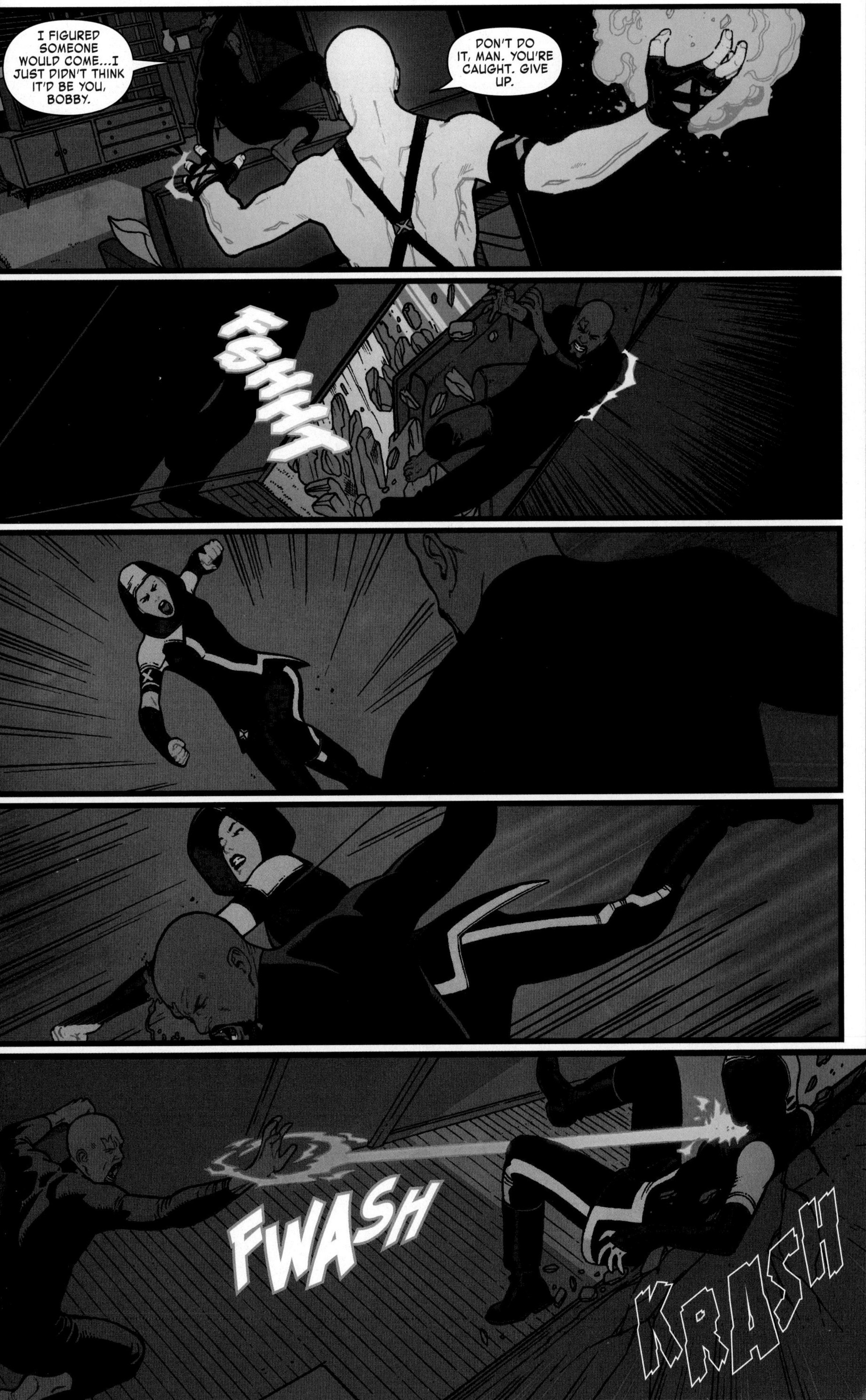
I FIGURED SOMEONE WOULD COME...I JUST DIDN'T THINK IT'D BE YOU, BOBBY.
DON'T DO IT, MAN. YOU'RE CAUGHT. GIVE UP.
FSHHT
FWASH
KRASH

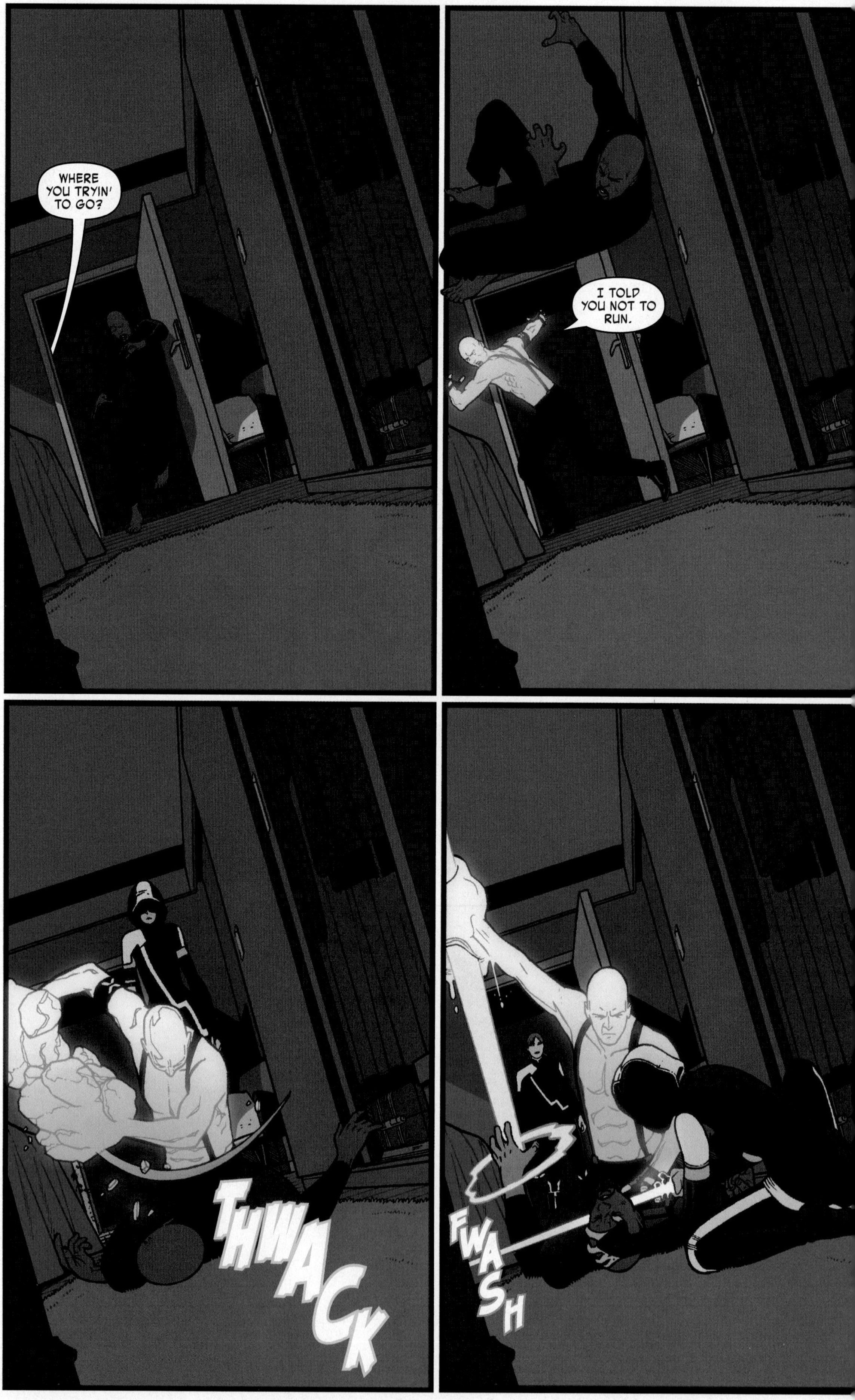

WHERE YOU TRYIN' TO GO?
I TOLD YOU NOT TO RUN.
THWACK
FWASH

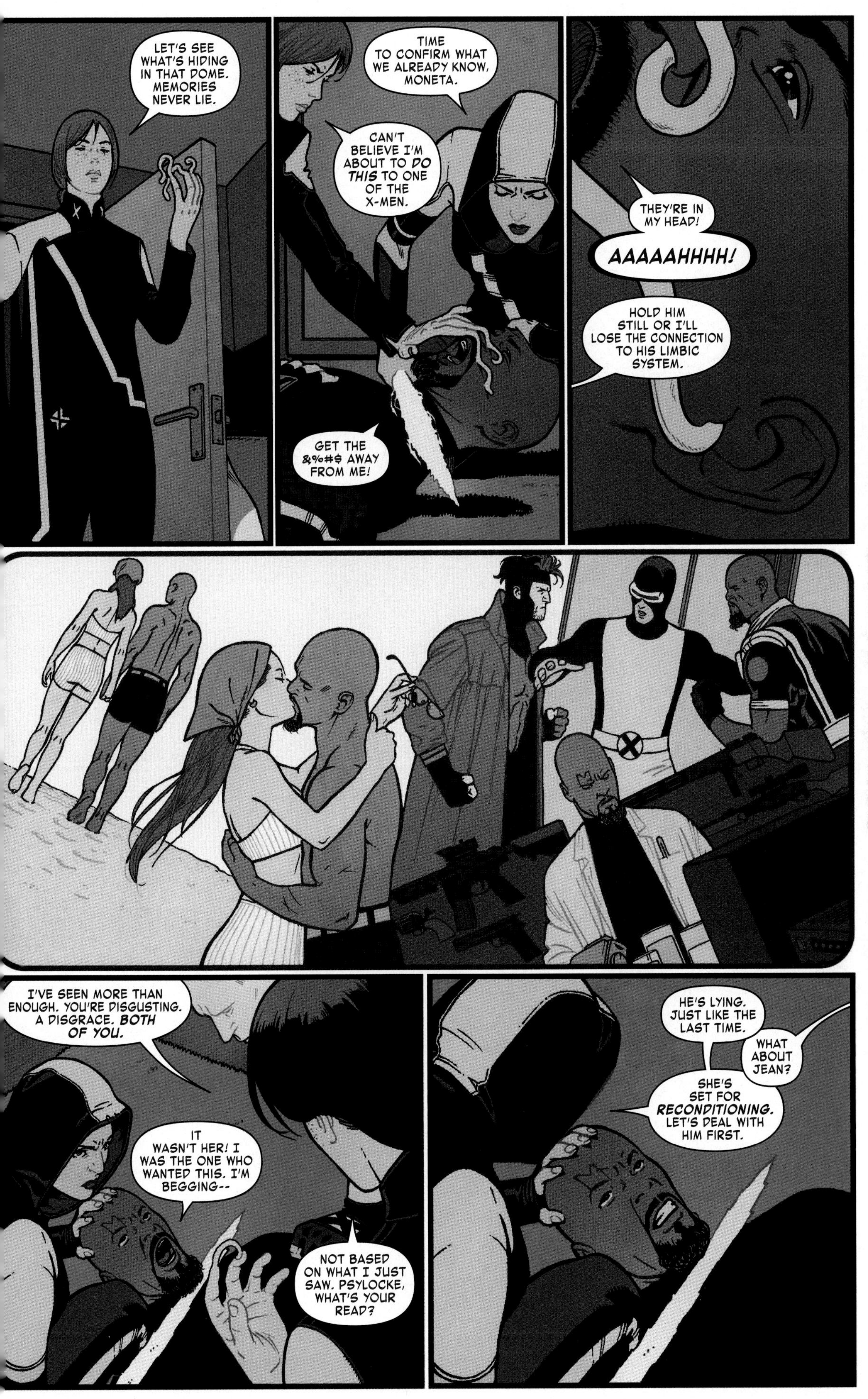

LET'S SEE WHAT'S HIDING IN THAT DOME. MEMORIES NEVER LIE.
TIME TO CONFIRM WHAT WE ALREADY KNOW, MONETA.
CAN'T BELIEVE I'M ABOUT TO DO THIS TO ONE OF THE X-MEN.
GET THE &%#$ AWAY FROM ME!
THEY'RE IN MY HEAD!
AAAAAHHHH!
HOLD HIM STILL OR I'LL LOSE THE CONNECTION TO HIS LIMBIC SYSTEM.
I'VE SEEN MORE THAN ENOUGH. YOU'RE DISGUSTING. A DISGRACE. BOTH OF YOU.
IT WASN'T HER! I WAS THE ONE WHO WANTED THIS. I'M BEGGING--
NOT BASED ON WHAT I JUST SAW. PSYLOCKE, WHAT'S YOUR READ?
HE'S LYING. JUST LIKE THE LAST TIME.
WHAT ABOUT JEAN?
SHE'S SET FOR RECONDITIONING. LET'S DEAL WITH HIM FIRST.

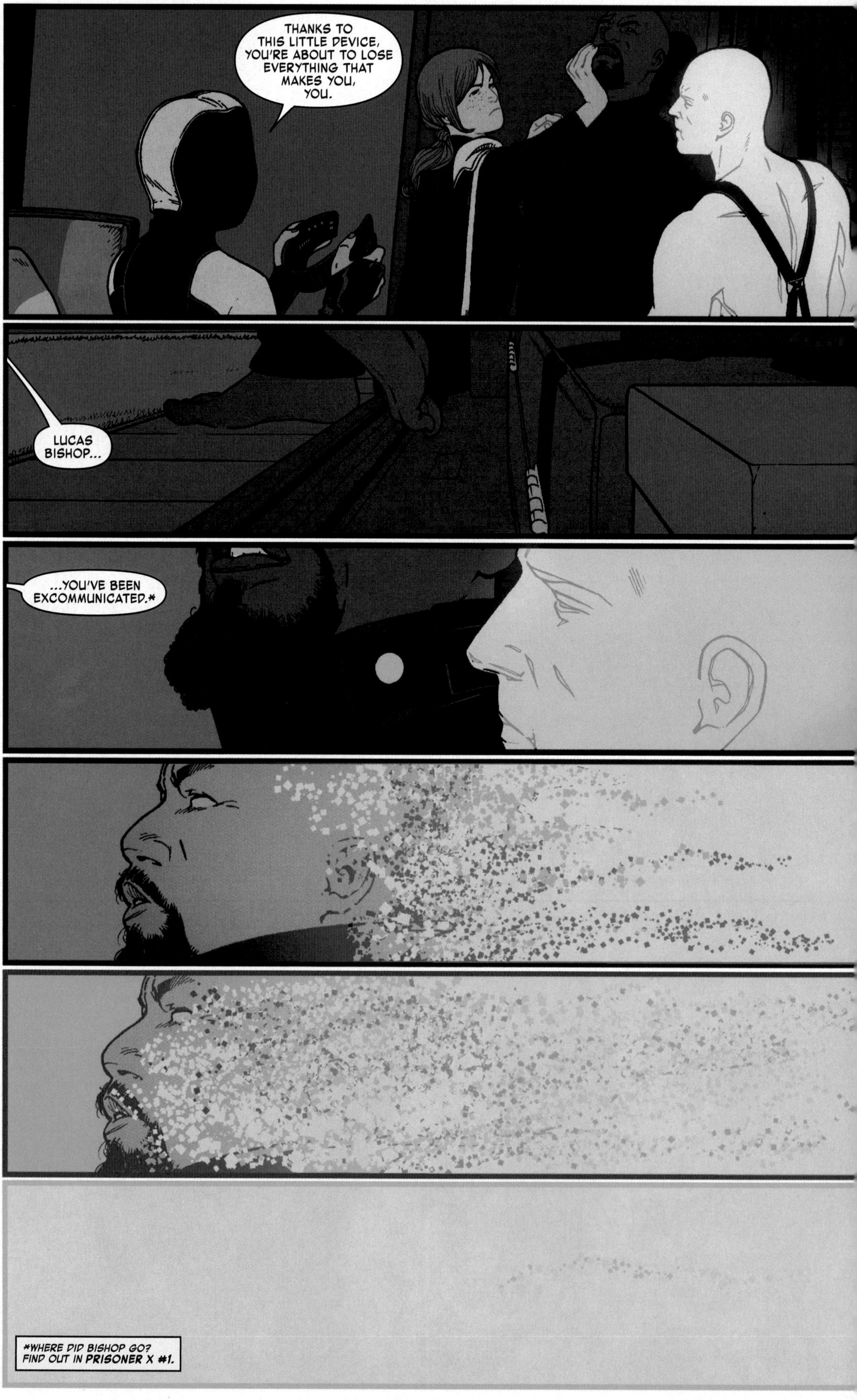
THANKS TO THIS LITTLE DEVICE, YOU'RE ABOUT TO LOSE EVERYTHING THAT MAKES YOU, YOU.
LUCAS BISHOP...
...YOU'VE BEEN EXCOMMUNICATED.*
*WHERE DID BISHOP GO? FIND OUT IN PRISONER X #1.

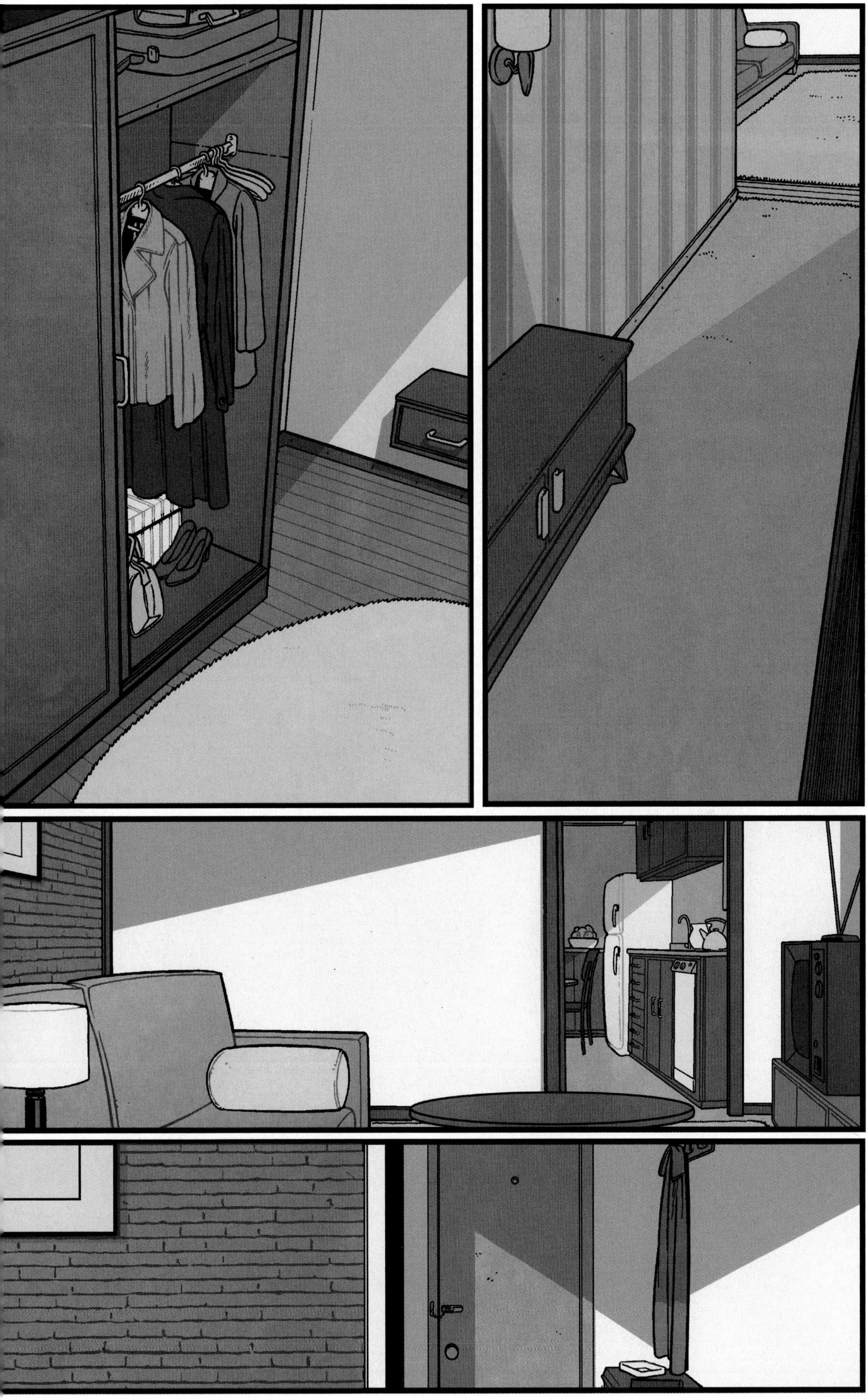

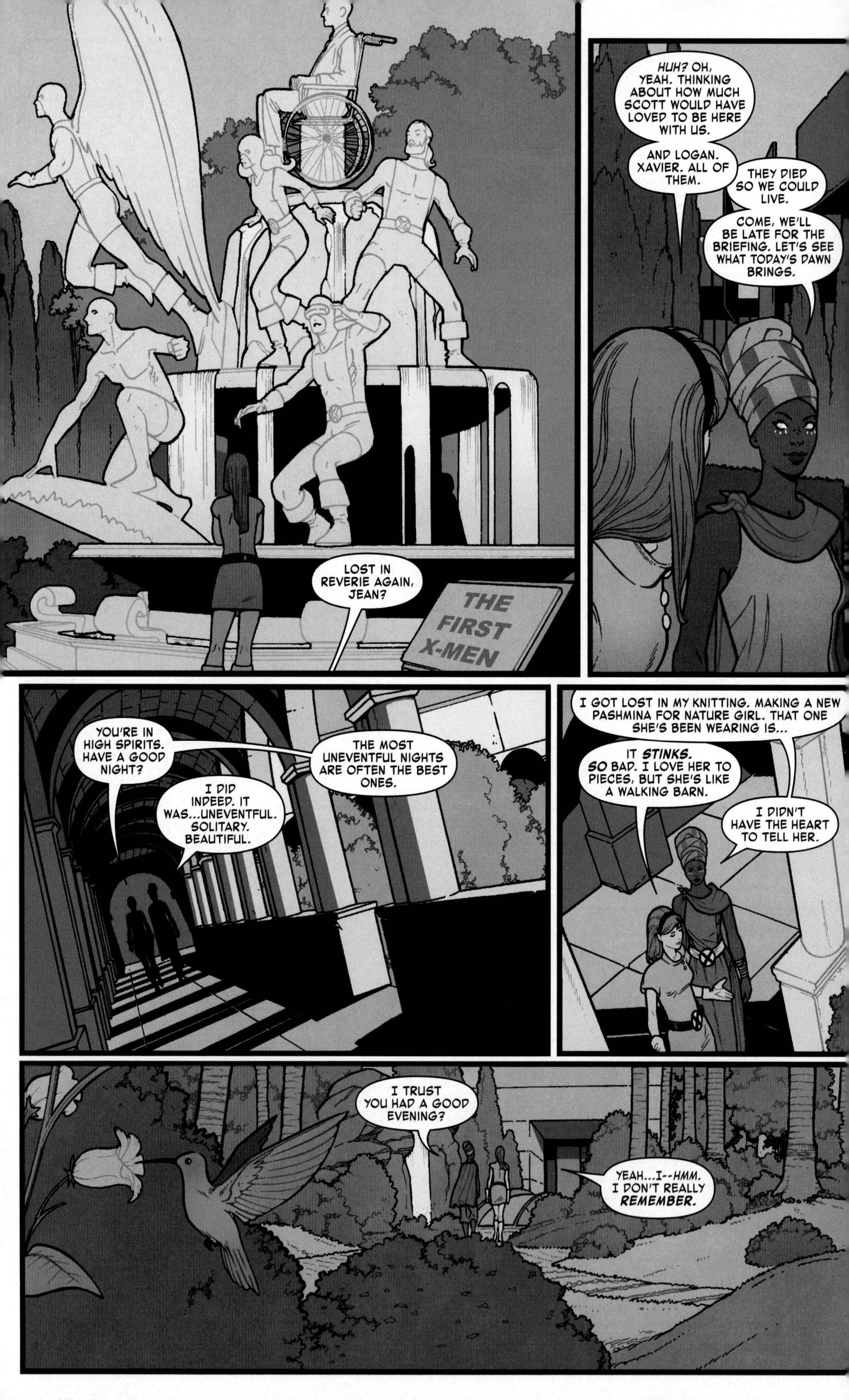
THE FIRST X-MEN
LOST IN REVERIE AGAIN, JEAN?
HUH? OH, YEAH. THINKING ABOUT HOW MUCH SCOTT WOULD HAVE LOVED TO BE HERE WITH US.
AND LOGAN. XAVIER. ALL OF THEM.
THEY DIED SO WE COULD LIVE.
COME, WE'LL BE LATE FOR THE BRIEFING. LET'S SEE WHAT TODAY'S DAWN BRINGS.
YOU'RE IN HIGH SPIRITS. HAVE A GOOD NIGHT?
I DID INDEED. IT WAS...UNEVENTFUL. SOLITARY. BEAUTIFUL.
THE MOST UNEVENTFUL NIGHTS ARE OFTEN THE BEST ONES.
I GOT LOST IN MY KNITTING. MAKING A NEW PASHMINA FOR NATURE GIRL. THAT ONE SHE'S BEEN WEARING IS...
IT *STINKS.* *SO* BAD. I LOVE HER TO PIECES, BUT SHE'S LIKE A WALKING BARN.
I DIDN'T HAVE THE HEART TO TELL HER.
I TRUST YOU HAD A GOOD EVENING?
YEAH...I--*HMM.* I DON'T REALLY ***REMEMBER.***

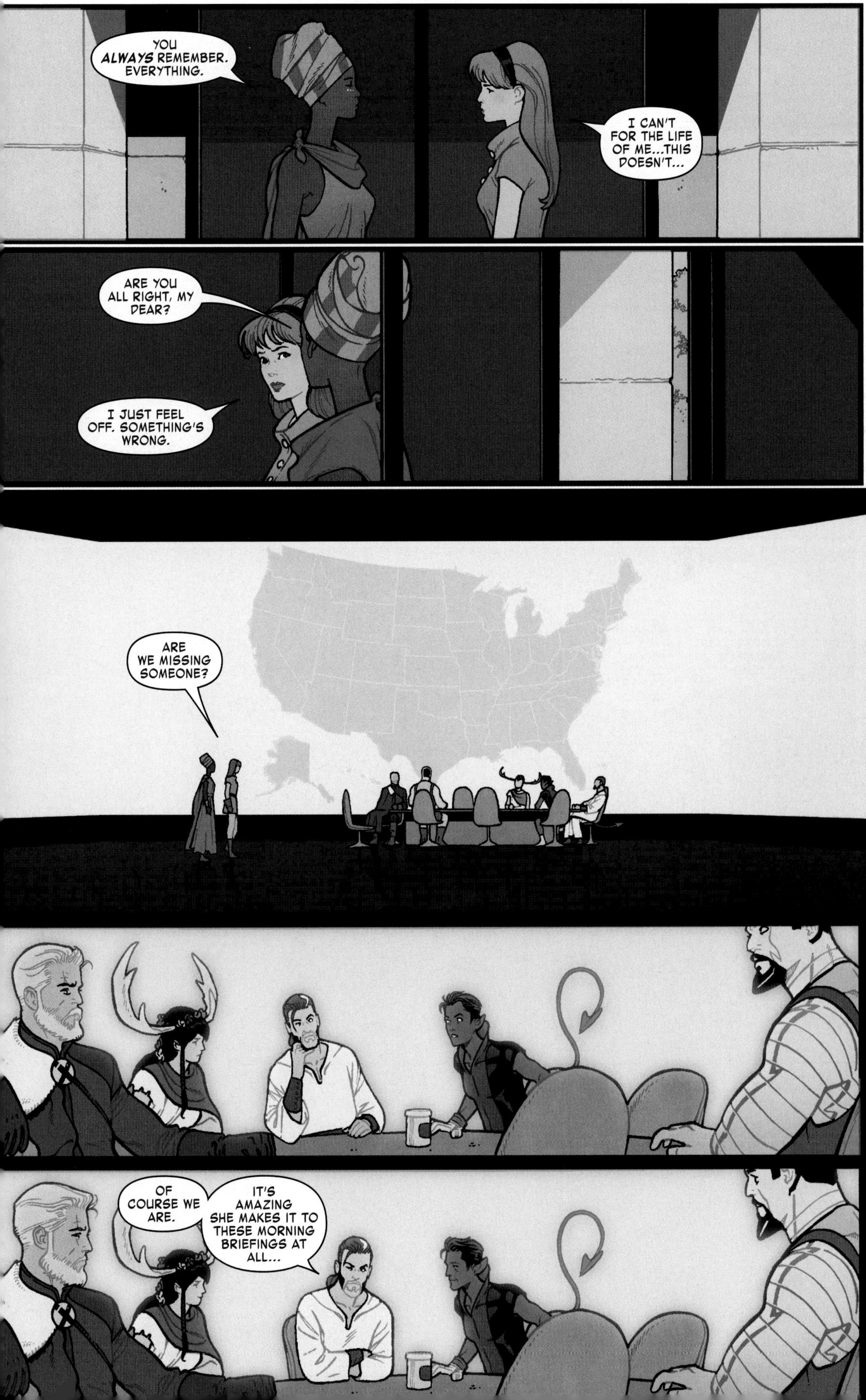
YOU ALWAYS REMEMBER. EVERYTHING.
I CAN'T FOR THE LIFE OF ME...THIS DOESN'T...
ARE YOU ALL RIGHT, MY DEAR?
I JUST FEEL OFF. SOMETHING'S WRONG.
ARE WE MISSING SOMEONE?
OF COURSE WE ARE.
IT'S AMAZING SHE MAKES IT TO THESE MORNING BRIEFINGS AT ALL...

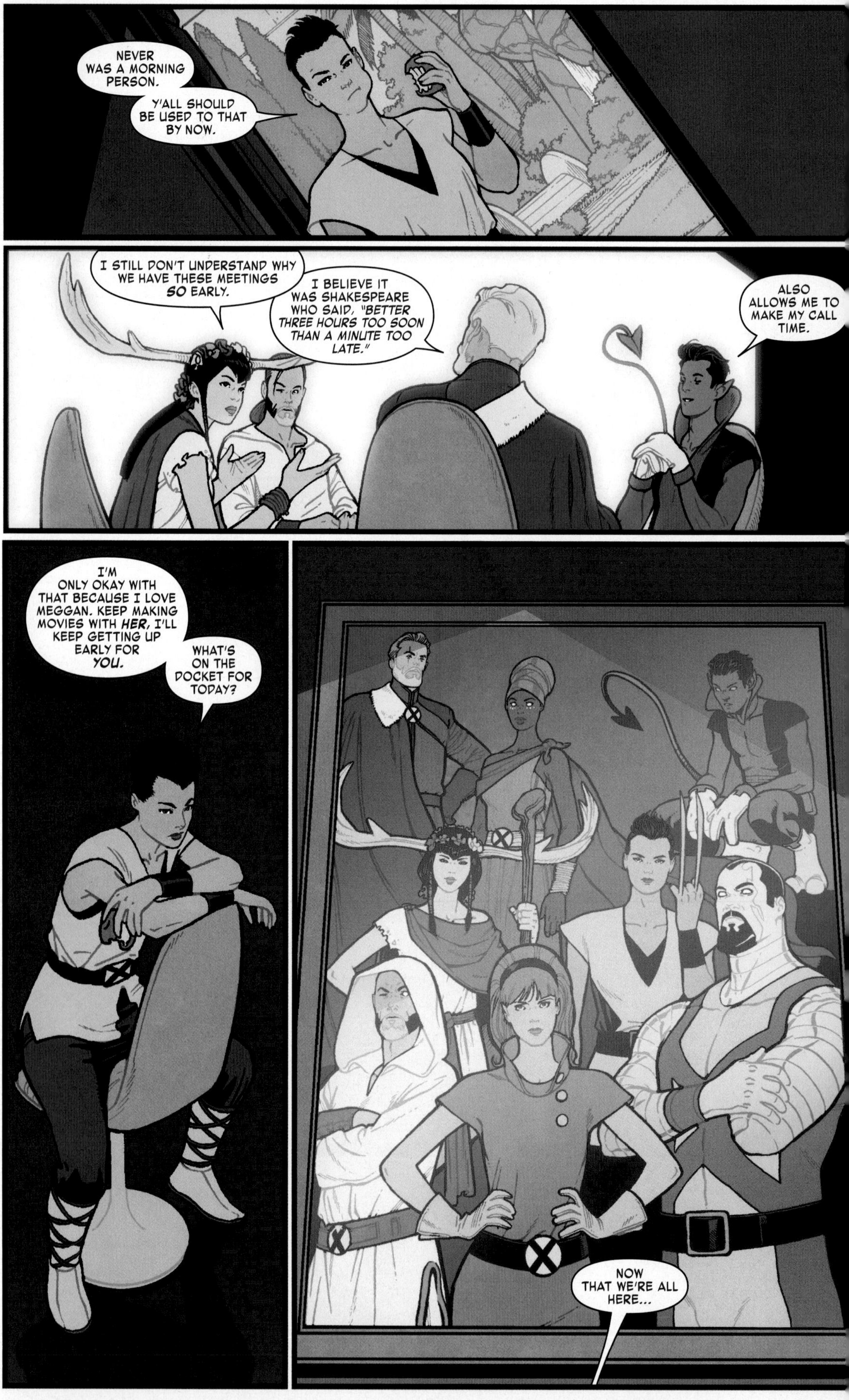
NEVER WAS A MORNING PERSON.
Y'ALL SHOULD BE USED TO THAT BY NOW.
I STILL DON'T UNDERSTAND WHY WE HAVE THESE MEETINGS *SO* EARLY.
I BELIEVE IT WAS SHAKESPEARE WHO SAID, *"BETTER THREE HOURS TOO SOON THAN A MINUTE TOO LATE."*
ALSO ALLOWS ME TO MAKE MY CALL TIME.
I'M ONLY OKAY WITH THAT BECAUSE I LOVE MEGGAN. KEEP MAKING MOVIES WITH *HER*, I'LL KEEP GETTING UP EARLY FOR *YOU.*
WHAT'S ON THE DOCKET FOR TODAY?
NOW THAT WE'RE ALL HERE...

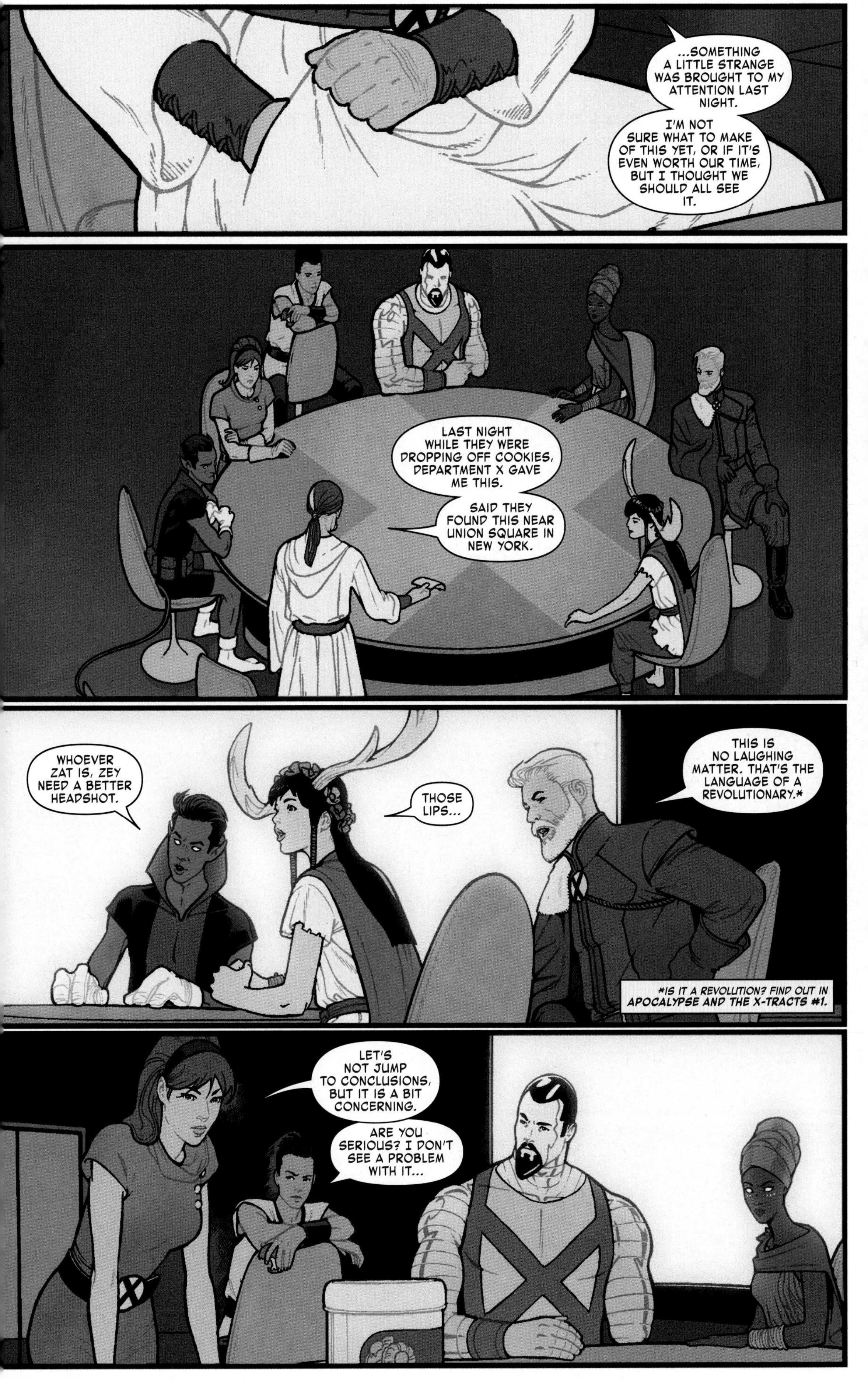
...SOMETHING A LITTLE STRANGE WAS BROUGHT TO MY ATTENTION LAST NIGHT.
I'M NOT SURE WHAT TO MAKE OF THIS YET, OR IF IT'S EVEN WORTH OUR TIME, BUT I THOUGHT WE SHOULD ALL SEE IT.
LAST NIGHT WHILE THEY WERE DROPPING OFF COOKIES, DEPARTMENT X GAVE ME THIS.
SAID THEY FOUND THIS NEAR UNION SQUARE IN NEW YORK.
WHOEVER ZAT IS, ZEY NEED A BETTER HEADSHOT.
THOSE LIPS...
THIS IS NO LAUGHING MATTER. THAT'S THE LANGUAGE OF A REVOLUTIONARY.*
*IS IT A REVOLUTION? FIND OUT IN APOCALYPSE AND THE X-TRACTS #1.
LET'S NOT JUMP TO CONCLUSIONS, BUT IT IS A BIT CONCERNING.
ARE YOU SERIOUS? I DON'T SEE A PROBLEM WITH IT...

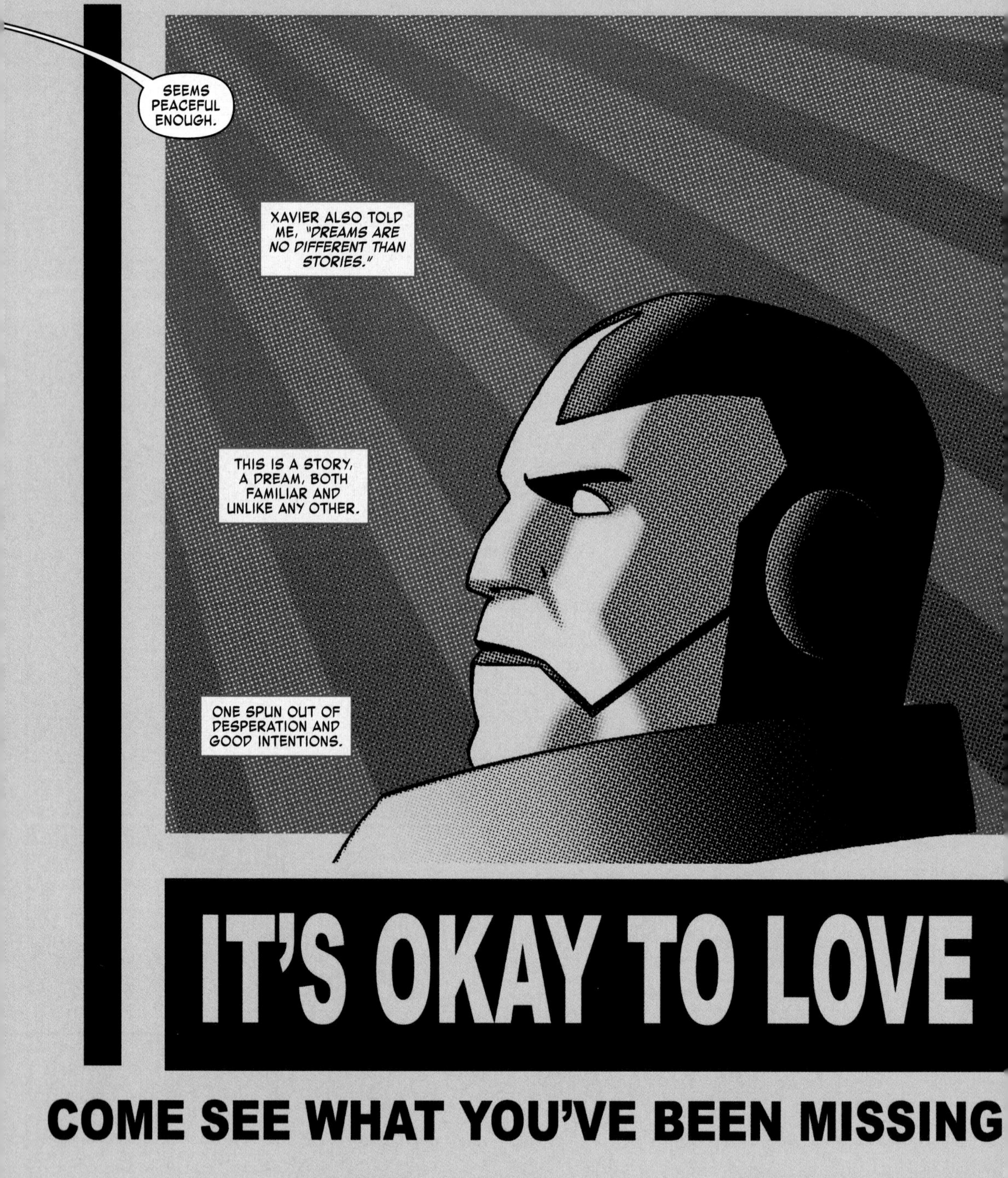
SEEMS PEACEFUL ENOUGH.
XAVIER ALSO TOLD ME, "DREAMS ARE NO DIFFERENT THAN STORIES."
THIS IS A STORY, A DREAM, BOTH FAMILIAR AND UNLIKE ANY OTHER.
ONE SPUN OUT OF DESPERATION AND GOOD INTENTIONS.
IT'S OKAY TO LOVE
COME SEE WHAT YOU'VE BEEN MISSING

"You cannot buy the revolution. You cannot make the revolution. You can only be the revolution. It is in your spirit, or it is nowhere."

—Ursula K. Le Guin, *'The Dispossessed'*

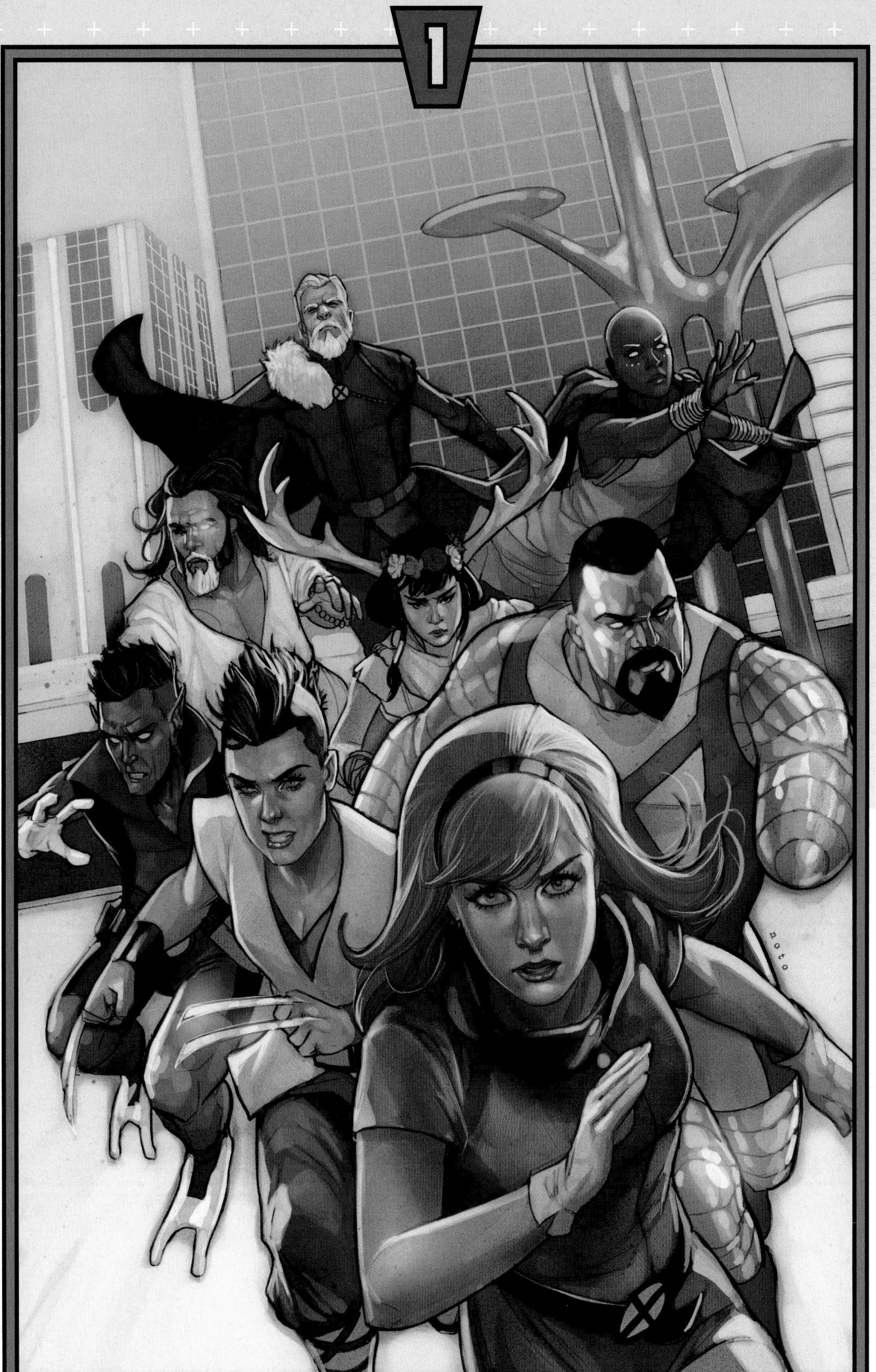
1

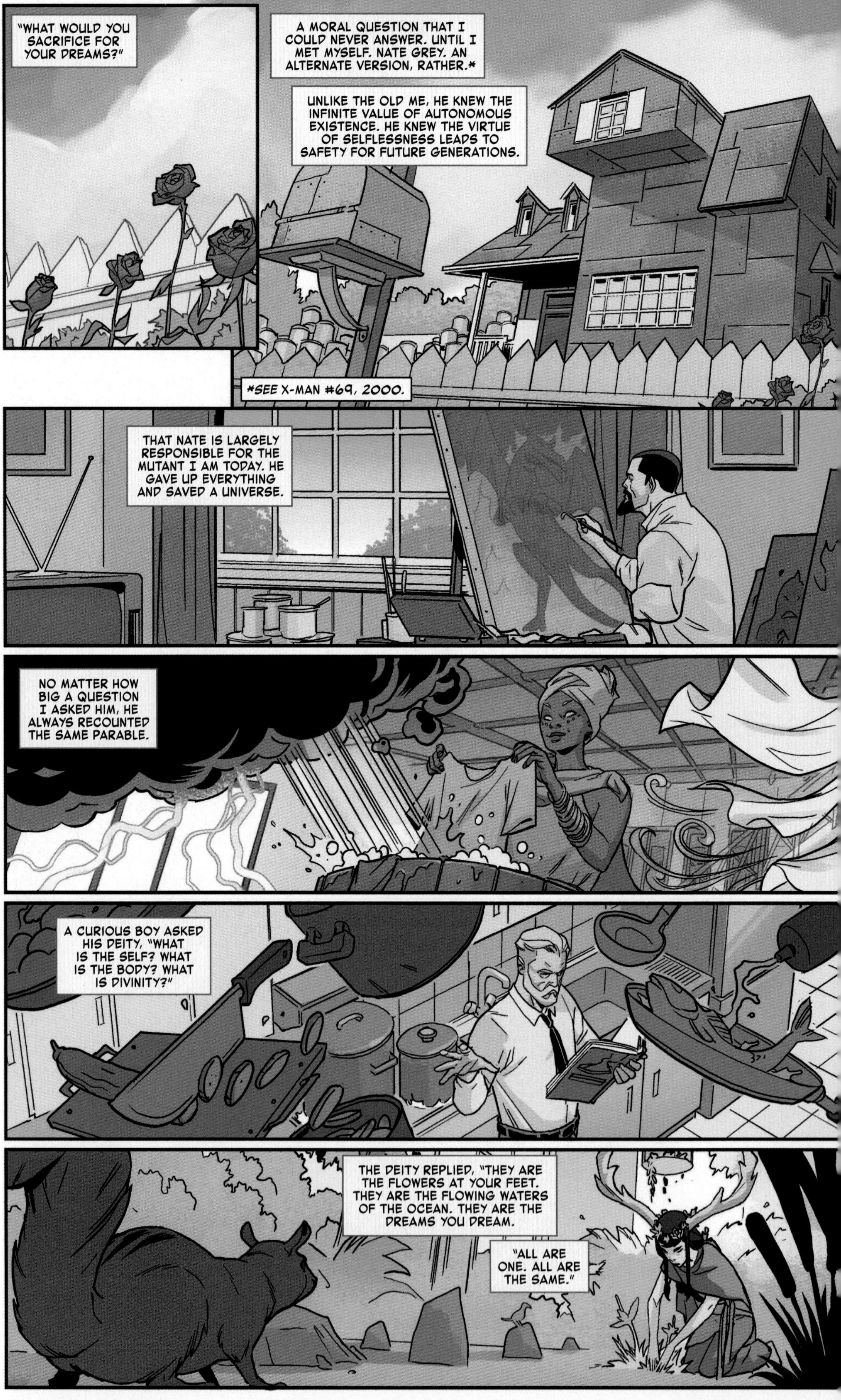
"WHAT WOULD YOU SACRIFICE FOR YOUR DREAMS?"
A MORAL QUESTION THAT I COULD NEVER ANSWER. UNTIL I MET MYSELF. NATE GREY. AN ALTERNATE VERSION, RATHER.*
UNLIKE THE OLD ME, HE KNEW THE INFINITE VALUE OF AUTONOMOUS EXISTENCE. HE KNEW THE VIRTUE OF SELFLESSNESS LEADS TO SAFETY FOR FUTURE GENERATIONS.
*SEE X-MAN #69, 2000.
THAT NATE IS LARGELY RESPONSIBLE FOR THE MUTANT I AM TODAY. HE GAVE UP EVERYTHING AND SAVED A UNIVERSE.
NO MATTER HOW BIG A QUESTION I ASKED HIM, HE ALWAYS RECOUNTED THE SAME PARABLE.
A CURIOUS BOY ASKED HIS DEITY, "WHAT IS THE SELF? WHAT IS THE BODY? WHAT IS DIVINITY?"
THE DEITY REPLIED, "THEY ARE THE FLOWERS AT YOUR FEET. THEY ARE THE FLOWING WATERS OF THE OCEAN. THEY ARE THE DREAMS YOU DREAM.
"ALL ARE ONE. ALL ARE THE SAME."

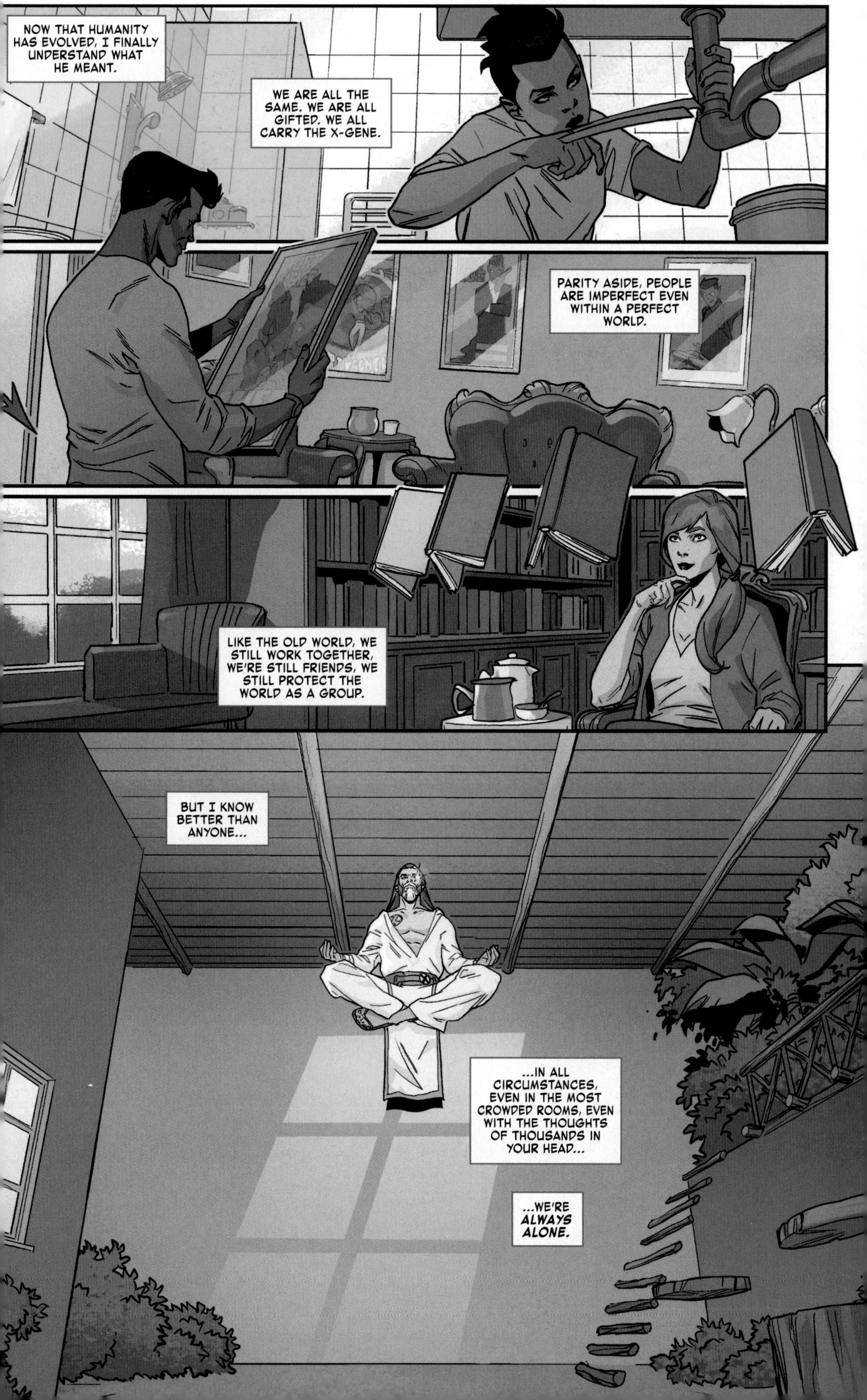
NOW THAT HUMANITY HAS EVOLVED, I FINALLY UNDERSTAND WHAT HE MEANT.
WE ARE ALL THE SAME. WE ARE ALL GIFTED. WE ALL CARRY THE X-GENE.
PARITY ASIDE, PEOPLE ARE IMPERFECT EVEN WITHIN A PERFECT WORLD.
LIKE THE OLD WORLD, WE STILL WORK TOGETHER, WE'RE STILL FRIENDS, WE STILL PROTECT THE WORLD AS A GROUP.
BUT I KNOW BETTER THAN ANYONE...
...IN ALL CIRCUMSTANCES, EVEN IN THE MOST CROWDED ROOMS, EVEN WITH THE THOUGHTS OF THOUSANDS IN YOUR HEAD...
...WE'RE ALWAYS ALONE.

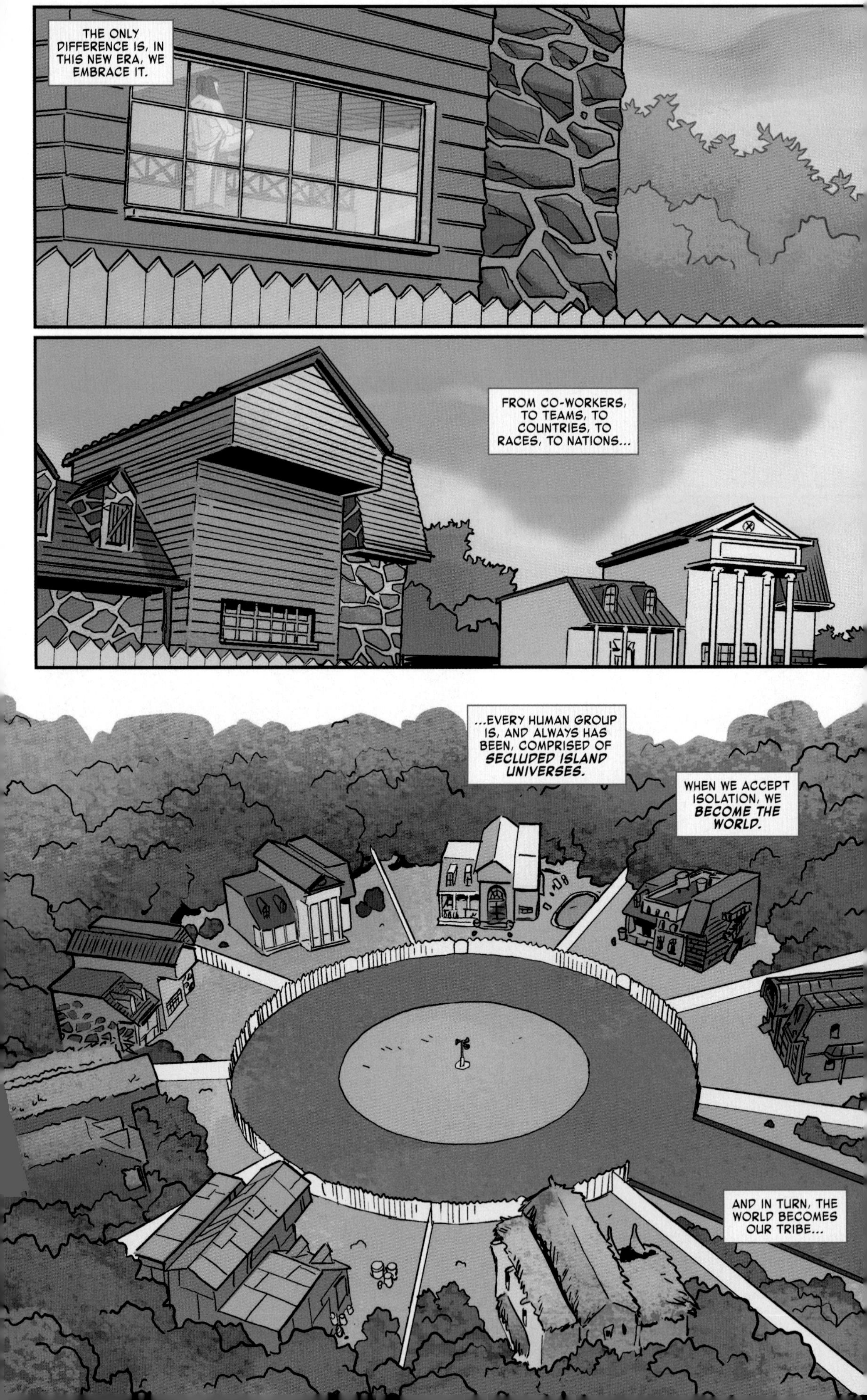
THE ONLY DIFFERENCE IS, IN THIS NEW ERA, WE EMBRACE IT.
FROM CO-WORKERS, TO TEAMS, TO COUNTRIES, TO RACES, TO NATIONS...
...EVERY HUMAN GROUP IS, AND ALWAYS HAS BEEN, COMPRISED OF *SECLUDED ISLAND UNIVERSES.*
WHEN WE ACCEPT ISOLATION, WE *BECOME THE WORLD.*
AND IN TURN, THE WORLD BECOMES OUR TRIBE...

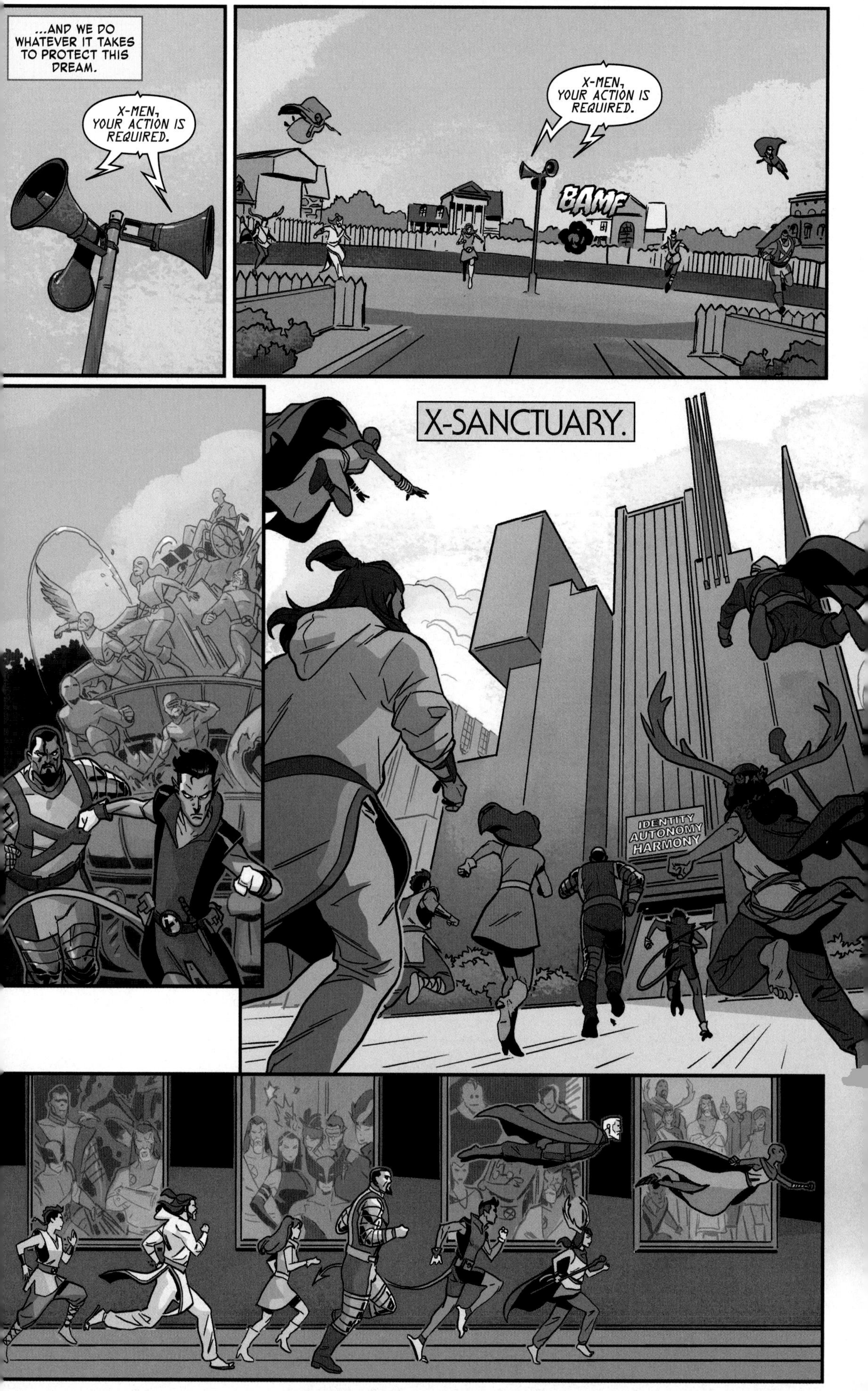
...AND WE DO WHATEVER IT TAKES TO PROTECT THIS DREAM.
X-MEN, YOUR ACTION IS REQUIRED.
X-MEN, YOUR ACTION IS REQUIRED.
BAMF
X-SANCTUARY.
IDENTITY AUTONOMY HARMONY

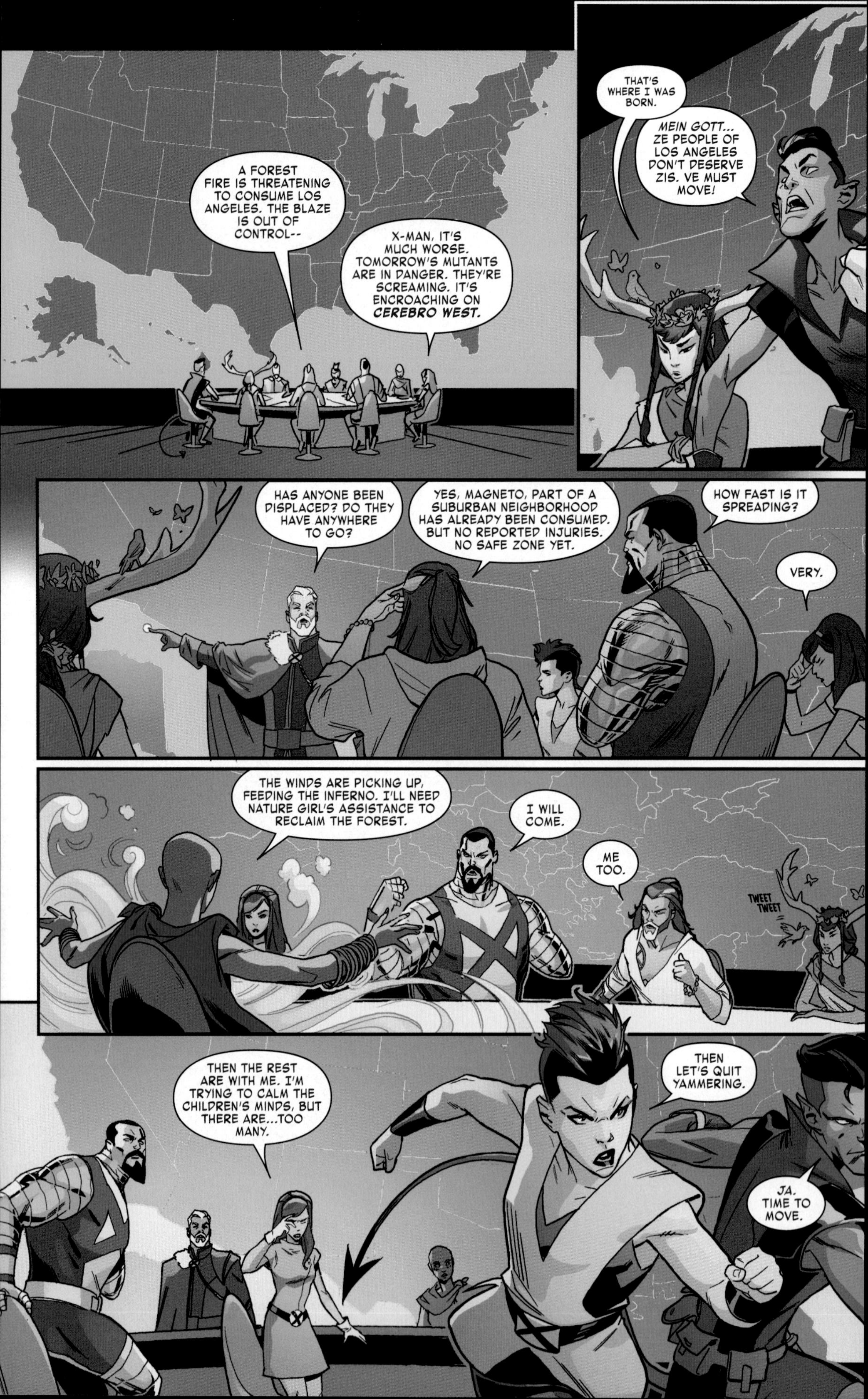
A FOREST FIRE IS THREATENING TO CONSUME LOS ANGELES. THE BLAZE IS OUT OF CONTROL--
X-MAN, IT'S MUCH WORSE. TOMORROW'S MUTANTS ARE IN DANGER. THEY'RE SCREAMING. IT'S ENCROACHING ON CEREBRO WEST.
THAT'S WHERE I WAS BORN.
MEIN GOTT... ZE PEOPLE OF LOS ANGELES DON'T DESERVE ZIS. VE MUST MOVE!
HAS ANYONE BEEN DISPLACED? DO THEY HAVE ANYWHERE TO GO?
YES, MAGNETO, PART OF A SUBURBAN NEIGHBORHOOD HAS ALREADY BEEN CONSUMED. BUT NO REPORTED INJURIES. NO SAFE ZONE YET.
HOW FAST IS IT SPREADING?
VERY.
THE WINDS ARE PICKING UP, FEEDING THE INFERNO. I'LL NEED NATURE GIRL'S ASSISTANCE TO RECLAIM THE FOREST.
I WILL COME.
ME TOO.
TWEET TWEET
THEN THE REST ARE WITH ME. I'M TRYING TO CALM THE CHILDREN'S MINDS, BUT THERE ARE...TOO MANY.
THEN LET'S QUIT YAMMERING.
JA. TIME TO MOVE.

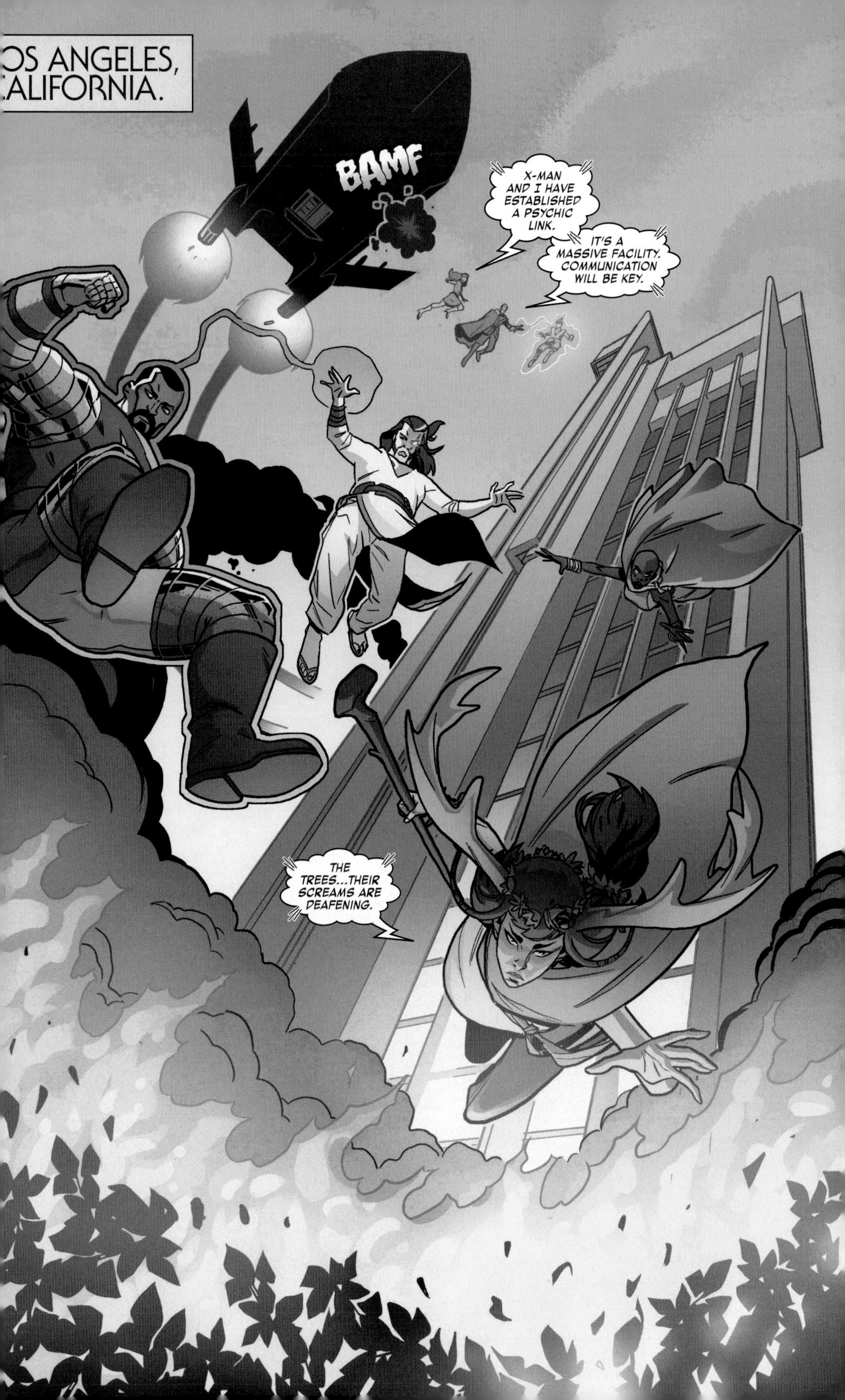
OS ANGELES,
ALIFORNIA.
BAMF
X-MAN AND I HAVE ESTABLISHED A PSYCHIC LINK.
IT'S A MASSIVE FACILITY. COMMUNICATION WILL BE KEY.
THE TREES...THEIR SCREAMS ARE DEAFENING.

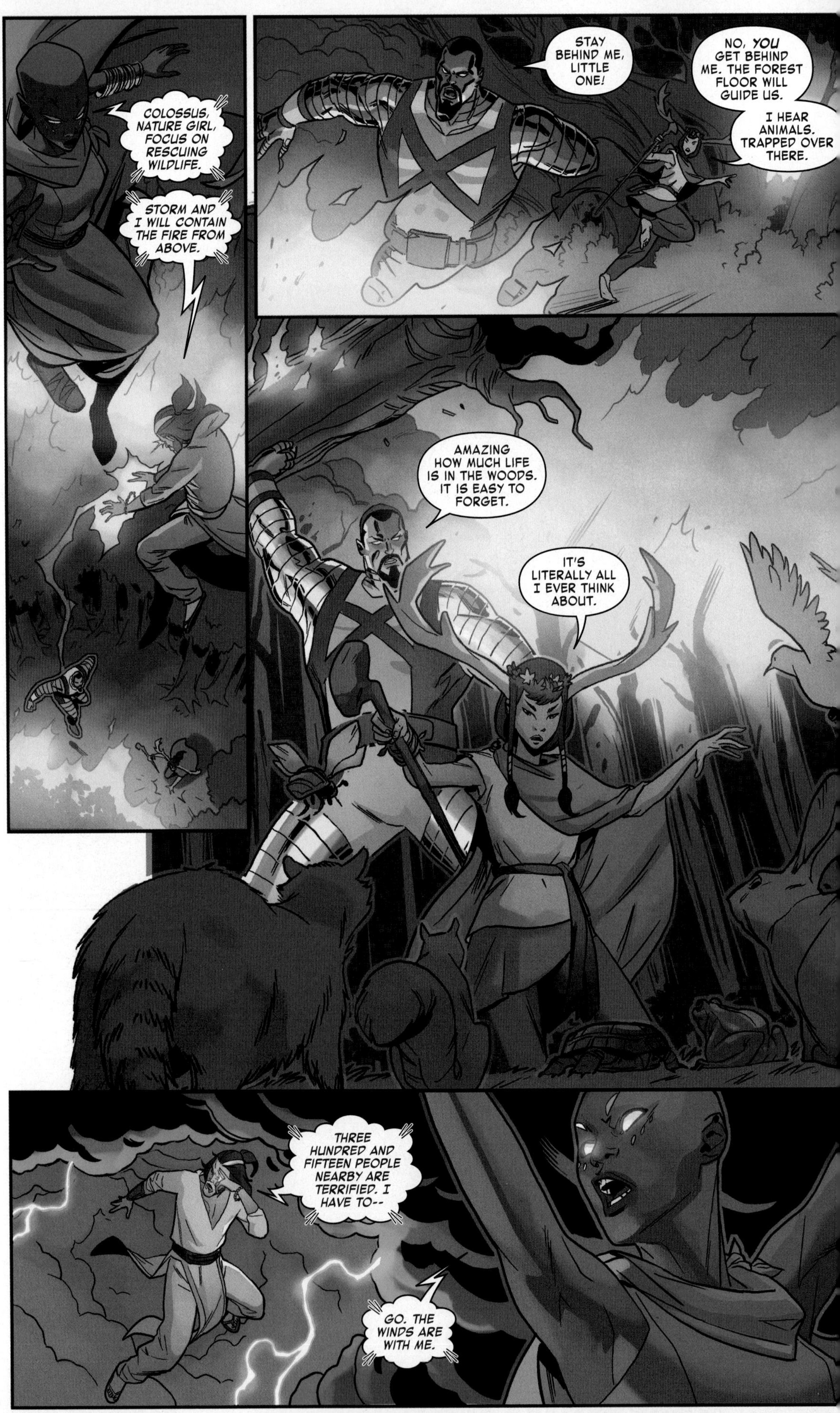
COLOSSUS, NATURE GIRL, FOCUS ON RESCUING WILDLIFE.
STORM AND I WILL CONTAIN THE FIRE FROM ABOVE.
STAY BEHIND ME, LITTLE ONE!
NO, YOU GET BEHIND ME. THE FOREST FLOOR WILL GUIDE US.
I HEAR ANIMALS. TRAPPED OVER THERE.
AMAZING HOW MUCH LIFE IS IN THE WOODS. IT IS EASY TO FORGET.
IT'S LITERALLY ALL I EVER THINK ABOUT.
THREE HUNDRED AND FIFTEEN PEOPLE NEARBY ARE TERRIFIED. I HAVE TO--
GO. THE WINDS ARE WITH ME.

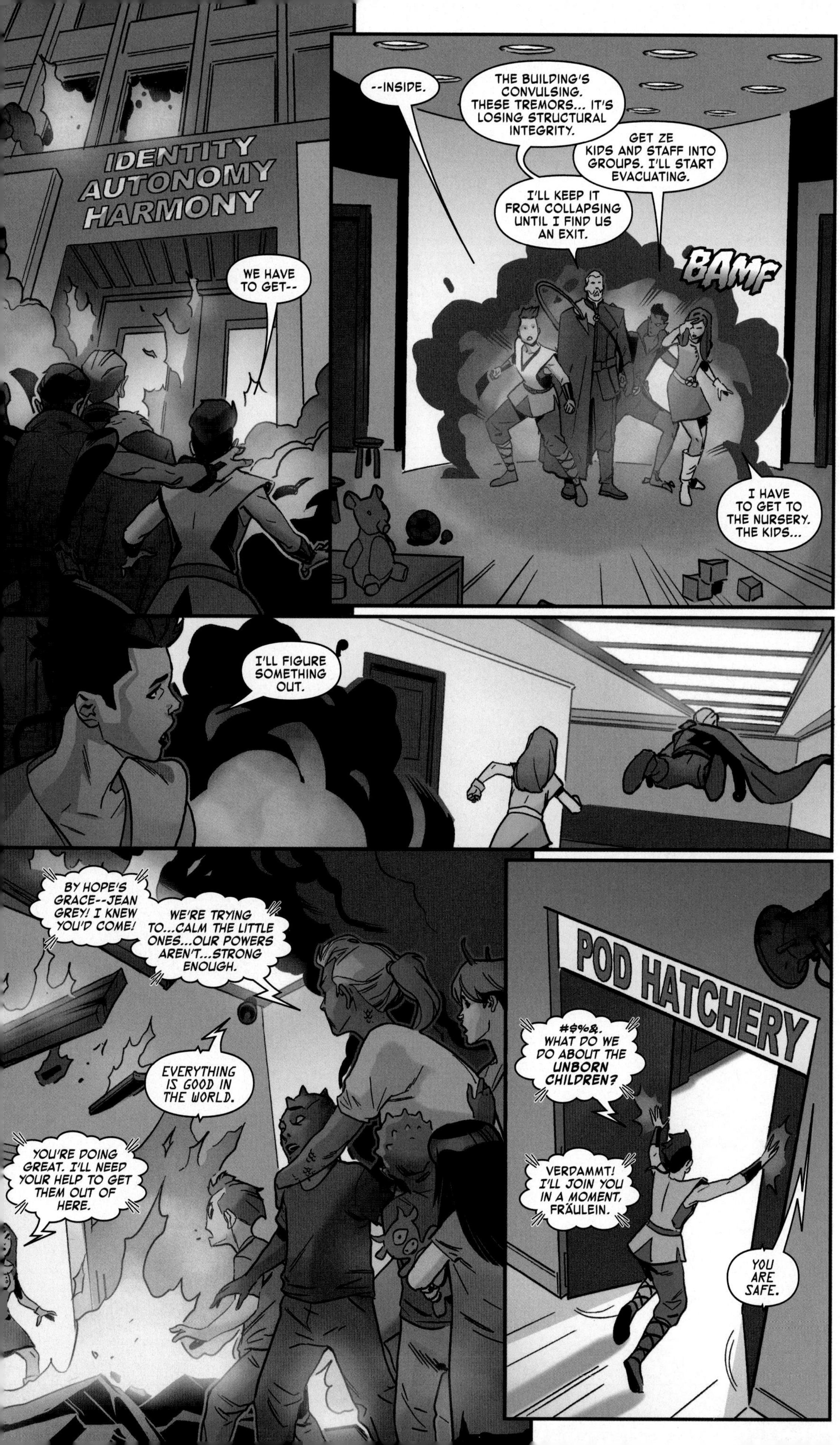
IDENTITY AUTONOMY HARMONY
WE HAVE TO GET--
--INSIDE.
THE BUILDING'S CONVULSING. THESE TREMORS... IT'S LOSING STRUCTURAL INTEGRITY.
GET ZE KIDS AND STAFF INTO GROUPS. I'LL START EVACUATING.
I'LL KEEP IT FROM COLLAPSING UNTIL I FIND US AN EXIT.
BAMF
I HAVE TO GET TO THE NURSERY. THE KIDS...
I'LL FIGURE SOMETHING OUT.
BY HOPE'S GRACE--JEAN GREY! I KNEW YOU'D COME!
WE'RE TRYING TO...CALM THE LITTLE ONES...OUR POWERS AREN'T...STRONG ENOUGH.
EVERYTHING IS GOOD IN THE WORLD.
YOU'RE DOING GREAT. I'LL NEED YOUR HELP TO GET THEM OUT OF HERE.
POD HATCHERY
#$%&. WHAT DO WE DO ABOUT THE UNBORN CHILDREN?
VERDAMMT! I'LL JOIN YOU IN A MOMENT, FRÄULEIN.
YOU ARE SAFE.

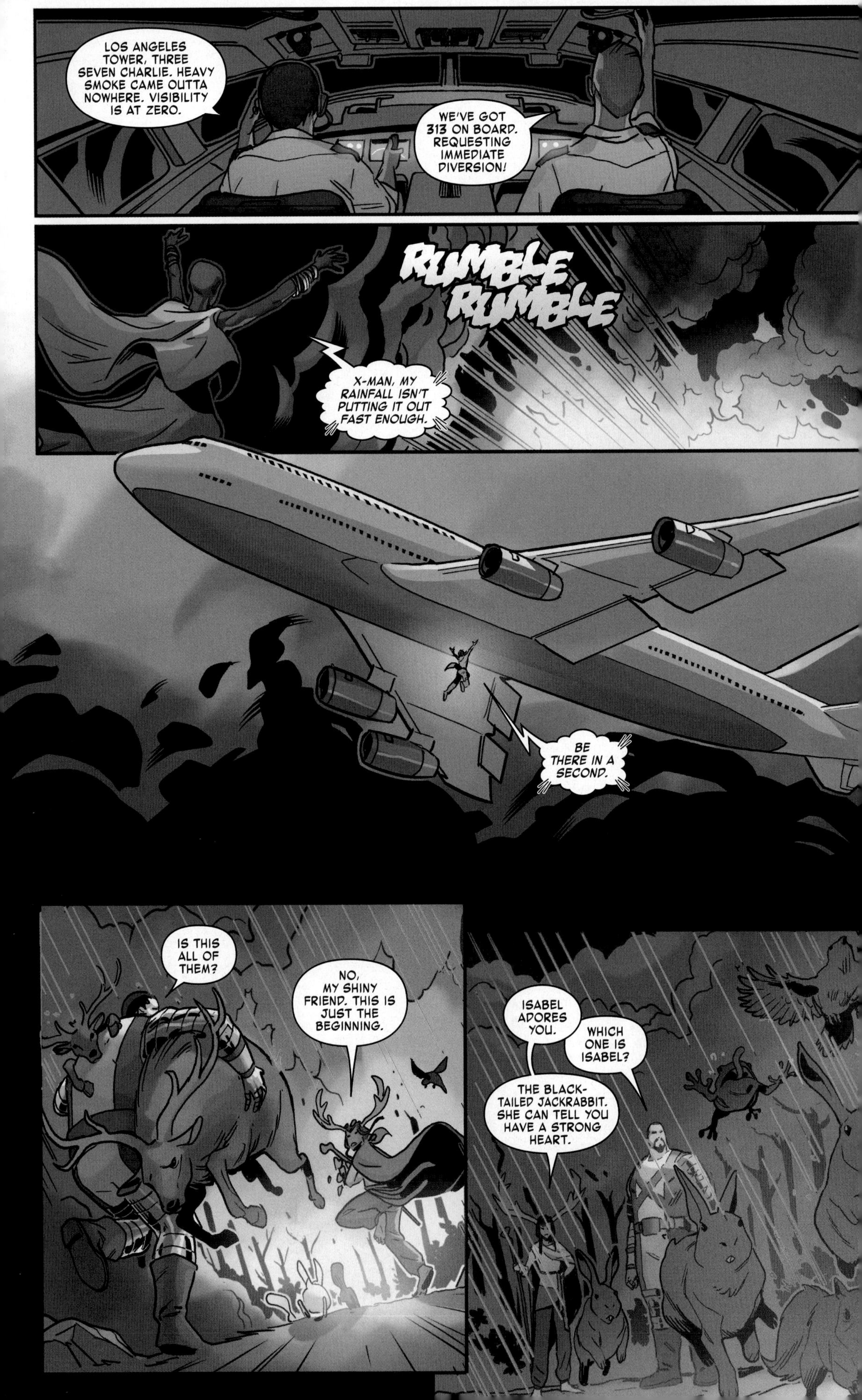
LOS ANGELES TOWER, THREE SEVEN CHARLIE. HEAVY SMOKE CAME OUTTA NOWHERE. VISIBILITY IS AT ZERO.
WE'VE GOT 313 ON BOARD. REQUESTING IMMEDIATE DIVERSION!
RUMBLE RUMBLE
X-MAN, MY RAINFALL ISN'T PUTTING IT OUT FAST ENOUGH.
BE THERE IN A SECOND.
IS THIS ALL OF THEM?
NO, MY SHINY FRIEND. THIS IS JUST THE BEGINNING.
ISABEL ADORES YOU.
WHICH ONE IS ISABEL?
THE BLACK-TAILED JACKRABBIT. SHE CAN TELL YOU HAVE A STRONG HEART.

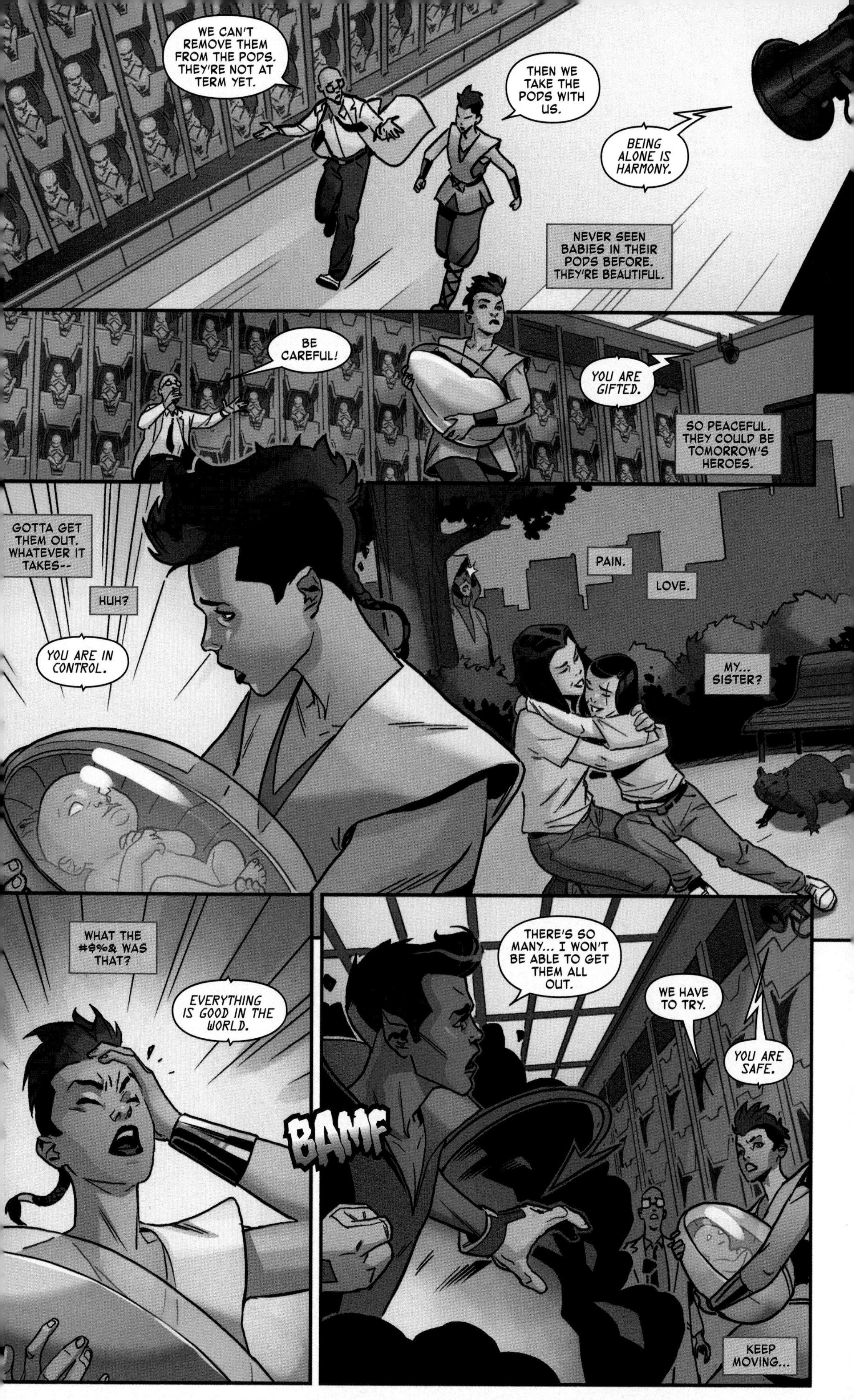
WE CAN'T REMOVE THEM FROM THE PODS. THEY'RE NOT AT TERM YET.
THEN WE TAKE THE PODS WITH US.
BEING ALONE IS HARMONY.
NEVER SEEN BABIES IN THEIR PODS BEFORE. THEY'RE BEAUTIFUL.
BE CAREFUL!
YOU ARE GIFTED.
SO PEACEFUL. THEY COULD BE TOMORROW'S HEROES.
GOTTA GET THEM OUT. WHATEVER IT TAKES--
HUH?
YOU ARE IN CONTROL.
PAIN.
LOVE.
MY... SISTER?
WHAT THE #$%& WAS THAT?
EVERYTHING IS GOOD IN THE WORLD.
BAMF
THERE'S SO MANY... I WON'T BE ABLE TO GET THEM ALL OUT.
WE HAVE TO TRY.
YOU ARE SAFE.
KEEP MOVING...

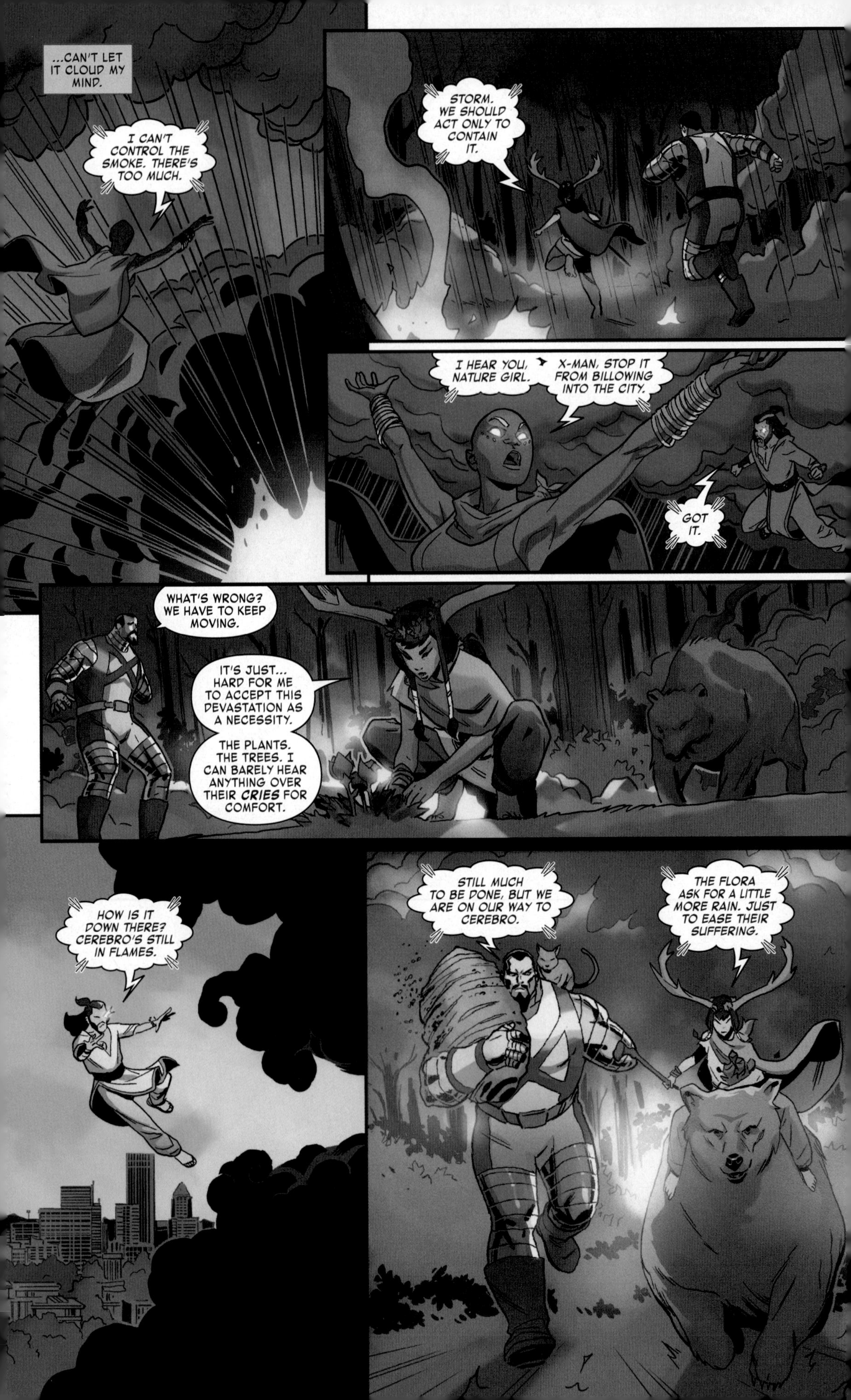
...CAN'T LET IT CLOUD MY MIND.
I CAN'T CONTROL THE SMOKE. THERE'S TOO MUCH.
STORM. WE SHOULD ACT ONLY TO CONTAIN IT.
I HEAR YOU, NATURE GIRL.
X-MAN, STOP IT FROM BILLOWING INTO THE CITY.
GOT IT.
WHAT'S WRONG? WE HAVE TO KEEP MOVING.
IT'S JUST... HARD FOR ME TO ACCEPT THIS DEVASTATION AS A NECESSITY.
THE PLANTS. THE TREES. I CAN BARELY HEAR ANYTHING OVER THEIR CRIES FOR COMFORT.
HOW IS IT DOWN THERE? CEREBRO'S STILL IN FLAMES.
STILL MUCH TO BE DONE, BUT WE ARE ON OUR WAY TO CEREBRO.
THE FLORA ASK FOR A LITTLE MORE RAIN. JUST TO EASE THEIR SUFFERING.

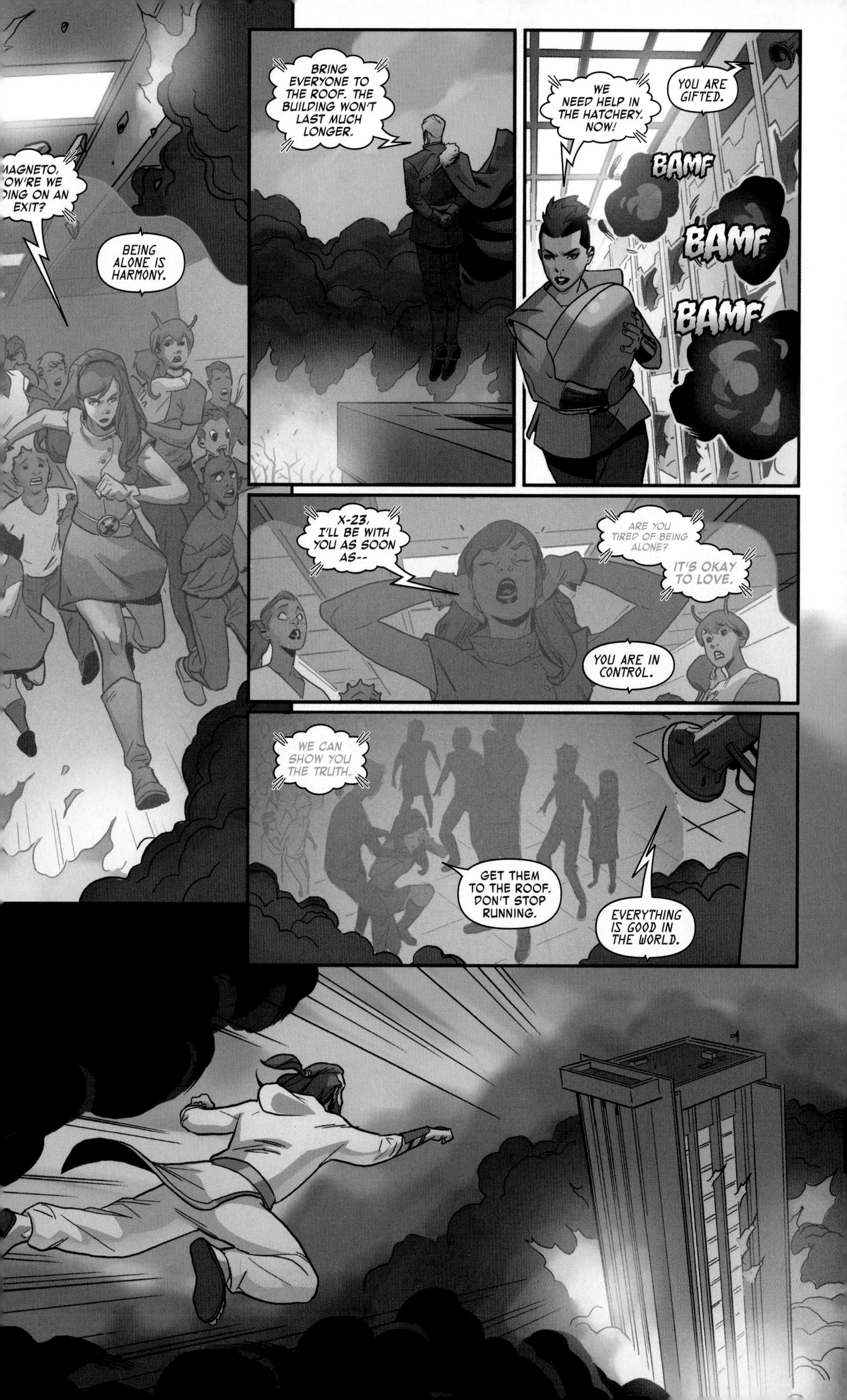
MAGNETO, OW'RE WE DING ON AN EXIT?
BEING ALONE IS HARMONY.
BRING EVERYONE TO THE ROOF. THE BUILDING WON'T LAST MUCH LONGER.
WE NEED HELP IN THE HATCHERY. NOW!
YOU ARE GIFTED.
BAMF
BAMF
BAMF
X-23, I'LL BE WITH YOU AS SOON AS--
ARE YOU TIRED OF BEING ALONE?
IT'S OKAY TO LOVE.
YOU ARE IN CONTROL.
WE CAN SHOW YOU THE TRUTH.
GET THEM TO THE ROOF. DON'T STOP RUNNING.
EVERYTHING IS GOOD IN THE WORLD.

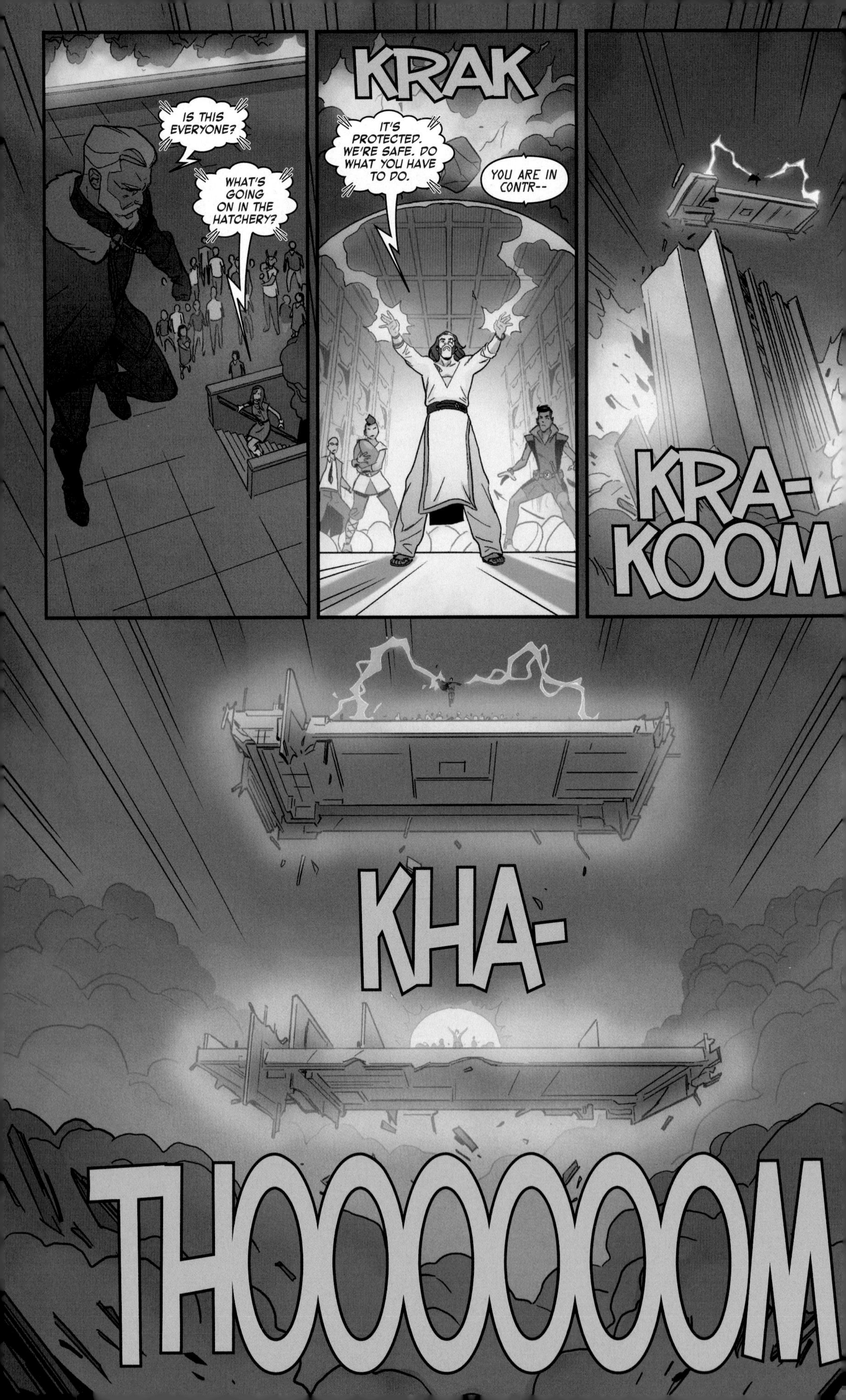
IS THIS EVERYONE?
WHAT'S GOING ON IN THE HATCHERY?
KRAK
IT'S PROTECTED. WE'RE SAFE. DO WHAT YOU HAVE TO DO.
YOU ARE IN CONTR--
KRA-KOOM
KHA-
THOOOOOOM

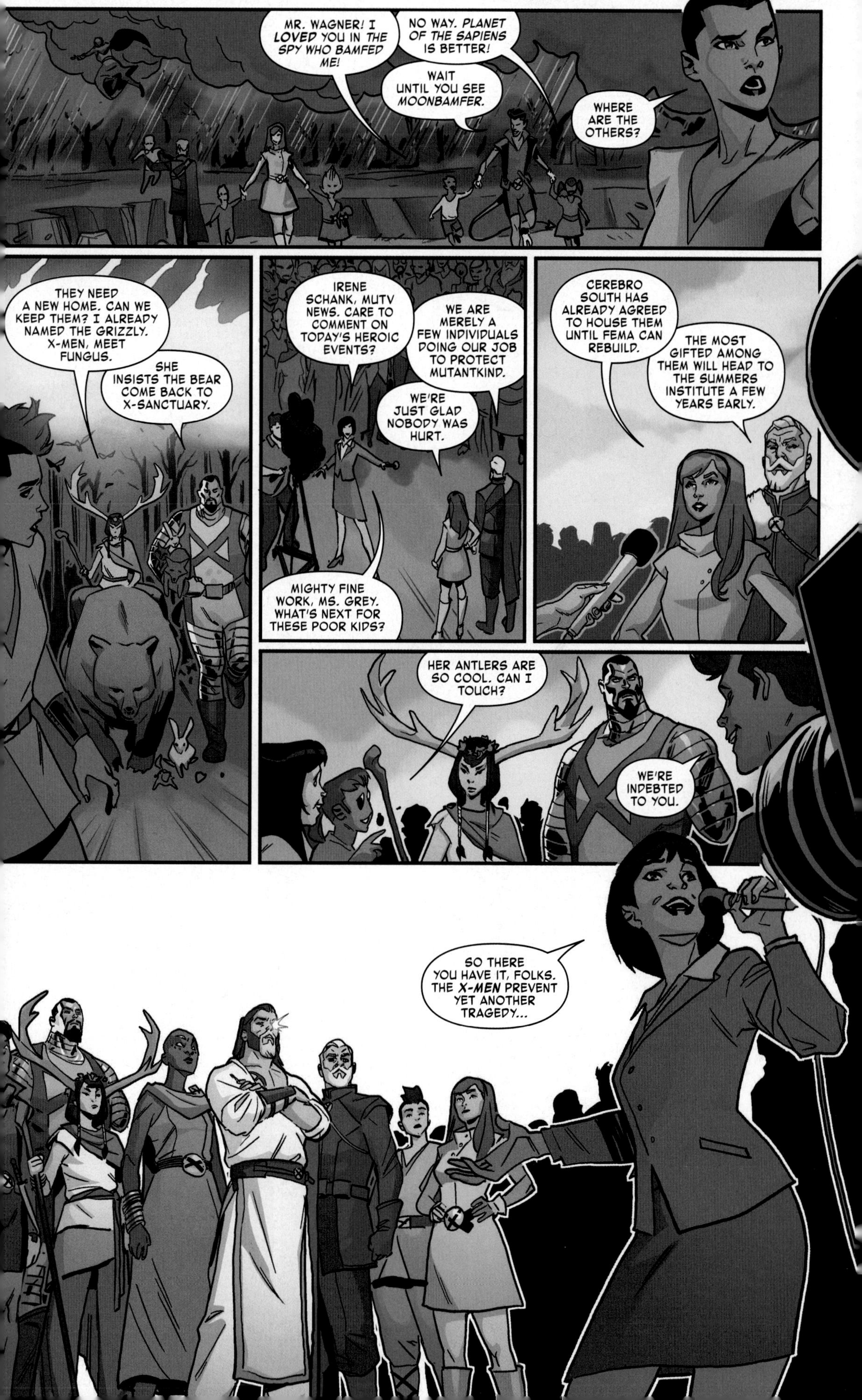
MR. WAGNER! I LOVED YOU IN THE SPY WHO BAMFED ME!
NO WAY. PLANET OF THE SAPIENS IS BETTER!
WAIT UNTIL YOU SEE MOONBAMFER.
WHERE ARE THE OTHERS?
THEY NEED A NEW HOME. CAN WE KEEP THEM? I ALREADY NAMED THE GRIZZLY. X-MEN, MEET FUNGUS.
SHE INSISTS THE BEAR COME BACK TO X-SANCTUARY.
IRENE SCHANK, MUTV NEWS. CARE TO COMMENT ON TODAY'S HEROIC EVENTS?
WE ARE MERELY A FEW INDIVIDUALS DOING OUR JOB TO PROTECT MUTANTKIND.
WE'RE JUST GLAD NOBODY WAS HURT.
MIGHTY FINE WORK, MS. GREY. WHAT'S NEXT FOR THESE POOR KIDS?
CEREBRO SOUTH HAS ALREADY AGREED TO HOUSE THEM UNTIL FEMA CAN REBUILD.
THE MOST GIFTED AMONG THEM WILL HEAD TO THE SUMMERS INSTITUTE A FEW YEARS EARLY.
HER ANTLERS ARE SO COOL. CAN I TOUCH?
WE'RE INDEBTED TO YOU.
SO THERE YOU HAVE IT, FOLKS. THE X-MEN PREVENT YET ANOTHER TRAGEDY...

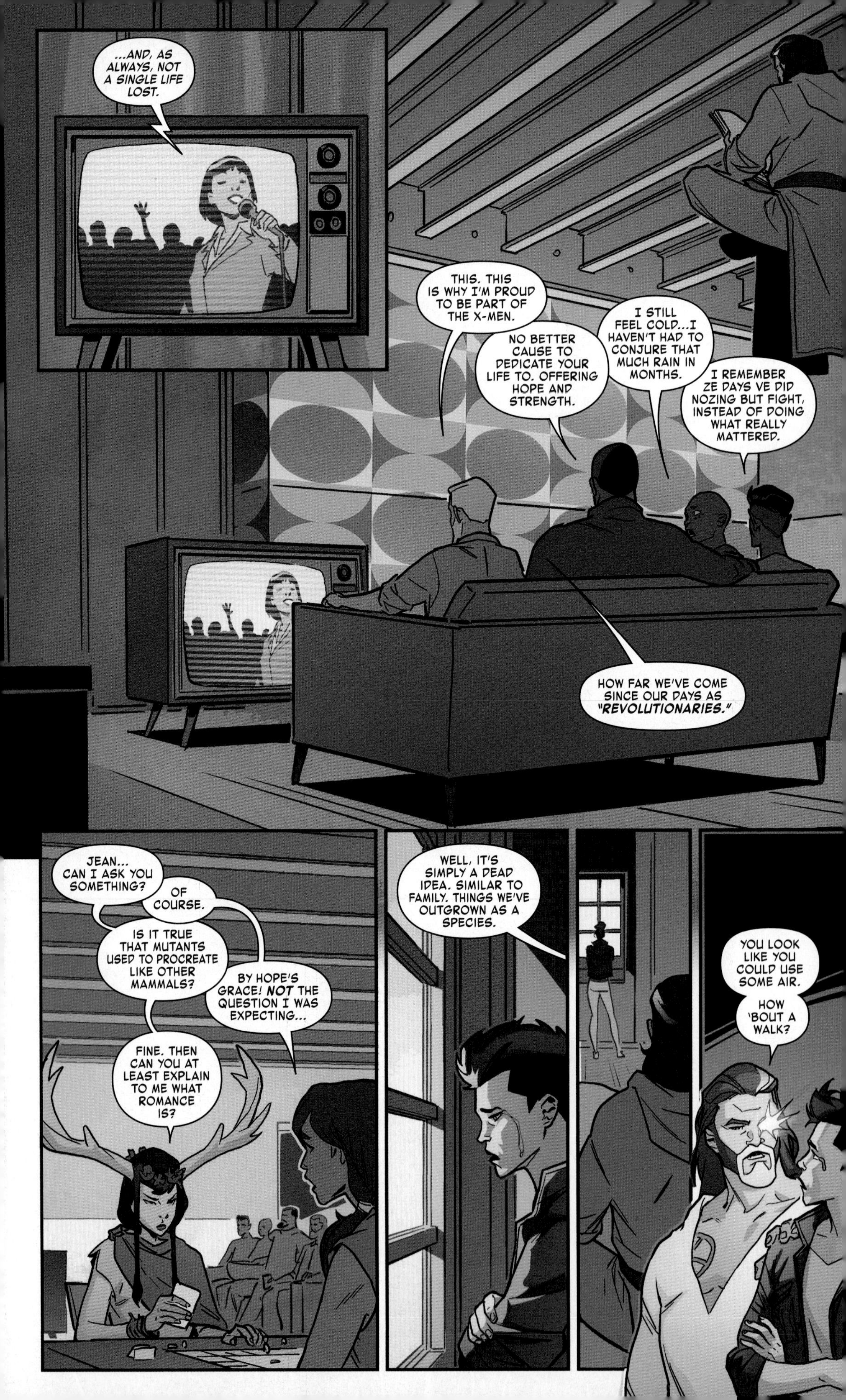
...AND, AS ALWAYS, NOT A SINGLE LIFE LOST.
THIS. THIS IS WHY I'M PROUD TO BE PART OF THE X-MEN.
NO BETTER CAUSE TO DEDICATE YOUR LIFE TO. OFFERING HOPE AND STRENGTH.
I STILL FEEL COLD...I HAVEN'T HAD TO CONJURE THAT MUCH RAIN IN MONTHS.
I REMEMBER ZE DAYS VE DID NOZING BUT FIGHT, INSTEAD OF DOING WHAT REALLY MATTERED.
HOW FAR WE'VE COME SINCE OUR DAYS AS "REVOLUTIONARIES."
JEAN... CAN I ASK YOU SOMETHING?
OF COURSE.
IS IT TRUE THAT MUTANTS USED TO PROCREATE LIKE OTHER MAMMALS?
BY HOPE'S GRACE! NOT THE QUESTION I WAS EXPECTING...
FINE. THEN CAN YOU AT LEAST EXPLAIN TO ME WHAT ROMANCE IS?
WELL, IT'S SIMPLY A DEAD IDEA. SIMILAR TO FAMILY. THINGS WE'VE OUTGROWN AS A SPECIES.
YOU LOOK LIKE YOU COULD USE SOME AIR.
HOW 'BOUT A WALK?

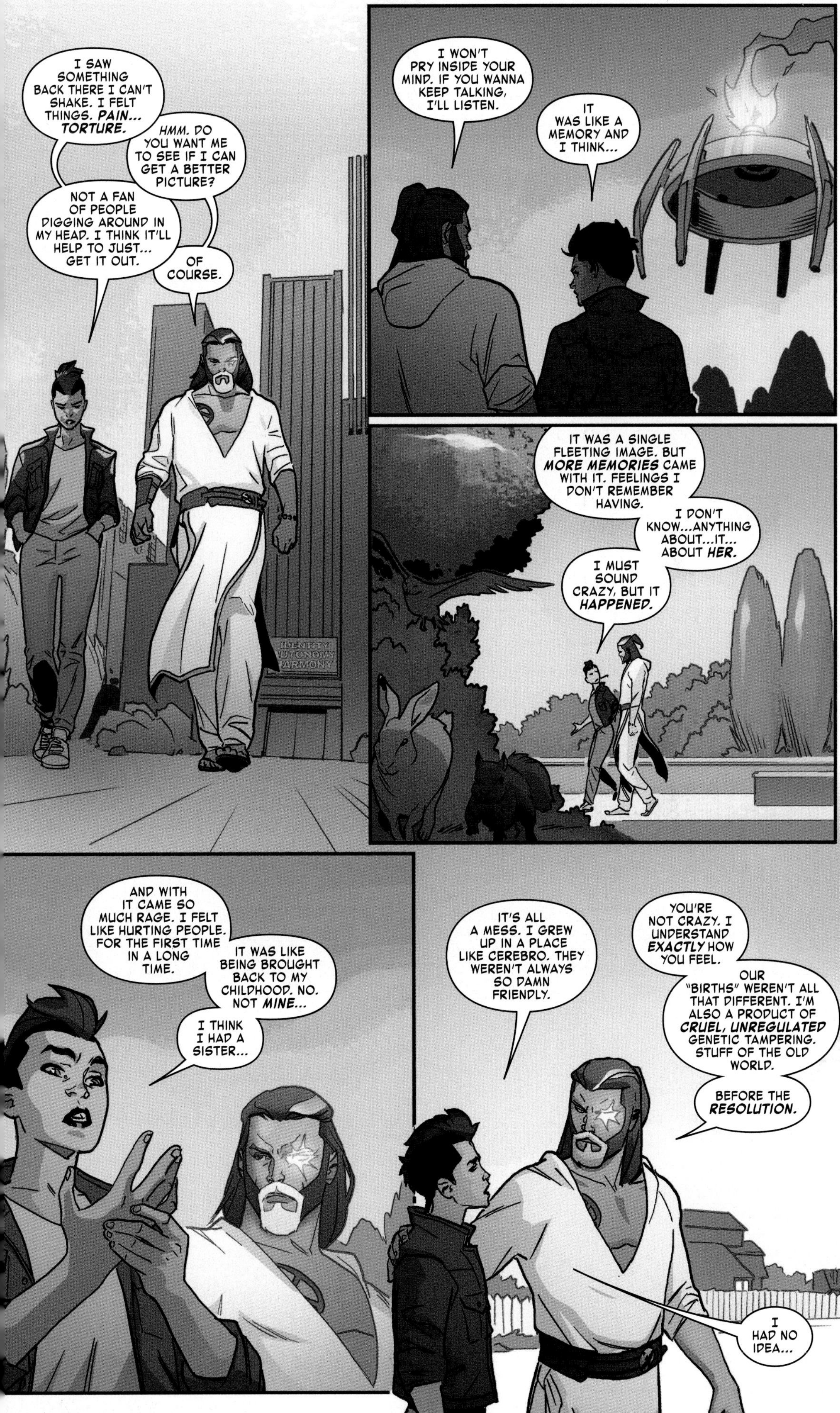
I SAW SOMETHING BACK THERE I CAN'T SHAKE. I FELT THINGS. *PAIN... TORTURE.*
HMM. DO YOU WANT ME TO SEE IF I CAN GET A BETTER PICTURE?
NOT A FAN OF PEOPLE DIGGING AROUND IN MY HEAD. I THINK IT'LL HELP TO JUST... GET IT OUT.
OF COURSE.
IDENTITY
I WON'T PRY INSIDE YOUR MIND. IF YOU WANNA KEEP TALKING, I'LL LISTEN.
IT WAS LIKE A MEMORY AND I THINK...
IT WAS A SINGLE FLEETING IMAGE. BUT *MORE MEMORIES* CAME WITH IT. FEELINGS I DON'T REMEMBER HAVING.
I DON'T KNOW...ANYTHING ABOUT...IT... ABOUT *HER.*
I MUST SOUND CRAZY, BUT IT *HAPPENED.*
AND WITH IT CAME SO MUCH RAGE. I FELT LIKE HURTING PEOPLE. FOR THE FIRST TIME IN A LONG TIME.
IT WAS LIKE BEING BROUGHT BACK TO MY CHILDHOOD. NO. NOT *MINE...*
I THINK I HAD A SISTER...
IT'S ALL A MESS. I GREW UP IN A PLACE LIKE CEREBRO. THEY WEREN'T ALWAYS SO DAMN FRIENDLY.
YOU'RE NOT CRAZY. I UNDERSTAND *EXACTLY* HOW YOU FEEL.
OUR "BIRTHS" WEREN'T ALL THAT DIFFERENT. I'M ALSO A PRODUCT OF *CRUEL, UNREGULATED* GENETIC TAMPERING. STUFF OF THE OLD WORLD.
BEFORE THE *RESOLUTION.*
I HAD NO IDEA...

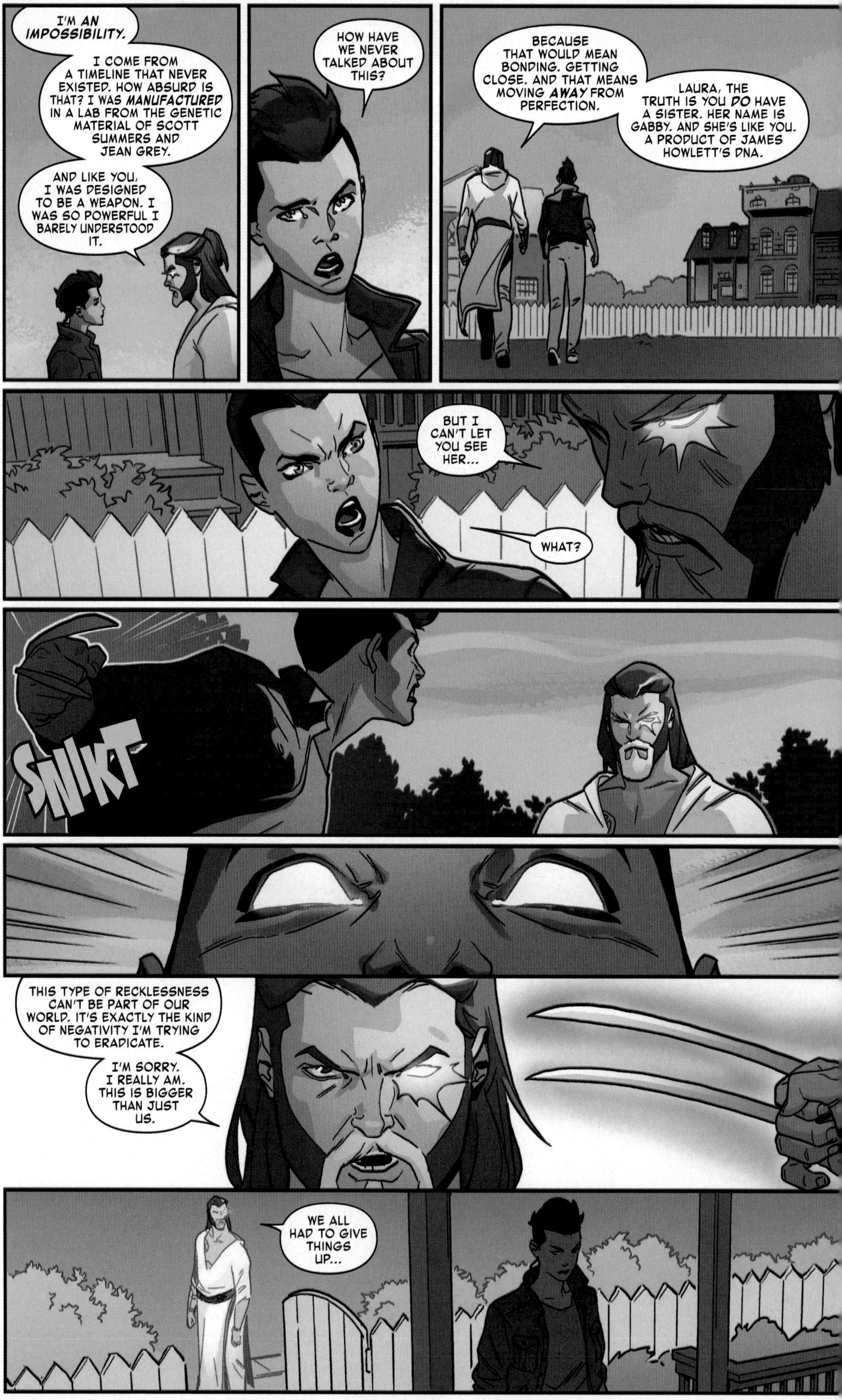
I'M AN IMPOSSIBILITY.
I COME FROM A TIMELINE THAT NEVER EXISTED. HOW ABSURD IS THAT? I WAS MANUFACTURED IN A LAB FROM THE GENETIC MATERIAL OF SCOTT SUMMERS AND JEAN GREY.
AND LIKE YOU, I WAS DESIGNED TO BE A WEAPON. I WAS SO POWERFUL I BARELY UNDERSTOOD IT.
HOW HAVE WE NEVER TALKED ABOUT THIS?
BECAUSE THAT WOULD MEAN BONDING. GETTING CLOSE. AND THAT MEANS MOVING AWAY FROM PERFECTION.
LAURA, THE TRUTH IS YOU DO HAVE A SISTER. HER NAME IS GABBY. AND SHE'S LIKE YOU. A PRODUCT OF JAMES HOWLETT'S DNA.
BUT I CAN'T LET YOU SEE HER...
WHAT?
SNIKT
THIS TYPE OF RECKLESSNESS CAN'T BE PART OF OUR WORLD. IT'S EXACTLY THE KIND OF NEGATIVITY I'M TRYING TO ERADICATE.
I'M SORRY. I REALLY AM. THIS IS BIGGER THAN JUST US.
WE ALL HAD TO GIVE THINGS UP...

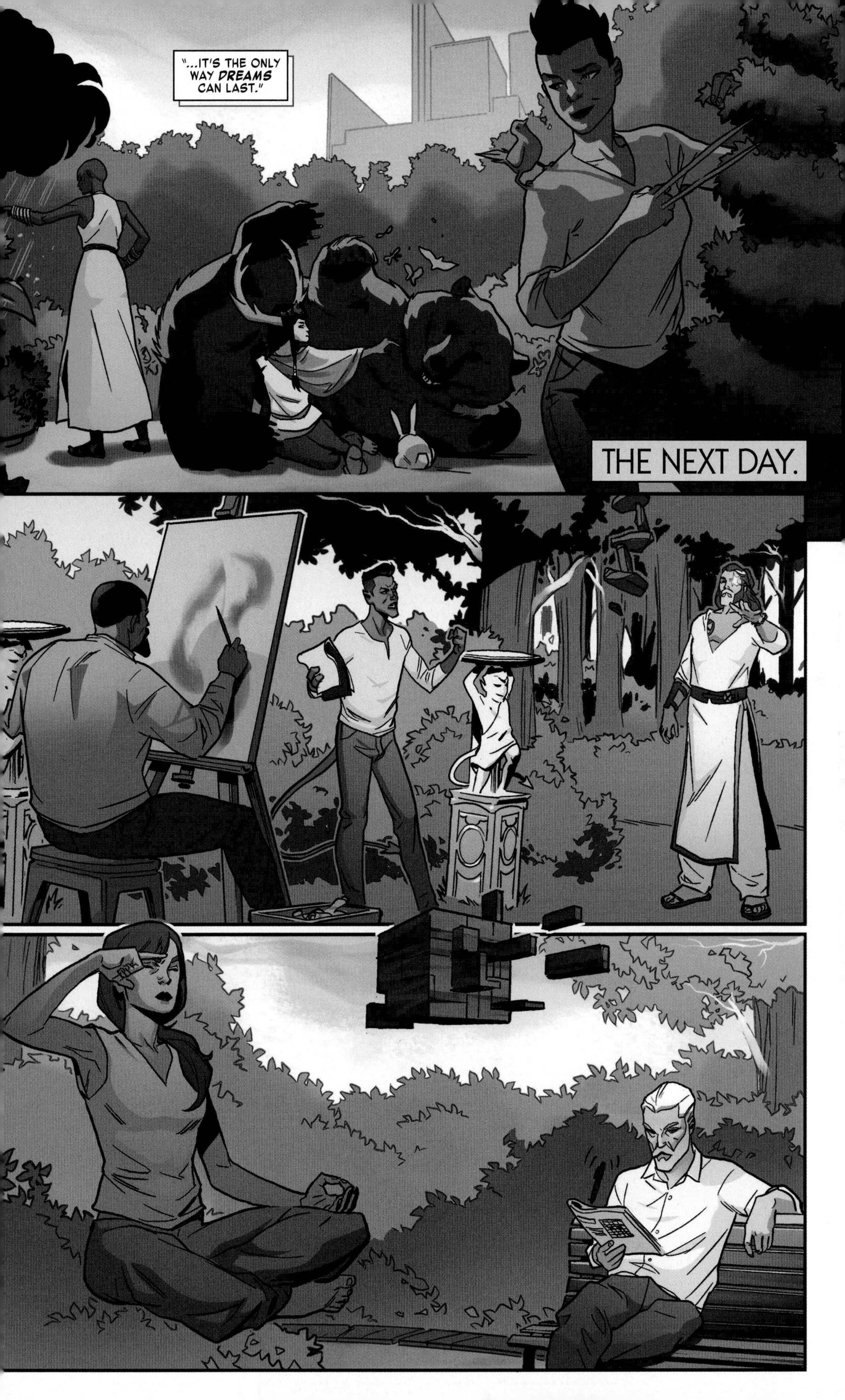
"...IT'S THE ONLY WAY DREAMS CAN LAST."
THE NEXT DAY.

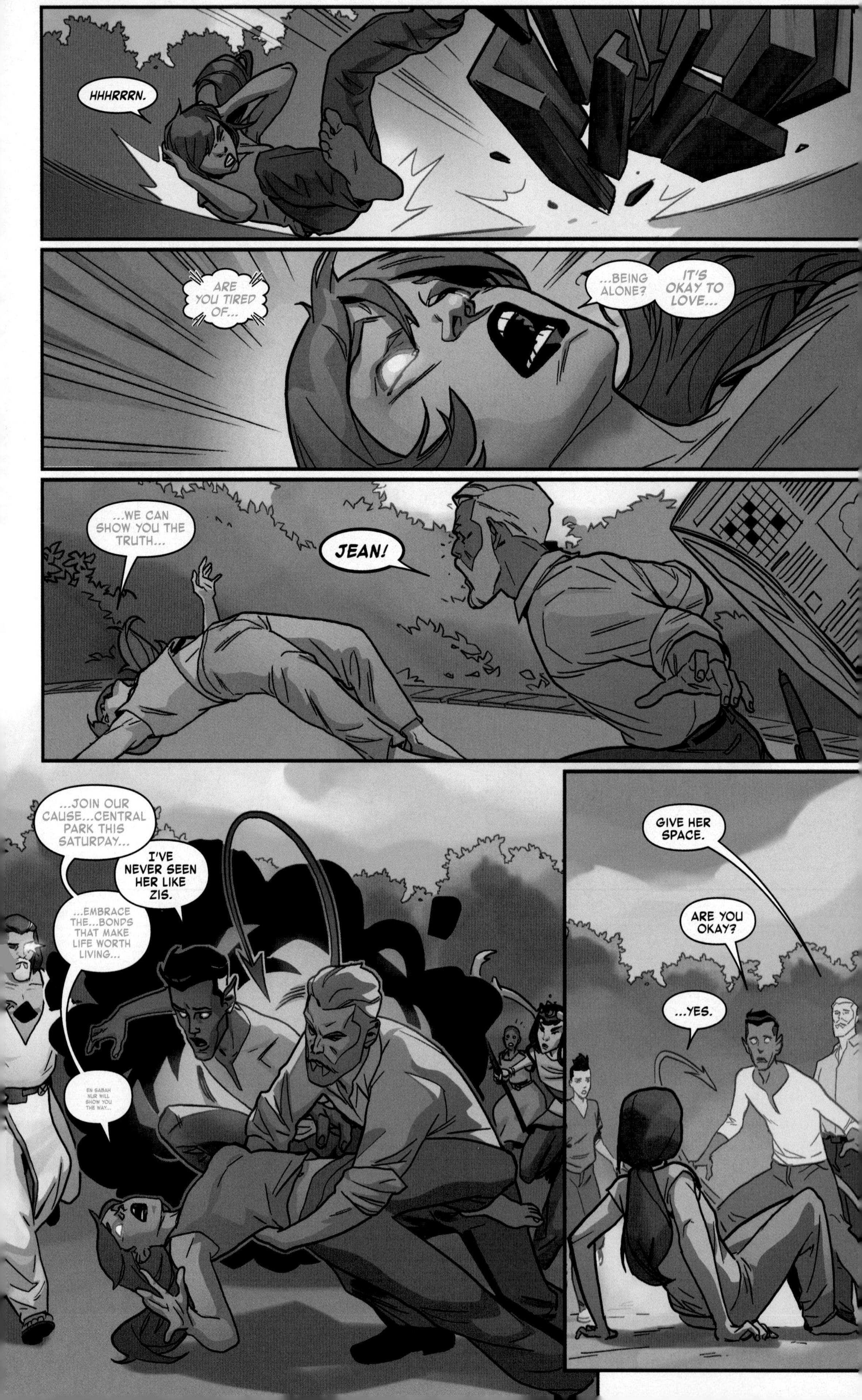
HHHRRRN.
ARE YOU TIRED OF...
...BEING ALONE?
IT'S OKAY TO LOVE...
...WE CAN SHOW YOU THE TRUTH...
JEAN!
...JOIN OUR CAUSE...CENTRAL PARK THIS SATURDAY...
I'VE NEVER SEEN HER LIKE ZIS.
...EMBRACE THE...BONDS THAT MAKE LIFE WORTH LIVING...
EN SABAH NUR WILL SHOW YOU THE WAY...
GIVE HER SPACE.
ARE YOU OKAY?
...YES.

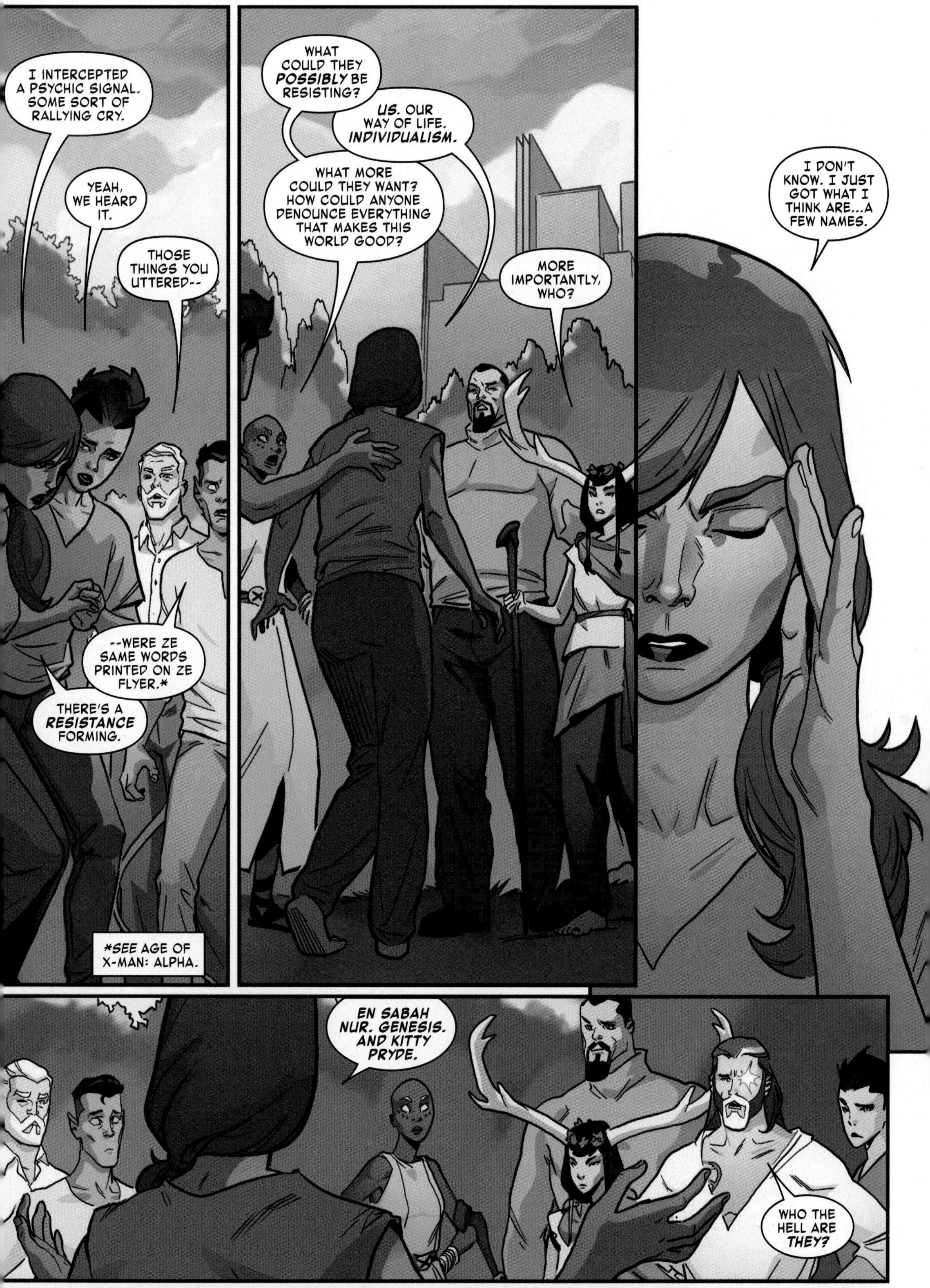
I INTERCEPTED A PSYCHIC SIGNAL. SOME SORT OF RALLYING CRY.
YEAH, WE HEARD IT.
THOSE THINGS YOU UTTERED--
--WERE ZE SAME WORDS PRINTED ON ZE FLYER.*
THERE'S A RESISTANCE FORMING.
*SEE AGE OF X-MAN: ALPHA.
WHAT COULD THEY POSSIBLY BE RESISTING?
US. OUR WAY OF LIFE. INDIVIDUALISM.
WHAT MORE COULD THEY WANT? HOW COULD ANYONE DENOUNCE EVERYTHING THAT MAKES THIS WORLD GOOD?
MORE IMPORTANTLY, WHO?
I DON'T KNOW. I JUST GOT WHAT I THINK ARE...A FEW NAMES.
EN SABAH NUR. GENESIS. AND KITTY PRYDE.
WHO THE HELL ARE THEY?

"There is a tyranny in the womb of every Utopia."

–Bertrand de Jouvenel

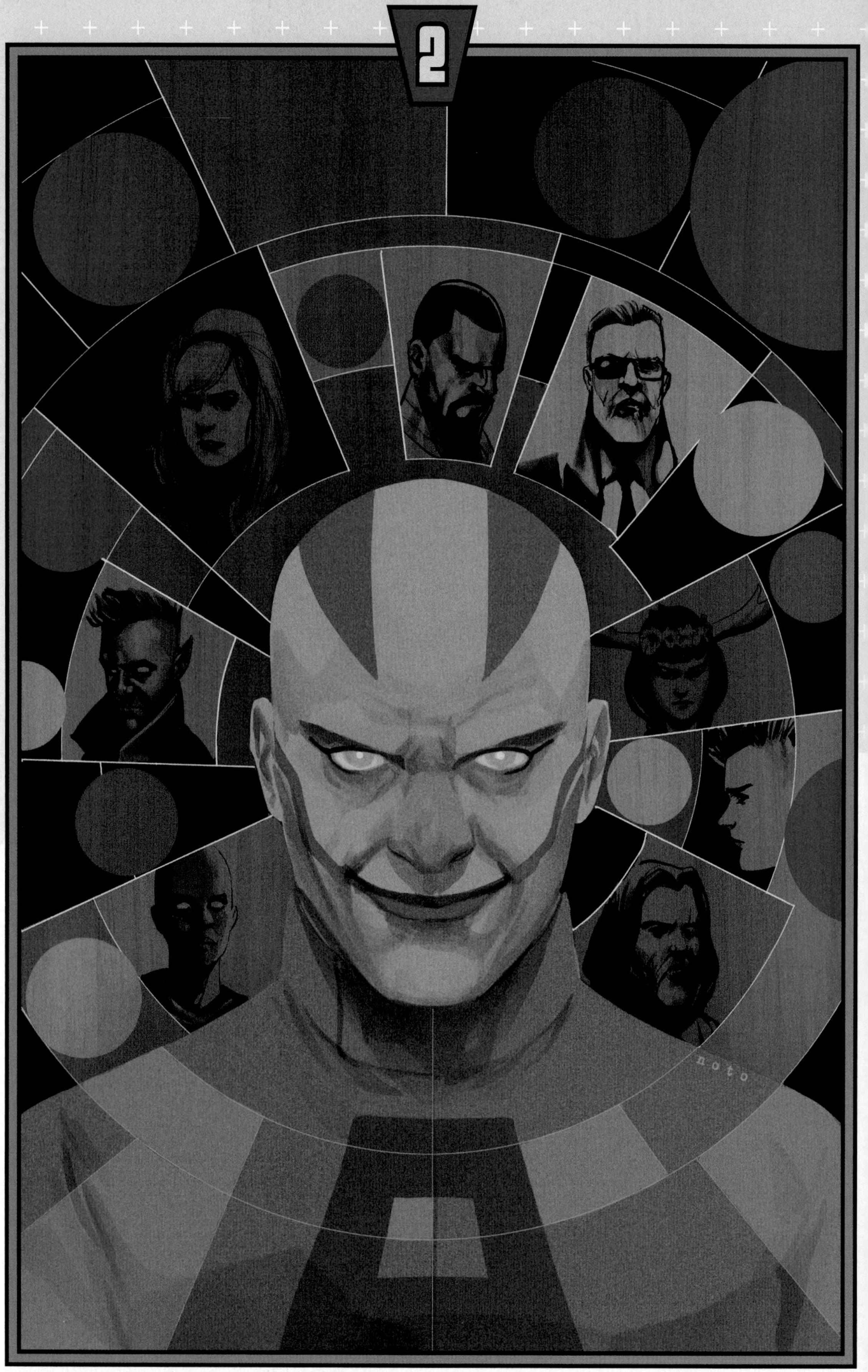
2
noto

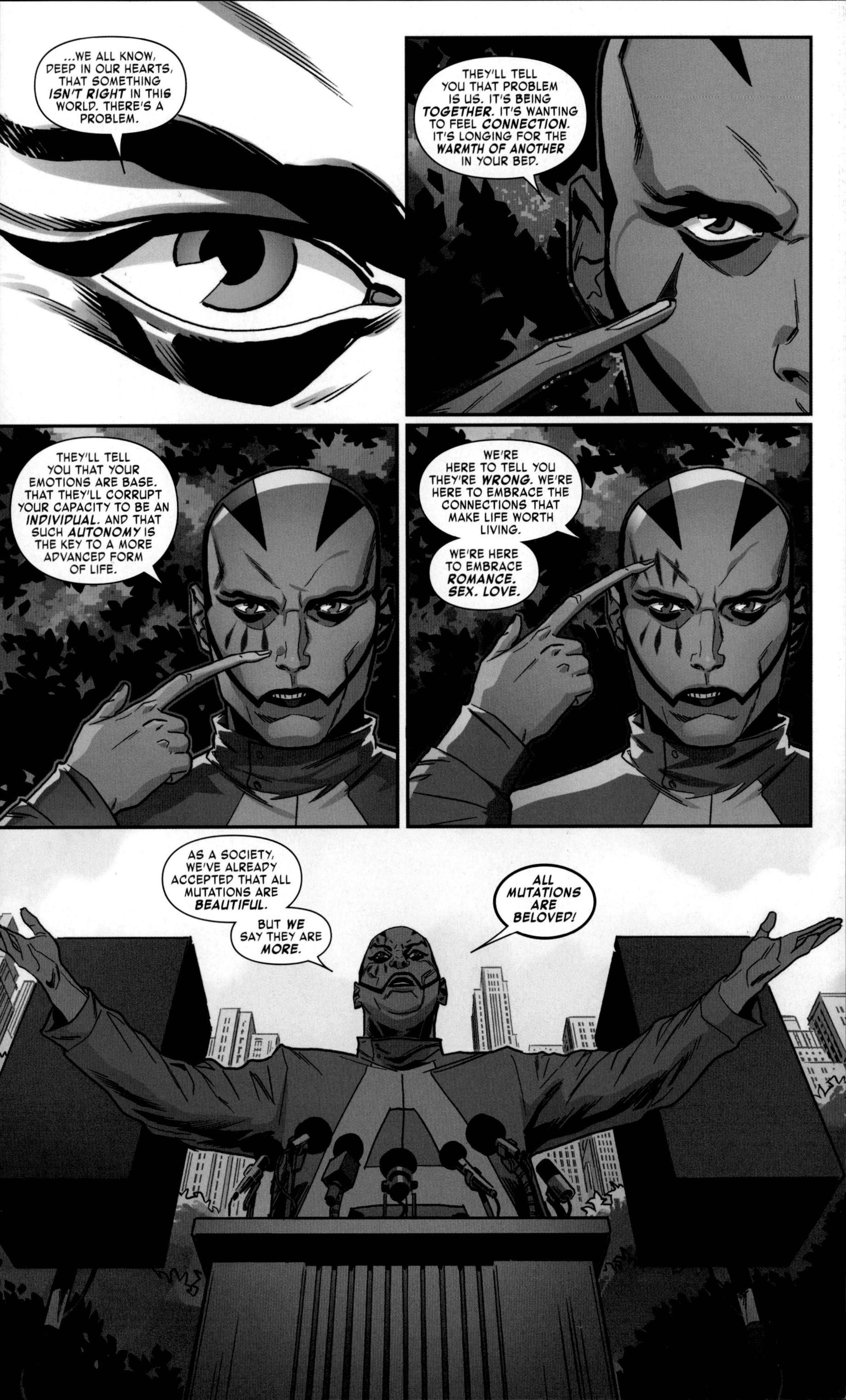
...WE ALL KNOW, DEEP IN OUR HEARTS, THAT SOMETHING *ISN'T RIGHT* IN THIS WORLD. THERE'S A PROBLEM.
THEY'LL TELL YOU THAT PROBLEM IS US. IT'S BEING *TOGETHER.* IT'S WANTING TO FEEL *CONNECTION.* IT'S LONGING FOR THE *WARMTH OF ANOTHER* IN YOUR BED.
THEY'LL TELL YOU THAT YOUR EMOTIONS ARE BASE. THAT THEY'LL CORRUPT YOUR CAPACITY TO BE AN *INDIVIDUAL.* AND THAT SUCH *AUTONOMY* IS THE KEY TO A MORE ADVANCED FORM OF LIFE.
WE'RE HERE TO TELL YOU THEY'RE *WRONG.* WE'RE HERE TO EMBRACE THE CONNECTIONS THAT MAKE LIFE WORTH LIVING.
WE'RE HERE TO EMBRACE *ROMANCE. SEX. LOVE.*
AS A SOCIETY, WE'VE ALREADY ACCEPTED THAT ALL MUTATIONS ARE *BEAUTIFUL.*
BUT *WE* SAY THEY ARE *MORE.*
ALL MUTATIONS ARE BELOVED!

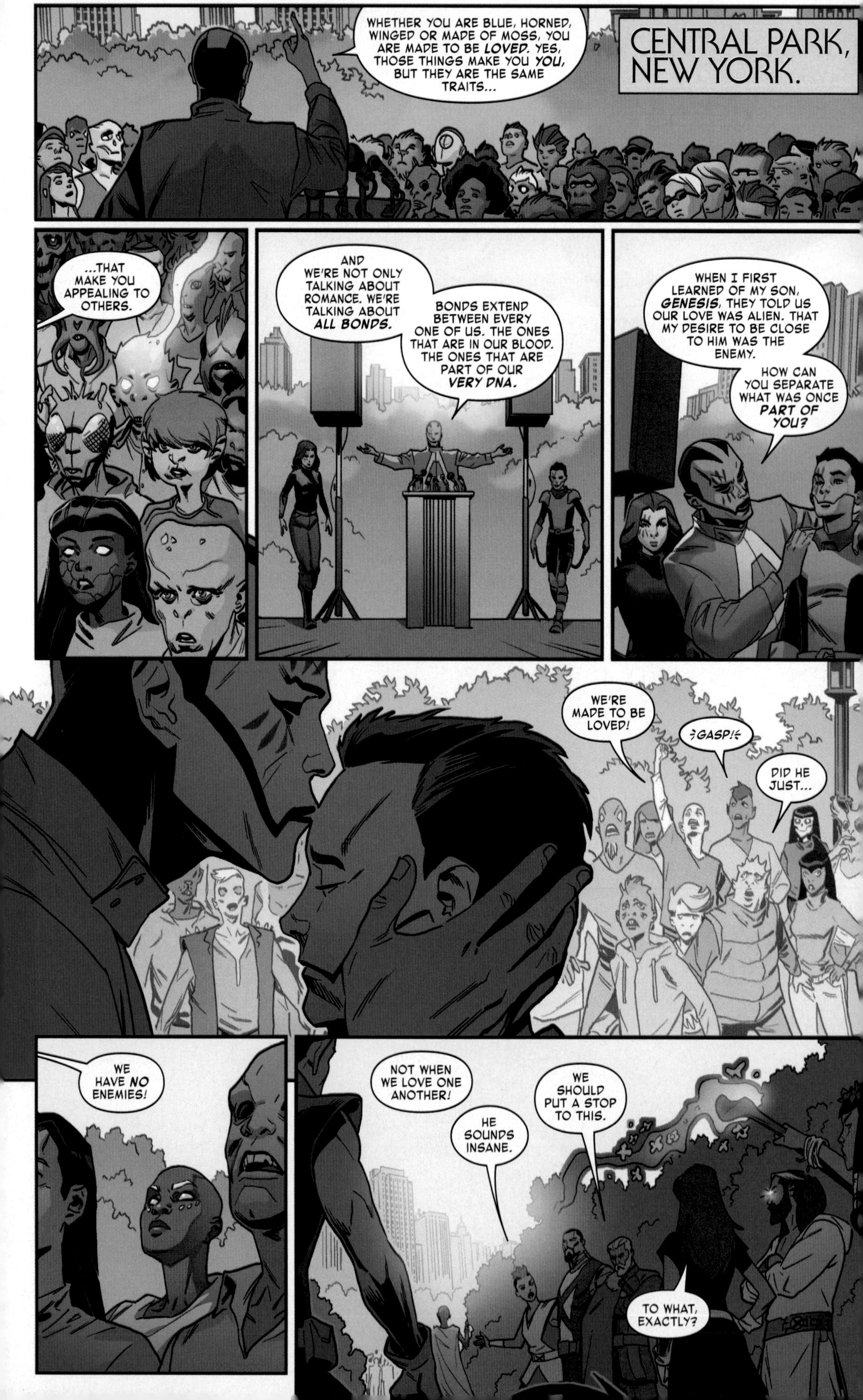
WHETHER YOU ARE BLUE, HORNED, WINGED OR MADE OF MOSS, YOU ARE MADE TO BE LOVED. YES, THOSE THINGS MAKE YOU YOU, BUT THEY ARE THE SAME TRAITS...
CENTRAL PARK, NEW YORK.
...THAT MAKE YOU APPEALING TO OTHERS.
AND WE'RE NOT ONLY TALKING ABOUT ROMANCE. WE'RE TALKING ABOUT ALL BONDS.
BONDS EXTEND BETWEEN EVERY ONE OF US. THE ONES THAT ARE IN OUR BLOOD. THE ONES THAT ARE PART OF OUR VERY DNA.
WHEN I FIRST LEARNED OF MY SON, GENESIS, THEY TOLD US OUR LOVE WAS ALIEN. THAT MY DESIRE TO BE CLOSE TO HIM WAS THE ENEMY.
HOW CAN YOU SEPARATE WHAT WAS ONCE PART OF YOU?
WE'RE MADE TO BE LOVED!
GASP!
DID HE JUST...
WE HAVE NO ENEMIES!
NOT WHEN WE LOVE ONE ANOTHER!
HE SOUNDS INSANE.
WE SHOULD PUT A STOP TO THIS.
TO WHAT, EXACTLY?

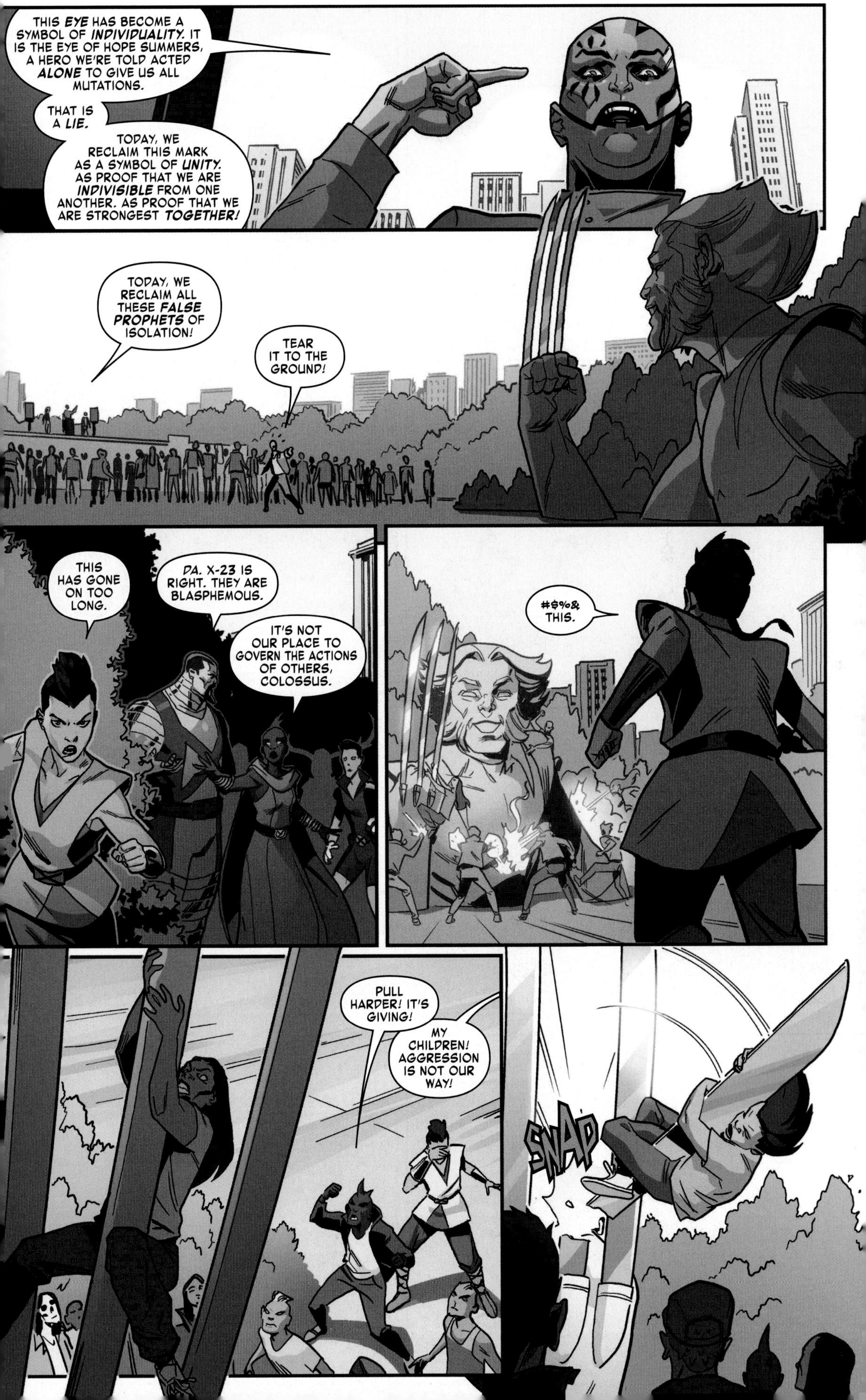
THIS EYE HAS BECOME A SYMBOL OF INDIVIDUALITY. IT IS THE EYE OF HOPE SUMMERS, A HERO WE'RE TOLD ACTED ALONE TO GIVE US ALL MUTATIONS.
THAT IS A LIE.
TODAY, WE RECLAIM THIS MARK AS A SYMBOL OF UNITY. AS PROOF THAT WE ARE INDIVISIBLE FROM ONE ANOTHER. AS PROOF THAT WE ARE STRONGEST TOGETHER!
TODAY, WE RECLAIM ALL THESE FALSE PROPHETS OF ISOLATION!
TEAR IT TO THE GROUND!
THIS HAS GONE ON TOO LONG.
DA. X-23 IS RIGHT. THEY ARE BLASPHEMOUS.
IT'S NOT OUR PLACE TO GOVERN THE ACTIONS OF OTHERS, COLOSSUS.
#$%& THIS.
PULL HARDER! IT'S GIVING!
MY CHILDREN! AGGRESSION IS NOT OUR WAY!
SNAP

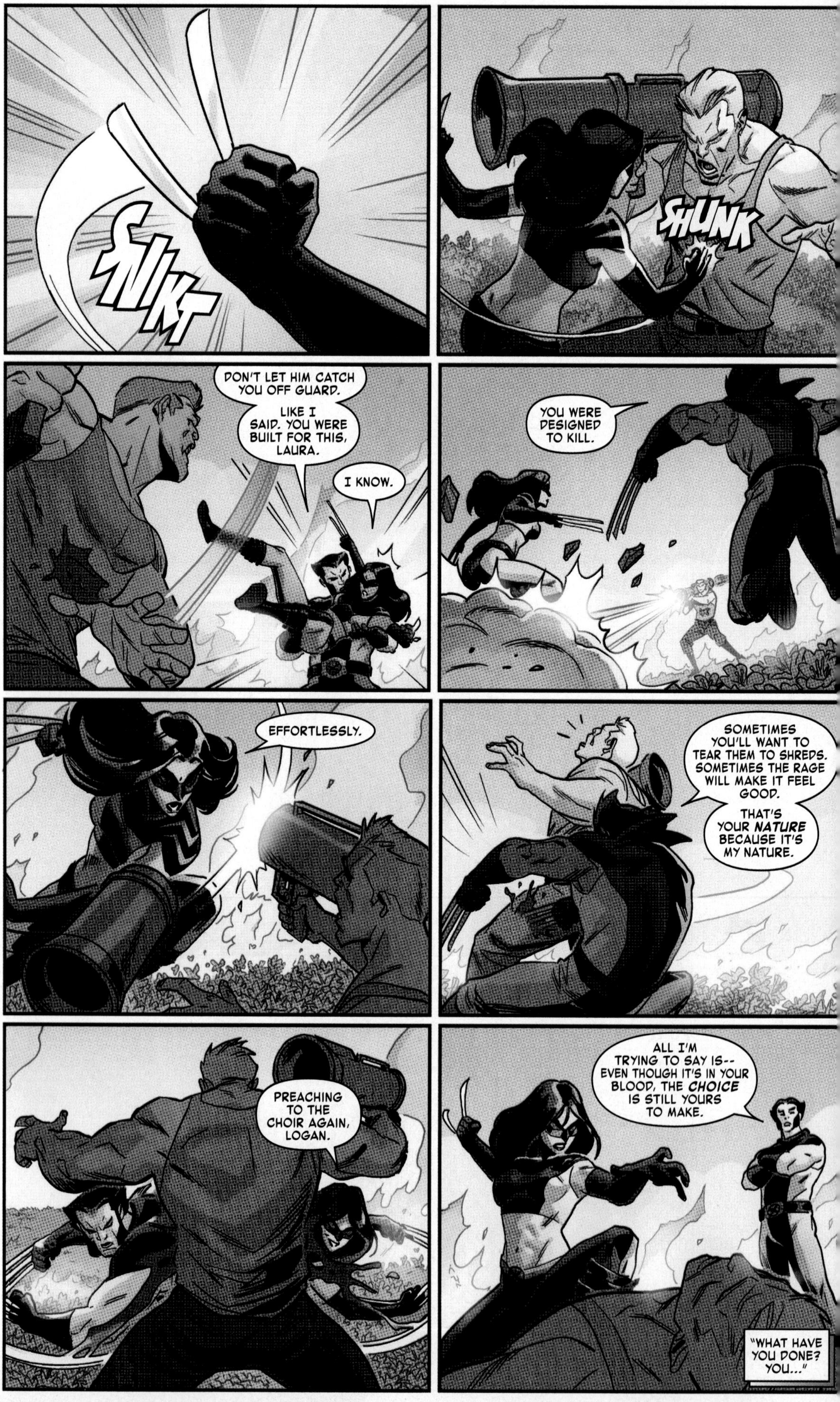
SNIKT
SHUNK
DON'T LET HIM CATCH YOU OFF GUARD.
LIKE I SAID. YOU WERE BUILT FOR THIS, LAURA.
I KNOW.
YOU WERE DESIGNED TO KILL.
EFFORTLESSLY.
SOMETIMES YOU'LL WANT TO TEAR THEM TO SHREDS. SOMETIMES THE RAGE WILL MAKE IT FEEL GOOD.
THAT'S YOUR *NATURE* BECAUSE IT'S MY NATURE.
PREACHING TO THE CHOIR AGAIN, LOGAN.
ALL I'M TRYING TO SAY IS-- EVEN THOUGH IT'S IN YOUR BLOOD, THE *CHOICE* IS STILL YOURS TO MAKE.
"WHAT HAVE YOU DONE? YOU..."

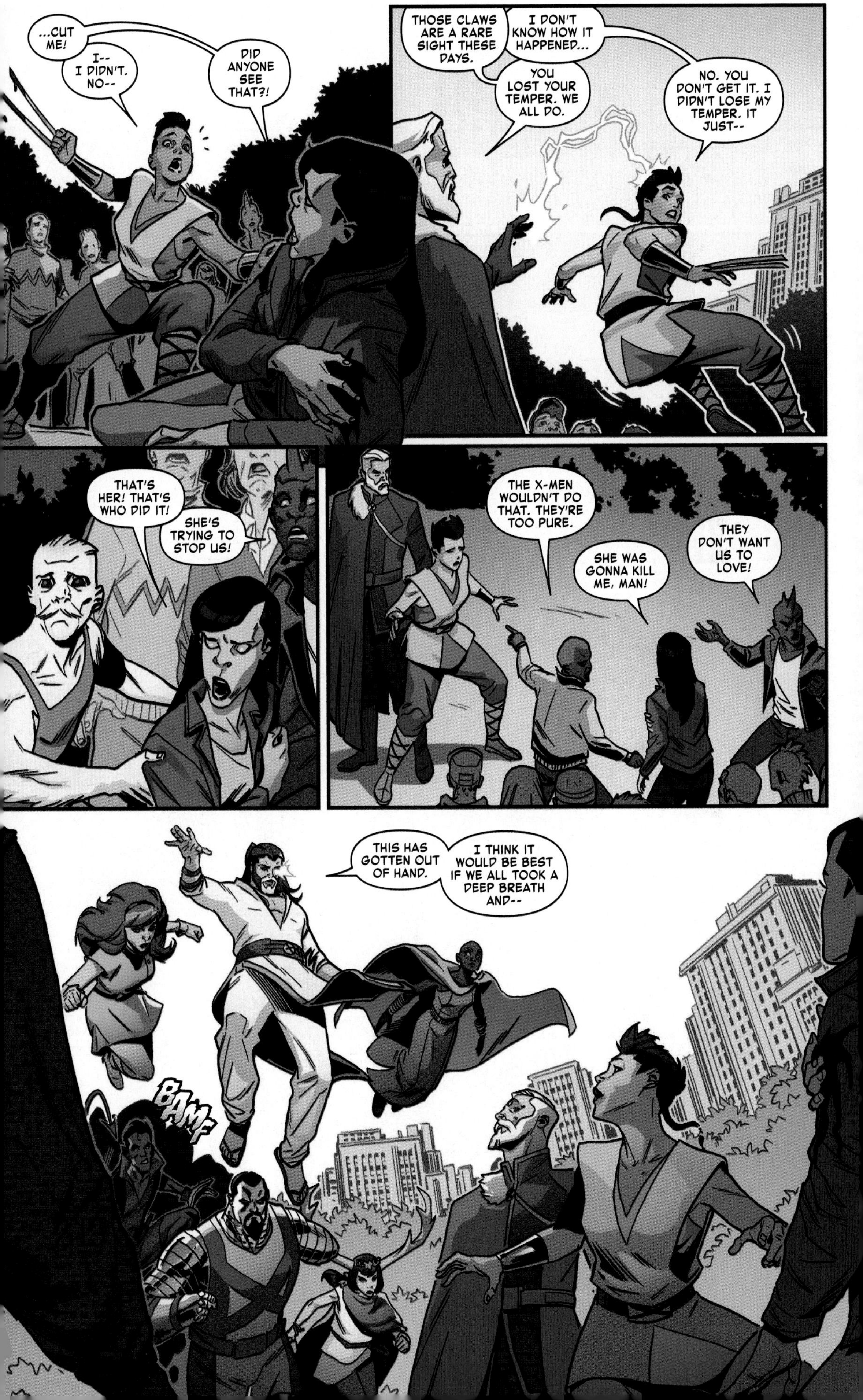
...CUT ME!
I-- I DIDN'T. NO--
DID ANYONE SEE THAT?!
THOSE CLAWS ARE A RARE SIGHT THESE DAYS.
I DON'T KNOW HOW IT HAPPENED...
YOU LOST YOUR TEMPER. WE ALL DO.
NO. YOU DON'T GET IT. I DIDN'T LOSE MY TEMPER. IT JUST--
THAT'S HER! THAT'S WHO DID IT!
SHE'S TRYING TO STOP US!
THE X-MEN WOULDN'T DO THAT. THEY'RE TOO PURE.
SHE WAS GONNA KILL ME, MAN!
THEY DON'T WANT US TO LOVE!
THIS HAS GOTTEN OUT OF HAND.
I THINK IT WOULD BE BEST IF WE ALL TOOK A DEEP BREATH AND--
BAMF

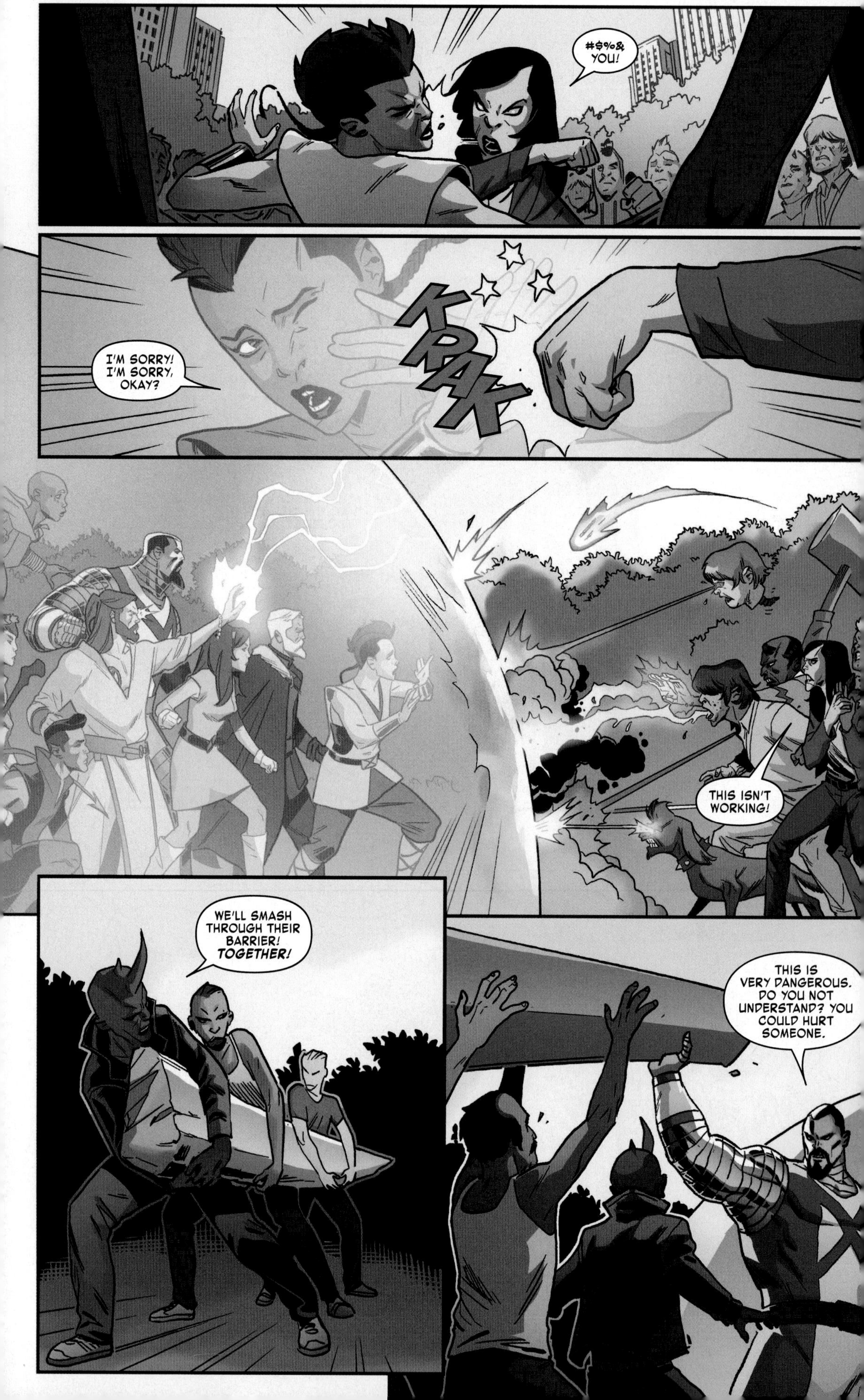
#$%& YOU!
I'M SORRY! I'M SORRY, OKAY?
KRAK
THIS ISN'T WORKING!
WE'LL SMASH THROUGH THEIR BARRIER! TOGETHER!
THIS IS VERY DANGEROUS. DO YOU NOT UNDERSTAND? YOU COULD HURT SOMEONE.

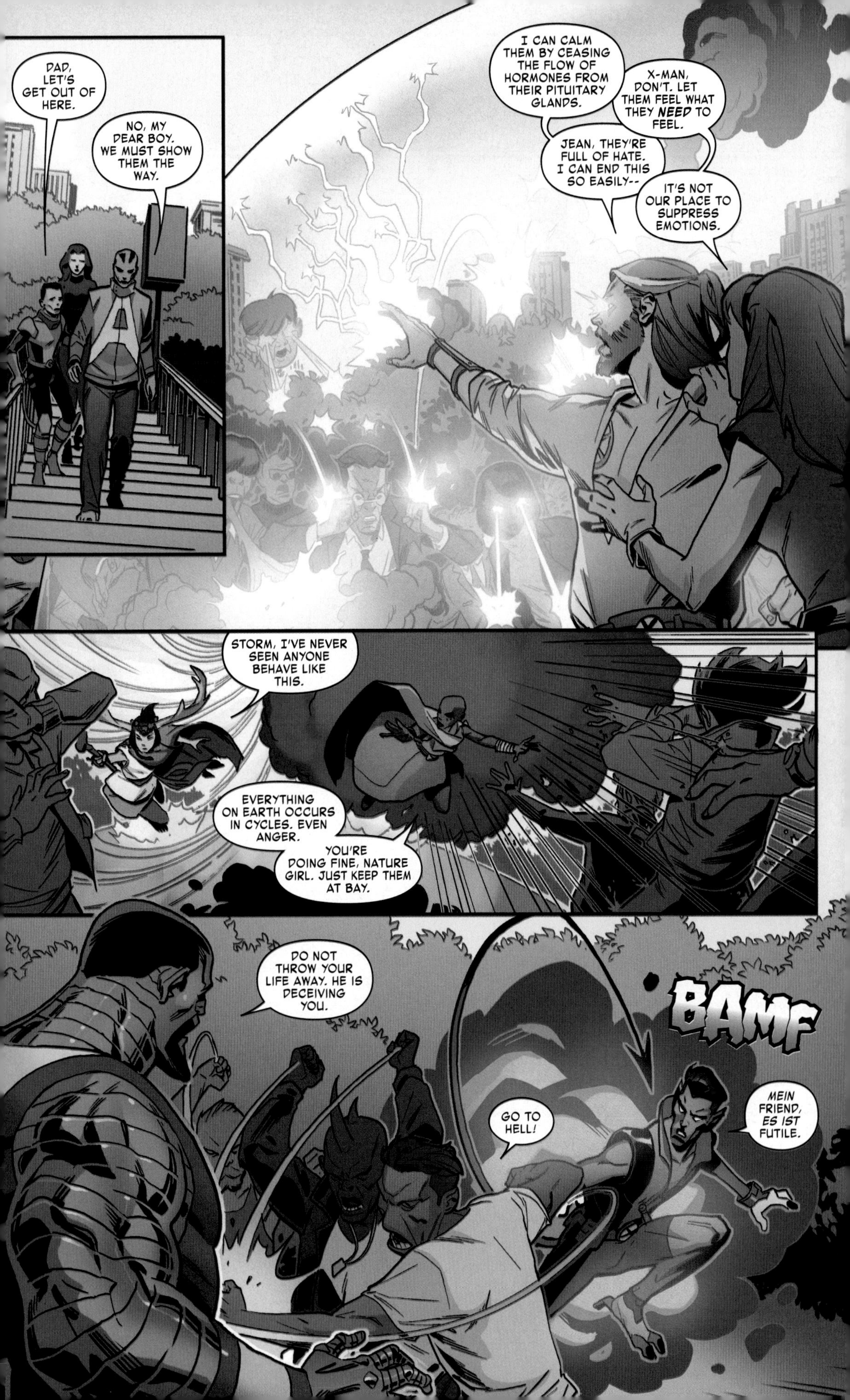
DAD, LET'S GET OUT OF HERE.
NO, MY DEAR BOY. WE MUST SHOW THEM THE WAY.
I CAN CALM THEM BY CEASING THE FLOW OF HORMONES FROM THEIR PITUITARY GLANDS.
X-MAN, DON'T. LET THEM FEEL WHAT THEY NEED TO FEEL.
JEAN, THEY'RE FULL OF HATE. I CAN END THIS SO EASILY--
IT'S NOT OUR PLACE TO SUPPRESS EMOTIONS.
STORM, I'VE NEVER SEEN ANYONE BEHAVE LIKE THIS.
EVERYTHING ON EARTH OCCURS IN CYCLES. EVEN ANGER.
YOU'RE DOING FINE, NATURE GIRL. JUST KEEP THEM AT BAY.
DO NOT THROW YOUR LIFE AWAY. HE IS DECEIVING YOU.
BAMF
GO TO HELL!
MEIN FRIEND, ES IST FUTILE.

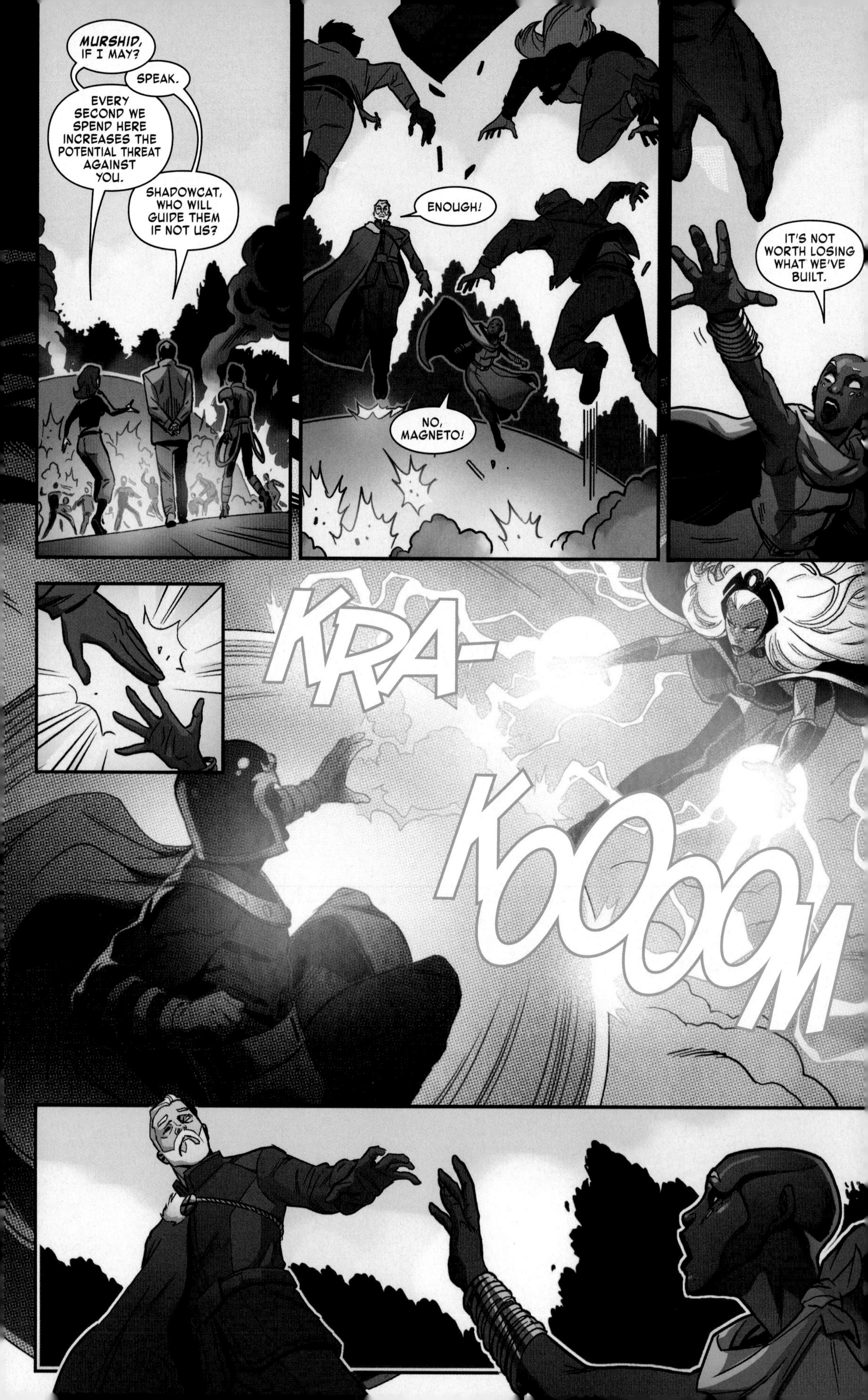
MURSHID, IF I MAY?
SPEAK.
EVERY SECOND WE SPEND HERE INCREASES THE POTENTIAL THREAT AGAINST YOU.
SHADOWCAT, WHO WILL GUIDE THEM IF NOT US?
ENOUGH!
NO, MAGNETO!
IT'S NOT WORTH LOSING WHAT WE'VE BUILT.
KRA-
KOOOOM

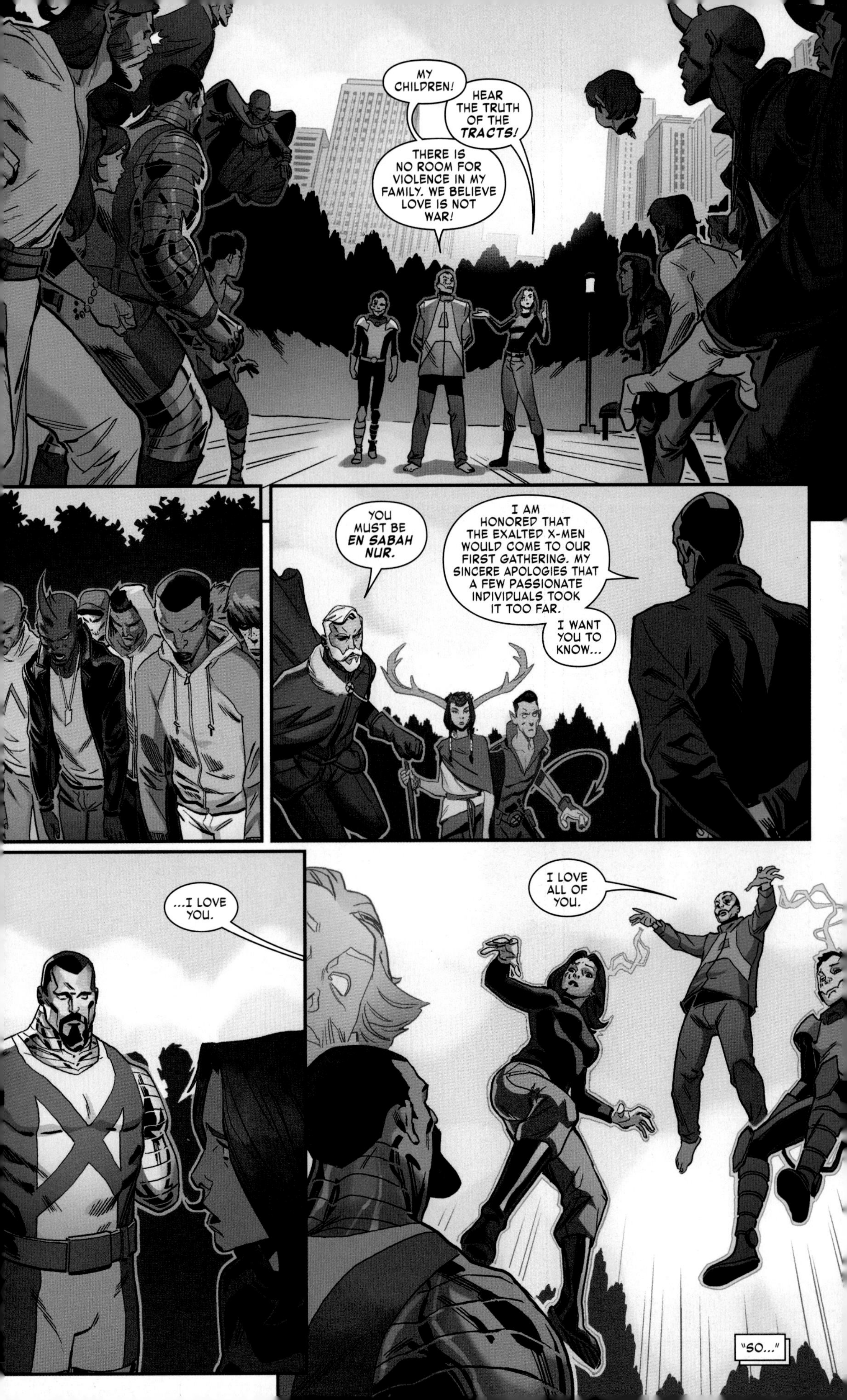
MY CHILDREN!
HEAR THE TRUTH OF THE TRACTS!
THERE IS NO ROOM FOR VIOLENCE IN MY FAMILY. WE BELIEVE LOVE IS NOT WAR!
YOU MUST BE EN SABAH NUR.
I AM HONORED THAT THE EXALTED X-MEN WOULD COME TO OUR FIRST GATHERING. MY SINCERE APOLOGIES THAT A FEW PASSIONATE INDIVIDUALS TOOK IT TOO FAR.
I WANT YOU TO KNOW...
...I LOVE YOU.
I LOVE ALL OF YOU.
"SO..."

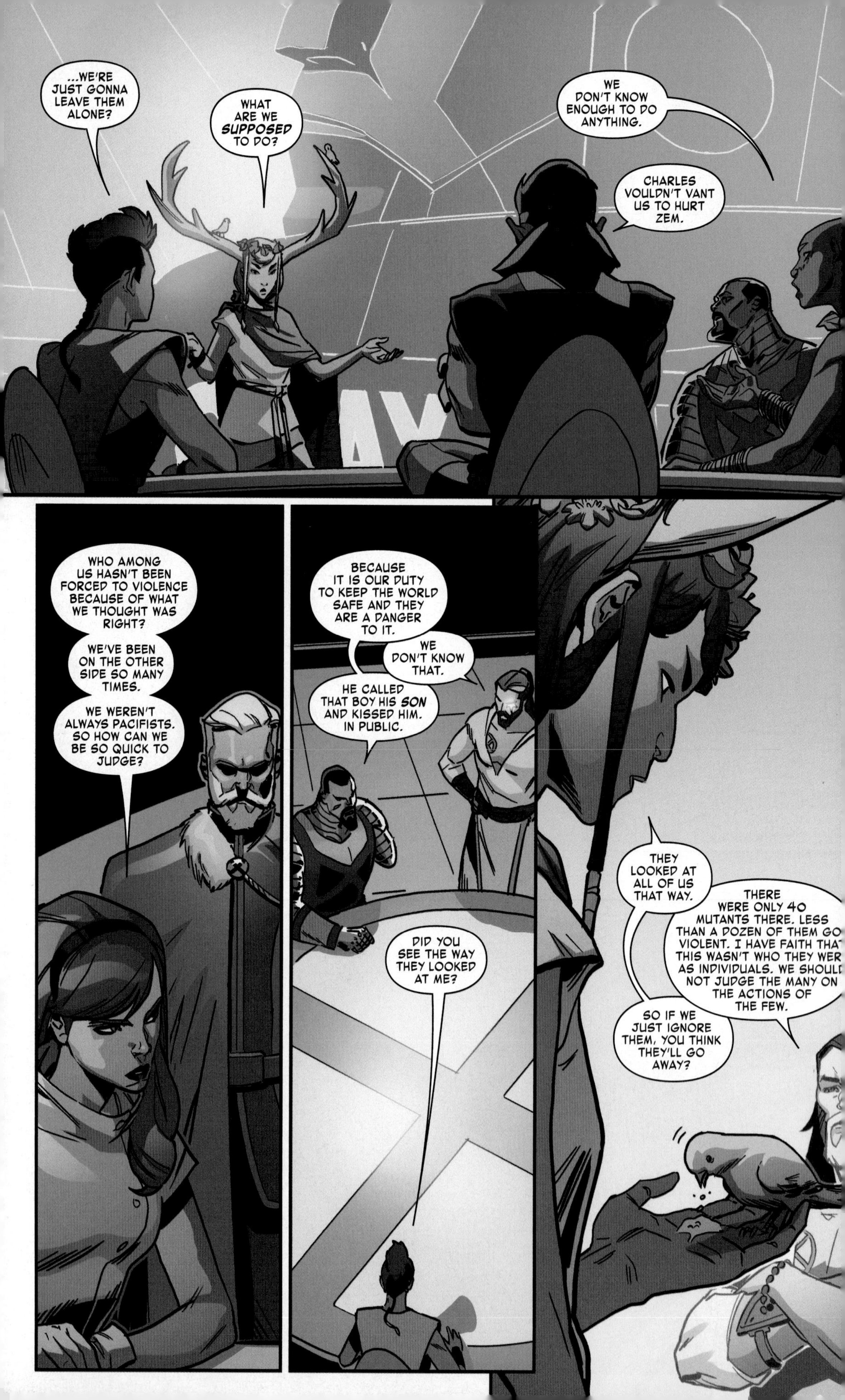
...WE'RE JUST GONNA LEAVE THEM ALONE?
WHAT ARE WE SUPPOSED TO DO?
WE DON'T KNOW ENOUGH TO DO ANYTHING.
CHARLES VOULDN'T VANT US TO HURT ZEM.
WHO AMONG US HASN'T BEEN FORCED TO VIOLENCE BECAUSE OF WHAT WE THOUGHT WAS RIGHT?
WE'VE BEEN ON THE OTHER SIDE SO MANY TIMES.
WE WEREN'T ALWAYS PACIFISTS. SO HOW CAN WE BE SO QUICK TO JUDGE?
BECAUSE IT IS OUR DUTY TO KEEP THE WORLD SAFE AND THEY ARE A DANGER TO IT.
WE DON'T KNOW THAT.
HE CALLED THAT BOY HIS SON AND KISSED HIM. IN PUBLIC.
DID YOU SEE THE WAY THEY LOOKED AT ME?
THEY LOOKED AT ALL OF US THAT WAY.
THERE WERE ONLY 40 MUTANTS THERE. LESS THAN A DOZEN OF THEM GO VIOLENT. I HAVE FAITH THAT THIS WASN'T WHO THEY WER AS INDIVIDUALS. WE SHOULD NOT JUDGE THE MANY ON THE ACTIONS OF THE FEW.
SO IF WE JUST IGNORE THEM, YOU THINK THEY'LL GO AWAY?

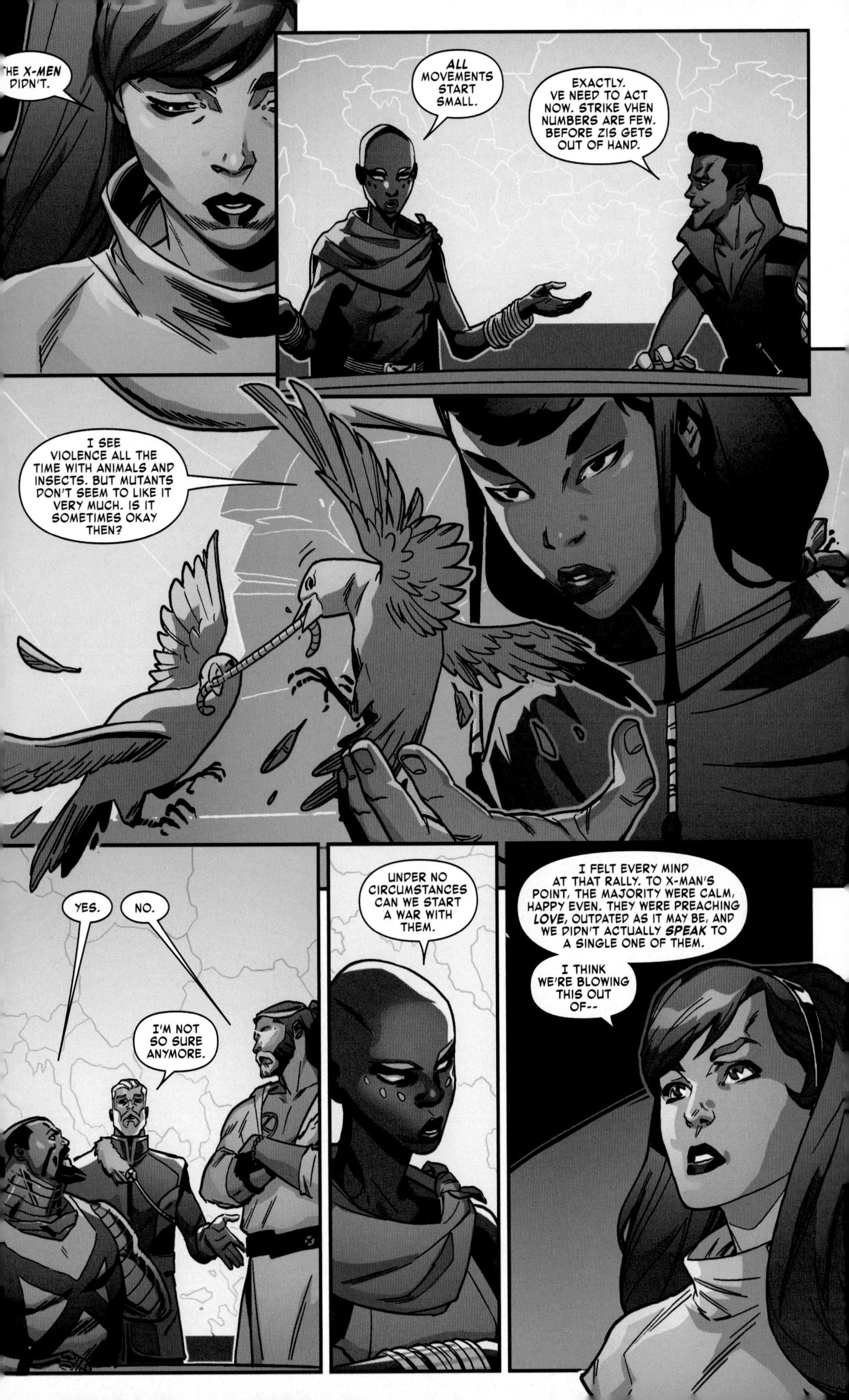
THE X-MEN DIDN'T.
ALL MOVEMENTS START SMALL.
EXACTLY. VE NEED TO ACT NOW. STRIKE VHEN NUMBERS ARE FEW. BEFORE ZIS GETS OUT OF HAND.
I SEE VIOLENCE ALL THE TIME WITH ANIMALS AND INSECTS. BUT MUTANTS DON'T SEEM TO LIKE IT VERY MUCH. IS IT SOMETIMES OKAY THEN?
YES.
NO.
I'M NOT SO SURE ANYMORE.
UNDER NO CIRCUMSTANCES CAN WE START A WAR WITH THEM.
I FELT EVERY MIND AT THAT RALLY. TO X-MAN'S POINT, THE MAJORITY WERE CALM, HAPPY EVEN. THEY WERE PREACHING LOVE, OUTDATED AS IT MAY BE, AND WE DIDN'T ACTUALLY SPEAK TO A SINGLE ONE OF THEM.
I THINK WE'RE BLOWING THIS OUT OF--

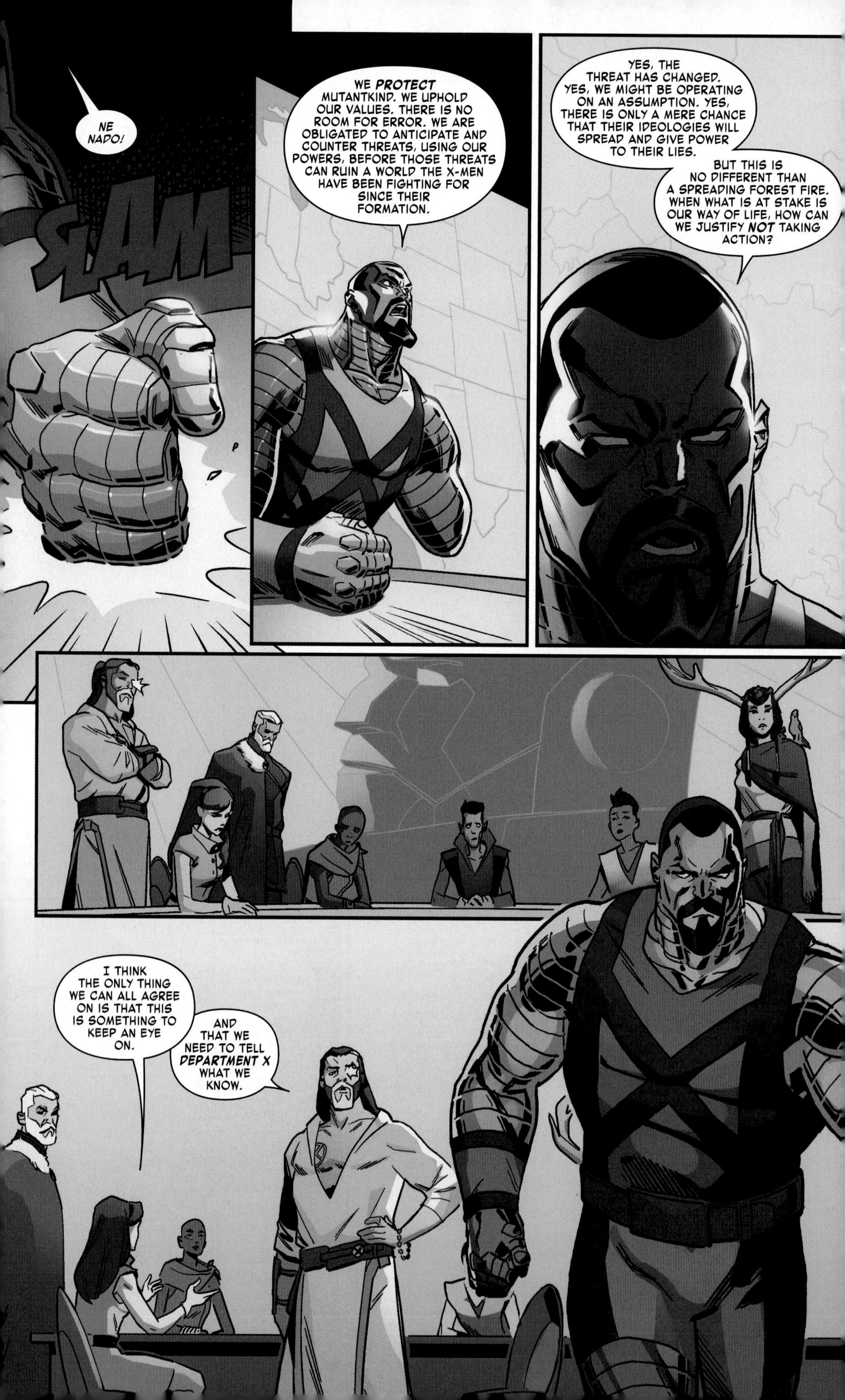
NE NADO!
SLAM
WE PROTECT MUTANTKIND. WE UPHOLD OUR VALUES. THERE IS NO ROOM FOR ERROR. WE ARE OBLIGATED TO ANTICIPATE AND COUNTER THREATS, USING OUR POWERS, BEFORE THOSE THREATS CAN RUIN A WORLD THE X-MEN HAVE BEEN FIGHTING FOR SINCE THEIR FORMATION.
YES, THE THREAT HAS CHANGED. YES, WE MIGHT BE OPERATING ON AN ASSUMPTION. YES, THERE IS ONLY A MERE CHANCE THAT THEIR IDEOLOGIES WILL SPREAD AND GIVE POWER TO THEIR LIES.
BUT THIS IS NO DIFFERENT THAN A SPREADING FOREST FIRE. WHEN WHAT IS AT STAKE IS OUR WAY OF LIFE, HOW CAN WE JUSTIFY NOT TAKING ACTION?
I THINK THE ONLY THING WE CAN ALL AGREE ON IS THAT THIS IS SOMETHING TO KEEP AN EYE ON.
AND THAT WE NEED TO TELL DEPARTMENT X WHAT WE KNOW.

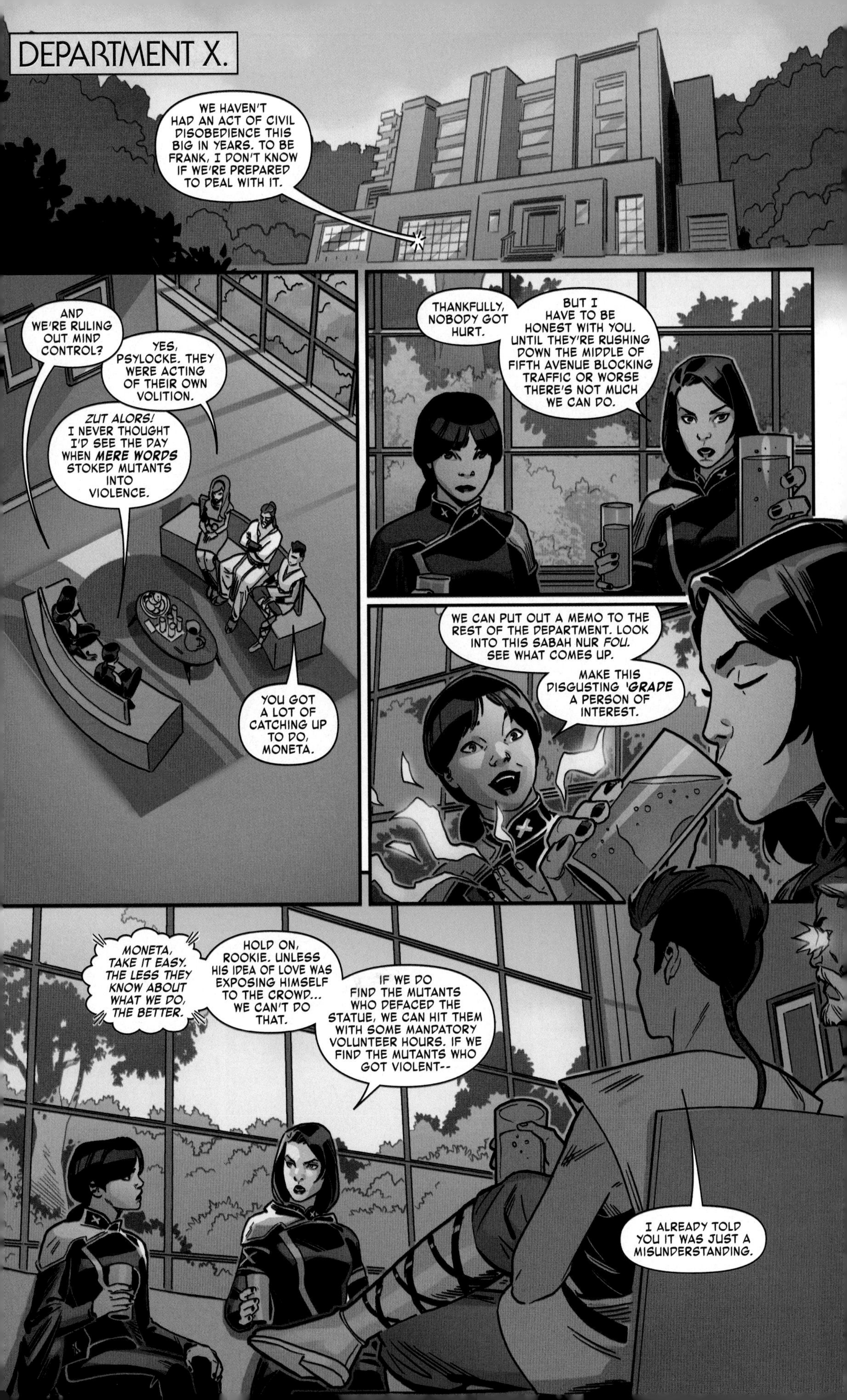
DEPARTMENT X.
WE HAVEN'T HAD AN ACT OF CIVIL DISOBEDIENCE THIS BIG IN YEARS. TO BE FRANK, I DON'T KNOW IF WE'RE PREPARED TO DEAL WITH IT.
AND WE'RE RULING OUT MIND CONTROL?
YES, PSYLOCKE. THEY WERE ACTING OF THEIR OWN VOLITION.
ZUT ALORS! I NEVER THOUGHT I'D SEE THE DAY WHEN MERE WORDS STOKED MUTANTS INTO VIOLENCE.
YOU GOT A LOT OF CATCHING UP TO DO, MONETA.
THANKFULLY, NOBODY GOT HURT.
BUT I HAVE TO BE HONEST WITH YOU. UNTIL THEY'RE RUSHING DOWN THE MIDDLE OF FIFTH AVENUE BLOCKING TRAFFIC OR WORSE THERE'S NOT MUCH WE CAN DO.
WE CAN PUT OUT A MEMO TO THE REST OF THE DEPARTMENT. LOOK INTO THIS SABAH NUR FOU. SEE WHAT COMES UP.
MAKE THIS DISGUSTING 'GRADE A PERSON OF INTEREST.
MONETA, TAKE IT EASY. THE LESS THEY KNOW ABOUT WHAT WE DO, THE BETTER.
HOLD ON, ROOKIE. UNLESS HIS IDEA OF LOVE WAS EXPOSING HIMSELF TO THE CROWD... WE CAN'T DO THAT.
IF WE DO FIND THE MUTANTS WHO DEFACED THE STATUE, WE CAN HIT THEM WITH SOME MANDATORY VOLUNTEER HOURS. IF WE FIND THE MUTANTS WHO GOT VIOLENT--
I ALREADY TOLD YOU IT WAS JUST A MISUNDERSTANDING.

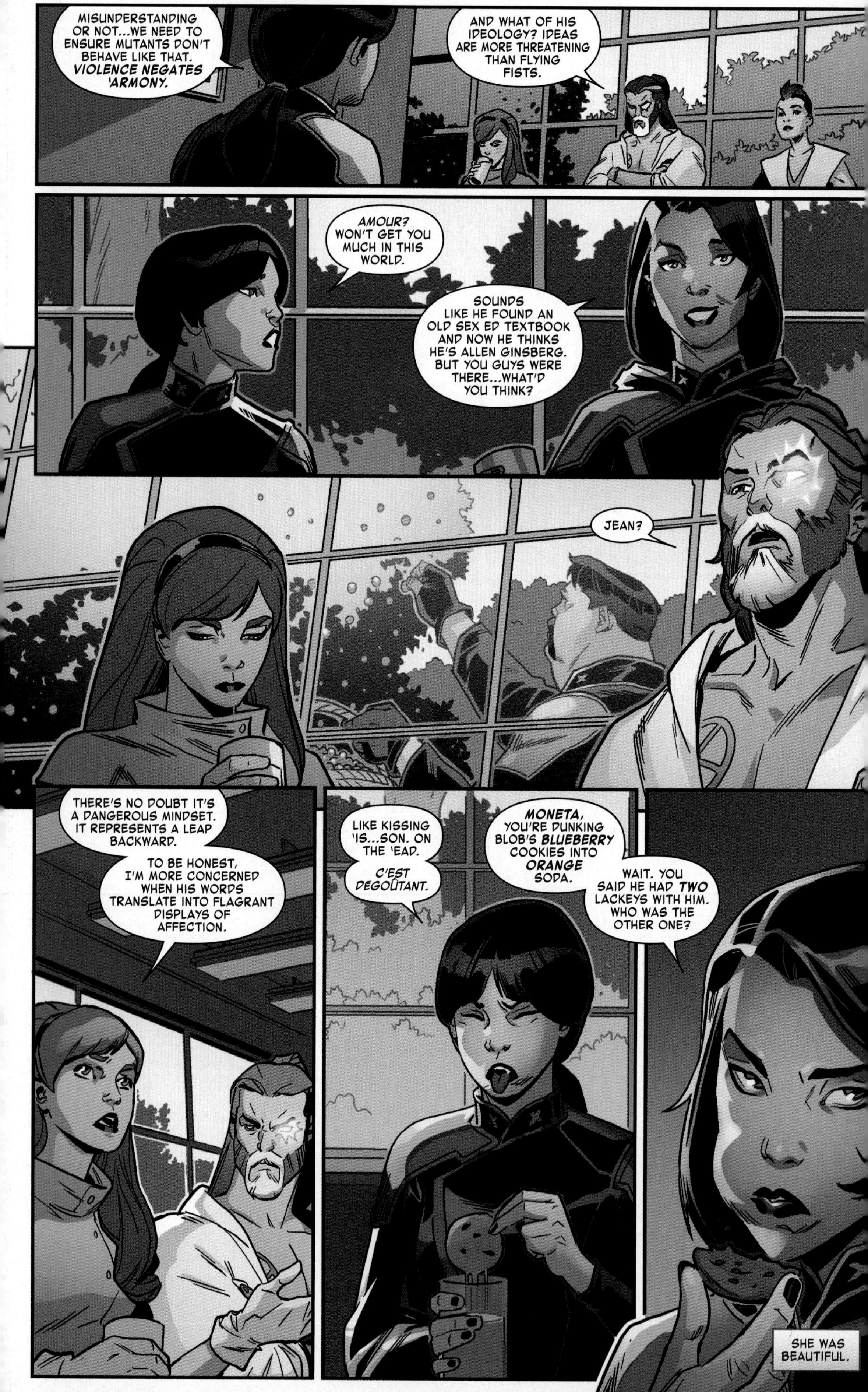
MISUNDERSTANDING OR NOT...WE NEED TO ENSURE MUTANTS DON'T BEHAVE LIKE THAT. VIOLENCE NEGATES 'ARMONY.
AND WHAT OF HIS IDEOLOGY? IDEAS ARE MORE THREATENING THAN FLYING FISTS.
AMOUR? WON'T GET YOU MUCH IN THIS WORLD.
SOUNDS LIKE HE FOUND AN OLD SEX ED TEXTBOOK AND NOW HE THINKS HE'S ALLEN GINSBERG. BUT YOU GUYS WERE THERE...WHAT'D YOU THINK?
JEAN?
THERE'S NO DOUBT IT'S A DANGEROUS MINDSET. IT REPRESENTS A LEAP BACKWARD.
TO BE HONEST, I'M MORE CONCERNED WHEN HIS WORDS TRANSLATE INTO FLAGRANT DISPLAYS OF AFFECTION.
LIKE KISSING 'IS...SON. ON THE 'EAD.
C'EST DEGOÛTANT.
MONETA, YOU'RE DUNKING BLOB'S BLUEBERRY COOKIES INTO ORANGE SODA.
WAIT. YOU SAID HE HAD TWO LACKEYS WITH HIM. WHO WAS THE OTHER ONE?
SHE WAS BEAUTIFUL.

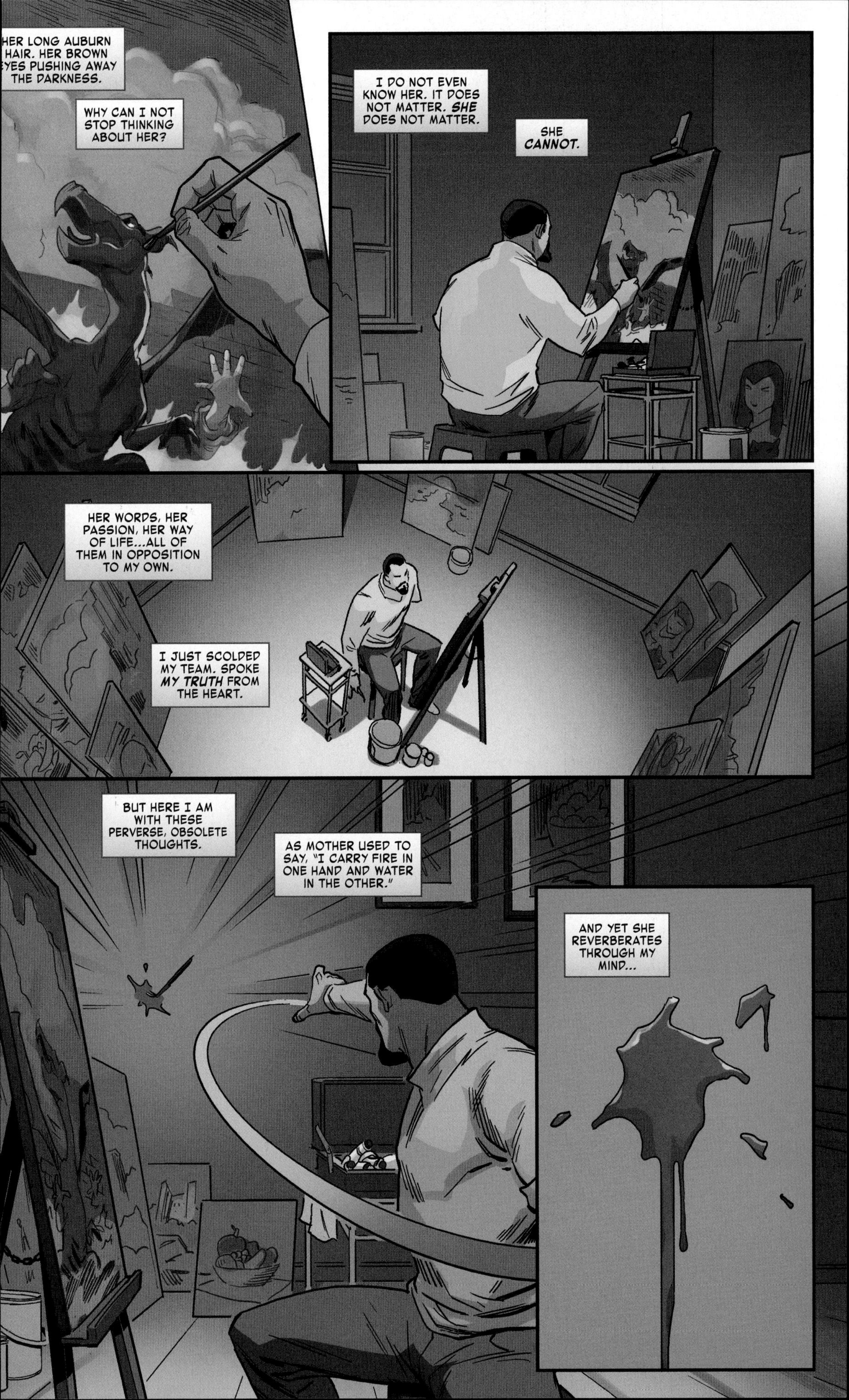
HER LONG AUBURN HAIR. HER BROWN EYES PUSHING AWAY THE DARKNESS.
WHY CAN I NOT STOP THINKING ABOUT HER?
I DO NOT EVEN KNOW HER. IT DOES NOT MATTER. SHE DOES NOT MATTER.
SHE CANNOT.
HER WORDS, HER PASSION, HER WAY OF LIFE...ALL OF THEM IN OPPOSITION TO MY OWN.
I JUST SCOLDED MY TEAM. SPOKE MY TRUTH FROM THE HEART.
BUT HERE I AM WITH THESE PERVERSE, OBSOLETE THOUGHTS.
AS MOTHER USED TO SAY, "I CARRY FIRE IN ONE HAND AND WATER IN THE OTHER."
AND YET SHE REVERBERATES THROUGH MY MIND...

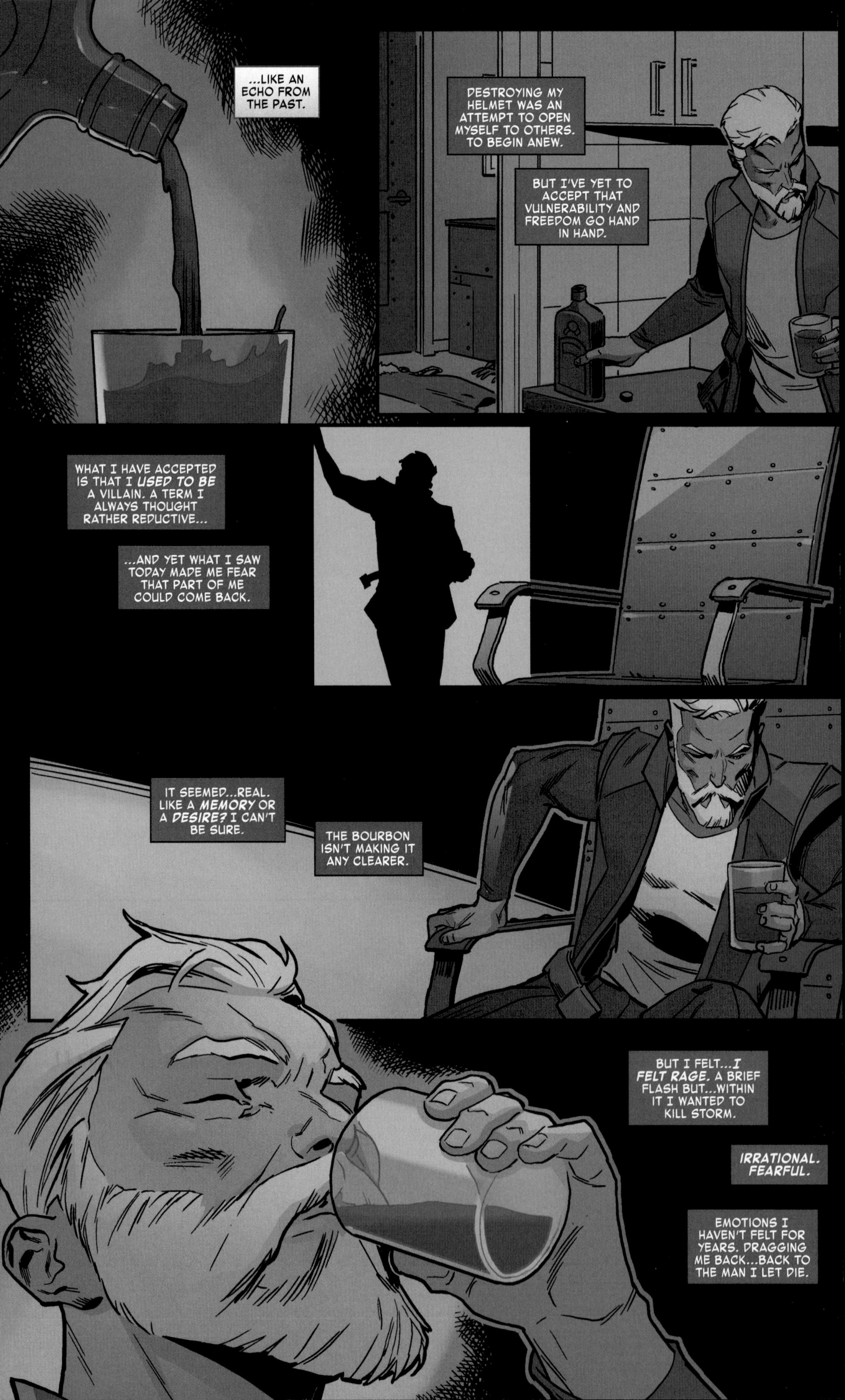
...LIKE AN ECHO FROM THE PAST.
DESTROYING MY HELMET WAS AN ATTEMPT TO OPEN MYSELF TO OTHERS. TO BEGIN ANEW.
BUT I'VE YET TO ACCEPT THAT VULNERABILITY AND FREEDOM GO HAND IN HAND.
WHAT I HAVE ACCEPTED IS THAT I *USED TO BE* A VILLAIN. A TERM I ALWAYS THOUGHT RATHER REDUCTIVE...
...AND YET WHAT I SAW TODAY MADE ME FEAR THAT PART OF ME COULD COME BACK.
IT SEEMED...REAL. LIKE A *MEMORY* OR A *DESIRE?* I CAN'T BE SURE.
THE BOURBON ISN'T MAKING IT ANY CLEARER.
BUT I FELT...*I FELT RAGE.* A BRIEF FLASH BUT...WITHIN IT I WANTED TO KILL STORM.
IRRATIONAL. FEARFUL.
EMOTIONS I HAVEN'T FELT FOR YEARS. DRAGGING ME BACK...BACK TO THE MAN I LET DIE.

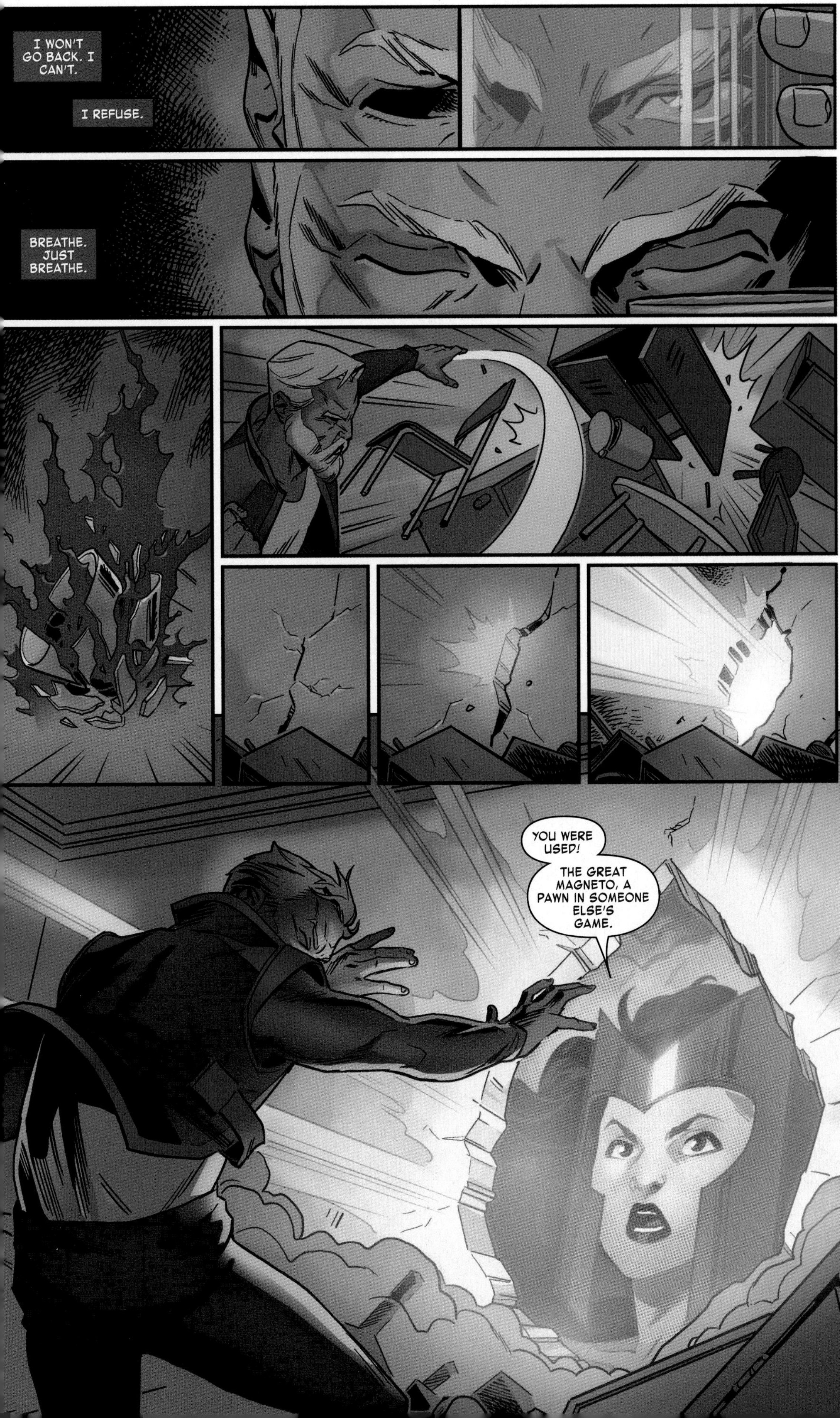
I WON'T GO BACK. I CAN'T.
I REFUSE.
BREATHE. JUST BREATHE.
YOU WERE USED!
THE GREAT MAGNETO, A PAWN IN SOMEONE ELSE'S GAME.

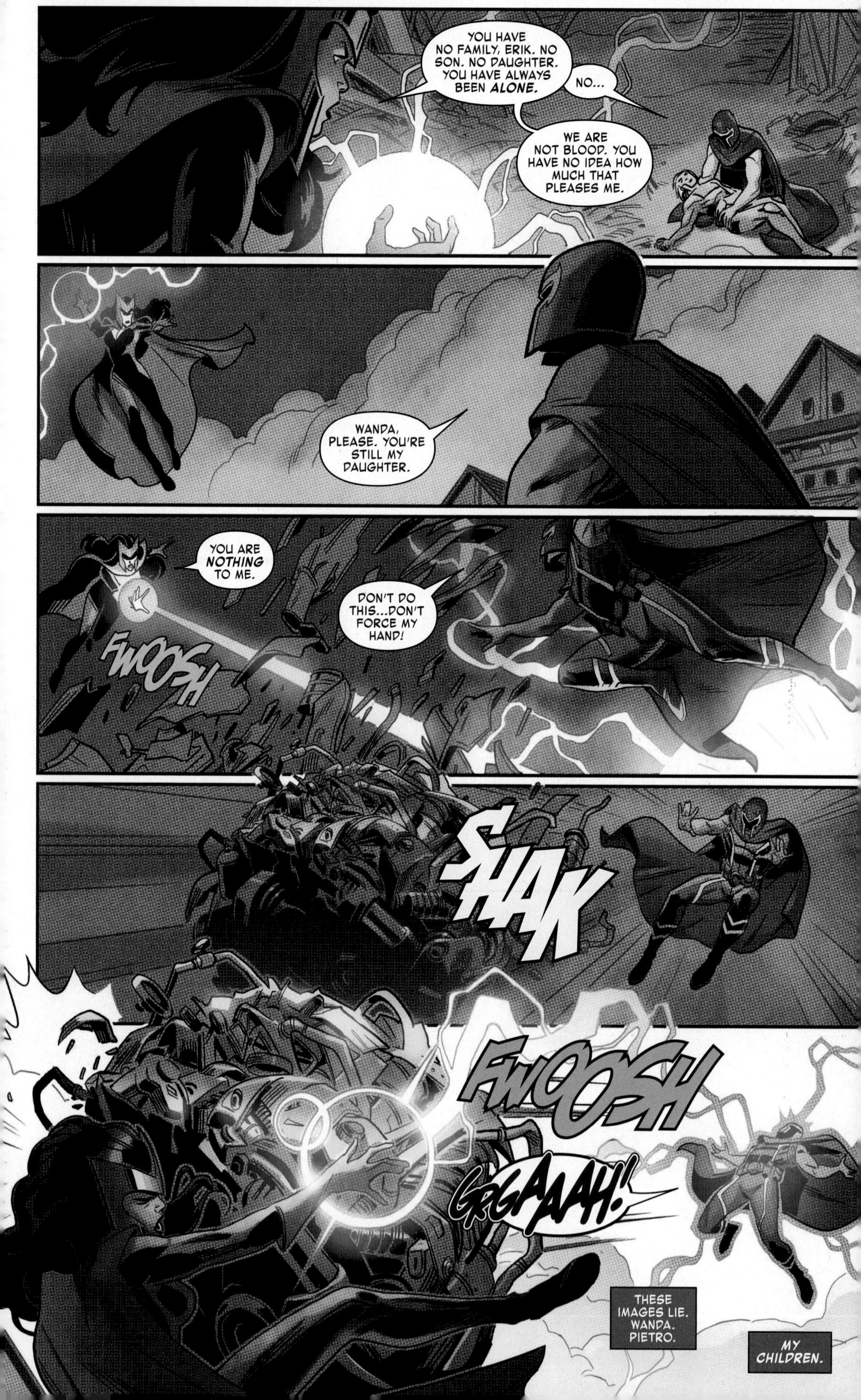
YOU HAVE NO FAMILY, ERIK. NO SON. NO DAUGHTER. YOU HAVE ALWAYS BEEN ALONE.
NO...
WE ARE NOT BLOOD. YOU HAVE NO IDEA HOW MUCH THAT PLEASES ME.
WANDA, PLEASE. YOU'RE STILL MY DAUGHTER.
YOU ARE NOTHING TO ME.
DON'T DO THIS...DON'T FORCE MY HAND!
FWOOSH
SHAK
FWOOSH
GRGAAAH!
THESE IMAGES LIE. WANDA. PIETRO.
MY CHILDREN.

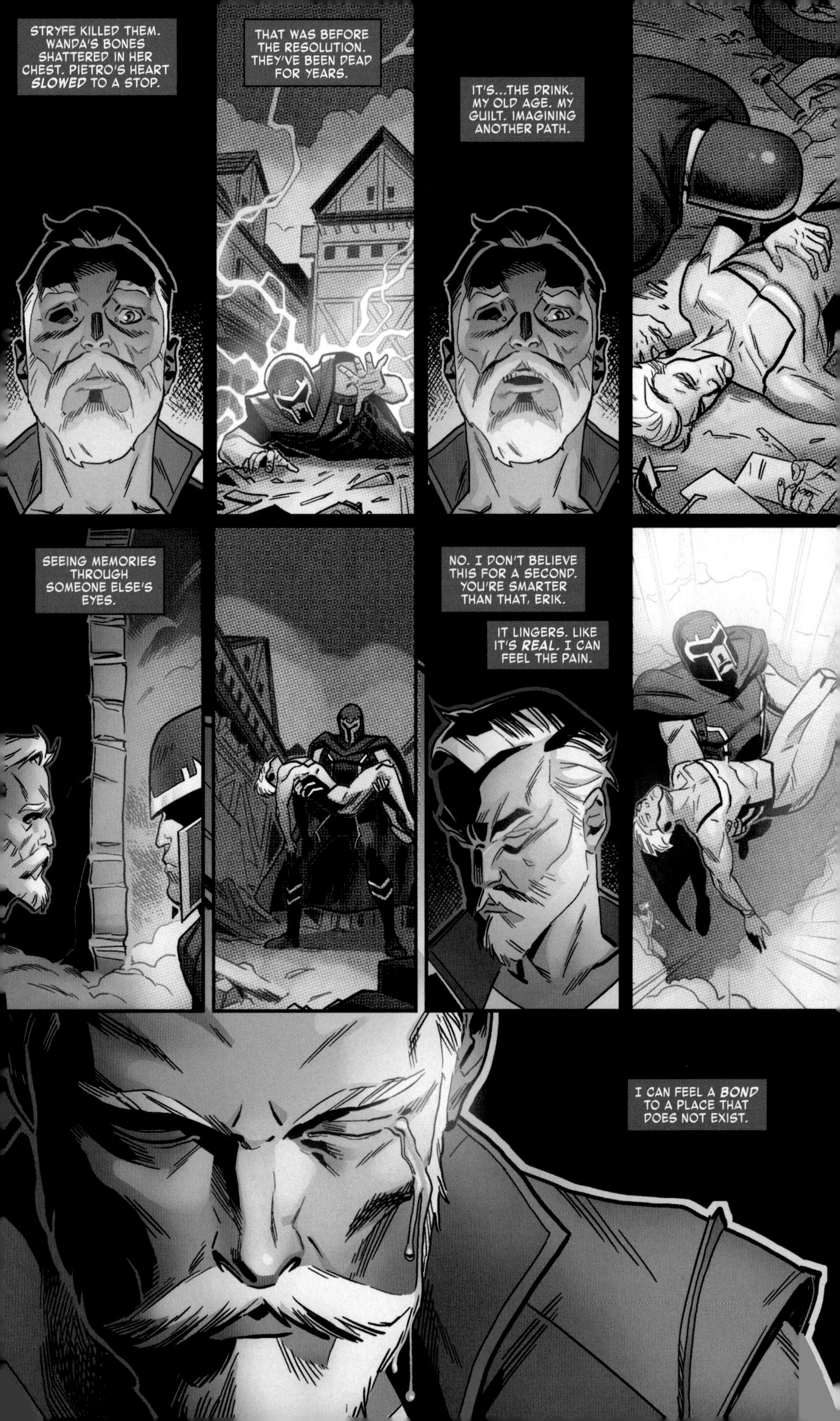
STRYFE KILLED THEM. WANDA'S BONES SHATTERED IN HER CHEST. PIETRO'S HEART *SLOWED* TO A STOP.
THAT WAS BEFORE THE RESOLUTION. THEY'VE BEEN DEAD FOR YEARS.
IT'S...THE DRINK. MY OLD AGE. MY GUILT. IMAGINING ANOTHER PATH.
SEEING MEMORIES THROUGH SOMEONE ELSE'S EYES.
NO. I DON'T BELIEVE THIS FOR A SECOND. YOU'RE SMARTER THAN THAT, ERIK.
IT LINGERS. LIKE IT'S *REAL*. I CAN FEEL THE PAIN.
I CAN FEEL A *BOND* TO A PLACE THAT DOES NOT EXIST.

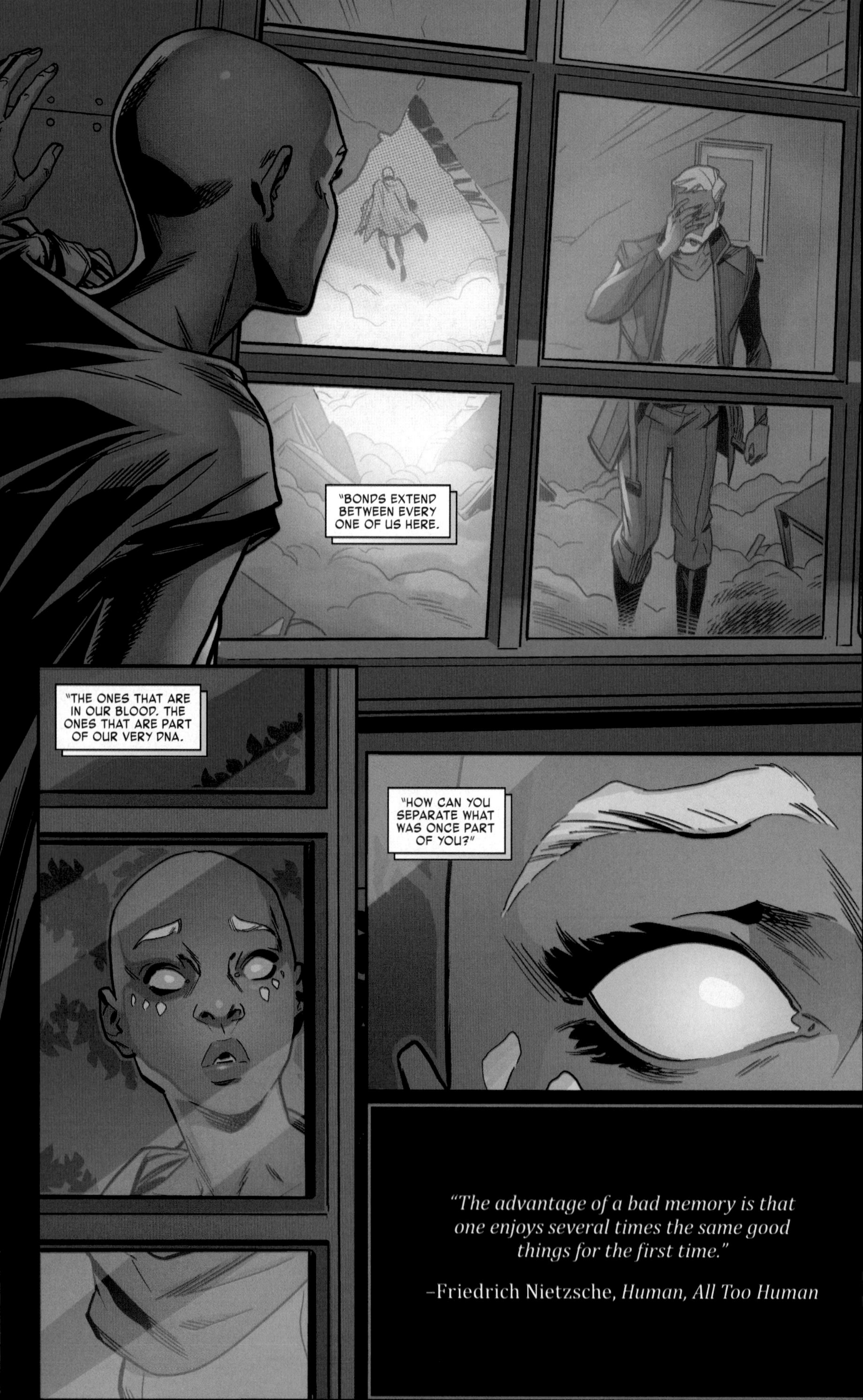
"BONDS EXTEND BETWEEN EVERY ONE OF US HERE.
"THE ONES THAT ARE IN OUR BLOOD. THE ONES THAT ARE PART OF OUR VERY DNA.
"HOW CAN YOU SEPARATE WHAT WAS ONCE PART OF YOU?"
"The advantage of a bad memory is that one enjoys several times the same good things for the first time."
–Friedrich Nietzsche, Human, All Too Human

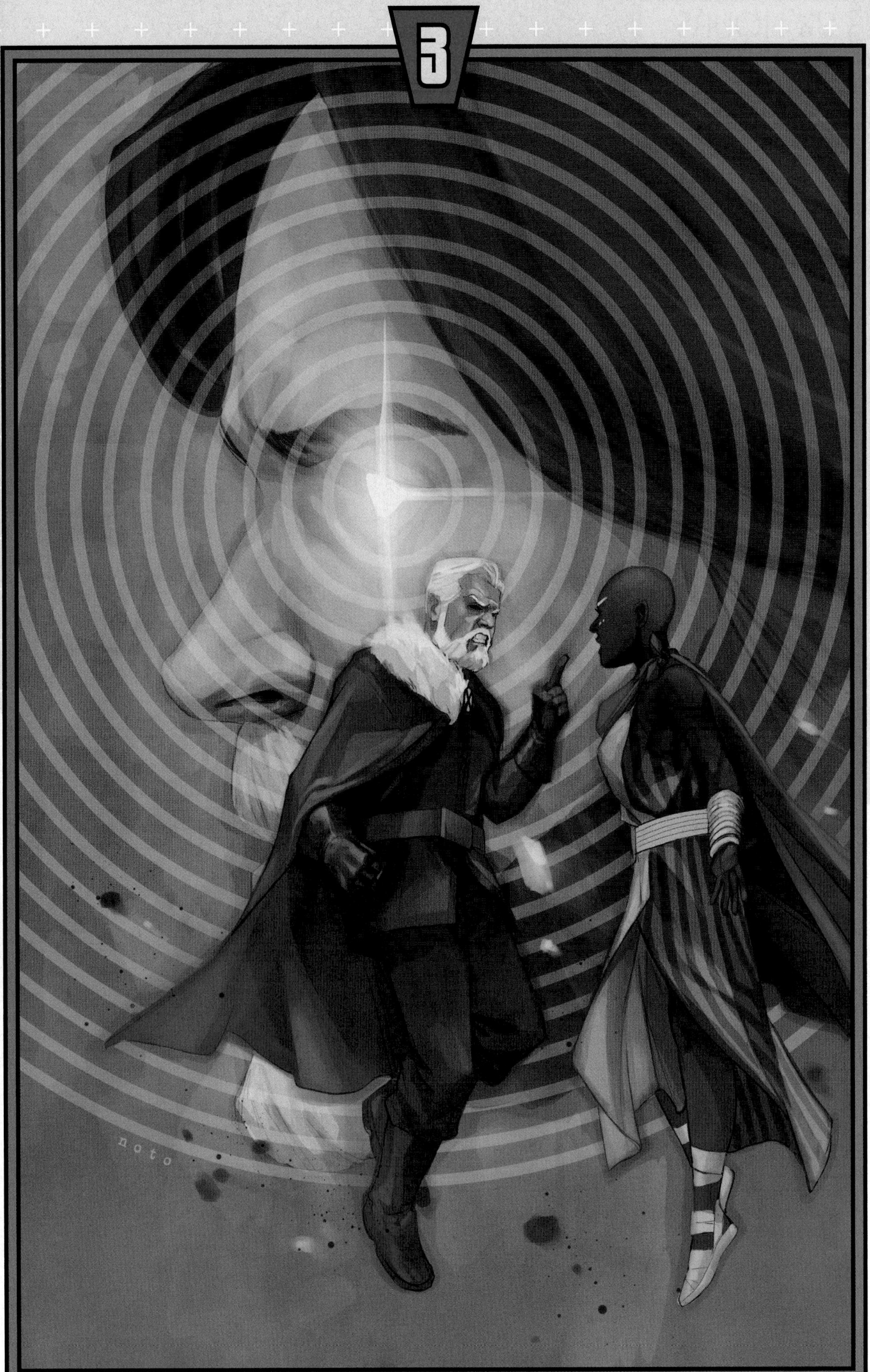
3
noto

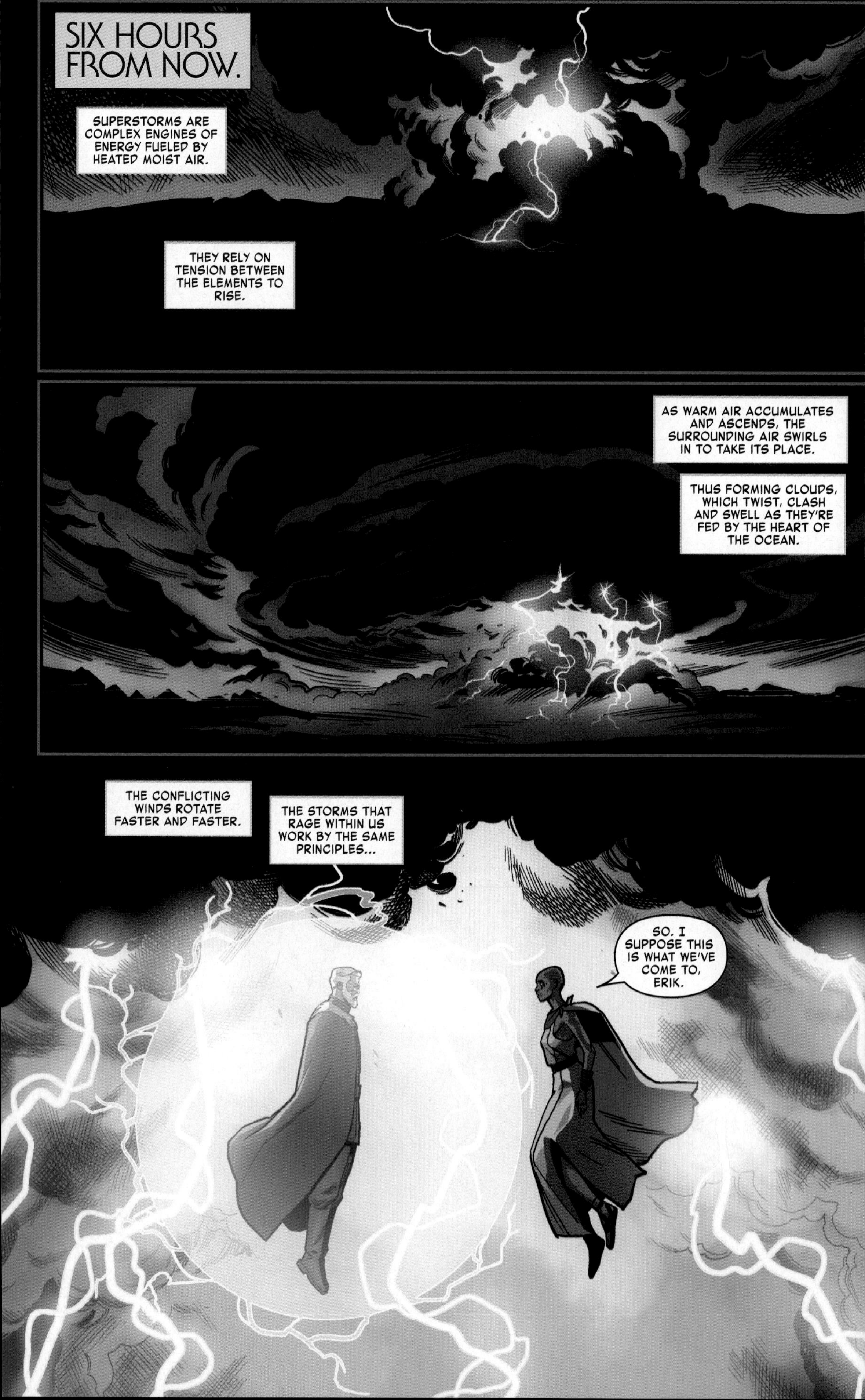
SIX HOURS FROM NOW.
SUPERSTORMS ARE COMPLEX ENGINES OF ENERGY FUELED BY HEATED MOIST AIR.
THEY RELY ON TENSION BETWEEN THE ELEMENTS TO RISE.
AS WARM AIR ACCUMULATES AND ASCENDS, THE SURROUNDING AIR SWIRLS IN TO TAKE ITS PLACE.
THUS FORMING CLOUDS, WHICH TWIST, CLASH AND SWELL AS THEY'RE FED BY THE HEART OF THE OCEAN.
THE CONFLICTING WINDS ROTATE FASTER AND FASTER.
THE STORMS THAT RAGE WITHIN US WORK BY THE SAME PRINCIPLES...
SO. I SUPPOSE THIS IS WHAT WE'VE COME TO, ERIK.

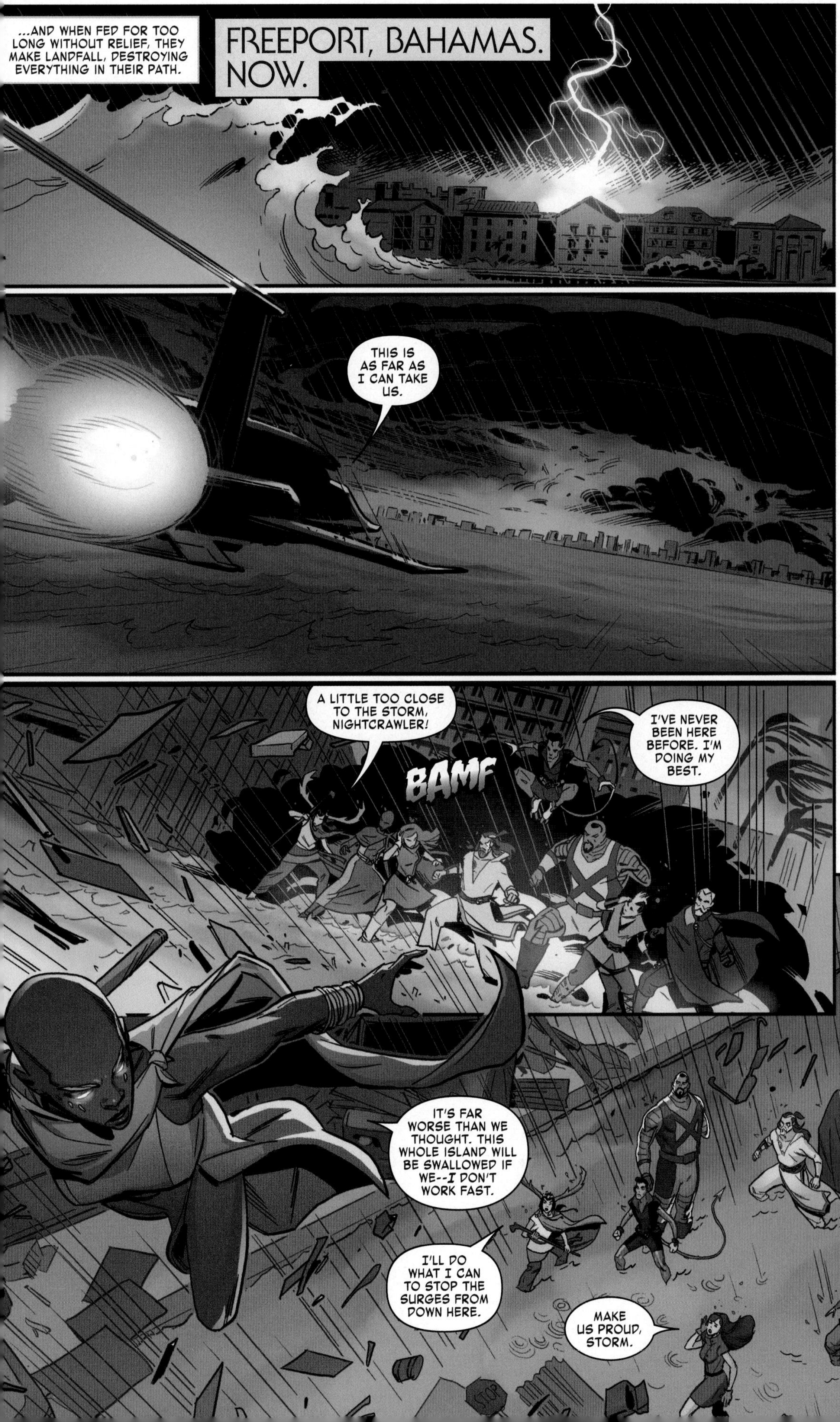
...AND WHEN FED FOR TOO LONG WITHOUT RELIEF, THEY MAKE LANDFALL, DESTROYING EVERYTHING IN THEIR PATH.
FREEPORT, BAHAMAS. NOW.
THIS IS AS FAR AS I CAN TAKE US.
A LITTLE TOO CLOSE TO THE STORM, NIGHTCRAWLER!
BAMF
I'VE NEVER BEEN HERE BEFORE. I'M DOING MY BEST.
IT'S FAR WORSE THAN WE THOUGHT. THIS WHOLE ISLAND WILL BE SWALLOWED IF WE--I DON'T WORK FAST.
I'LL DO WHAT I CAN TO STOP THE SURGES FROM DOWN HERE.
MAKE US PROUD, STORM.

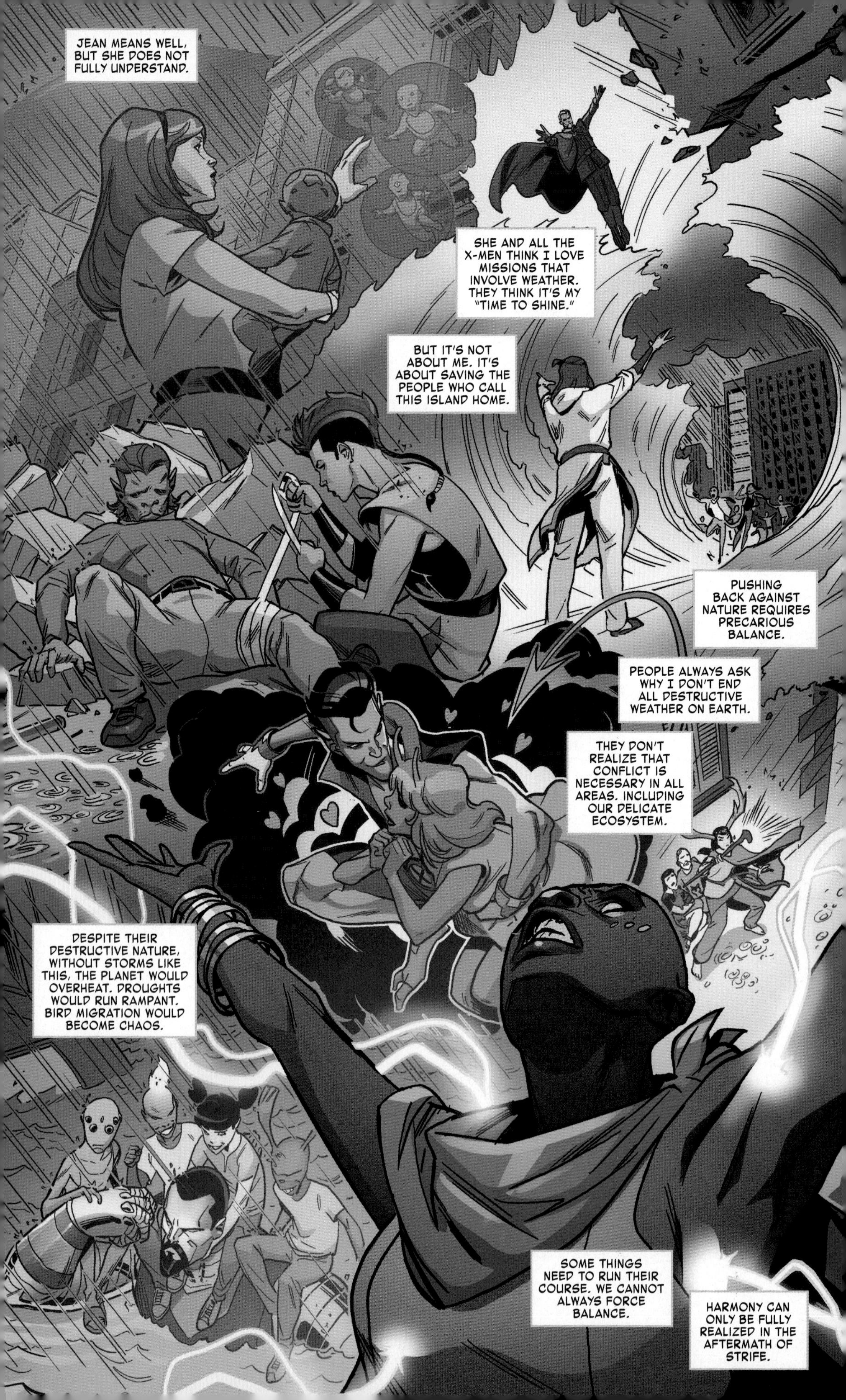
JEAN MEANS WELL, BUT SHE DOES NOT FULLY UNDERSTAND.
SHE AND ALL THE X-MEN THINK I LOVE MISSIONS THAT INVOLVE WEATHER. THEY THINK IT'S MY "TIME TO SHINE."
BUT IT'S NOT ABOUT ME. IT'S ABOUT SAVING THE PEOPLE WHO CALL THIS ISLAND HOME.
PUSHING BACK AGAINST NATURE REQUIRES PRECARIOUS BALANCE.
PEOPLE ALWAYS ASK WHY I DON'T END ALL DESTRUCTIVE WEATHER ON EARTH.
THEY DON'T REALIZE THAT CONFLICT IS NECESSARY IN ALL AREAS. INCLUDING OUR DELICATE ECOSYSTEM.
DESPITE THEIR DESTRUCTIVE NATURE, WITHOUT STORMS LIKE THIS, THE PLANET WOULD OVERHEAT. DROUGHTS WOULD RUN RAMPANT. BIRD MIGRATION WOULD BECOME CHAOS.
SOME THINGS NEED TO RUN THEIR COURSE. WE CANNOT ALWAYS FORCE BALANCE.
HARMONY CAN ONLY BE FULLY REALIZED IN THE AFTERMATH OF STRIFE.

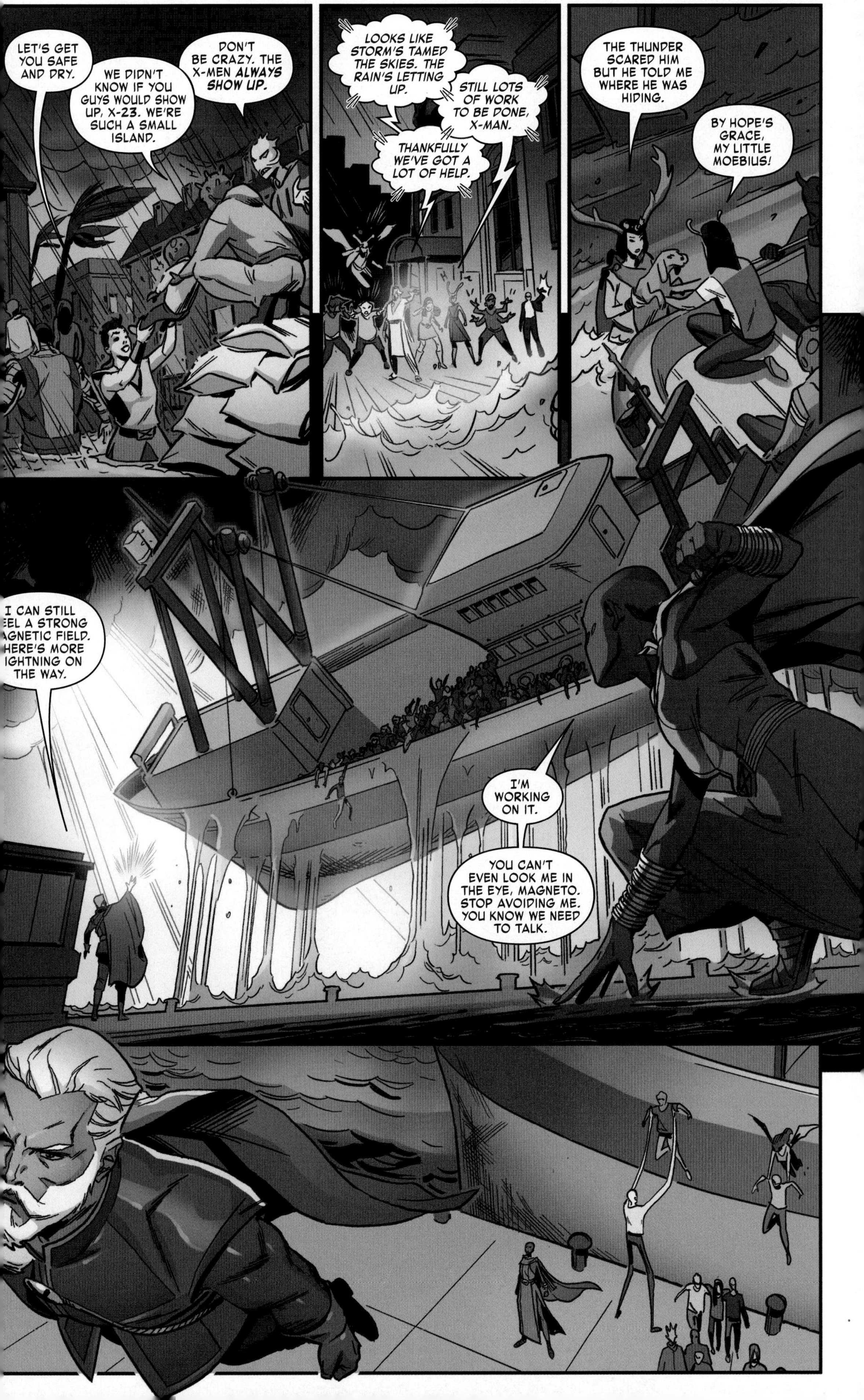
LET'S GET YOU SAFE AND DRY.
WE DIDN'T KNOW IF YOU GUYS WOULD SHOW UP, X-23. WE'RE SUCH A SMALL ISLAND.
DON'T BE CRAZY. THE X-MEN ALWAYS SHOW UP.
LOOKS LIKE STORM'S TAMED THE SKIES. THE RAIN'S LETTING UP.
THANKFULLY WE'VE GOT A LOT OF HELP.
STILL LOTS OF WORK TO BE DONE, X-MAN.
THE THUNDER SCARED HIM BUT HE TOLD ME WHERE HE WAS HIDING.
BY HOPE'S GRACE, MY LITTLE MOEBIUS!
I CAN STILL EEL A STRONG AGNETIC FIELD. HERE'S MORE IGHTNING ON THE WAY.
I'M WORKING ON IT.
YOU CAN'T EVEN LOOK ME IN THE EYE, MAGNETO. STOP AVOIDING ME. YOU KNOW WE NEED TO TALK.

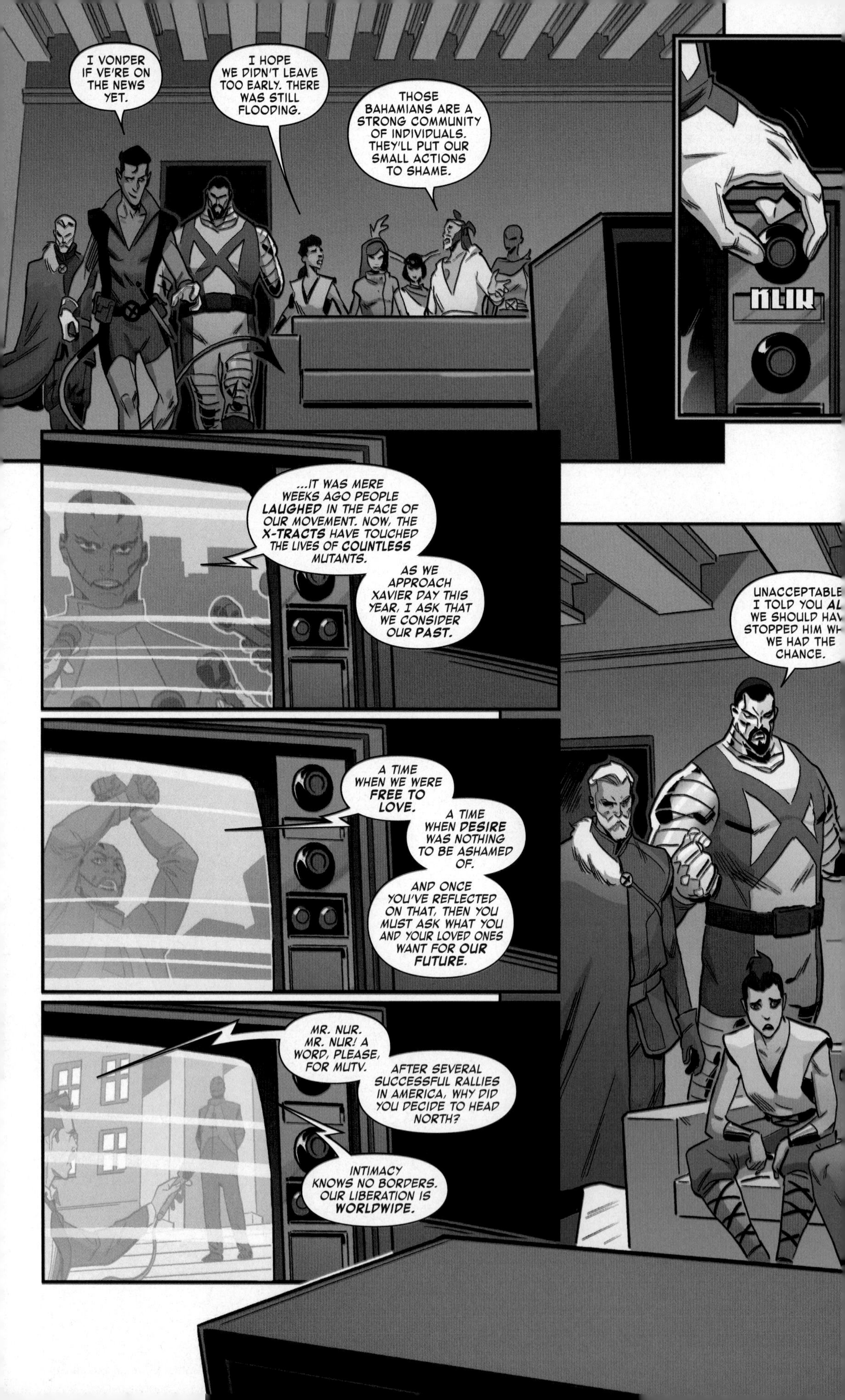
I VONDER IF VE'RE ON THE NEWS YET.
I HOPE WE DIDN'T LEAVE TOO EARLY. THERE WAS STILL FLOODING.
THOSE BAHAMIANS ARE A STRONG COMMUNITY OF INDIVIDUALS. THEY'LL PUT OUR SMALL ACTIONS TO SHAME.
KLIK
...IT WAS MERE WEEKS AGO PEOPLE LAUGHED IN THE FACE OF OUR MOVEMENT. NOW, THE X-TRACTS HAVE TOUCHED THE LIVES OF COUNTLESS MUTANTS.
AS WE APPROACH XAVIER DAY THIS YEAR, I ASK THAT WE CONSIDER OUR PAST.
A TIME WHEN WE WERE FREE TO LOVE.
A TIME WHEN DESIRE WAS NOTHING TO BE ASHAMED OF.
AND ONCE YOU'VE REFLECTED ON THAT, THEN YOU MUST ASK WHAT YOU AND YOUR LOVED ONES WANT FOR OUR FUTURE.
MR. NUR. MR. NUR! A WORD, PLEASE, FOR MUTV.
AFTER SEVERAL SUCCESSFUL RALLIES IN AMERICA, WHY DID YOU DECIDE TO HEAD NORTH?
INTIMACY KNOWS NO BORDERS. OUR LIBERATION IS WORLDWIDE.

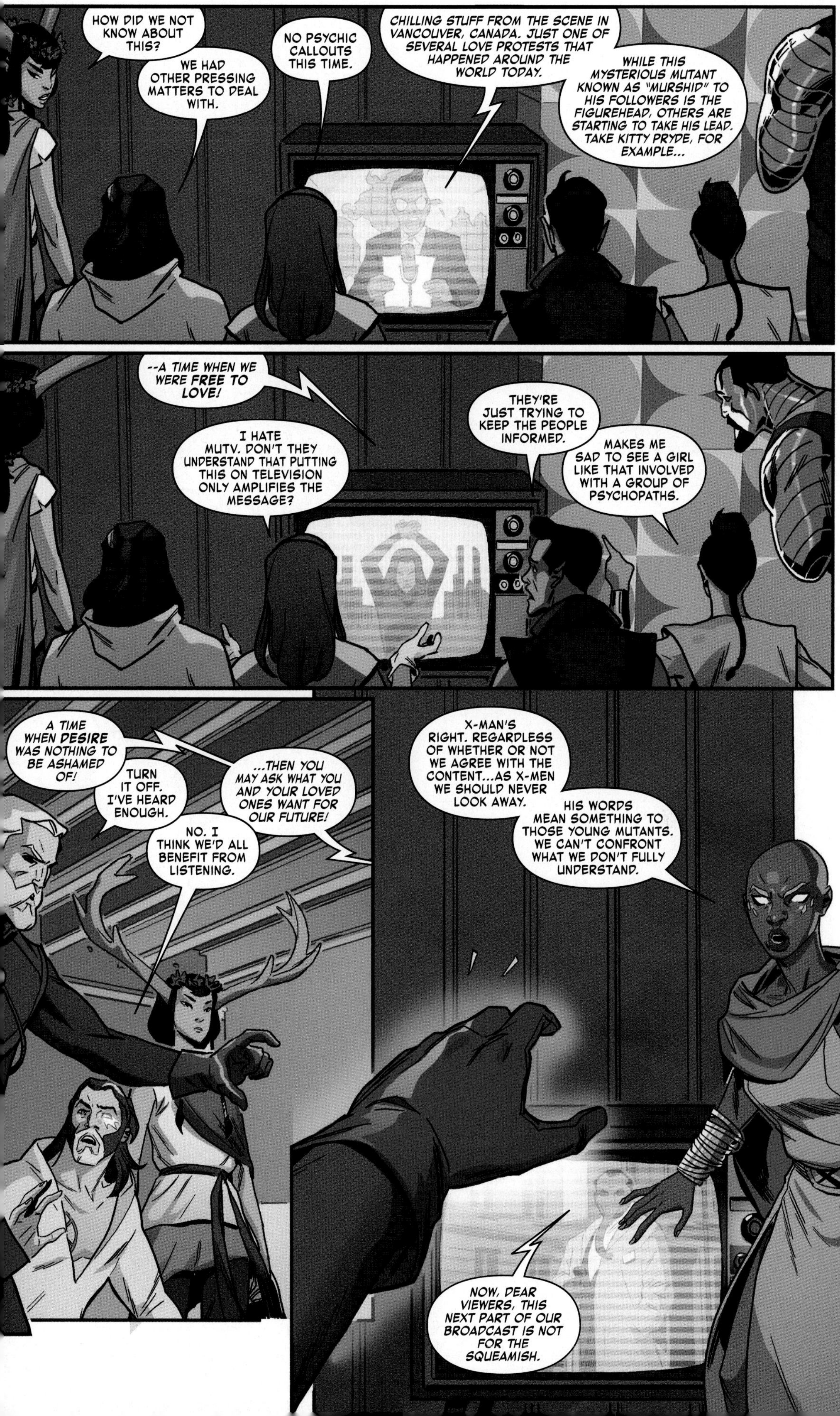
HOW DID WE NOT KNOW ABOUT THIS?
WE HAD OTHER PRESSING MATTERS TO DEAL WITH.
NO PSYCHIC CALLOUTS THIS TIME.
CHILLING STUFF FROM THE SCENE IN VANCOUVER, CANADA. JUST ONE OF SEVERAL LOVE PROTESTS THAT HAPPENED AROUND THE WORLD TODAY.
WHILE THIS MYSTERIOUS MUTANT KNOWN AS "MURSHID" TO HIS FOLLOWERS IS THE FIGUREHEAD, OTHERS ARE STARTING TO TAKE HIS LEAD. TAKE KITTY PRYDE, FOR EXAMPLE...
--A TIME WHEN WE WERE FREE TO LOVE!
I HATE MUTV. DON'T THEY UNDERSTAND THAT PUTTING THIS ON TELEVISION ONLY AMPLIFIES THE MESSAGE?
THEY'RE JUST TRYING TO KEEP THE PEOPLE INFORMED.
MAKES ME SAD TO SEE A GIRL LIKE THAT INVOLVED WITH A GROUP OF PSYCHOPATHS.
A TIME WHEN DESIRE WAS NOTHING TO BE ASHAMED OF!
TURN IT OFF. I'VE HEARD ENOUGH.
...THEN YOU MAY ASK WHAT YOU AND YOUR LOVED ONES WANT FOR OUR FUTURE!
NO. I THINK WE'D ALL BENEFIT FROM LISTENING.
X-MAN'S RIGHT. REGARDLESS OF WHETHER OR NOT WE AGREE WITH THE CONTENT...AS X-MEN WE SHOULD NEVER LOOK AWAY.
HIS WORDS MEAN SOMETHING TO THOSE YOUNG MUTANTS. WE CAN'T CONFRONT WHAT WE DON'T FULLY UNDERSTAND.
NOW, DEAR VIEWERS, THIS NEXT PART OF OUR BROADCAST IS NOT FOR THE SQUEAMISH.

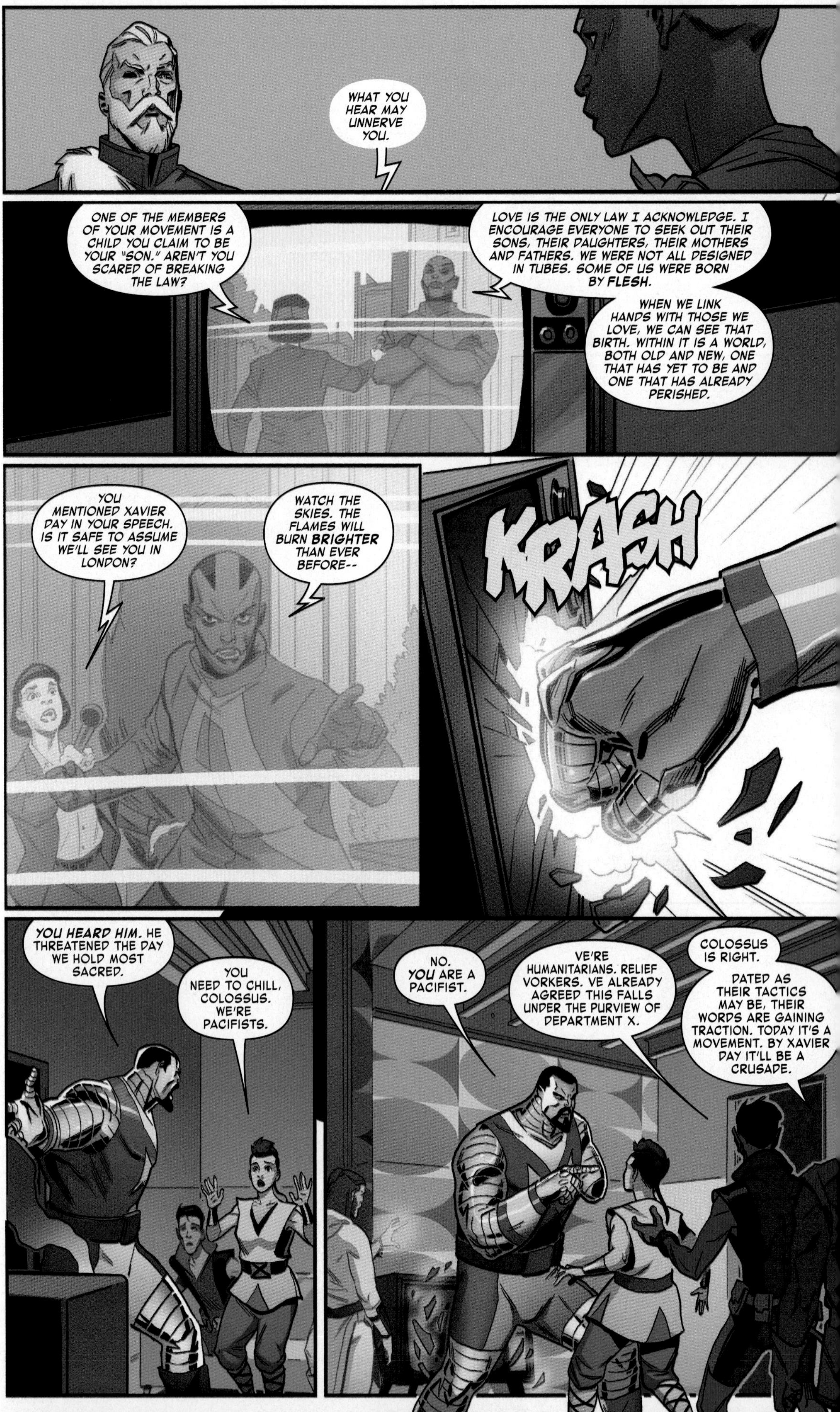
WHAT YOU HEAR MAY UNNERVE YOU.
ONE OF THE MEMBERS OF YOUR MOVEMENT IS A CHILD YOU CLAIM TO BE YOUR "SON." AREN'T YOU SCARED OF BREAKING THE LAW?
LOVE IS THE ONLY LAW I ACKNOWLEDGE. I ENCOURAGE EVERYONE TO SEEK OUT THEIR SONS, THEIR DAUGHTERS, THEIR MOTHERS AND FATHERS. WE WERE NOT ALL DESIGNED IN TUBES. SOME OF US WERE BORN BY FLESH.
WHEN WE LINK HANDS WITH THOSE WE LOVE, WE CAN SEE THAT BIRTH. WITHIN IT IS A WORLD, BOTH OLD AND NEW, ONE THAT HAS YET TO BE AND ONE THAT HAS ALREADY PERISHED.
YOU MENTIONED XAVIER DAY IN YOUR SPEECH. IS IT SAFE TO ASSUME WE'LL SEE YOU IN LONDON?
WATCH THE SKIES. THE FLAMES WILL BURN BRIGHTER THAN EVER BEFORE--
KRASH
YOU HEARD HIM. HE THREATENED THE DAY WE HOLD MOST SACRED.
YOU NEED TO CHILL, COLOSSUS. WE'RE PACIFISTS.
NO. YOU ARE A PACIFIST.
VE'RE HUMANITARIANS. RELIEF VORKERS. VE ALREADY AGREED THIS FALLS UNDER THE PURVIEW OF DEPARTMENT X.
COLOSSUS IS RIGHT.
DATED AS THEIR TACTICS MAY BE, THEIR WORDS ARE GAINING TRACTION. TODAY IT'S A MOVEMENT. BY XAVIER DAY IT'LL BE A CRUSADE.

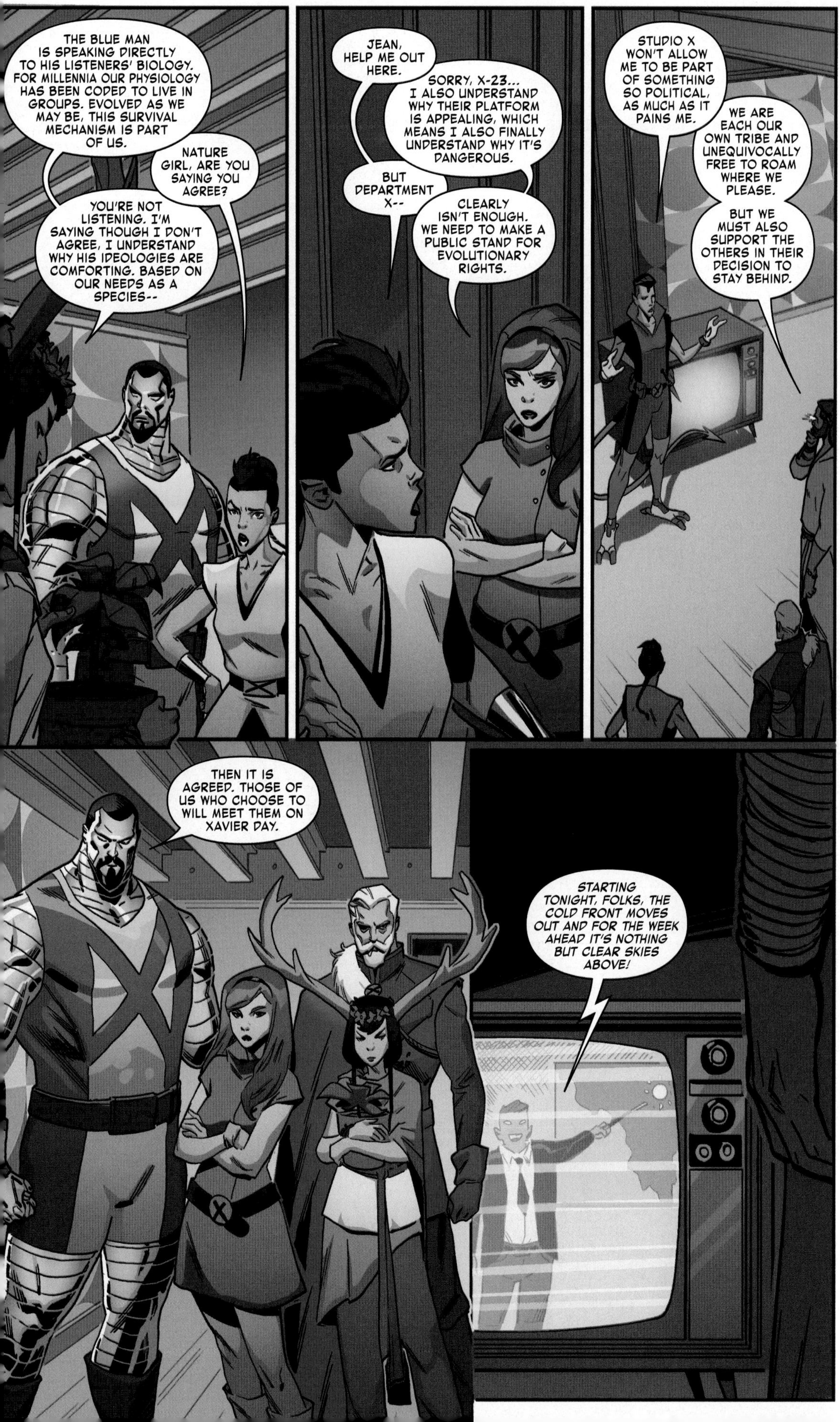
THE BLUE MAN IS SPEAKING DIRECTLY TO HIS LISTENERS' BIOLOGY. FOR MILLENNIA OUR PHYSIOLOGY HAS BEEN CODED TO LIVE IN GROUPS. EVOLVED AS WE MAY BE, THIS SURVIVAL MECHANISM IS PART OF US.
NATURE GIRL, ARE YOU SAYING YOU AGREE?
YOU'RE NOT LISTENING. I'M SAYING THOUGH I DON'T AGREE, I UNDERSTAND WHY HIS IDEOLOGIES ARE COMFORTING. BASED ON OUR NEEDS AS A SPECIES--
JEAN, HELP ME OUT HERE.
SORRY, X-23... I ALSO UNDERSTAND WHY THEIR PLATFORM IS APPEALING, WHICH MEANS I ALSO FINALLY UNDERSTAND WHY IT'S DANGEROUS.
BUT DEPARTMENT X--
CLEARLY ISN'T ENOUGH. WE NEED TO MAKE A PUBLIC STAND FOR EVOLUTIONARY RIGHTS.
STUDIO X WON'T ALLOW ME TO BE PART OF SOMETHING SO POLITICAL, AS MUCH AS IT PAINS ME.
WE ARE EACH OUR OWN TRIBE AND UNEQUIVOCALLY FREE TO ROAM WHERE WE PLEASE.
BUT WE MUST ALSO SUPPORT THE OTHERS IN THEIR DECISION TO STAY BEHIND.
THEN IT IS AGREED. THOSE OF US WHO CHOOSE TO WILL MEET THEM ON XAVIER DAY.
STARTING TONIGHT, FOLKS, THE COLD FRONT MOVES OUT AND FOR THE WEEK AHEAD IT'S NOTHING BUT CLEAR SKIES ABOVE!

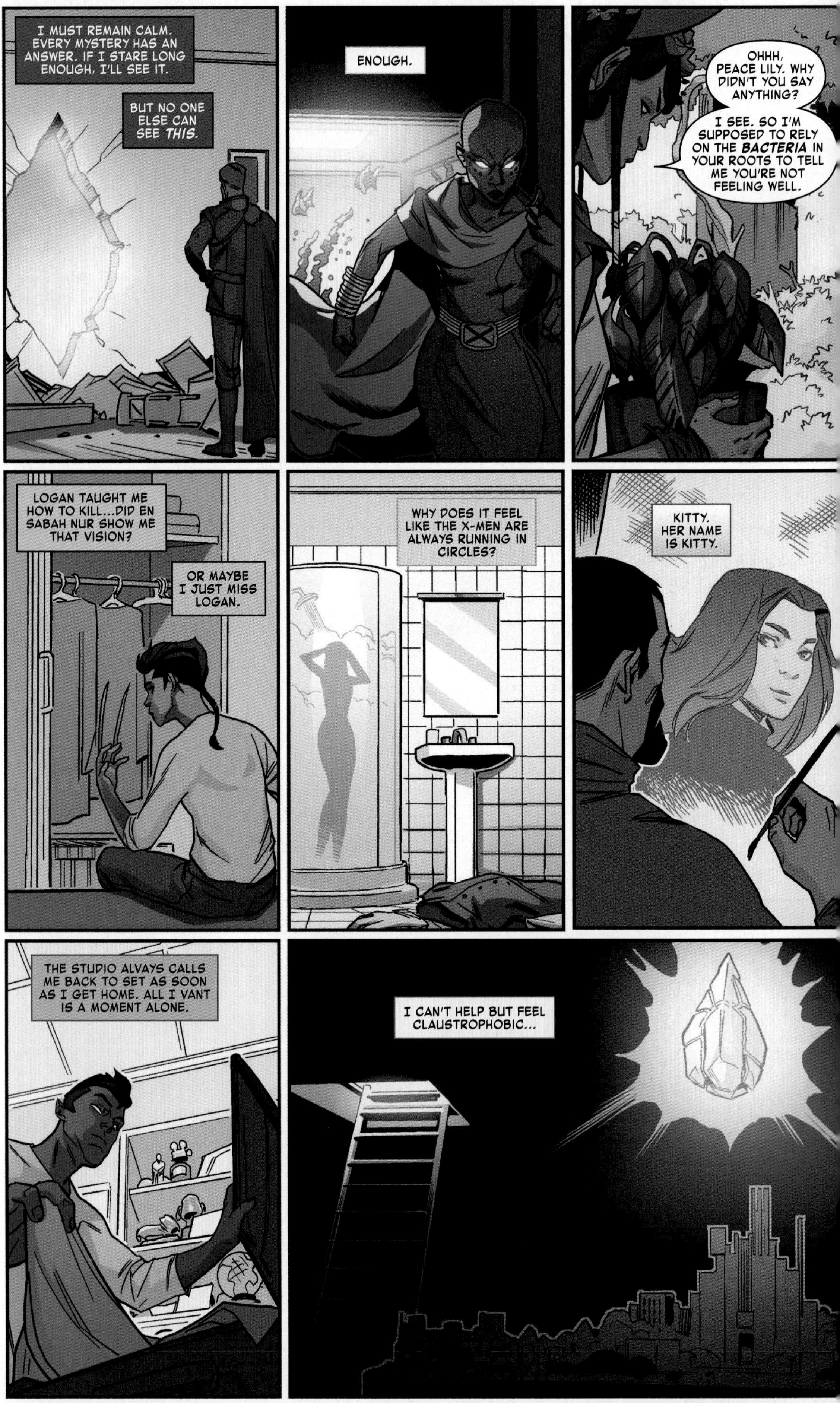
I MUST REMAIN CALM. EVERY MYSTERY HAS AN ANSWER. IF I STARE LONG ENOUGH, I'LL SEE IT.
BUT NO ONE ELSE CAN SEE *THIS*.
ENOUGH.
OHHH, PEACE LILY. WHY DIDN'T YOU SAY ANYTHING?
I SEE. SO I'M SUPPOSED TO RELY ON THE *BACTERIA* IN YOUR ROOTS TO TELL ME YOU'RE NOT FEELING WELL.
LOGAN TAUGHT ME HOW TO KILL...DID EN SABAH NUR SHOW ME THAT VISION?
OR MAYBE I JUST MISS LOGAN.
WHY DOES IT FEEL LIKE THE X-MEN ARE ALWAYS RUNNING IN CIRCLES?
KITTY. HER NAME IS KITTY.
THE STUDIO ALVAYS CALLS ME BACK TO SET AS SOON AS I GET HOME. ALL I VANT IS A MOMENT ALONE.
I CAN'T HELP BUT FEEL CLAUSTROPHOBIC...

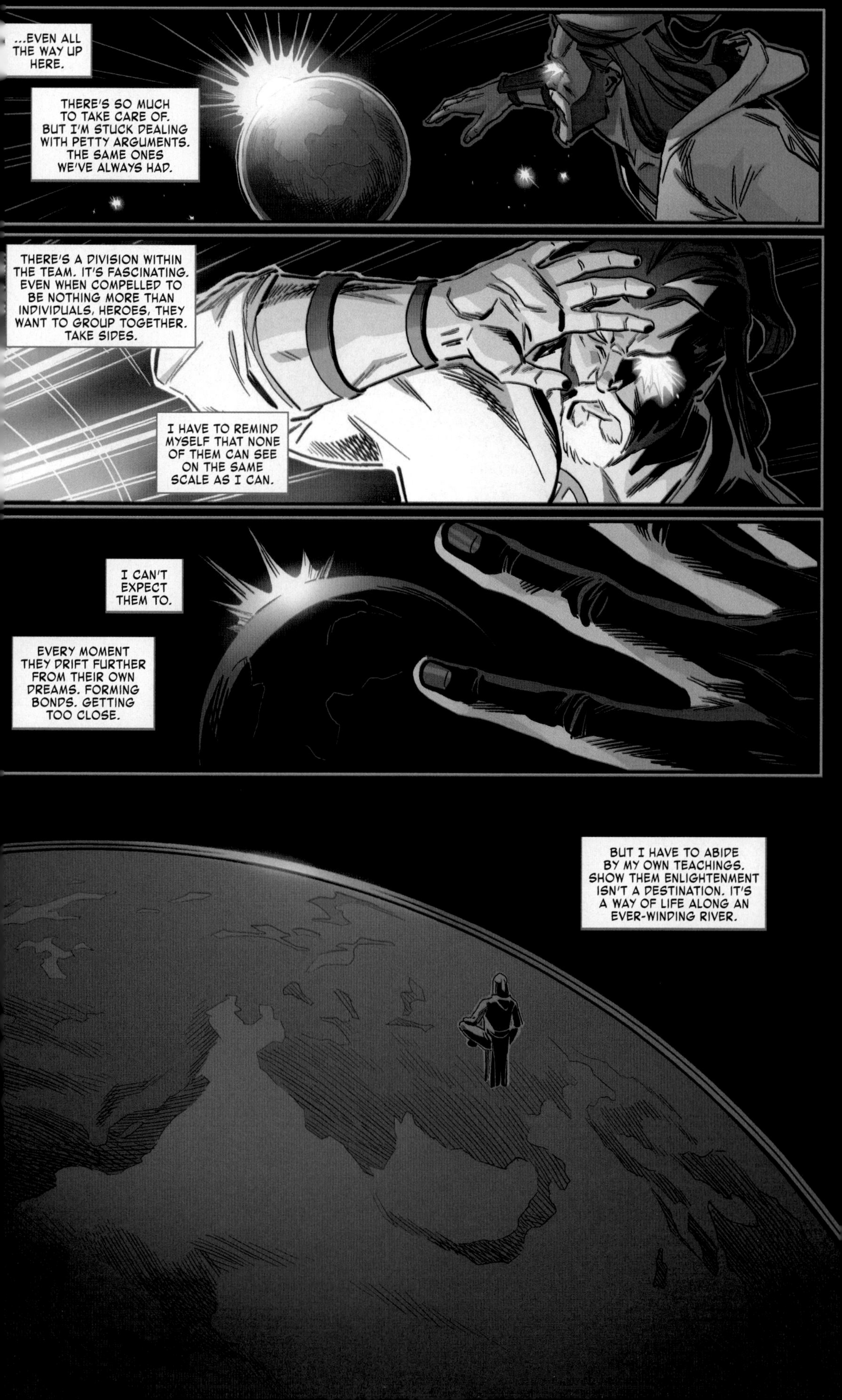
...EVEN ALL THE WAY UP HERE.
THERE'S SO MUCH TO TAKE CARE OF. BUT I'M STUCK DEALING WITH PETTY ARGUMENTS. THE SAME ONES WE'VE ALWAYS HAD.
THERE'S A DIVISION WITHIN THE TEAM. IT'S FASCINATING. EVEN WHEN COMPELLED TO BE NOTHING MORE THAN INDIVIDUALS, HEROES, THEY WANT TO GROUP TOGETHER. TAKE SIDES.
I HAVE TO REMIND MYSELF THAT NONE OF THEM CAN SEE ON THE SAME SCALE AS I CAN.
I CAN'T EXPECT THEM TO.
EVERY MOMENT THEY DRIFT FURTHER FROM THEIR OWN DREAMS. FORMING BONDS. GETTING TOO CLOSE.
BUT I HAVE TO ABIDE BY MY OWN TEACHINGS. SHOW THEM ENLIGHTENMENT ISN'T A DESTINATION. IT'S A WAY OF LIFE ALONG AN EVER-WINDING RIVER.

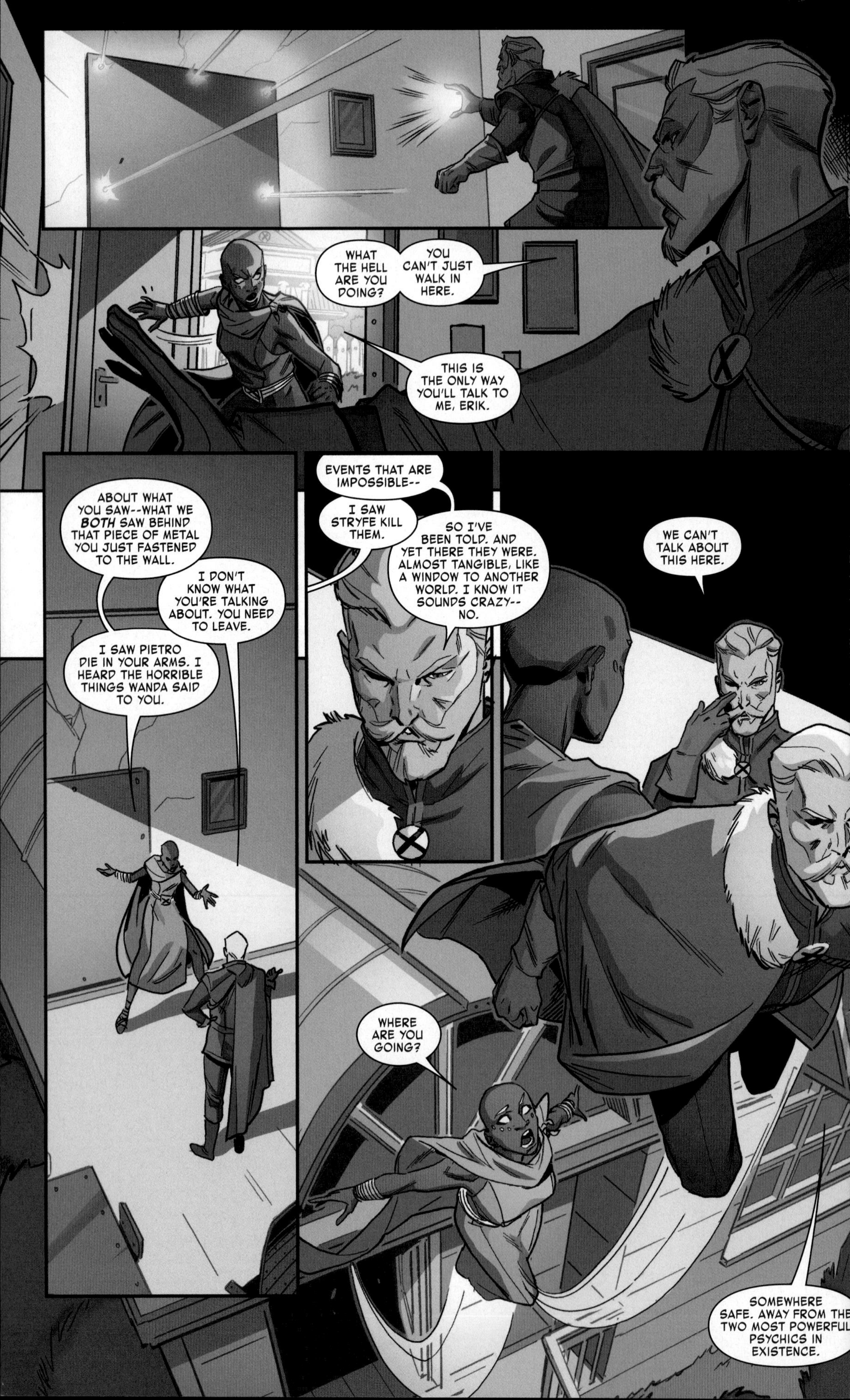
WHAT THE HELL ARE YOU DOING?
YOU CAN'T JUST WALK IN HERE.
THIS IS THE ONLY WAY YOU'LL TALK TO ME, ERIK.
ABOUT WHAT YOU SAW--WHAT WE *BOTH* SAW BEHIND THAT PIECE OF METAL YOU JUST FASTENED TO THE WALL.
I DON'T KNOW WHAT YOU'RE TALKING ABOUT. YOU NEED TO LEAVE.
I SAW PIETRO DIE IN YOUR ARMS. I HEARD THE HORRIBLE THINGS WANDA SAID TO YOU.
EVENTS THAT ARE IMPOSSIBLE--
I SAW STRYFE KILL THEM.
SO I'VE BEEN TOLD. AND YET THERE THEY WERE. ALMOST TANGIBLE, LIKE A WINDOW TO ANOTHER WORLD. I KNOW IT SOUNDS CRAZY--
NO.
WE CAN'T TALK ABOUT THIS HERE.
WHERE ARE YOU GOING?
SOMEWHERE SAFE. AWAY FROM THE TWO MOST POWERFUL PSYCHICS IN EXISTENCE.

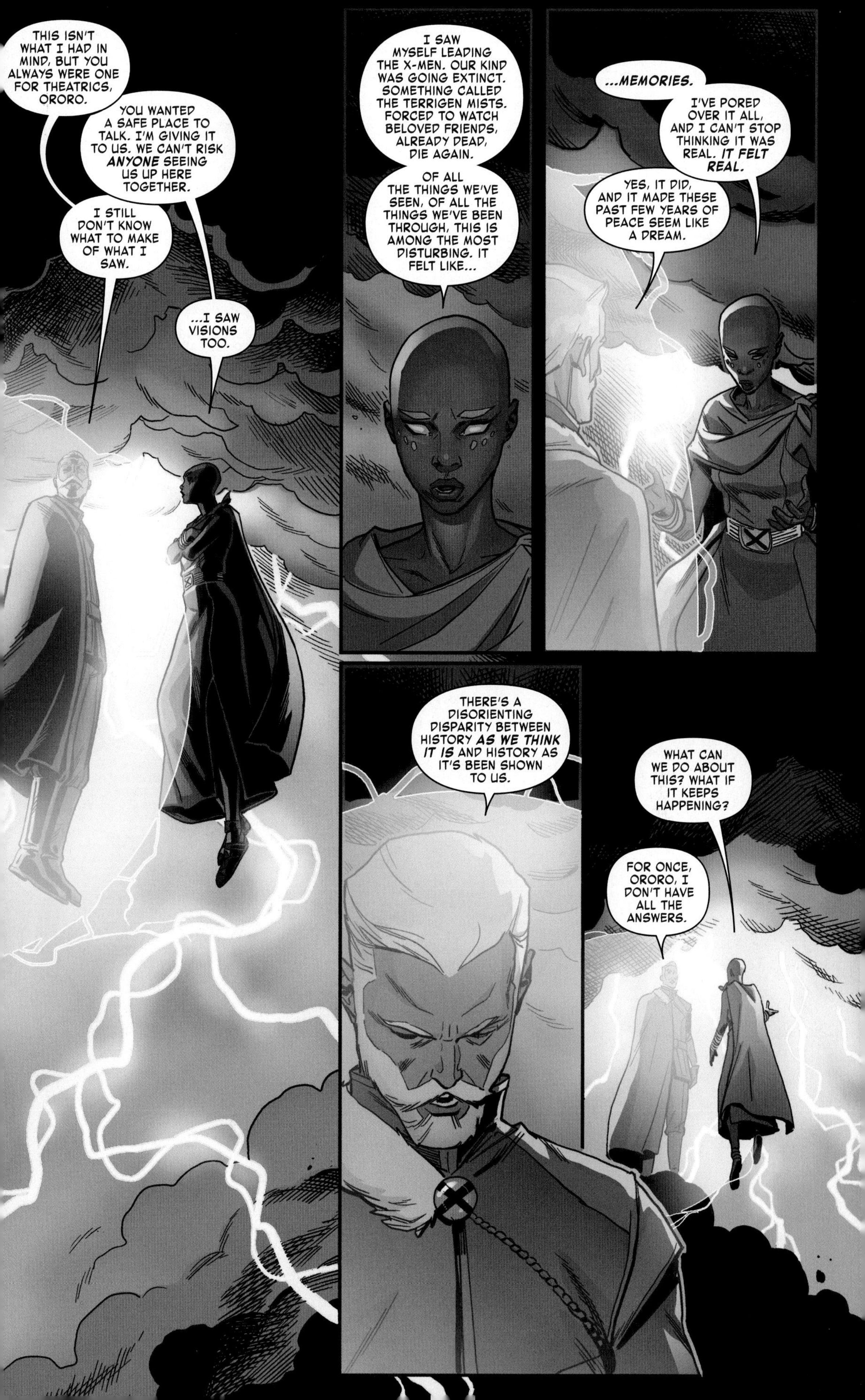
THIS ISN'T WHAT I HAD IN MIND, BUT YOU ALWAYS WERE ONE FOR THEATRICS, ORORO.
YOU WANTED A SAFE PLACE TO TALK. I'M GIVING IT TO US. WE CAN'T RISK ANYONE SEEING US UP HERE TOGETHER.
I STILL DON'T KNOW WHAT TO MAKE OF WHAT I SAW.
...I SAW VISIONS TOO.
I SAW MYSELF LEADING THE X-MEN. OUR KIND WAS GOING EXTINCT. SOMETHING CALLED THE TERRIGEN MISTS. FORCED TO WATCH BELOVED FRIENDS, ALREADY DEAD, DIE AGAIN.
OF ALL THE THINGS WE'VE SEEN, OF ALL THE THINGS WE'VE BEEN THROUGH, THIS IS AMONG THE MOST DISTURBING. IT FELT LIKE...
...MEMORIES.
I'VE PORED OVER IT ALL, AND I CAN'T STOP THINKING IT WAS REAL. IT FELT REAL.
YES, IT DID, AND IT MADE THESE PAST FEW YEARS OF PEACE SEEM LIKE A DREAM.
THERE'S A DISORIENTING DISPARITY BETWEEN HISTORY AS WE THINK IT IS AND HISTORY AS IT'S BEEN SHOWN TO US.
WHAT CAN WE DO ABOUT THIS? WHAT IF IT KEEPS HAPPENING?
FOR ONCE, ORORO, I DON'T HAVE ALL THE ANSWERS.

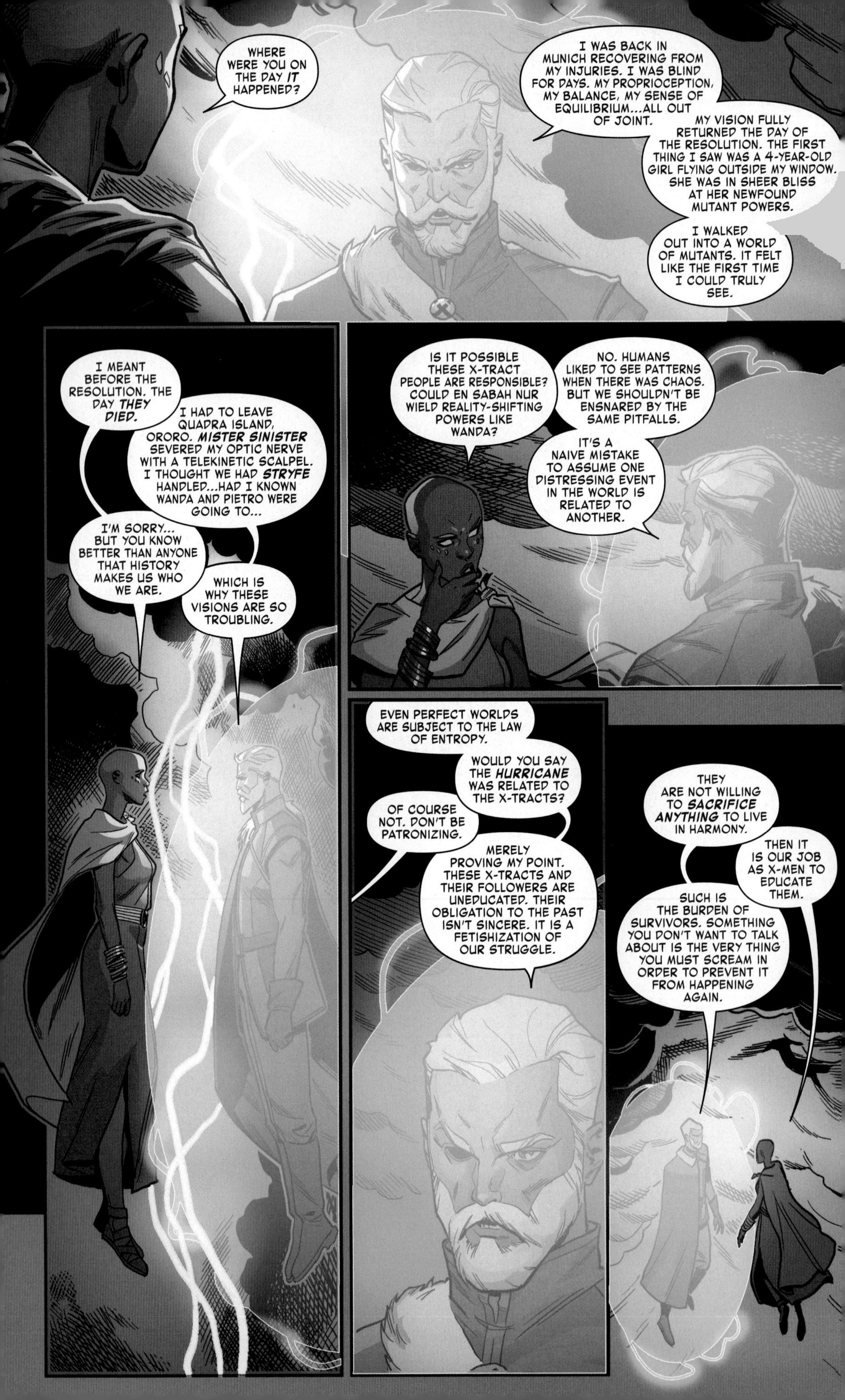
WHERE WERE YOU ON THE DAY IT HAPPENED?
I WAS BACK IN MUNICH RECOVERING FROM MY INJURIES. I WAS BLIND FOR DAYS. MY PROPRIOCEPTION, MY BALANCE, MY SENSE OF EQUILIBRIUM...ALL OUT OF JOINT.
MY VISION FULLY RETURNED THE DAY OF THE RESOLUTION. THE FIRST THING I SAW WAS A 4-YEAR-OLD GIRL FLYING OUTSIDE MY WINDOW. SHE WAS IN SHEER BLISS AT HER NEWFOUND MUTANT POWERS.
I WALKED OUT INTO A WORLD OF MUTANTS. IT FELT LIKE THE FIRST TIME I COULD TRULY SEE.
I MEANT BEFORE THE RESOLUTION. THE DAY THEY DIED.
I HAD TO LEAVE QUADRA ISLAND, ORORO. MISTER SINISTER SEVERED MY OPTIC NERVE WITH A TELEKINETIC SCALPEL. I THOUGHT WE HAD STRYFE HANDLED...HAD I KNOWN WANDA AND PIETRO WERE GOING TO...
I'M SORRY... BUT YOU KNOW BETTER THAN ANYONE THAT HISTORY MAKES US WHO WE ARE.
WHICH IS WHY THESE VISIONS ARE SO TROUBLING.
IS IT POSSIBLE THESE X-TRACT PEOPLE ARE RESPONSIBLE? COULD EN SABAH NUR WIELD REALITY-SHIFTING POWERS LIKE WANDA?
NO. HUMANS LIKED TO SEE PATTERNS WHEN THERE WAS CHAOS. BUT WE SHOULDN'T BE ENSNARED BY THE SAME PITFALLS.
IT'S A NAIVE MISTAKE TO ASSUME ONE DISTRESSING EVENT IN THE WORLD IS RELATED TO ANOTHER.
EVEN PERFECT WORLDS ARE SUBJECT TO THE LAW OF ENTROPY.
WOULD YOU SAY THE HURRICANE WAS RELATED TO THE X-TRACTS?
OF COURSE NOT. DON'T BE PATRONIZING.
MERELY PROVING MY POINT. THESE X-TRACTS AND THEIR FOLLOWERS ARE UNEDUCATED. THEIR OBLIGATION TO THE PAST ISN'T SINCERE. IT IS A FETISHIZATION OF OUR STRUGGLE.
THEY ARE NOT WILLING TO SACRIFICE ANYTHING TO LIVE IN HARMONY.
THEN IT IS OUR JOB AS X-MEN TO EDUCATE THEM.
SUCH IS THE BURDEN OF SURVIVORS. SOMETHING YOU DON'T WANT TO TALK ABOUT IS THE VERY THING YOU MUST SCREAM IN ORDER TO PREVENT IT FROM HAPPENING AGAIN.

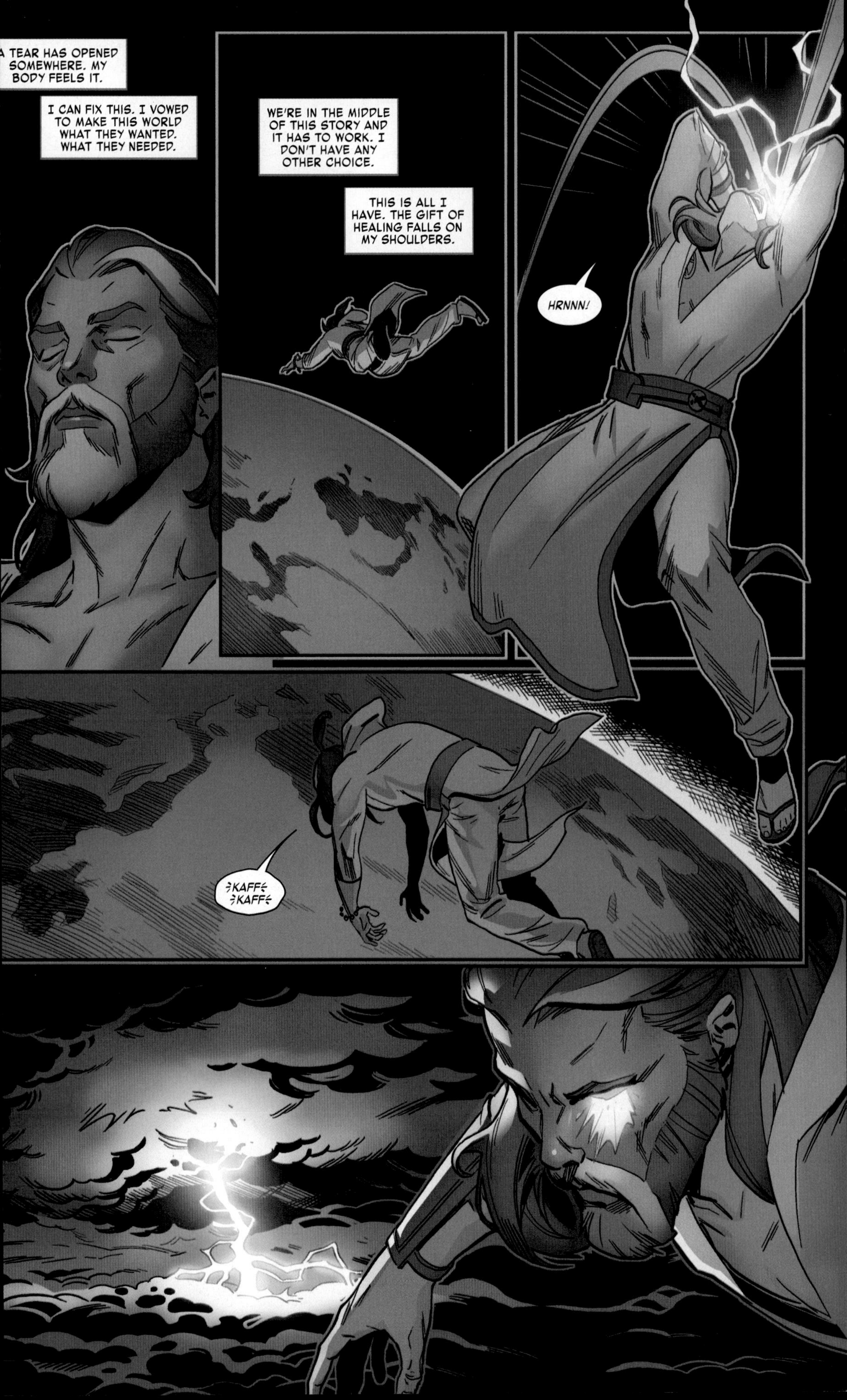
A TEAR HAS OPENED SOMEWHERE. MY BODY FEELS IT.
I CAN FIX THIS. I VOWED TO MAKE THIS WORLD WHAT THEY WANTED. WHAT THEY NEEDED.
WE'RE IN THE MIDDLE OF THIS STORY AND IT HAS TO WORK. I DON'T HAVE ANY OTHER CHOICE.
THIS IS ALL I HAVE. THE GIFT OF HEALING FALLS ON MY SHOULDERS.
HRNNN!
KAFF KAFF

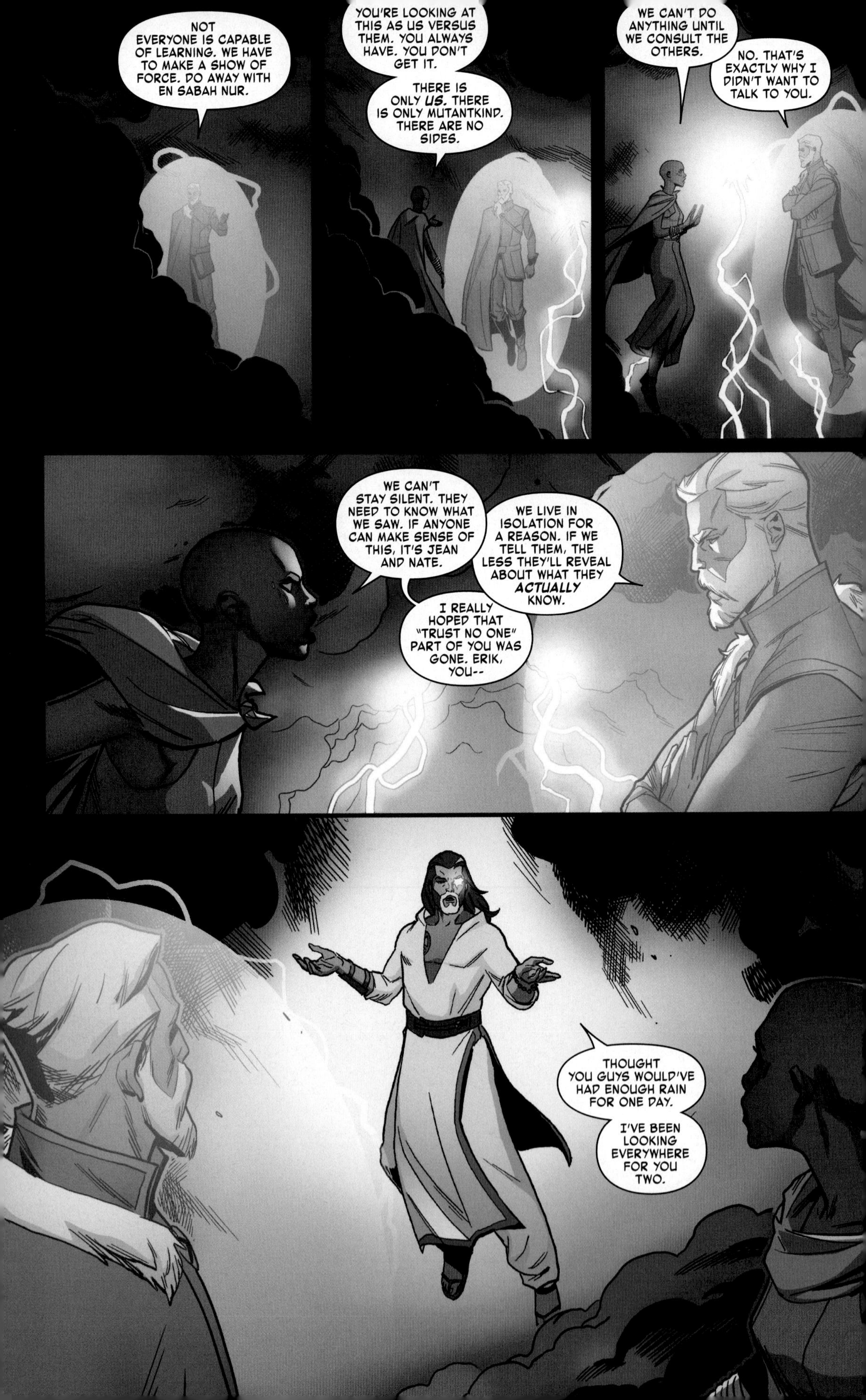
NOT EVERYONE IS CAPABLE OF LEARNING. WE HAVE TO MAKE A SHOW OF FORCE. DO AWAY WITH EN SABAH NUR.
YOU'RE LOOKING AT THIS AS US VERSUS THEM. YOU ALWAYS HAVE. YOU DON'T GET IT.
THERE IS ONLY US. THERE IS ONLY MUTANTKIND. THERE ARE NO SIDES.
WE CAN'T DO ANYTHING UNTIL WE CONSULT THE OTHERS.
NO. THAT'S EXACTLY WHY I DIDN'T WANT TO TALK TO YOU.
WE CAN'T STAY SILENT. THEY NEED TO KNOW WHAT WE SAW. IF ANYONE CAN MAKE SENSE OF THIS, IT'S JEAN AND NATE.
WE LIVE IN ISOLATION FOR A REASON. IF WE TELL THEM, THE LESS THEY'LL REVEAL ABOUT WHAT THEY ACTUALLY KNOW.
I REALLY HOPED THAT "TRUST NO ONE" PART OF YOU WAS GONE. ERIK, YOU--
THOUGHT YOU GUYS WOULD'VE HAD ENOUGH RAIN FOR ONE DAY.
I'VE BEEN LOOKING EVERYWHERE FOR YOU TWO.

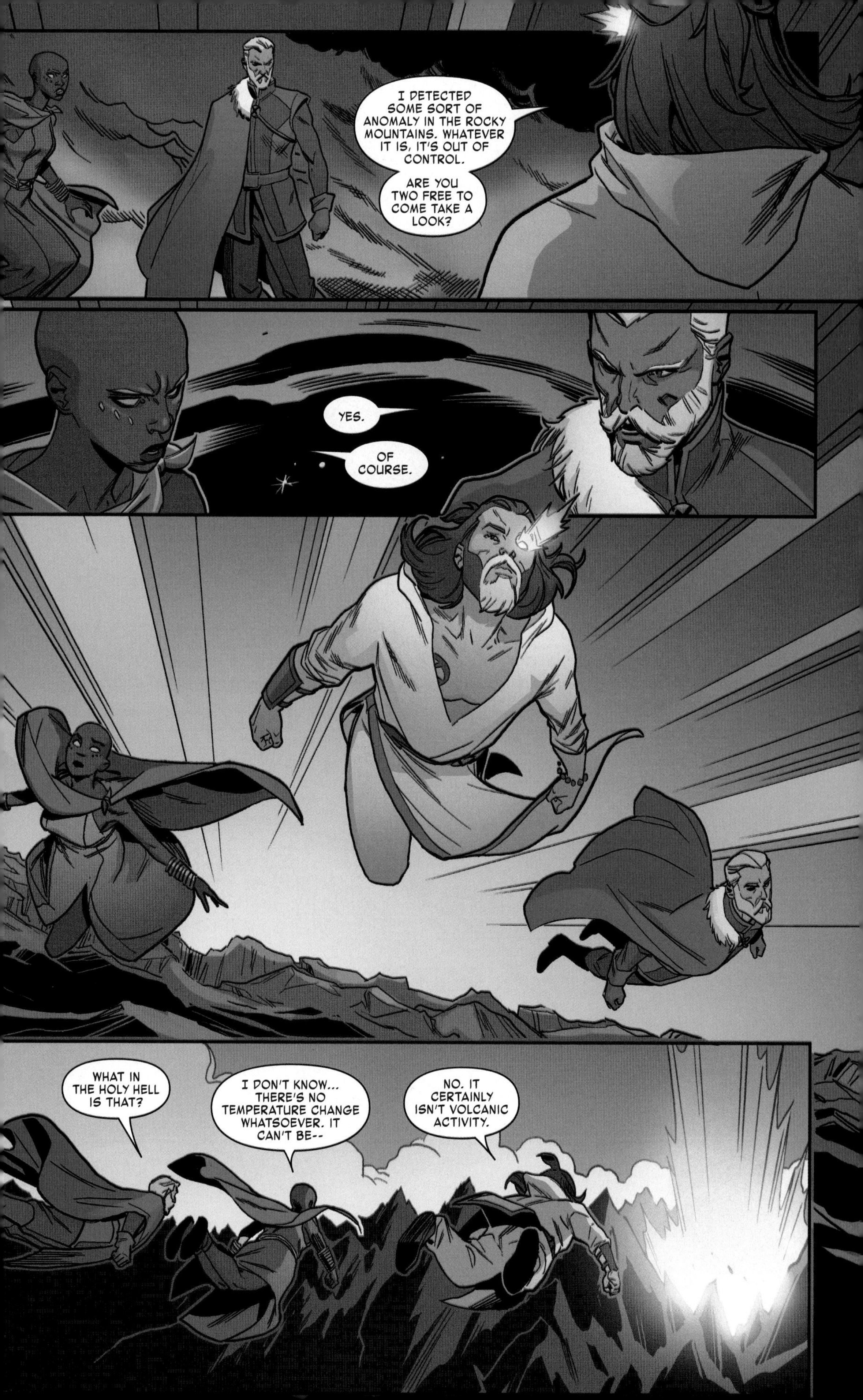
I DETECTED SOME SORT OF ANOMALY IN THE ROCKY MOUNTAINS. WHATEVER IT IS, IT'S OUT OF CONTROL.
ARE YOU TWO FREE TO COME TAKE A LOOK?
YES.
OF COURSE.
WHAT IN THE HOLY HELL IS THAT?
I DON'T KNOW... THERE'S NO TEMPERATURE CHANGE WHATSOEVER. IT CAN'T BE--
NO. IT CERTAINLY ISN'T VOLCANIC ACTIVITY.

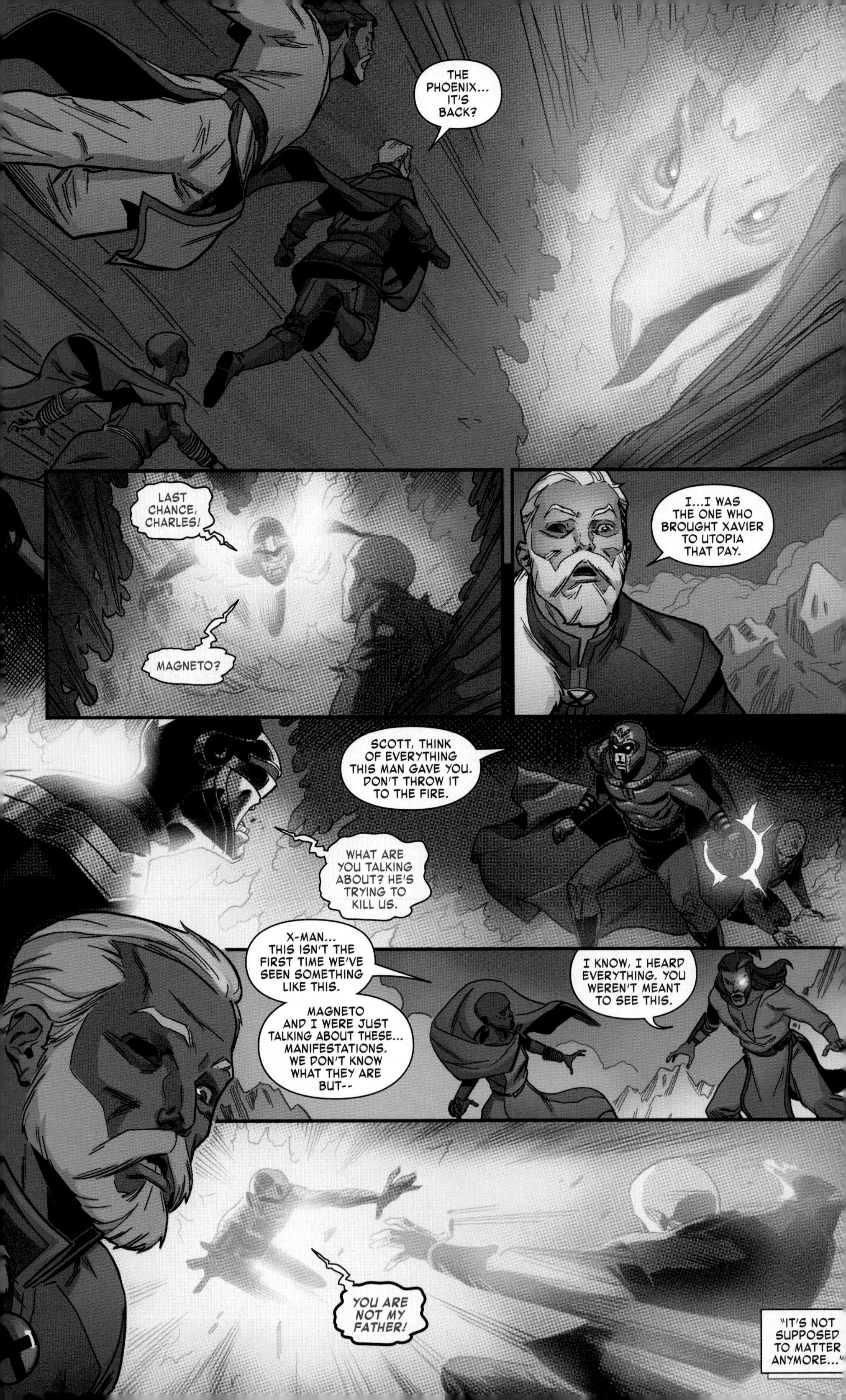
THE PHOENIX... IT'S BACK?
LAST CHANCE, CHARLES!
MAGNETO?
I...I WAS THE ONE WHO BROUGHT XAVIER TO UTOPIA THAT DAY.
SCOTT, THINK OF EVERYTHING THIS MAN GAVE YOU. DON'T THROW IT TO THE FIRE.
WHAT ARE YOU TALKING ABOUT? HE'S TRYING TO KILL US.
X-MAN... THIS ISN'T THE FIRST TIME WE'VE SEEN SOMETHING LIKE THIS.
MAGNETO AND I WERE JUST TALKING ABOUT THESE... MANIFESTATIONS. WE DON'T KNOW WHAT THEY ARE BUT--
I KNOW. I HEARD EVERYTHING. YOU WEREN'T MEANT TO SEE THIS.
YOU ARE NOT MY FATHER!
"IT'S NOT SUPPOSED TO MATTER ANYMORE..."

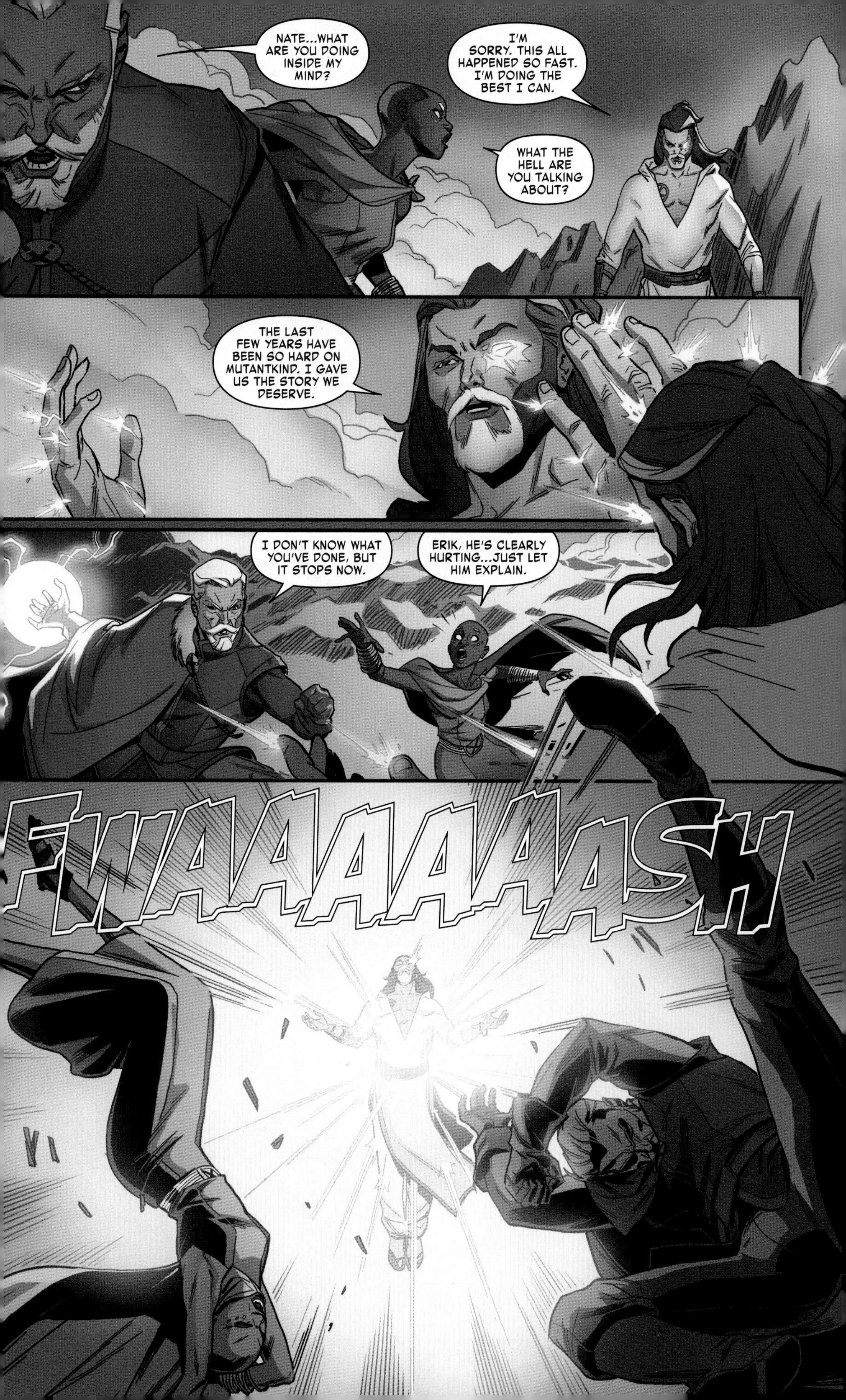
NATE...WHAT ARE YOU DOING INSIDE MY MIND?
I'M SORRY. THIS ALL HAPPENED SO FAST. I'M DOING THE BEST I CAN.
WHAT THE HELL ARE YOU TALKING ABOUT?
THE LAST FEW YEARS HAVE BEEN SO HARD ON MUTANTKIND. I GAVE US THE STORY WE DESERVE.
I DON'T KNOW WHAT YOU'VE DONE, BUT IT STOPS NOW.
ERIK, HE'S CLEARLY HURTING...JUST LET HIM EXPLAIN.
FWAAAAAASH

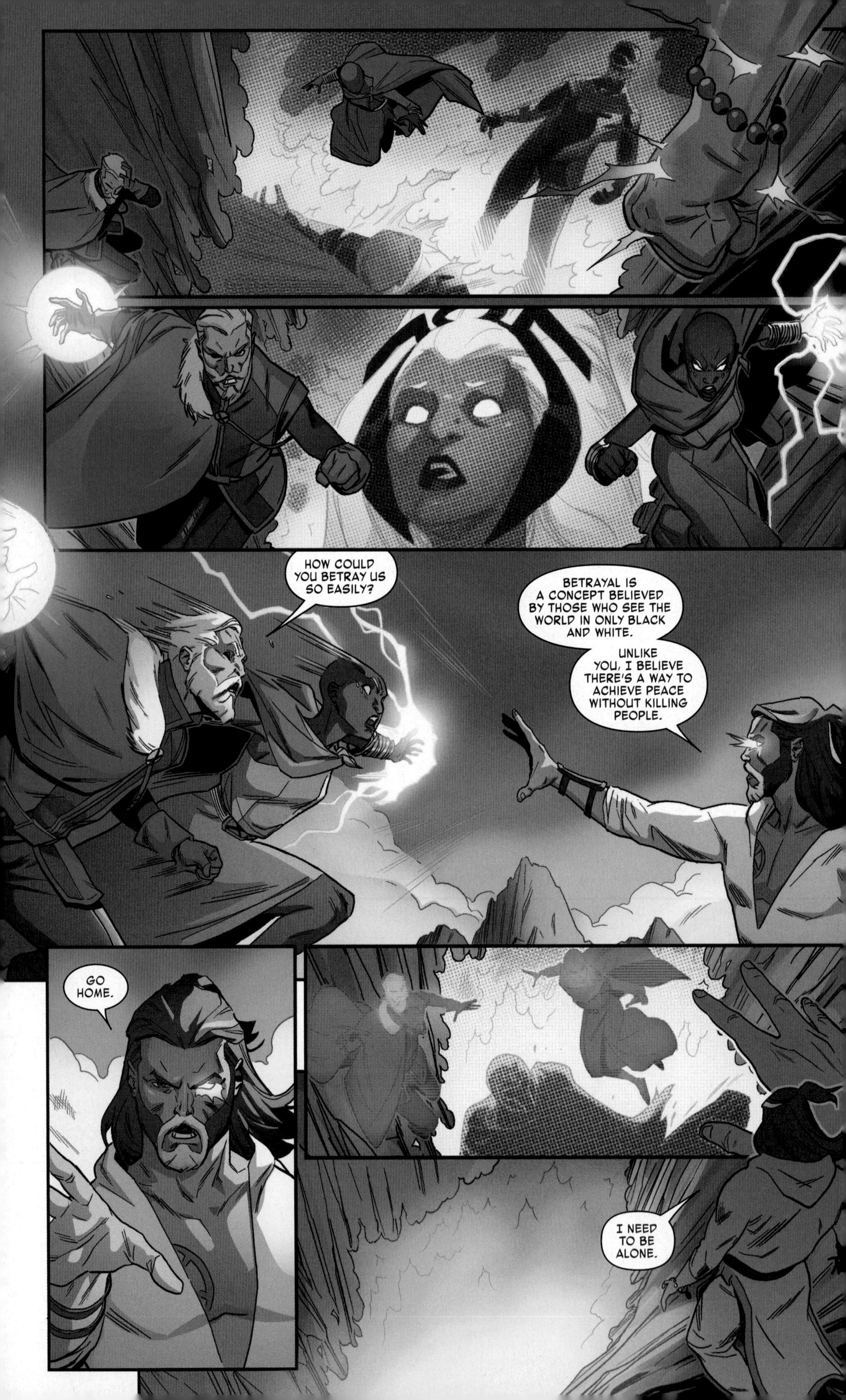
HOW COULD YOU BETRAY US SO EASILY?
BETRAYAL IS A CONCEPT BELIEVED BY THOSE WHO SEE THE WORLD IN ONLY BLACK AND WHITE.
UNLIKE YOU, I BELIEVE THERE'S A WAY TO ACHIEVE PEACE WITHOUT KILLING PEOPLE.
GO HOME.
I NEED TO BE ALONE.

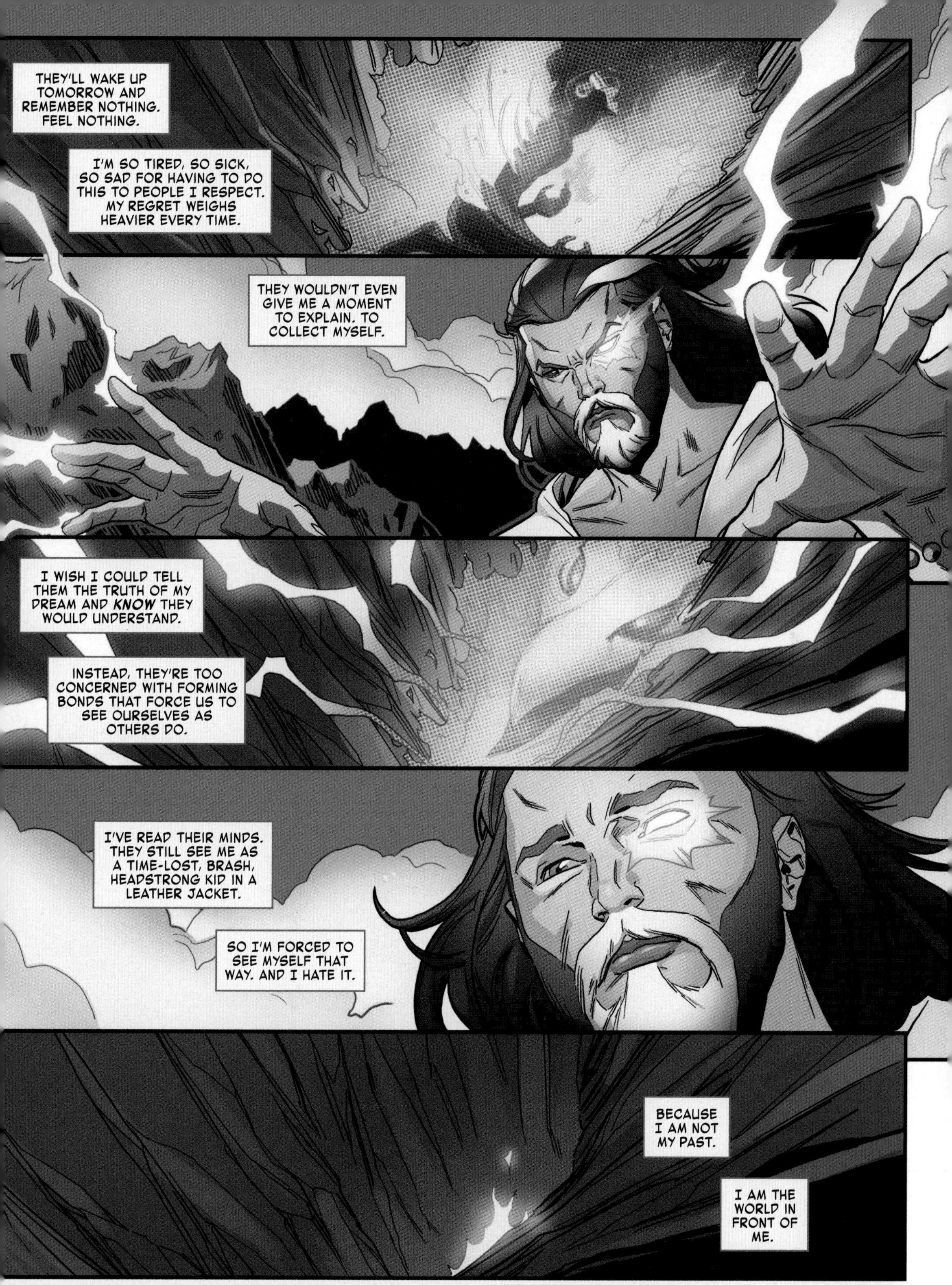
THEY'LL WAKE UP TOMORROW AND REMEMBER NOTHING. FEEL NOTHING.
I'M SO TIRED, SO SICK, SO SAD FOR HAVING TO DO THIS TO PEOPLE I RESPECT. MY REGRET WEIGHS HEAVIER EVERY TIME.
THEY WOULDN'T EVEN GIVE ME A MOMENT TO EXPLAIN. TO COLLECT MYSELF.
I WISH I COULD TELL THEM THE TRUTH OF MY DREAM AND *KNOW* THEY WOULD UNDERSTAND.
INSTEAD, THEY'RE TOO CONCERNED WITH FORMING BONDS THAT FORCE US TO SEE OURSELVES AS OTHERS DO.
I'VE READ THEIR MINDS. THEY STILL SEE ME AS A TIME-LOST, BRASH, HEADSTRONG KID IN A LEATHER JACKET.
SO I'M FORCED TO SEE MYSELF THAT WAY. AND I HATE IT.
BECAUSE I AM NOT MY PAST.
I AM THE WORLD IN FRONT OF ME.

"Hell is other people."

–Jean-Paul Sartre, *No Exit*

4

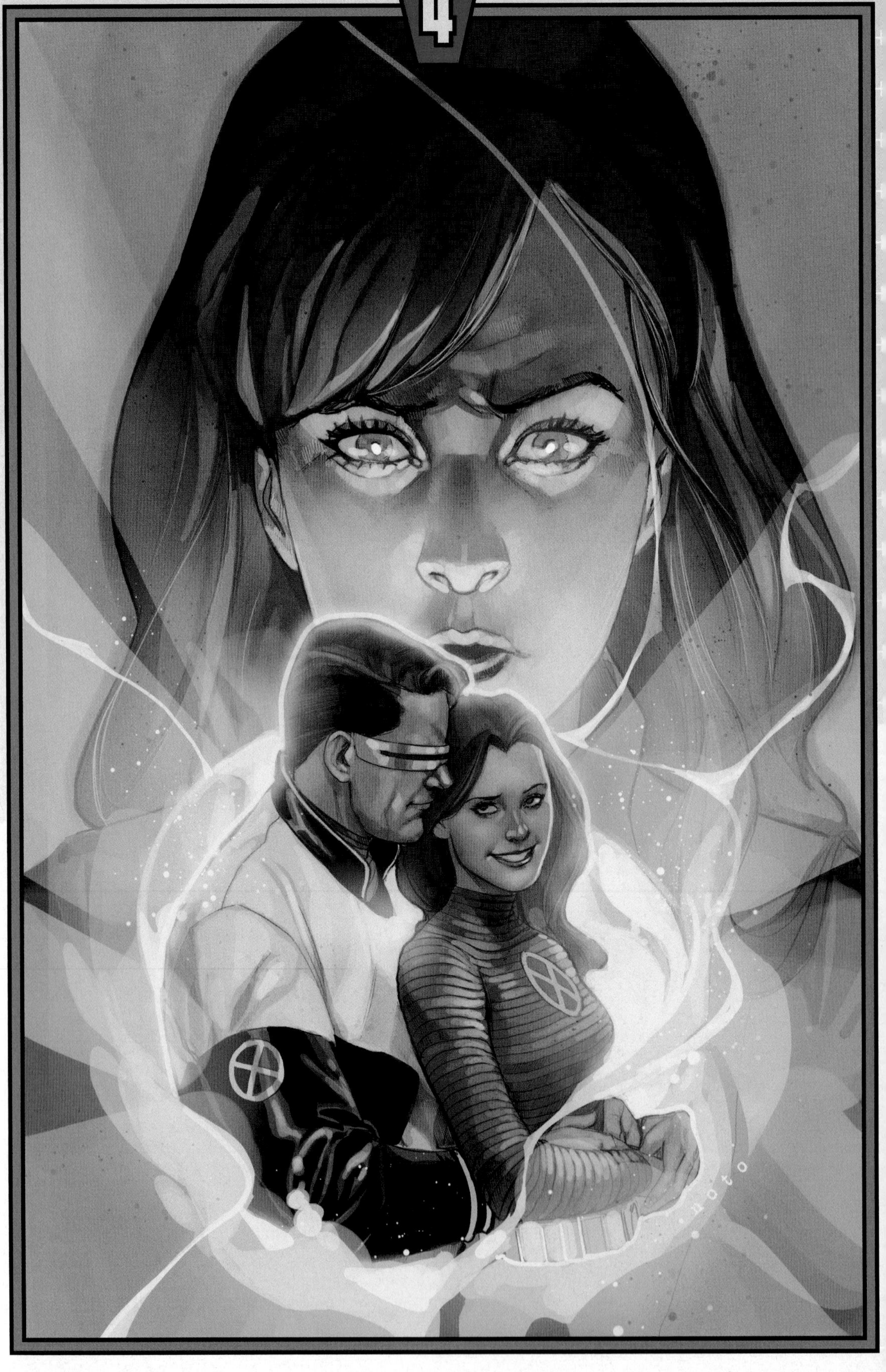

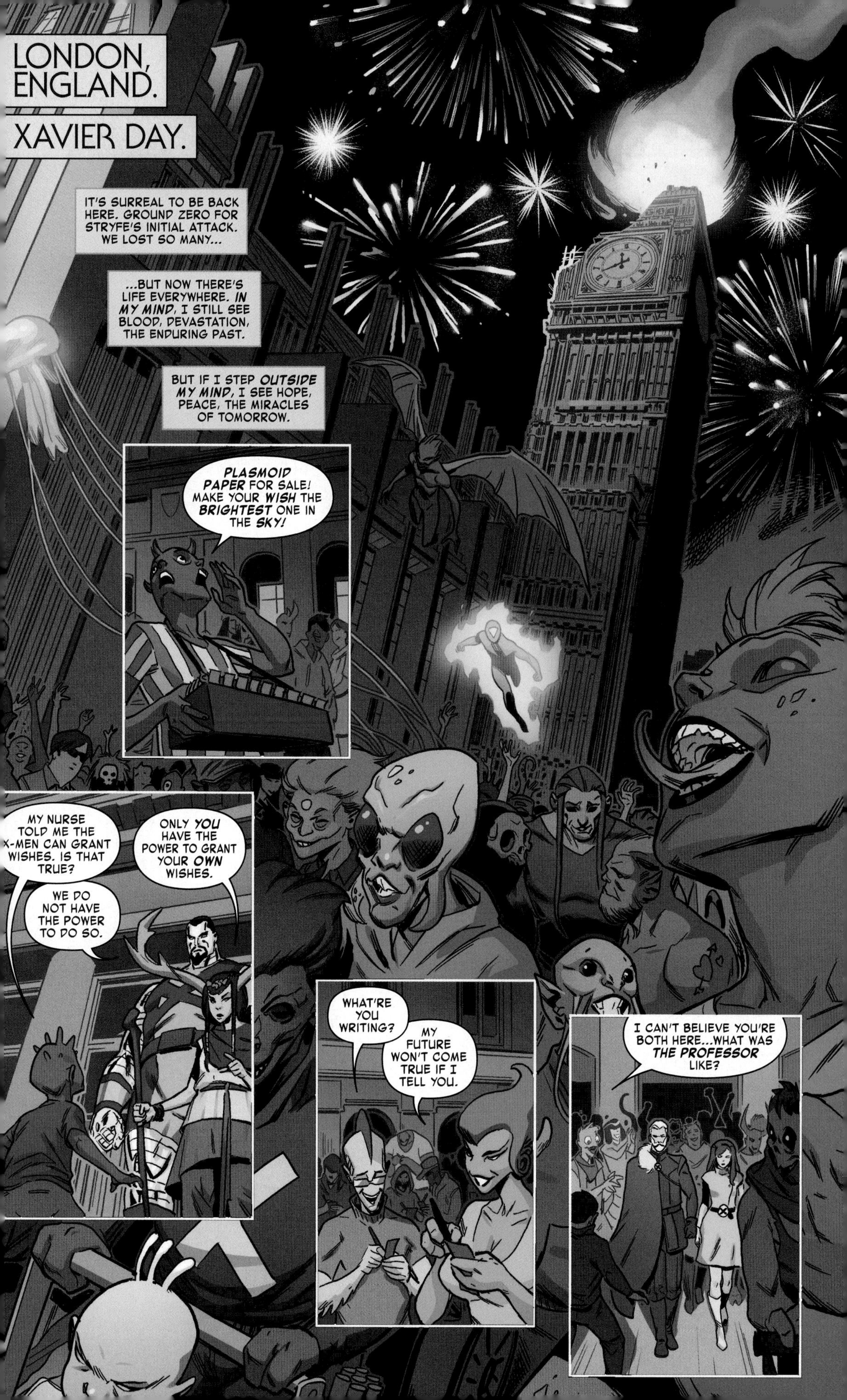
LONDON, ENGLAND.
XAVIER DAY.
IT'S SURREAL TO BE BACK HERE. GROUND ZERO FOR STRYFE'S INITIAL ATTACK. WE LOST SO MANY...
...BUT NOW THERE'S LIFE EVERYWHERE. IN MY MIND, I STILL SEE BLOOD, DEVASTATION, THE ENDURING PAST.
BUT IF I STEP OUTSIDE MY MIND, I SEE HOPE, PEACE, THE MIRACLES OF TOMORROW.
PLASMOID PAPER FOR SALE! MAKE YOUR WISH THE BRIGHTEST ONE IN THE SKY!
MY NURSE TOLD ME THE X-MEN CAN GRANT WISHES. IS THAT TRUE?
WE DO NOT HAVE THE POWER TO DO SO.
ONLY YOU HAVE THE POWER TO GRANT YOUR OWN WISHES.
WHAT'RE YOU WRITING?
MY FUTURE WON'T COME TRUE IF I TELL YOU.
I CAN'T BELIEVE YOU'RE BOTH HERE...WHAT WAS THE PROFESSOR LIKE?

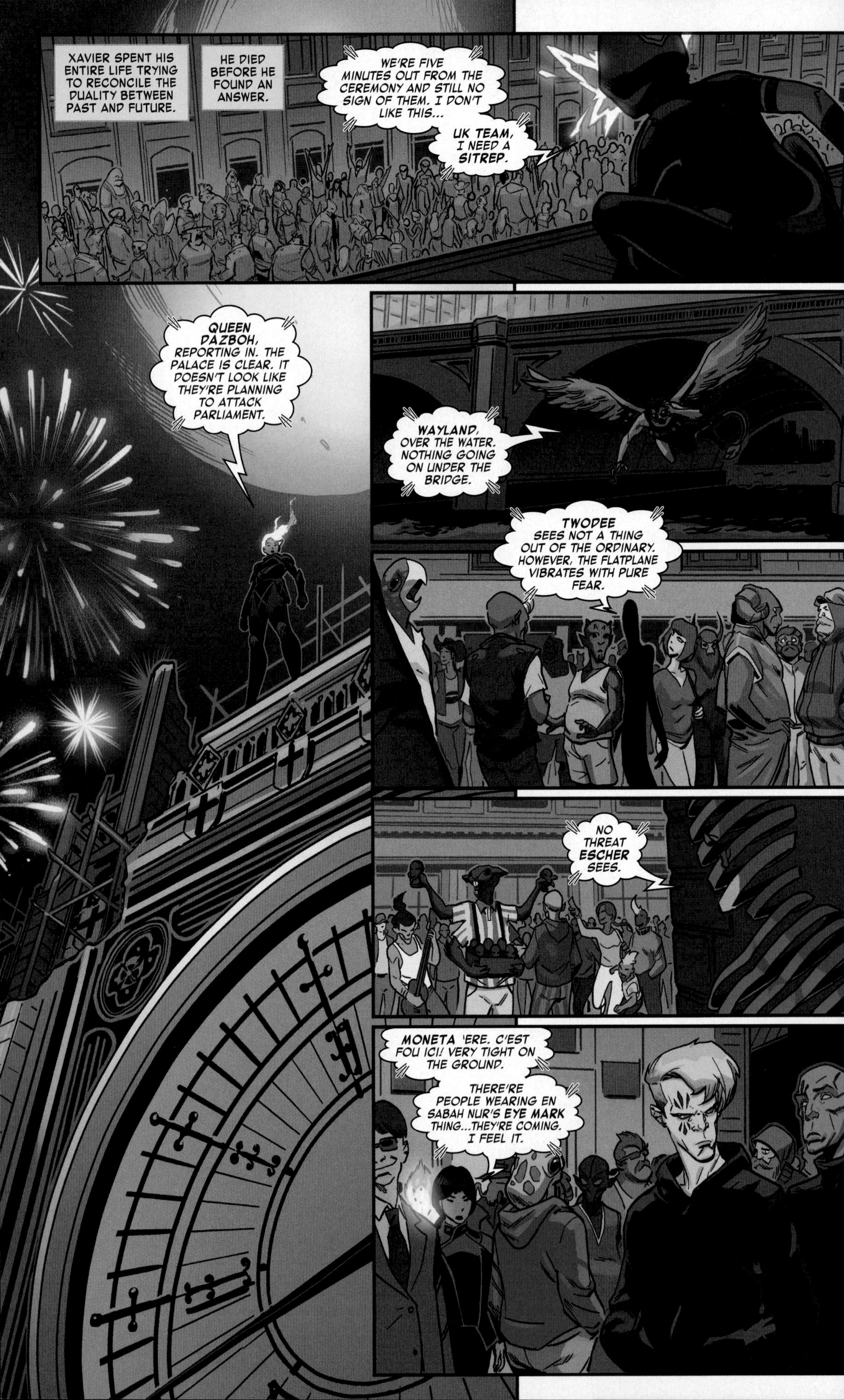
XAVIER SPENT HIS ENTIRE LIFE TRYING TO RECONCILE THE DUALITY BETWEEN PAST AND FUTURE.
HE DIED BEFORE HE FOUND AN ANSWER.
WE'RE FIVE MINUTES OUT FROM THE CEREMONY AND STILL NO SIGN OF THEM. I DON'T LIKE THIS...
UK TEAM, I NEED A SITREP.
QUEEN DAZBOH, REPORTING IN. THE PALACE IS CLEAR. IT DOESN'T LOOK LIKE THEY'RE PLANNING TO ATTACK PARLIAMENT.
WAYLAND, OVER THE WATER. NOTHING GOING ON UNDER THE BRIDGE.
TWODEE SEES NOT A THING OUT OF THE ORDINARY. HOWEVER, THE FLATPLANE VIBRATES WITH PURE FEAR.
NO THREAT ESCHER SEES.
MONETA 'ERE. C'EST FOU ICI! VERY TIGHT ON THE GROUND.
THERE'RE PEOPLE WEARING EN SABAH NUR'S EYE MARK THING...THEY'RE COMING. I FEEL IT.

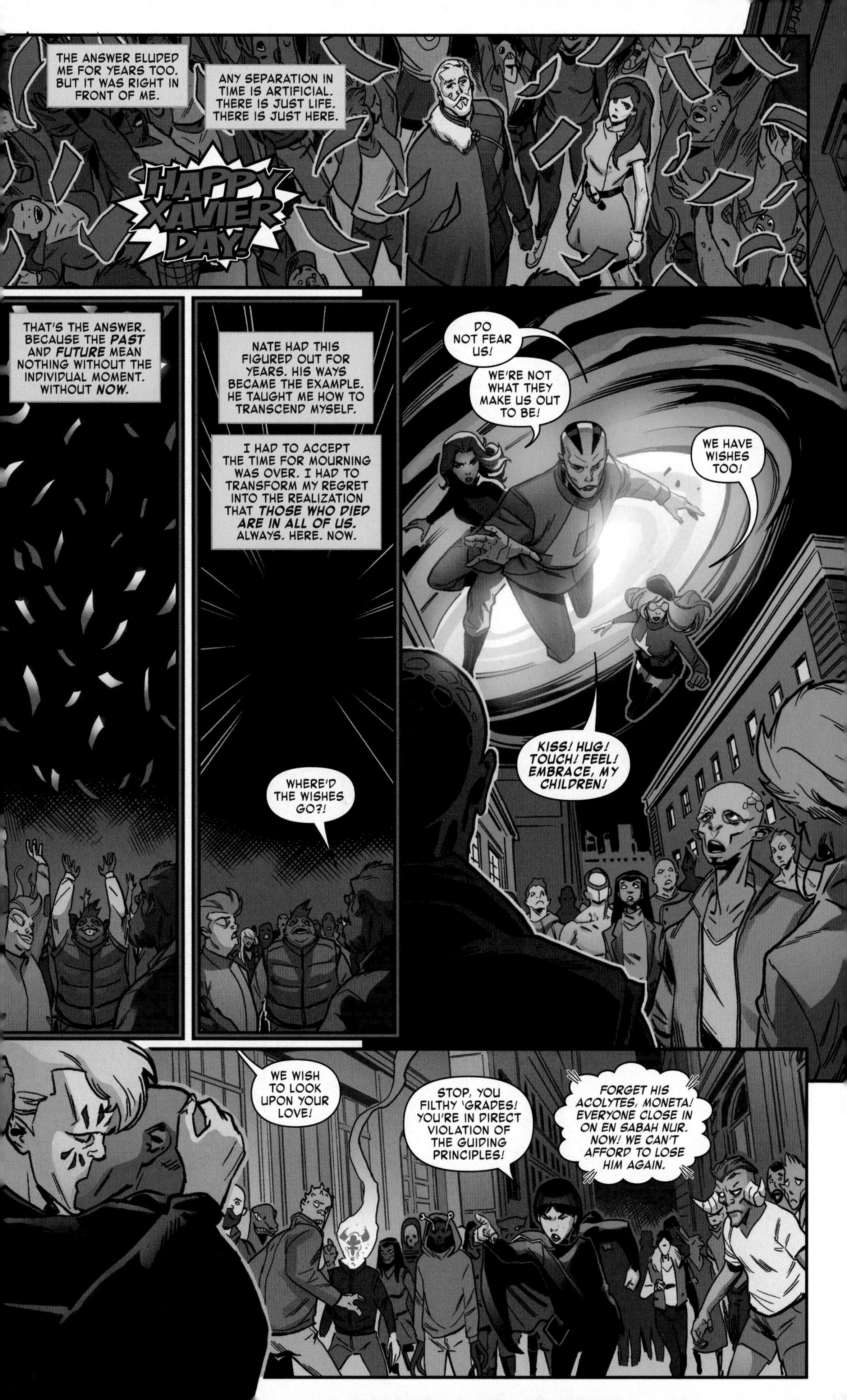
THE ANSWER ELUDED ME FOR YEARS TOO. BUT IT WAS RIGHT IN FRONT OF ME.
ANY SEPARATION IN TIME IS ARTIFICIAL. THERE IS JUST LIFE. THERE IS JUST HERE.
HAPPY XAVIER DAY!
THAT'S THE ANSWER. BECAUSE THE *PAST* AND *FUTURE* MEAN NOTHING WITHOUT THE INDIVIDUAL MOMENT. WITHOUT *NOW*.
NATE HAD THIS FIGURED OUT FOR YEARS. HIS WAYS BECAME THE EXAMPLE. HE TAUGHT ME HOW TO TRANSCEND MYSELF.
I HAD TO ACCEPT THE TIME FOR MOURNING WAS OVER. I HAD TO TRANSFORM MY REGRET INTO THE REALIZATION THAT *THOSE WHO DIED ARE IN ALL OF US.* ALWAYS. HERE. NOW.
WHERE'D THE WISHES GO?!
DO NOT FEAR US!
WE'RE NOT WHAT THEY MAKE US OUT TO BE!
WE HAVE WISHES TOO!
KISS! HUG! TOUCH! FEEL! EMBRACE, MY CHILDREN!
WE WISH TO LOOK UPON YOUR LOVE!
STOP, YOU FILTHY 'GRADES! YOU'RE IN DIRECT VIOLATION OF THE GUIDING PRINCIPLES!
FORGET HIS ACOLYTES, MONETA! EVERYONE CLOSE IN ON EN SABAH NUR. NOW! WE CAN'T AFFORD TO LOSE HIM AGAIN.

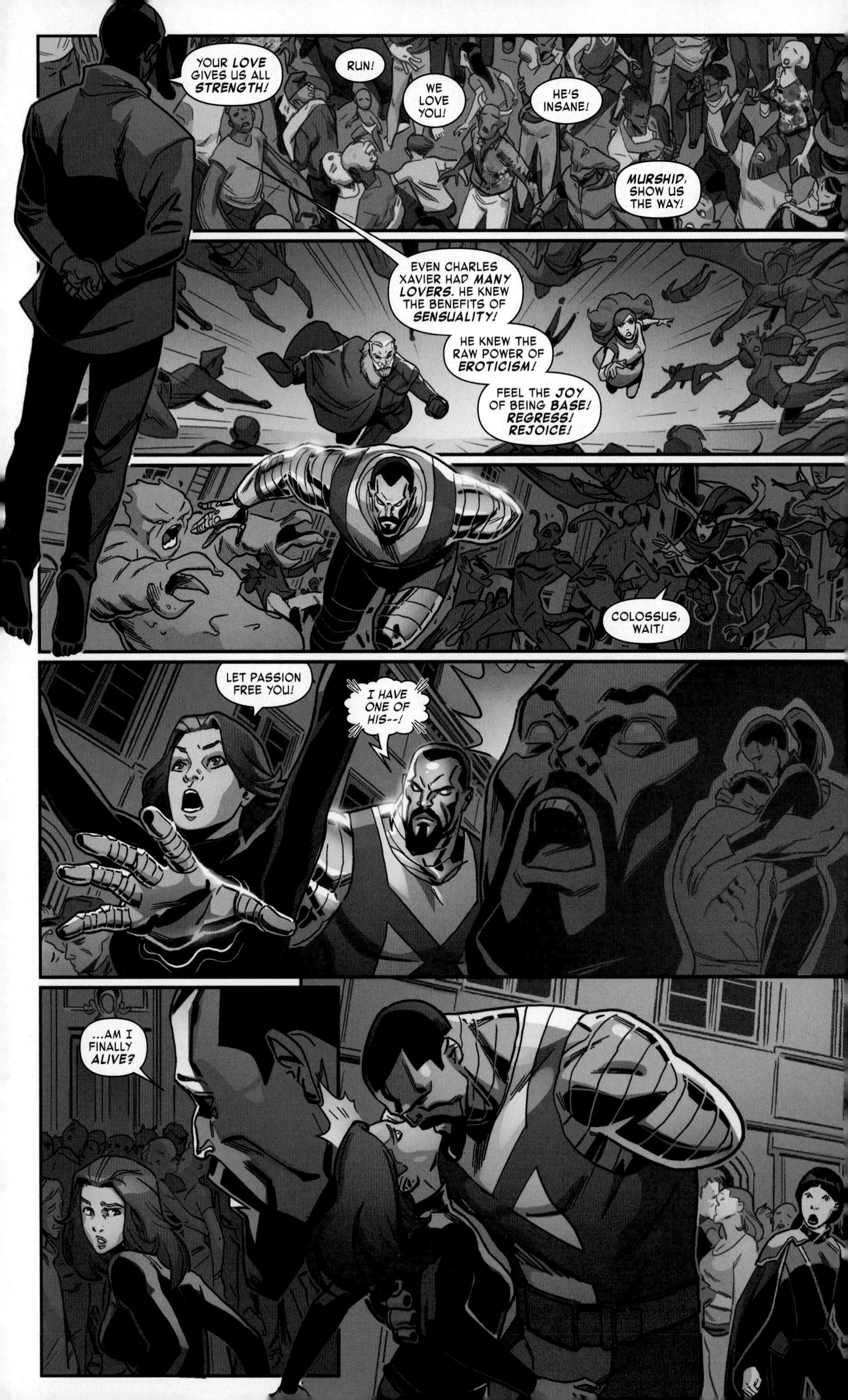
YOUR LOVE GIVES US ALL STRENGTH!
RUN!
WE LOVE YOU!
HE'S INSANE!
MURSHID, SHOW US THE WAY!
EVEN CHARLES XAVIER HAD MANY LOVERS. HE KNEW THE BENEFITS OF SENSUALITY!
HE KNEW THE RAW POWER OF EROTICISM!
FEEL THE JOY OF BEING BASE! REGRESS! REJOICE!
COLOSSUS, WAIT!
LET PASSION FREE YOU!
I HAVE ONE OF HIS--!
...AM I FINALLY ALIVE?

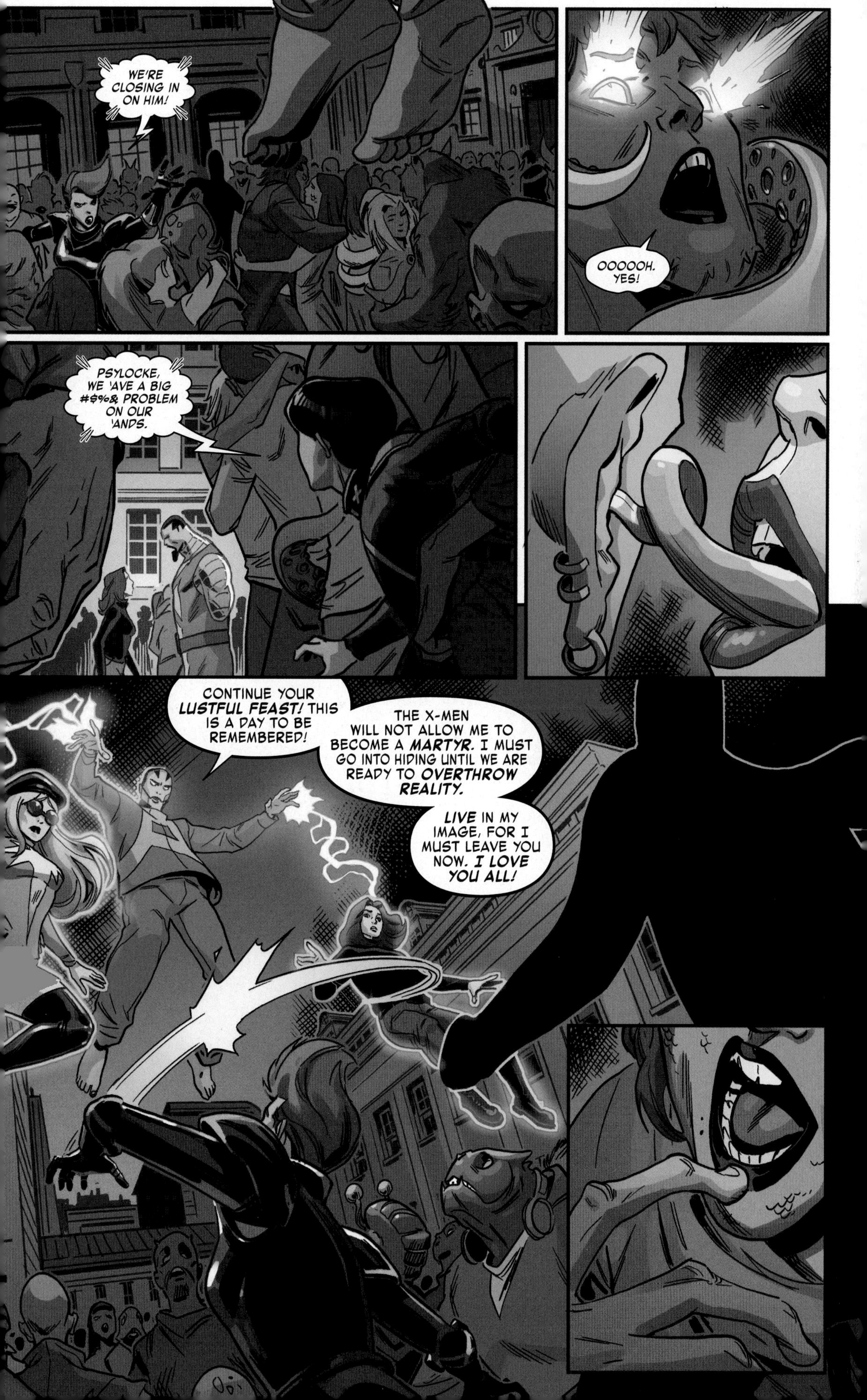
WE'RE CLOSING IN ON HIM!
OOOOOH. YES!
PSYLOCKE, WE 'AVE A BIG #$%& PROBLEM ON OUR 'ANDS.
CONTINUE YOUR LUSTFUL FEAST! THIS IS A DAY TO BE REMEMBERED!
THE X-MEN WILL NOT ALLOW ME TO BECOME A MARTYR. I MUST GO INTO HIDING UNTIL WE ARE READY TO OVERTHROW REALITY.
LIVE IN MY IMAGE, FOR I MUST LEAVE YOU NOW. I LOVE YOU ALL!

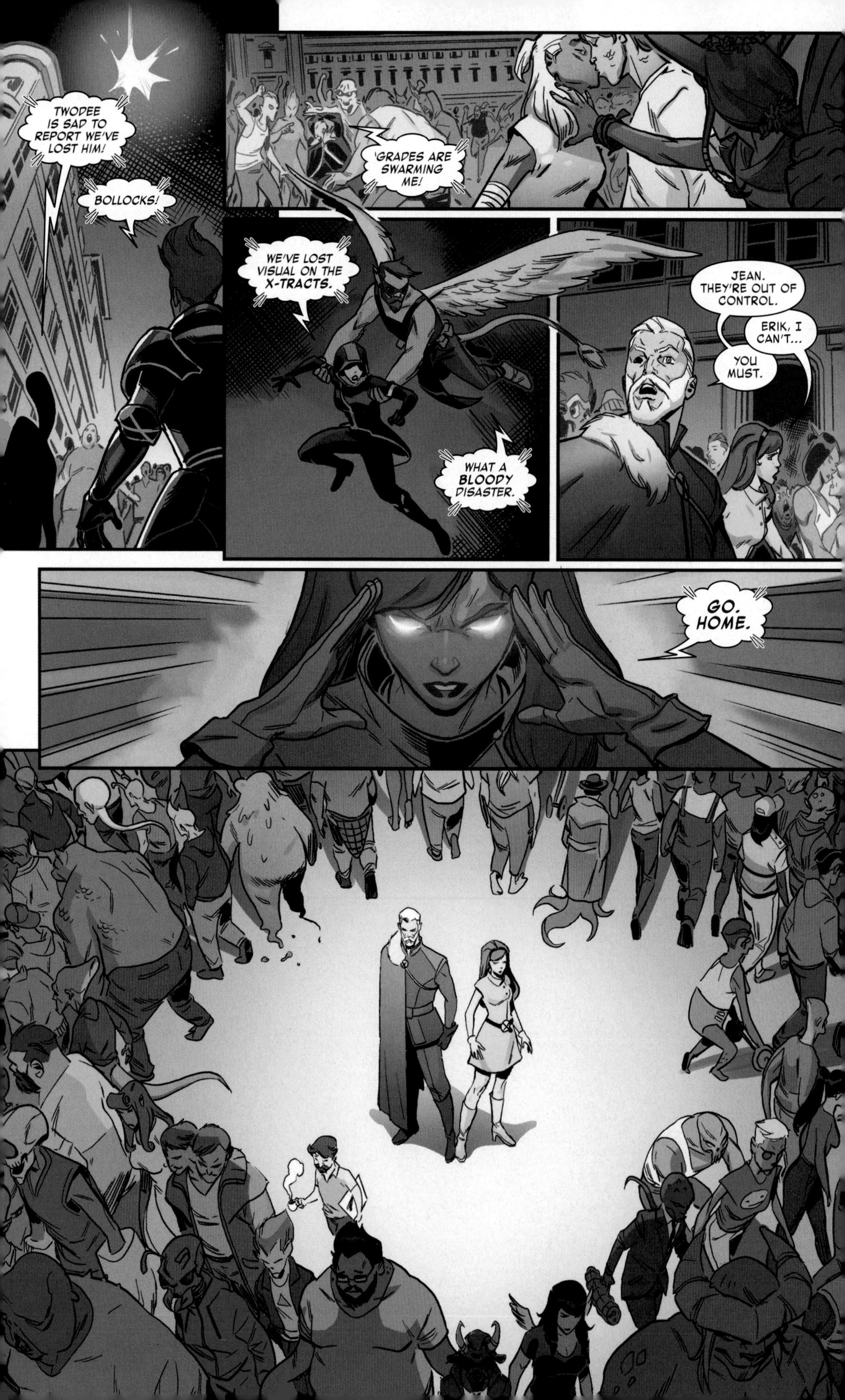
TWODEE IS SAD TO REPORT WE'VE LOST HIM!
BOLLOCKS!
'GRADES ARE SWARMING ME!
WE'VE LOST VISUAL ON THE X-TRACTS.
WHAT A BLOODY DISASTER.
JEAN. THEY'RE OUT OF CONTROL.
ERIK, I CAN'T...
YOU MUST.
GO. HOME.

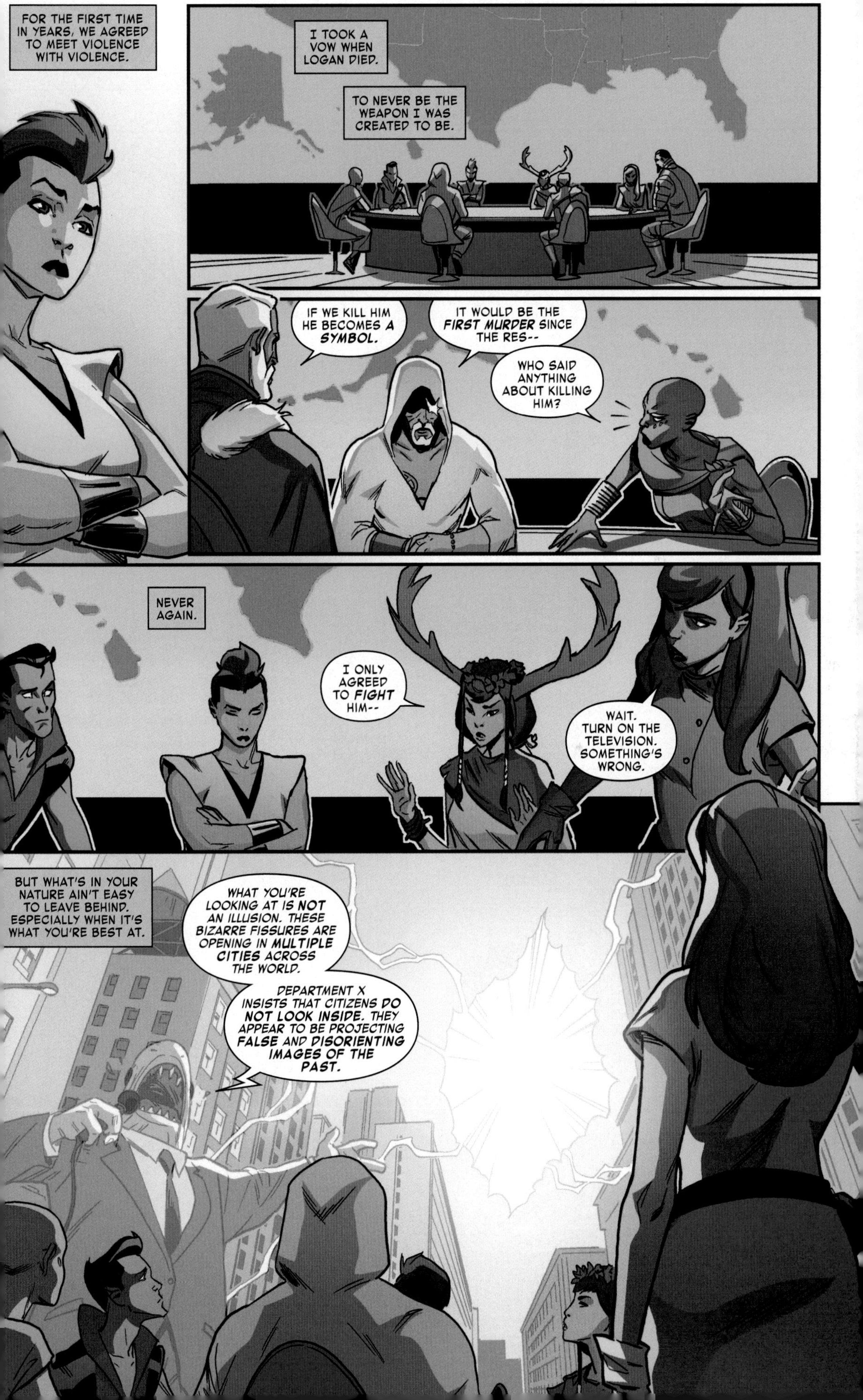
FOR THE FIRST TIME IN YEARS, WE AGREED TO MEET VIOLENCE WITH VIOLENCE.
I TOOK A VOW WHEN LOGAN DIED.
TO NEVER BE THE WEAPON I WAS CREATED TO BE.
IF WE KILL HIM HE BECOMES A SYMBOL.
IT WOULD BE THE FIRST MURDER SINCE THE RES--
WHO SAID ANYTHING ABOUT KILLING HIM?
NEVER AGAIN.
I ONLY AGREED TO FIGHT HIM--
WAIT. TURN ON THE TELEVISION. SOMETHING'S WRONG.
BUT WHAT'S IN YOUR NATURE AIN'T EASY TO LEAVE BEHIND. ESPECIALLY WHEN IT'S WHAT YOU'RE BEST AT.
WHAT YOU'RE LOOKING AT IS NOT AN ILLUSION. THESE BIZARRE FISSURES ARE OPENING IN MULTIPLE CITIES ACROSS THE WORLD.
DEPARTMENT X INSISTS THAT CITIZENS DO NOT LOOK INSIDE. THEY APPEAR TO BE PROJECTING FALSE AND DISORIENTING IMAGES OF THE PAST.

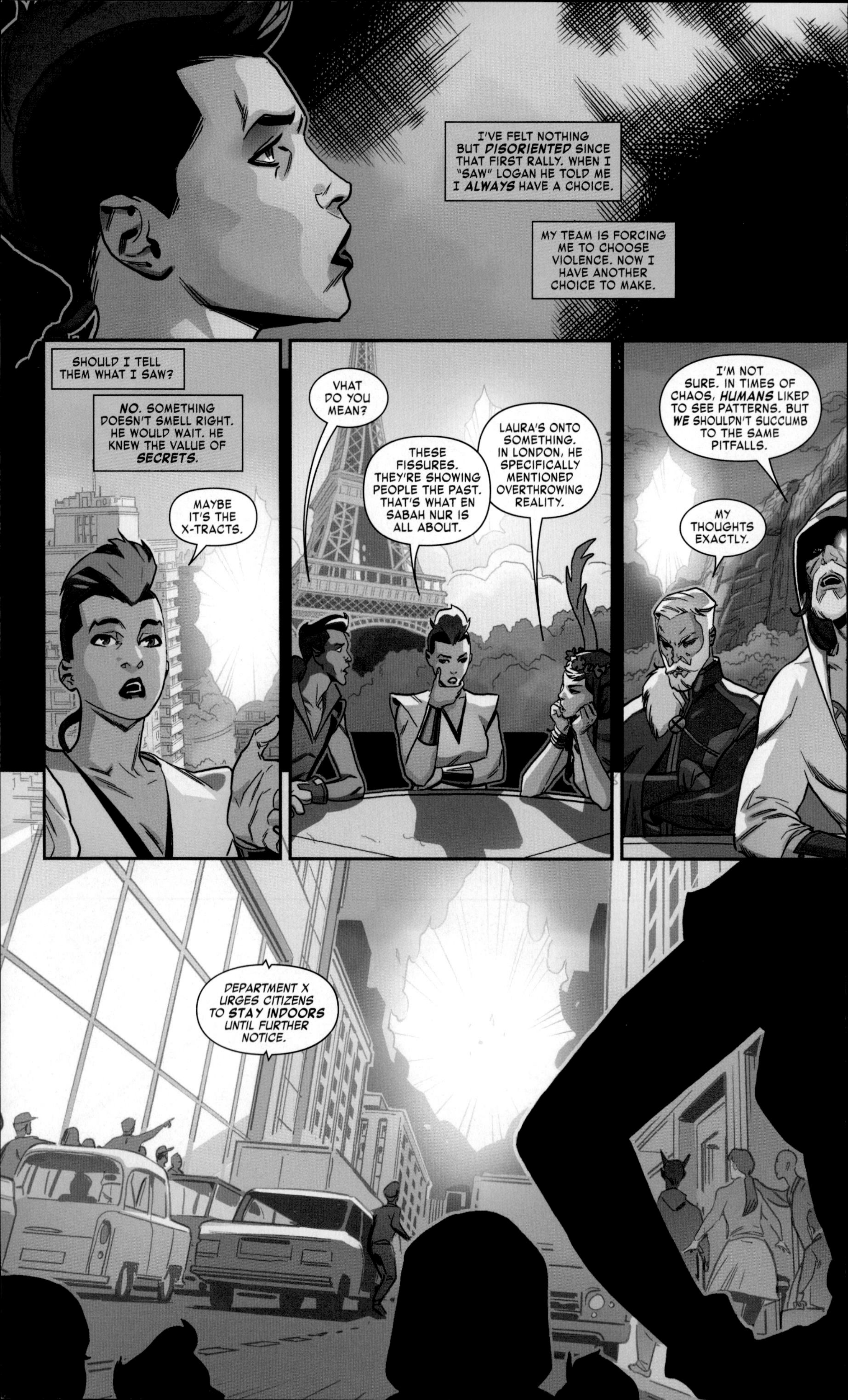
I'VE FELT NOTHING BUT DISORIENTED SINCE THAT FIRST RALLY. WHEN I "SAW" LOGAN HE TOLD ME I ALWAYS HAVE A CHOICE.
MY TEAM IS FORCING ME TO CHOOSE VIOLENCE. NOW I HAVE ANOTHER CHOICE TO MAKE.
SHOULD I TELL THEM WHAT I SAW?
NO. SOMETHING DOESN'T SMELL RIGHT. HE WOULD WAIT. HE KNEW THE VALUE OF SECRETS.
MAYBE IT'S THE X-TRACTS.
WHAT DO YOU MEAN?
THESE FISSURES. THEY'RE SHOWING PEOPLE THE PAST. THAT'S WHAT EN SABAH NUR IS ALL ABOUT.
LAURA'S ONTO SOMETHING. IN LONDON, HE SPECIFICALLY MENTIONED OVERTHROWING REALITY.
I'M NOT SURE. IN TIMES OF CHAOS, HUMANS LIKED TO SEE PATTERNS. BUT WE SHOULDN'T SUCCUMB TO THE SAME PITFALLS.
MY THOUGHTS EXACTLY.
DEPARTMENT X URGES CITIZENS TO STAY INDOORS UNTIL FURTHER NOTICE.

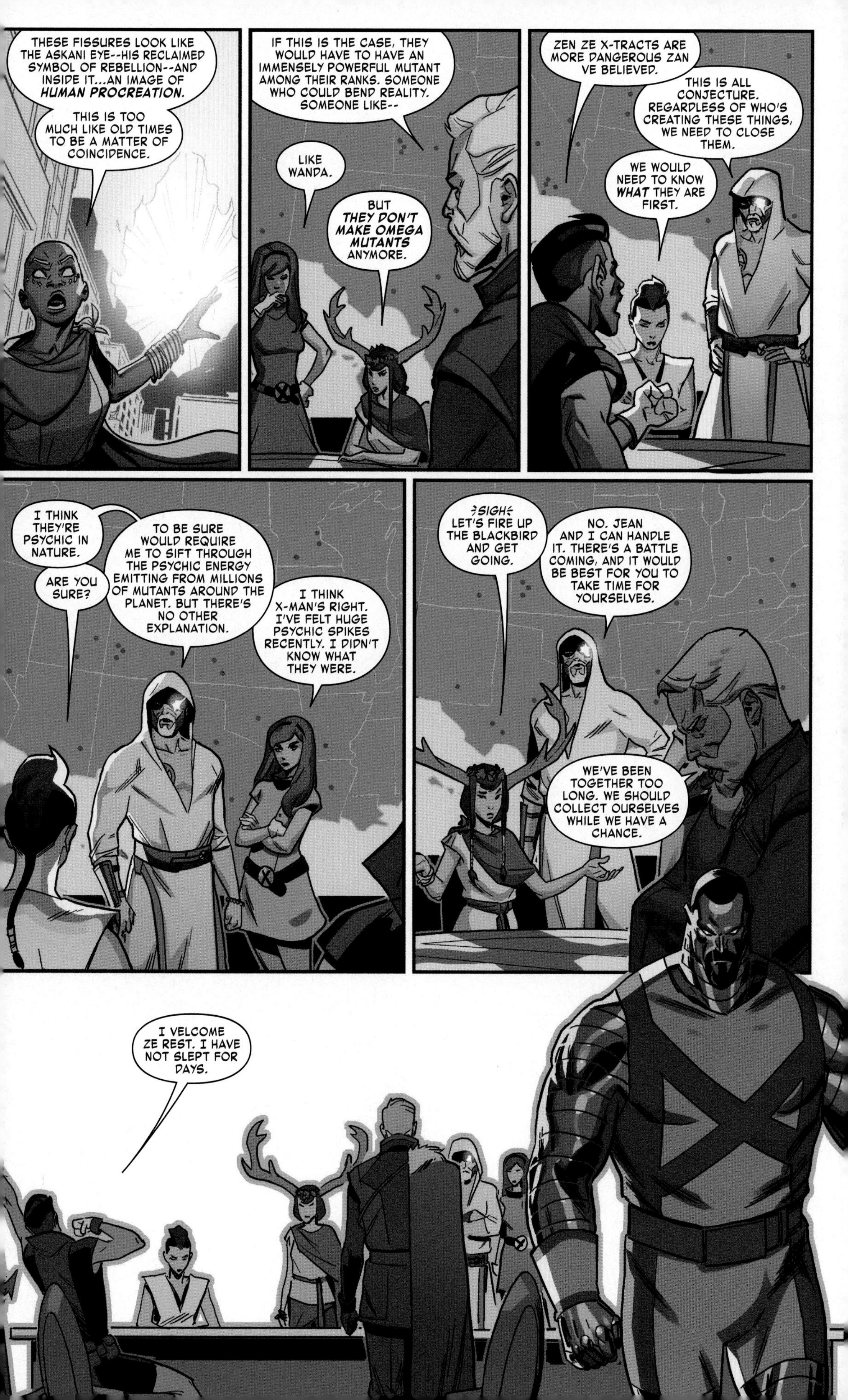
THESE FISSURES LOOK LIKE THE ASKANI EYE--HIS RECLAIMED SYMBOL OF REBELLION--AND INSIDE IT...AN IMAGE OF HUMAN PROCREATION.
THIS IS TOO MUCH LIKE OLD TIMES TO BE A MATTER OF COINCIDENCE.
IF THIS IS THE CASE, THEY WOULD HAVE TO HAVE AN IMMENSELY POWERFUL MUTANT AMONG THEIR RANKS. SOMEONE WHO COULD BEND REALITY. SOMEONE LIKE--
LIKE WANDA.
BUT THEY DON'T MAKE OMEGA MUTANTS ANYMORE.
ZEN ZE X-TRACTS ARE MORE DANGEROUS ZAN VE BELIEVED.
THIS IS ALL CONJECTURE. REGARDLESS OF WHO'S CREATING THESE THINGS, WE NEED TO CLOSE THEM.
WE WOULD NEED TO KNOW WHAT THEY ARE FIRST.
I THINK THEY'RE PSYCHIC IN NATURE.
ARE YOU SURE?
TO BE SURE WOULD REQUIRE ME TO SIFT THROUGH THE PSYCHIC ENERGY EMITTING FROM MILLIONS OF MUTANTS AROUND THE PLANET. BUT THERE'S NO OTHER EXPLANATION.
I THINK X-MAN'S RIGHT. I'VE FELT HUGE PSYCHIC SPIKES RECENTLY. I DIDN'T KNOW WHAT THEY WERE.
SIGH
LET'S FIRE UP THE BLACKBIRD AND GET GOING.
NO. JEAN AND I CAN HANDLE IT. THERE'S A BATTLE COMING, AND IT WOULD BE BEST FOR YOU TO TAKE TIME FOR YOURSELVES.
WE'VE BEEN TOGETHER TOO LONG. WE SHOULD COLLECT OURSELVES WHILE WE HAVE A CHANCE.
I VELCOME ZE REST. I HAVE NOT SLEPT FOR DAYS.

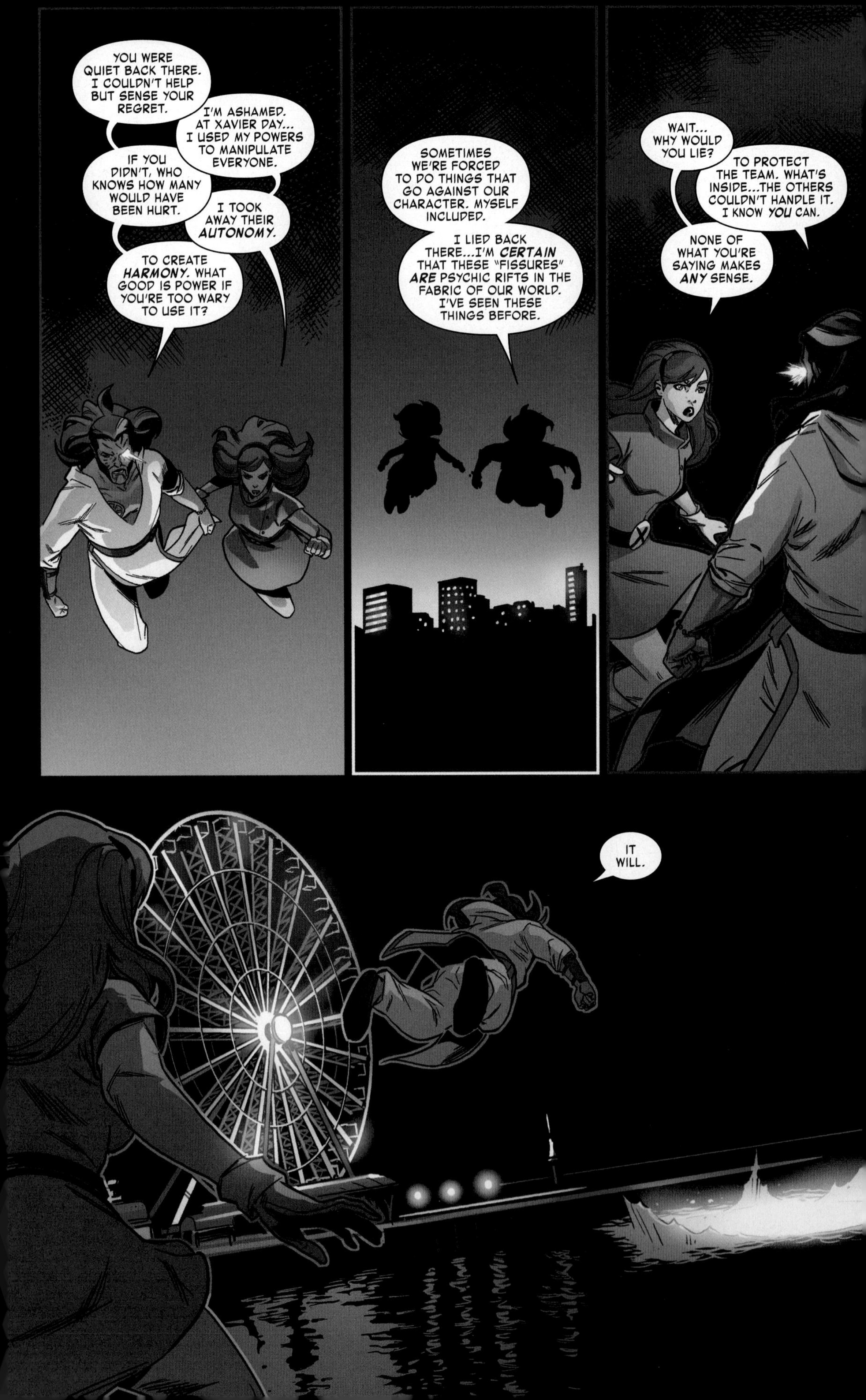
YOU WERE QUIET BACK THERE. I COULDN'T HELP BUT SENSE YOUR REGRET.
I'M ASHAMED. AT XAVIER DAY... I USED MY POWERS TO MANIPULATE EVERYONE.
IF YOU DIDN'T, WHO KNOWS HOW MANY WOULD HAVE BEEN HURT.
I TOOK AWAY THEIR AUTONOMY.
TO CREATE HARMONY. WHAT GOOD IS POWER IF YOU'RE TOO WARY TO USE IT?
SOMETIMES WE'RE FORCED TO DO THINGS THAT GO AGAINST OUR CHARACTER. MYSELF INCLUDED.
I LIED BACK THERE...I'M CERTAIN THAT THESE "FISSURES" ARE PSYCHIC RIFTS IN THE FABRIC OF OUR WORLD. I'VE SEEN THESE THINGS BEFORE.
WAIT... WHY WOULD YOU LIE?
TO PROTECT THE TEAM. WHAT'S INSIDE...THE OTHERS COULDN'T HANDLE IT. I KNOW YOU CAN.
NONE OF WHAT YOU'RE SAYING MAKES ANY SENSE.
IT WILL.

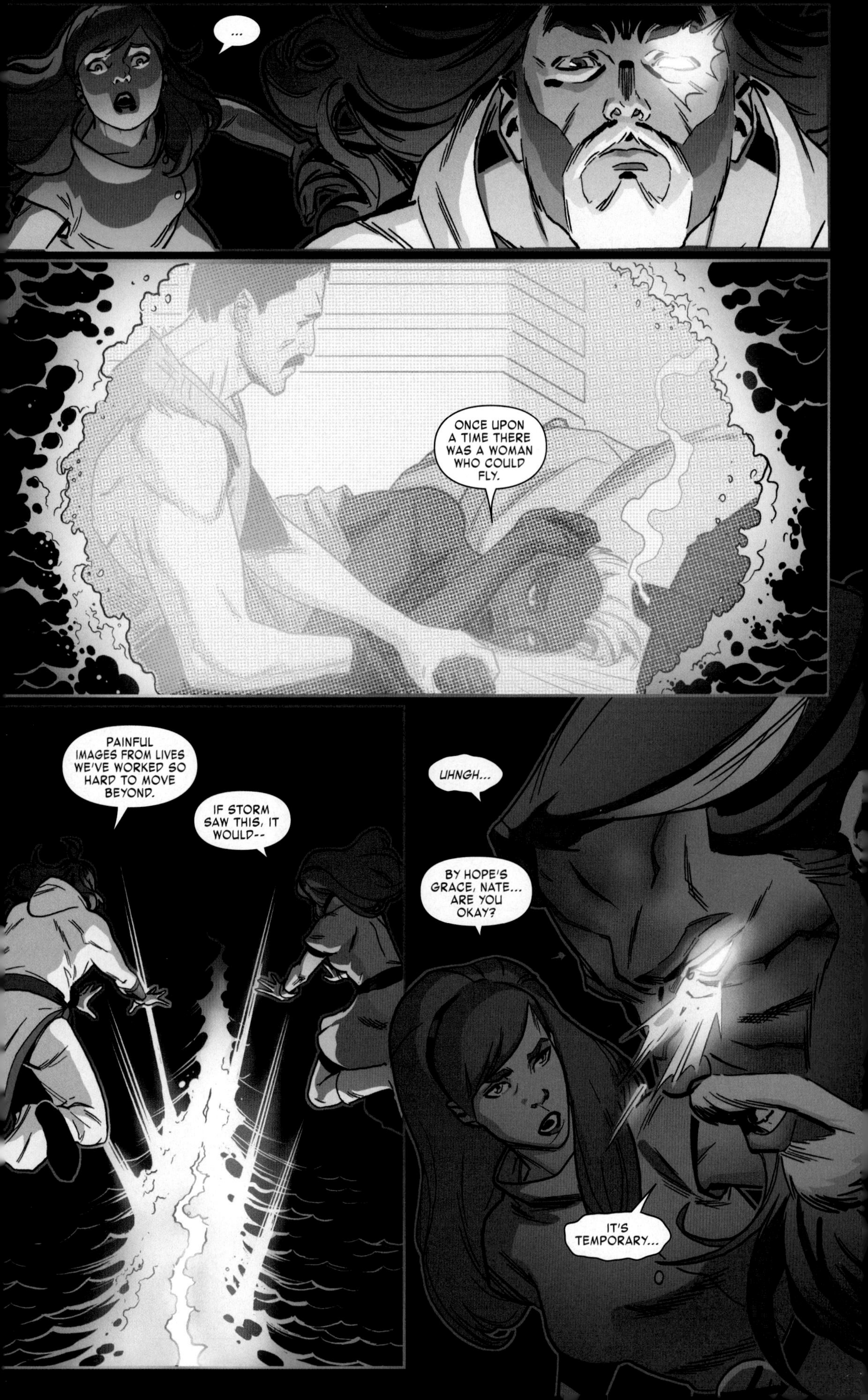
...
ONCE UPON A TIME THERE WAS A WOMAN WHO COULD FLY.
PAINFUL IMAGES FROM LIVES WE'VE WORKED SO HARD TO MOVE BEYOND.
IF STORM SAW THIS, IT WOULD--
UHNGH...
BY HOPE'S GRACE, NATE... ARE YOU OKAY?
IT'S TEMPORARY...

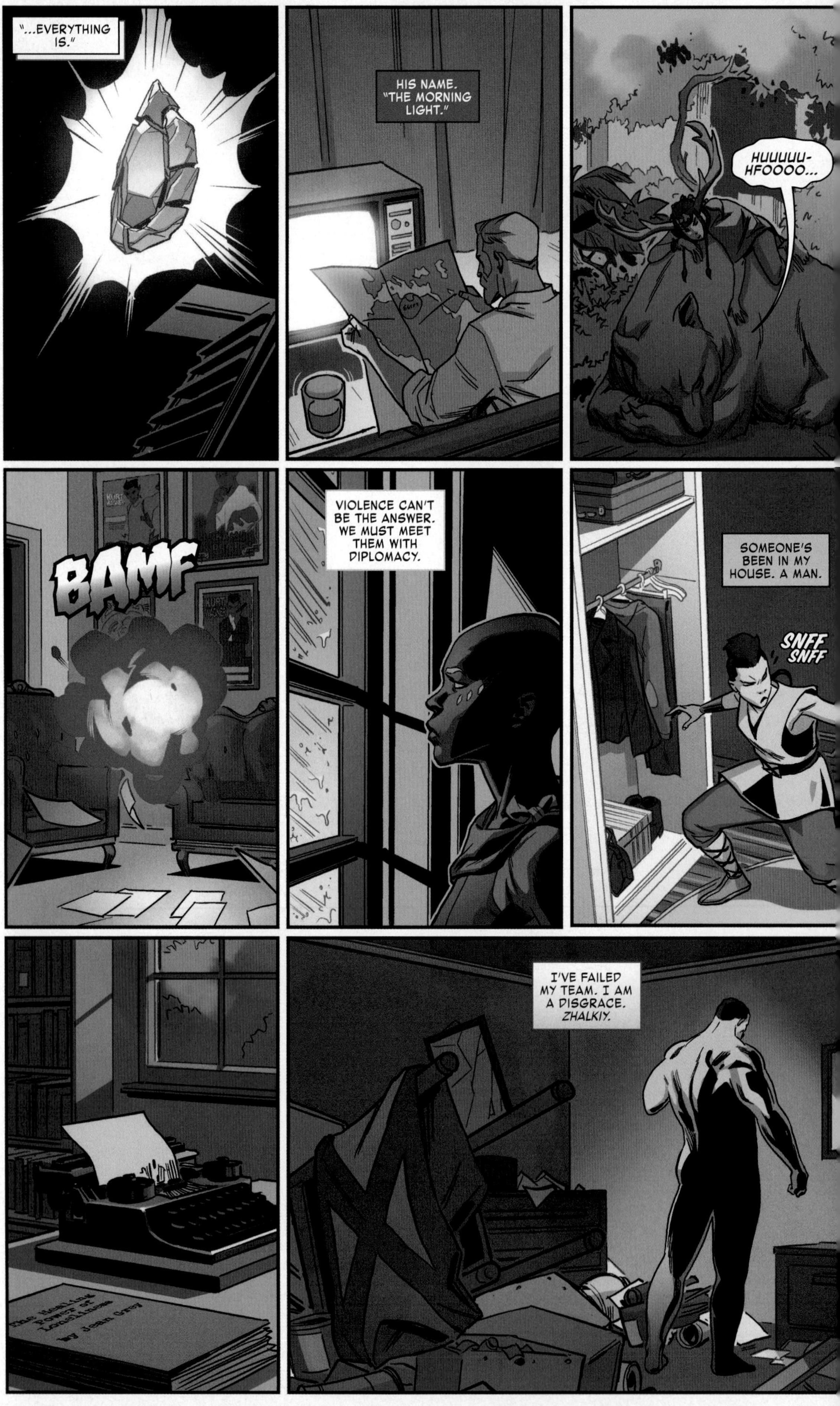
"...EVERYTHING IS."
HIS NAME. "THE MORNING LIGHT."
HUUUUU-HFOOOO...
BAMF
VIOLENCE CAN'T BE THE ANSWER. WE MUST MEET THEM WITH DIPLOMACY.
SOMEONE'S BEEN IN MY HOUSE. A MAN.
SNFF SNFF
The Healing Power of Loneliness by Jean Grey
I'VE FAILED MY TEAM. I AM A DISGRACE. ZHALKIY.

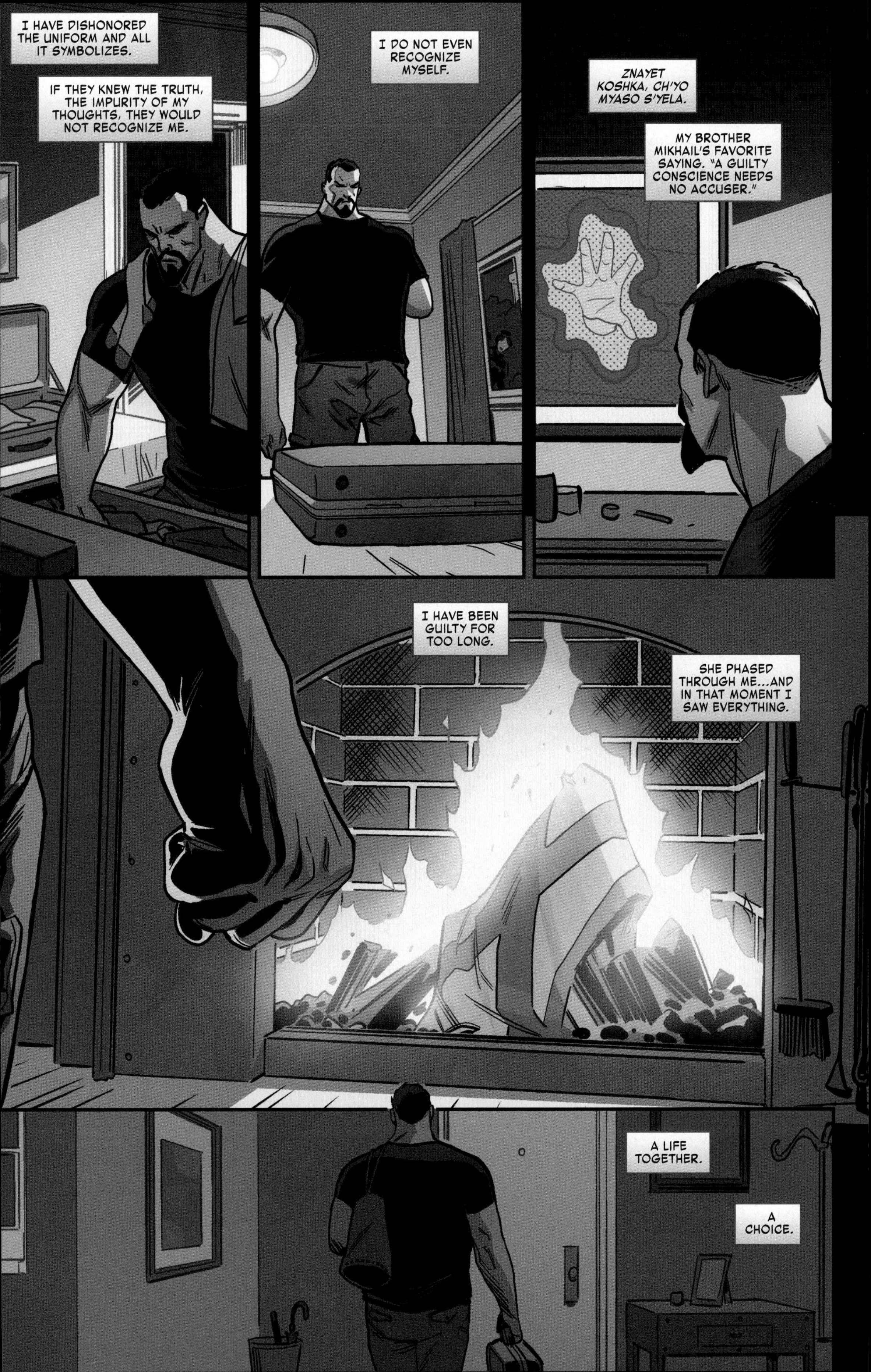
I HAVE DISHONORED THE UNIFORM AND ALL IT SYMBOLIZES.
IF THEY KNEW THE TRUTH, THE IMPURITY OF MY THOUGHTS, THEY WOULD NOT RECOGNIZE ME.
I DO NOT EVEN RECOGNIZE MYSELF.
ZNAYET KOSHKA, CH'YO MYASO S'YELA.
MY BROTHER MIKHAIL'S FAVORITE SAYING. "A GUILTY CONSCIENCE NEEDS NO ACCUSER."
I HAVE BEEN GUILTY FOR TOO LONG.
SHE PHASED THROUGH ME...AND IN THAT MOMENT I SAW EVERYTHING.
A LIFE TOGETHER.
A CHOICE.

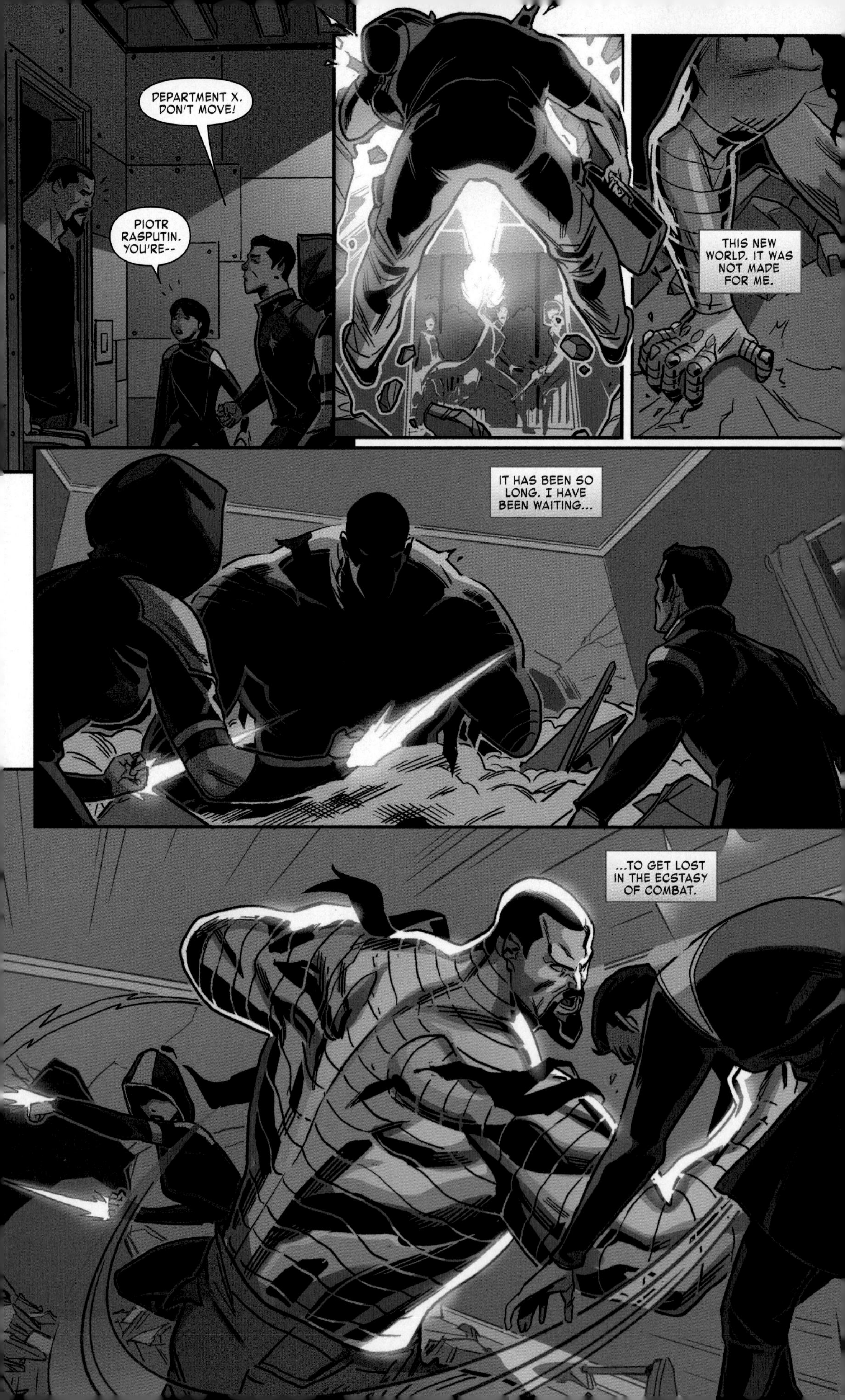
DEPARTMENT X. DON'T MOVE!
PIOTR RASPUTIN. YOU'RE--
THIS NEW WORLD. IT WAS NOT MADE FOR ME.
IT HAS BEEN SO LONG. I HAVE BEEN WAITING...
...TO GET LOST IN THE ECSTASY OF COMBAT.

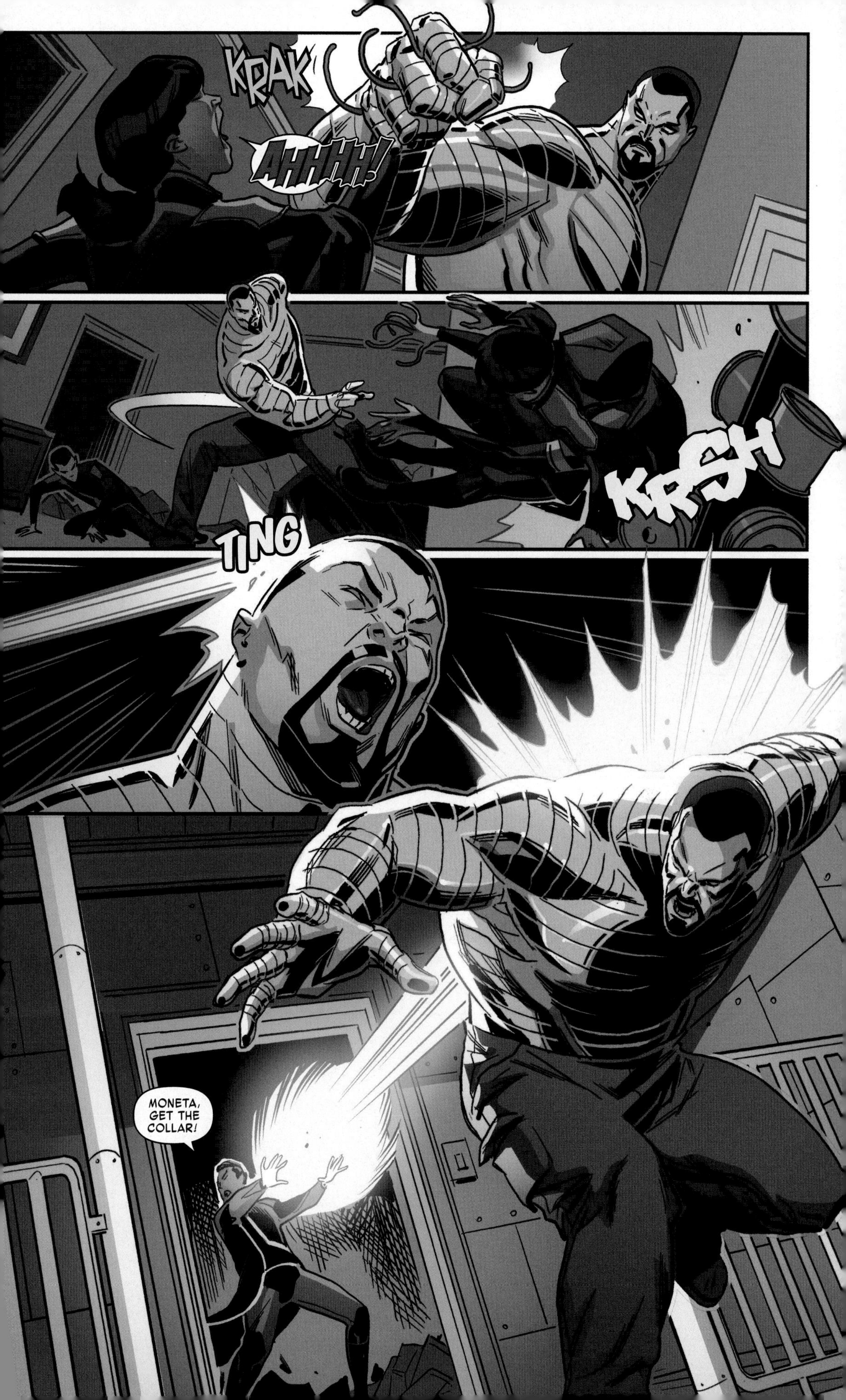
KRAK
AHHHH!
KRSH
TING
MONETA, GET THE COLLAR!

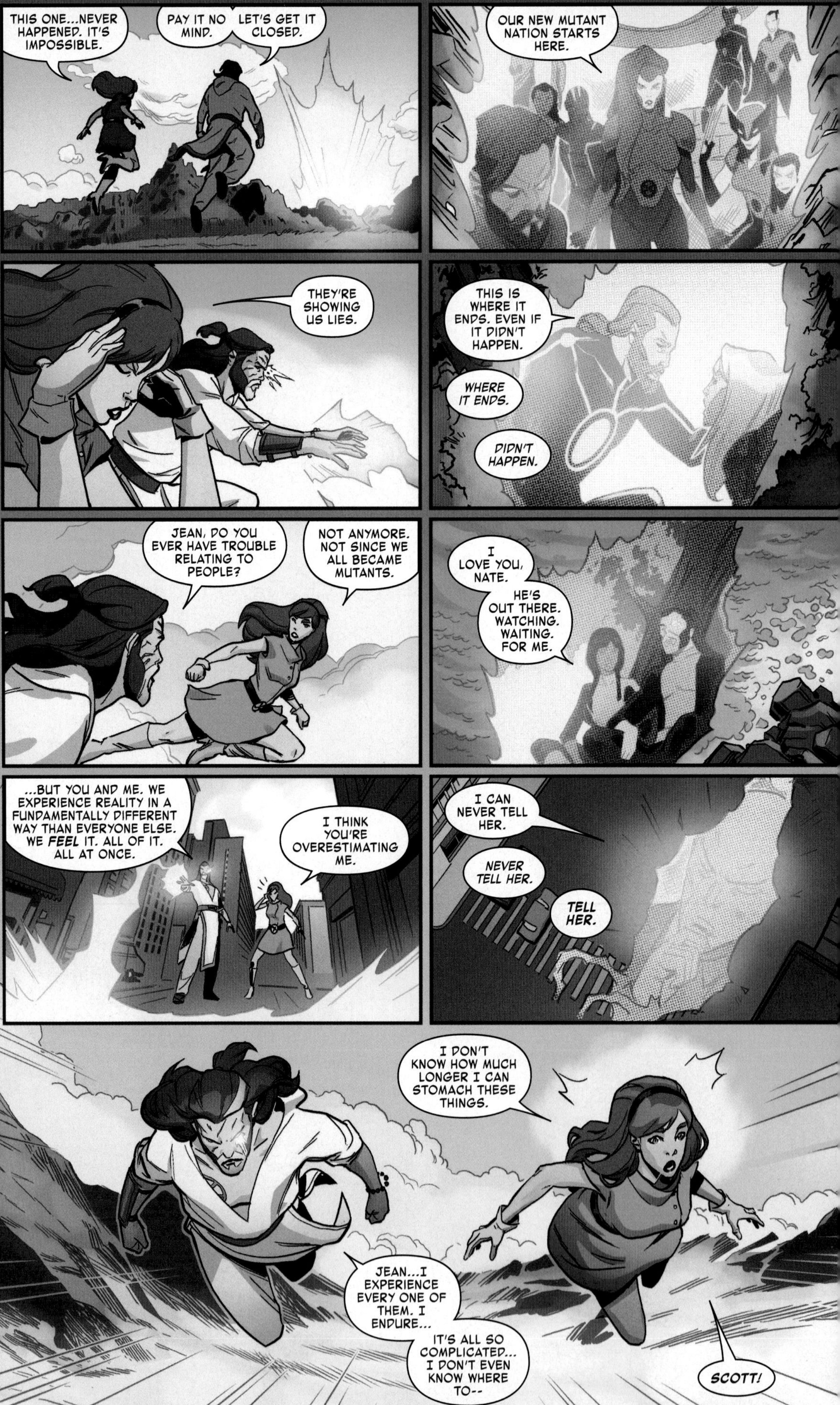

THIS ONE...NEVER HAPPENED. IT'S IMPOSSIBLE.
PAY IT NO MIND.
LET'S GET IT CLOSED.
OUR NEW MUTANT NATION STARTS HERE.
THEY'RE SHOWING US LIES.
THIS IS WHERE IT ENDS. EVEN IF IT DIDN'T HAPPEN.
WHERE IT ENDS.
DIDN'T HAPPEN.
JEAN, DO YOU EVER HAVE TROUBLE RELATING TO PEOPLE?
NOT ANYMORE. NOT SINCE WE ALL BECAME MUTANTS.
I LOVE YOU, NATE.
HE'S OUT THERE. WATCHING. WAITING. FOR ME.
...BUT YOU AND ME. WE EXPERIENCE REALITY IN A FUNDAMENTALLY DIFFERENT WAY THAN EVERYONE ELSE. WE FEEL IT. ALL OF IT. ALL AT ONCE.
I THINK YOU'RE OVERESTIMATING ME.
I CAN NEVER TELL HER.
NEVER TELL HER.
TELL HER.
I DON'T KNOW HOW MUCH LONGER I CAN STOMACH THESE THINGS.
JEAN...I EXPERIENCE EVERY ONE OF THEM. I ENDURE...
IT'S ALL SO COMPLICATED... I DON'T EVEN KNOW WHERE TO--
SCOTT!

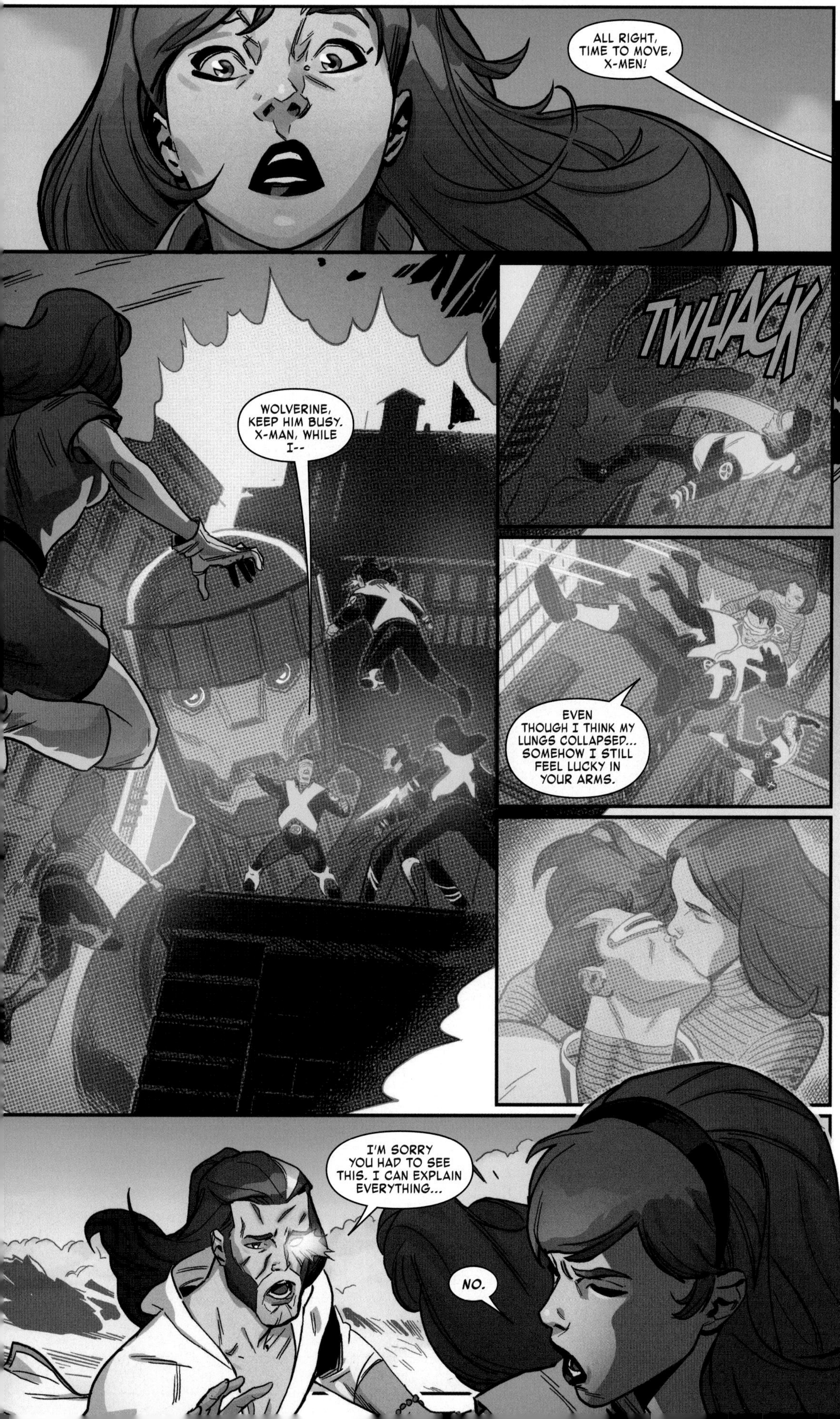
ALL RIGHT, TIME TO MOVE, X-MEN!
WOLVERINE, KEEP HIM BUSY. X-MAN, WHILE I--
TWHACK
EVEN THOUGH I THINK MY LUNGS COLLAPSED... SOMEHOW I STILL FEEL LUCKY IN YOUR ARMS.
I'M SORRY YOU HAD TO SEE THIS. I CAN EXPLAIN EVERYTHING...
NO.

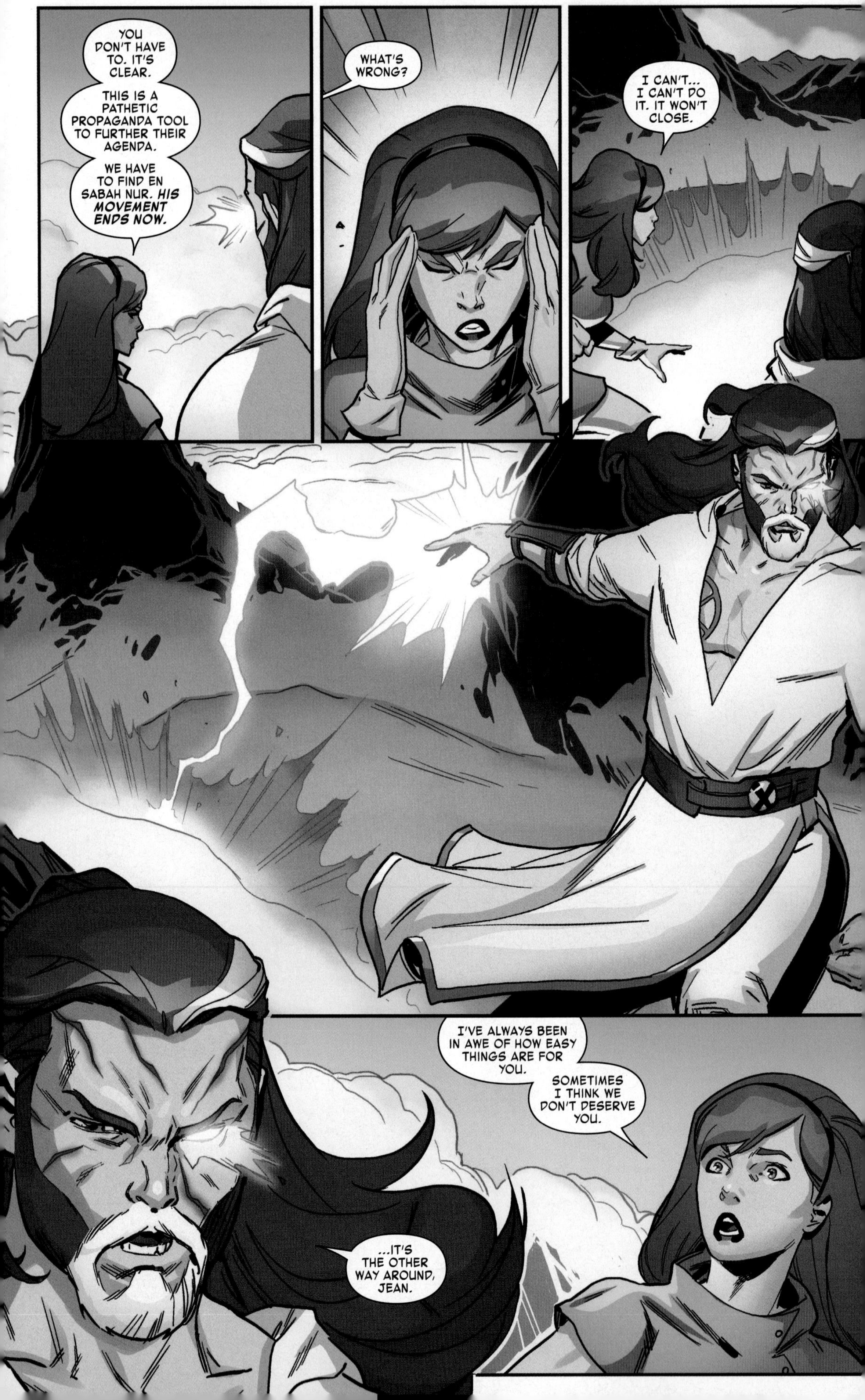
YOU DON'T HAVE TO. IT'S CLEAR.
THIS IS A PATHETIC PROPAGANDA TOOL TO FURTHER THEIR AGENDA.
WE HAVE TO FIND EN SABAH NUR. *HIS MOVEMENT ENDS NOW.*
WHAT'S WRONG?
I CAN'T... I CAN'T DO IT. IT WON'T CLOSE.
I'VE ALWAYS BEEN IN AWE OF HOW EASY THINGS ARE FOR YOU.
SOMETIMES I THINK WE DON'T DESERVE YOU.
...IT'S THE OTHER WAY AROUND, JEAN.

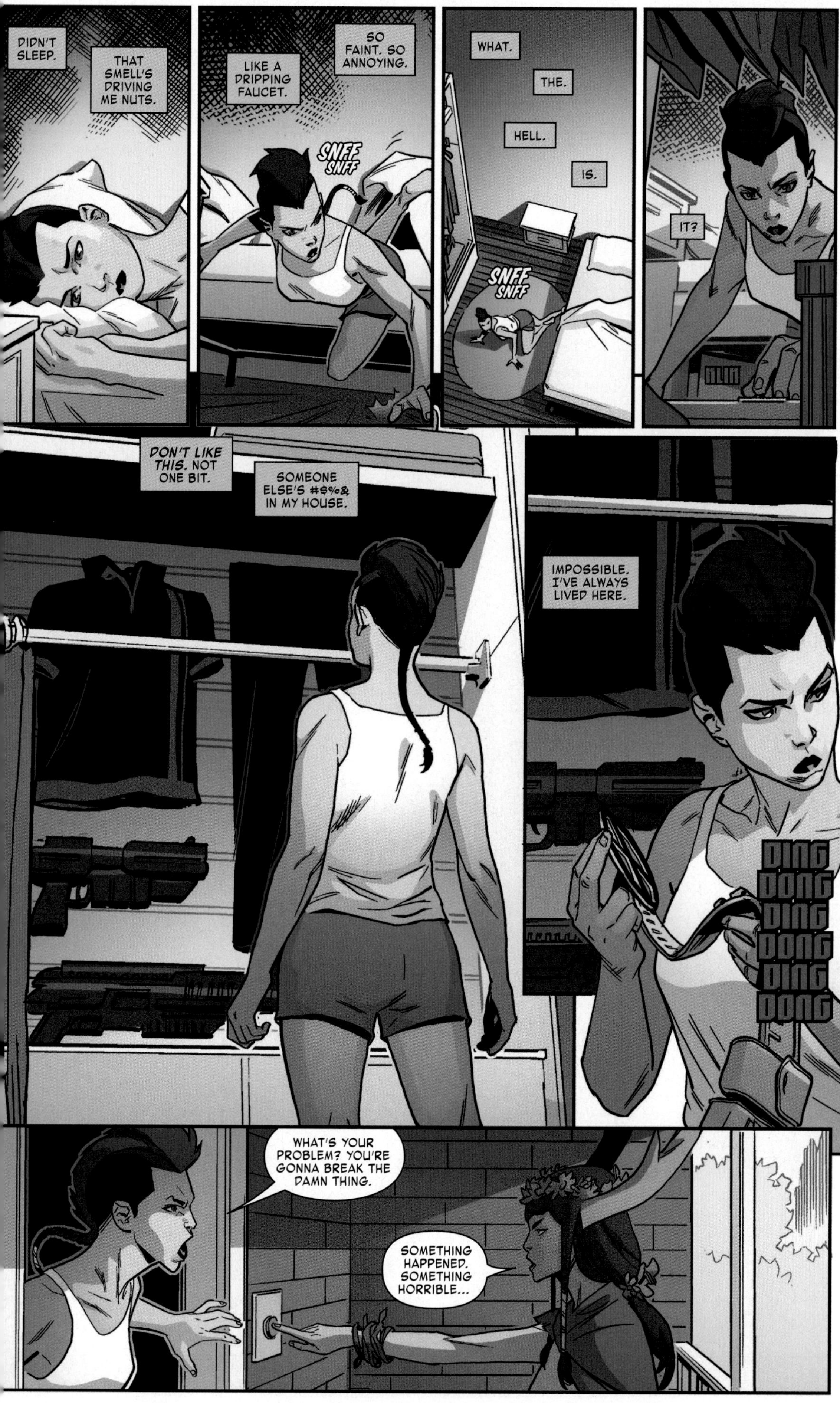

DIDN'T SLEEP.
THAT SMELL'S DRIVING ME NUTS.
LIKE A DRIPPING FAUCET.
SO FAINT. SO ANNOYING.
SNFF SNFF
WHAT.
THE.
HELL.
IS.
SNFF SNFF
IT?
DON'T LIKE THIS. NOT ONE BIT.
SOMEONE ELSE'S #$%& IN MY HOUSE.
IMPOSSIBLE. I'VE ALWAYS LIVED HERE.
DING DONG DING DONG DING DONG
WHAT'S YOUR PROBLEM? YOU'RE GONNA BREAK THE DAMN THING.
SOMETHING HAPPENED. SOMETHING HORRIBLE...

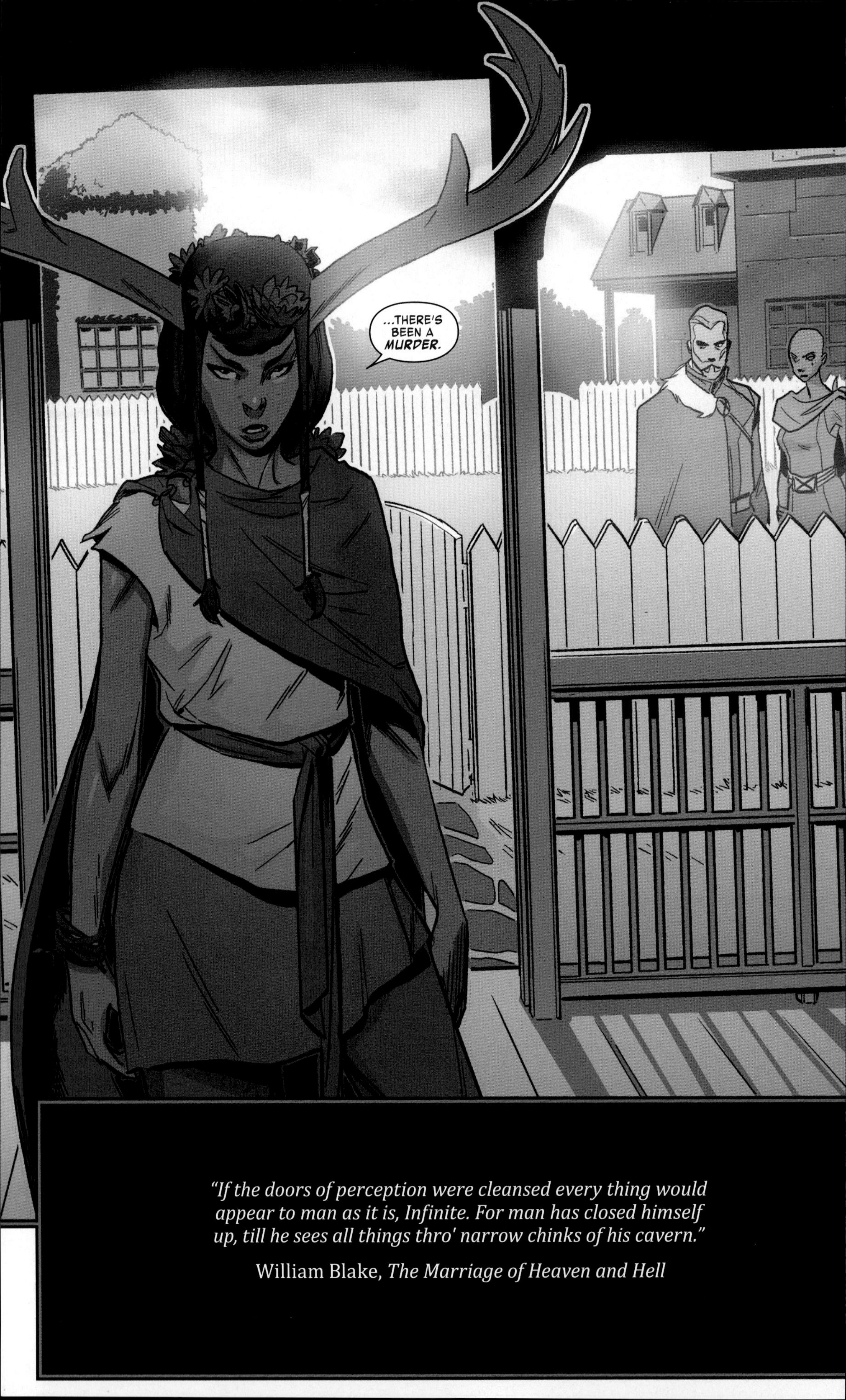
...THERE'S BEEN A MURDER.

"If the doors of perception were cleansed every thing would appear to man as it is, Infinite. For man has closed himself up, till he sees all things thro' narrow chinks of his cavern."

William Blake, *The Marriage of Heaven and Hell*

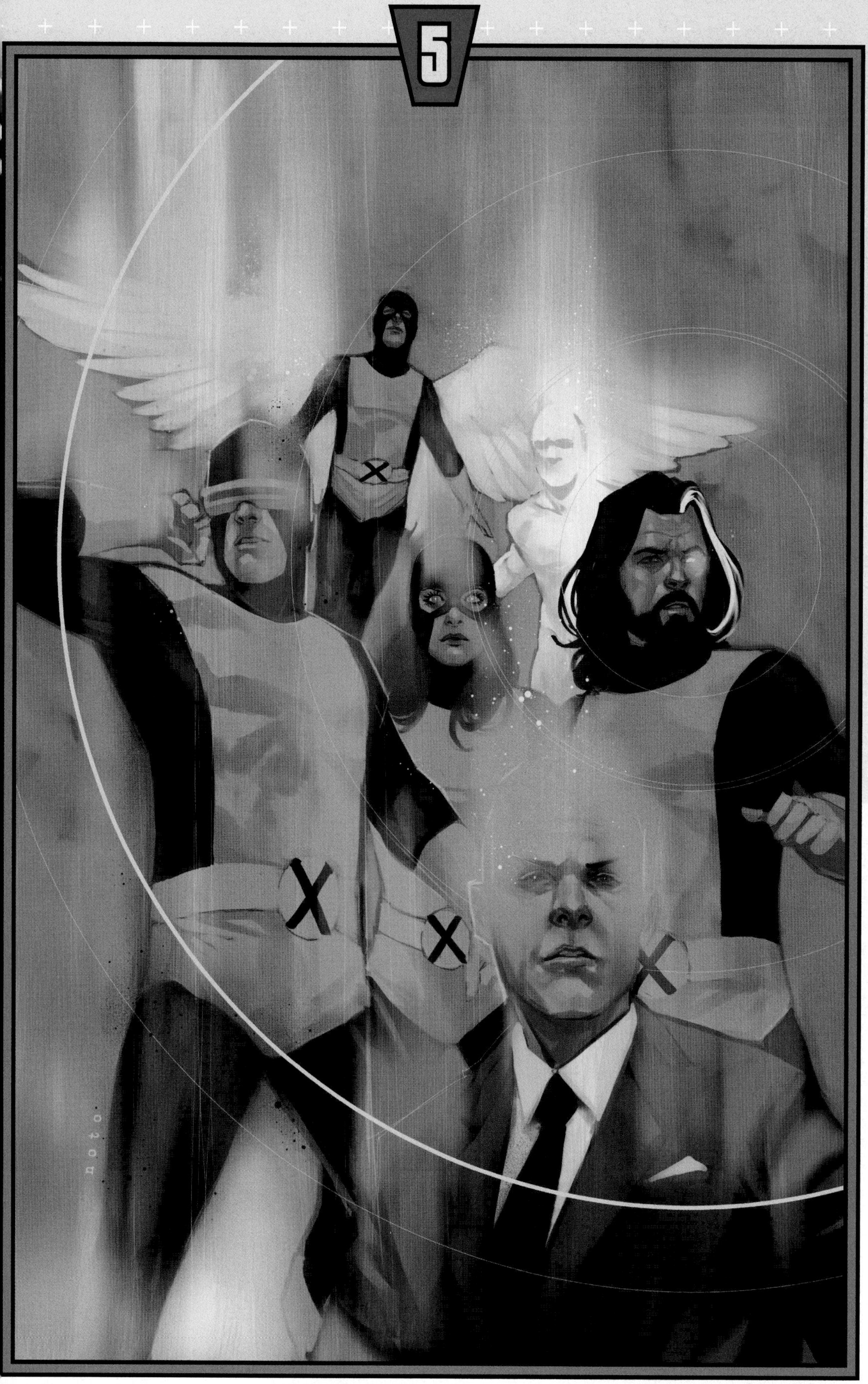
5

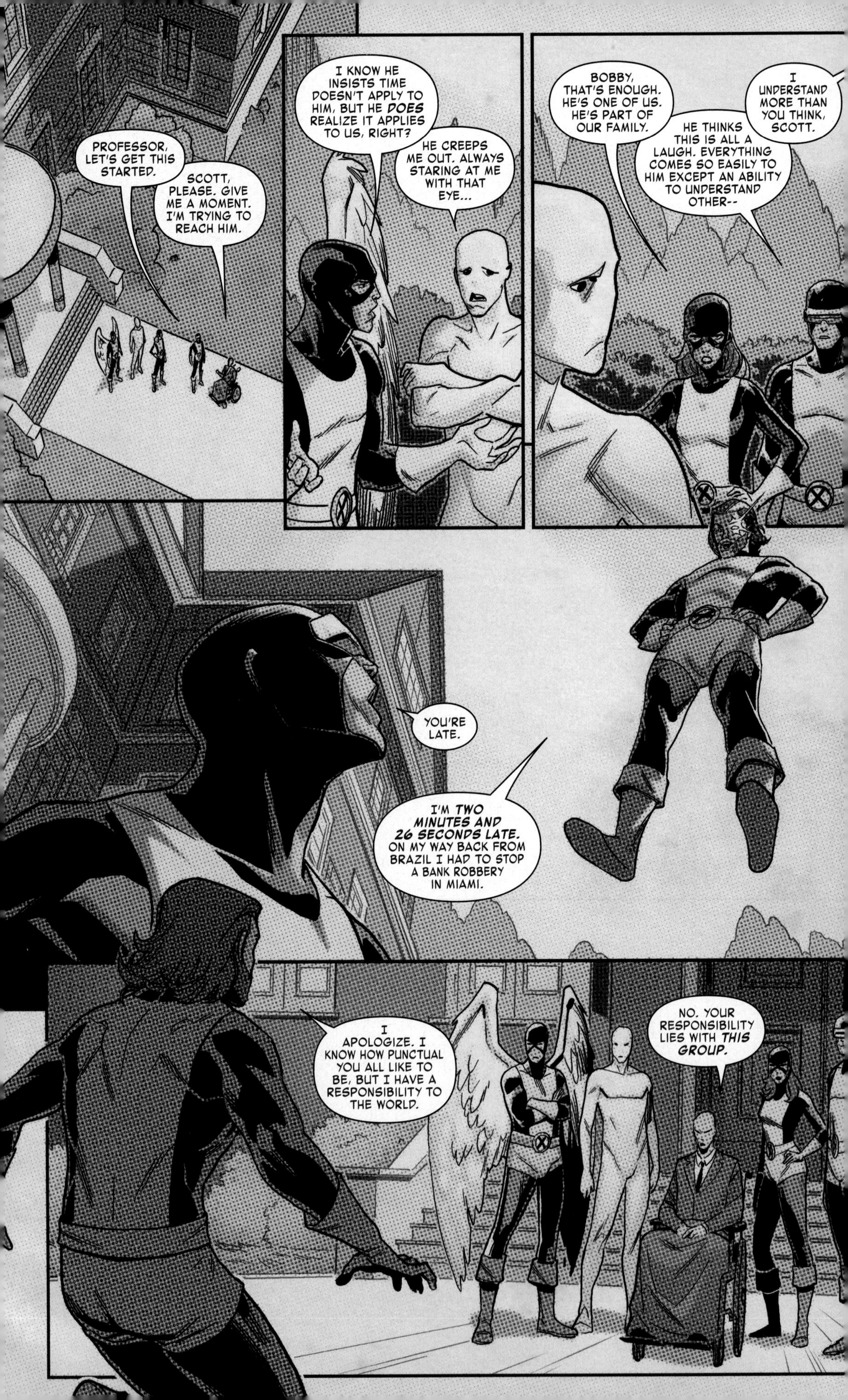
PROFESSOR, LET'S GET THIS STARTED.
SCOTT, PLEASE. GIVE ME A MOMENT. I'M TRYING TO REACH HIM.
I KNOW HE INSISTS TIME DOESN'T APPLY TO HIM, BUT HE *DOES* REALIZE IT APPLIES TO US, RIGHT?
HE CREEPS ME OUT. ALWAYS STARING AT ME WITH THAT EYE...
BOBBY, THAT'S ENOUGH. HE'S ONE OF US. HE'S PART OF OUR FAMILY.
HE THINKS THIS IS ALL A LAUGH. EVERYTHING COMES SO EASILY TO HIM EXCEPT AN ABILITY TO UNDERSTAND OTHER--
I UNDERSTAND MORE THAN YOU THINK, SCOTT.
YOU'RE LATE.
I'M ***TWO MINUTES AND 26 SECONDS LATE.*** ON MY WAY BACK FROM BRAZIL I HAD TO STOP A BANK ROBBERY IN MIAMI.
I APOLOGIZE. I KNOW HOW PUNCTUAL YOU ALL LIKE TO BE, BUT I HAVE A RESPONSIBILITY TO THE WORLD.
NO. YOUR RESPONSIBILITY LIES WITH ***THIS GROUP.***

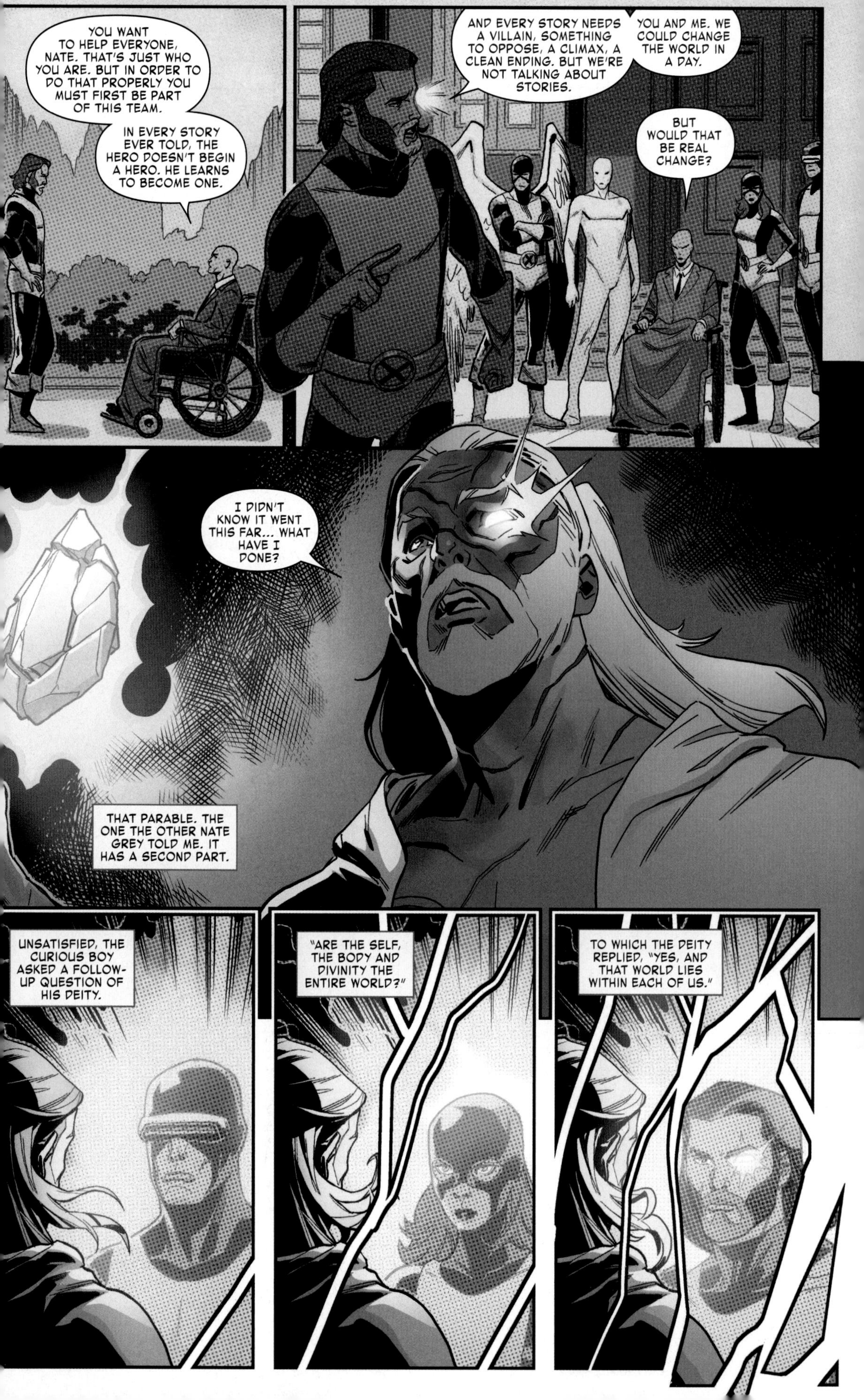
YOU WANT TO HELP EVERYONE, NATE. THAT'S JUST WHO YOU ARE. BUT IN ORDER TO DO THAT PROPERLY YOU MUST FIRST BE PART OF THIS TEAM.
IN EVERY STORY EVER TOLD, THE HERO DOESN'T BEGIN A HERO. HE LEARNS TO BECOME ONE.
AND EVERY STORY NEEDS A VILLAIN, SOMETHING TO OPPOSE, A CLIMAX, A CLEAN ENDING. BUT WE'RE NOT TALKING ABOUT STORIES.
YOU AND ME. WE COULD CHANGE THE WORLD IN A DAY.
BUT WOULD THAT BE REAL CHANGE?
I DIDN'T KNOW IT WENT THIS FAR... WHAT HAVE I DONE?
THAT PARABLE. THE ONE THE OTHER NATE GREY TOLD ME. IT HAS A SECOND PART.
UNSATISFIED, THE CURIOUS BOY ASKED A FOLLOW-UP QUESTION OF HIS DEITY.
"ARE THE SELF, THE BODY AND DIVINITY THE ENTIRE WORLD?"
TO WHICH THE DEITY REPLIED, "YES, AND THAT WORLD LIES WITHIN EACH OF US."

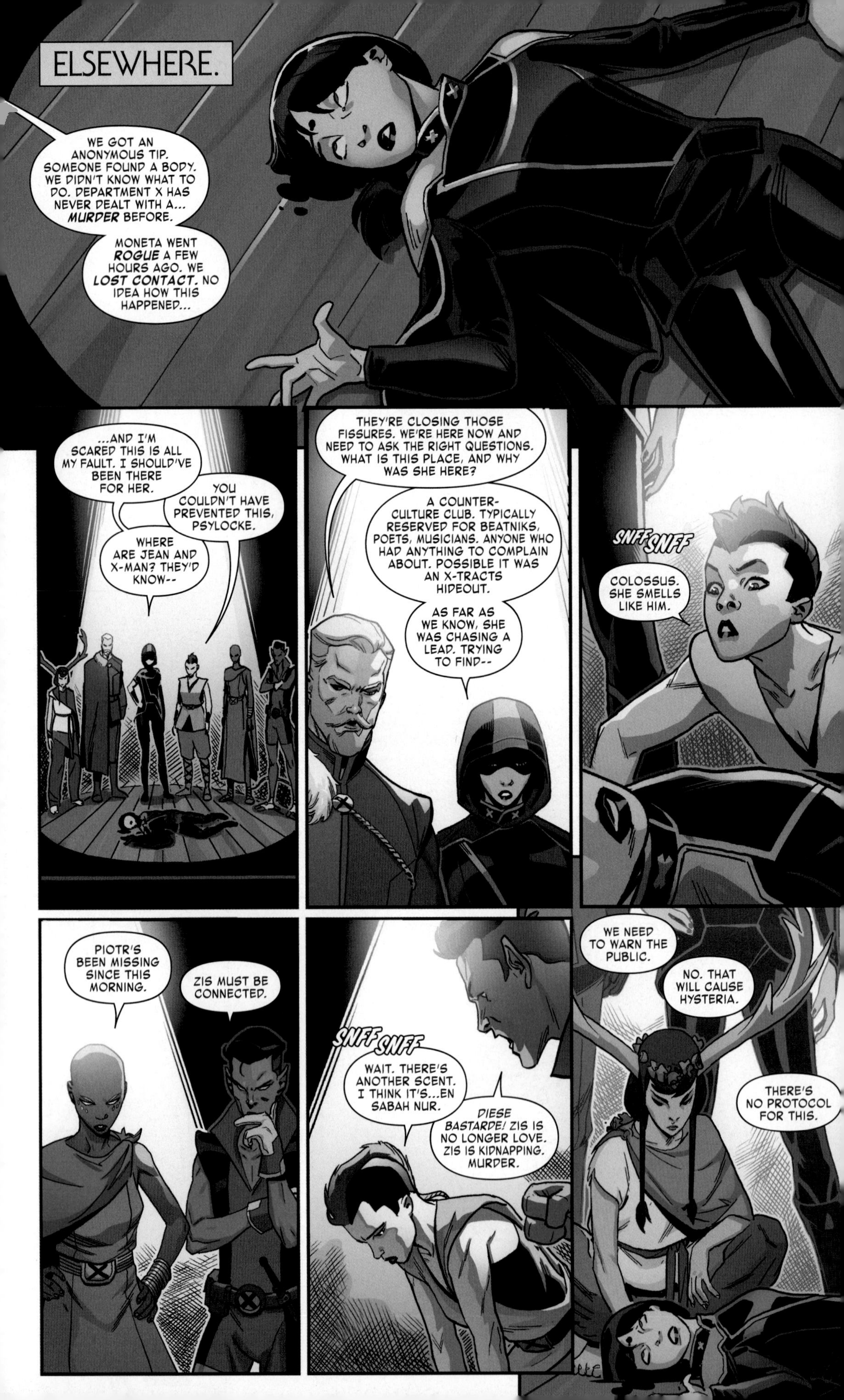
ELSEWHERE.
WE GOT AN ANONYMOUS TIP. SOMEONE FOUND A BODY. WE DIDN'T KNOW WHAT TO DO. DEPARTMENT X HAS NEVER DEALT WITH A... MURDER BEFORE.
MONETA WENT ROGUE A FEW HOURS AGO. WE LOST CONTACT. NO IDEA HOW THIS HAPPENED...
...AND I'M SCARED THIS IS ALL MY FAULT. I SHOULD'VE BEEN THERE FOR HER.
YOU COULDN'T HAVE PREVENTED THIS, PSYLOCKE.
WHERE ARE JEAN AND X-MAN? THEY'D KNOW--
THEY'RE CLOSING THOSE FISSURES. WE'RE HERE NOW AND NEED TO ASK THE RIGHT QUESTIONS. WHAT IS THIS PLACE, AND WHY WAS SHE HERE?
A COUNTER-CULTURE CLUB. TYPICALLY RESERVED FOR BEATNIKS, POETS, MUSICIANS. ANYONE WHO HAD ANYTHING TO COMPLAIN ABOUT. POSSIBLE IT WAS AN X-TRACTS HIDEOUT.
AS FAR AS WE KNOW, SHE WAS CHASING A LEAD. TRYING TO FIND--
SNFF SNFF
COLOSSUS. SHE SMELLS LIKE HIM.
PIOTR'S BEEN MISSING SINCE THIS MORNING.
ZIS MUST BE CONNECTED.
SNFF SNFF
WAIT. THERE'S ANOTHER SCENT. I THINK IT'S...EN SABAH NUR.
DIESE BASTARDE! ZIS IS NO LONGER LOVE. ZIS IS KIDNAPPING. MURDER.
WE NEED TO WARN THE PUBLIC.
NO. THAT WILL CAUSE HYSTERIA.
THERE'S NO PROTOCOL FOR THIS.

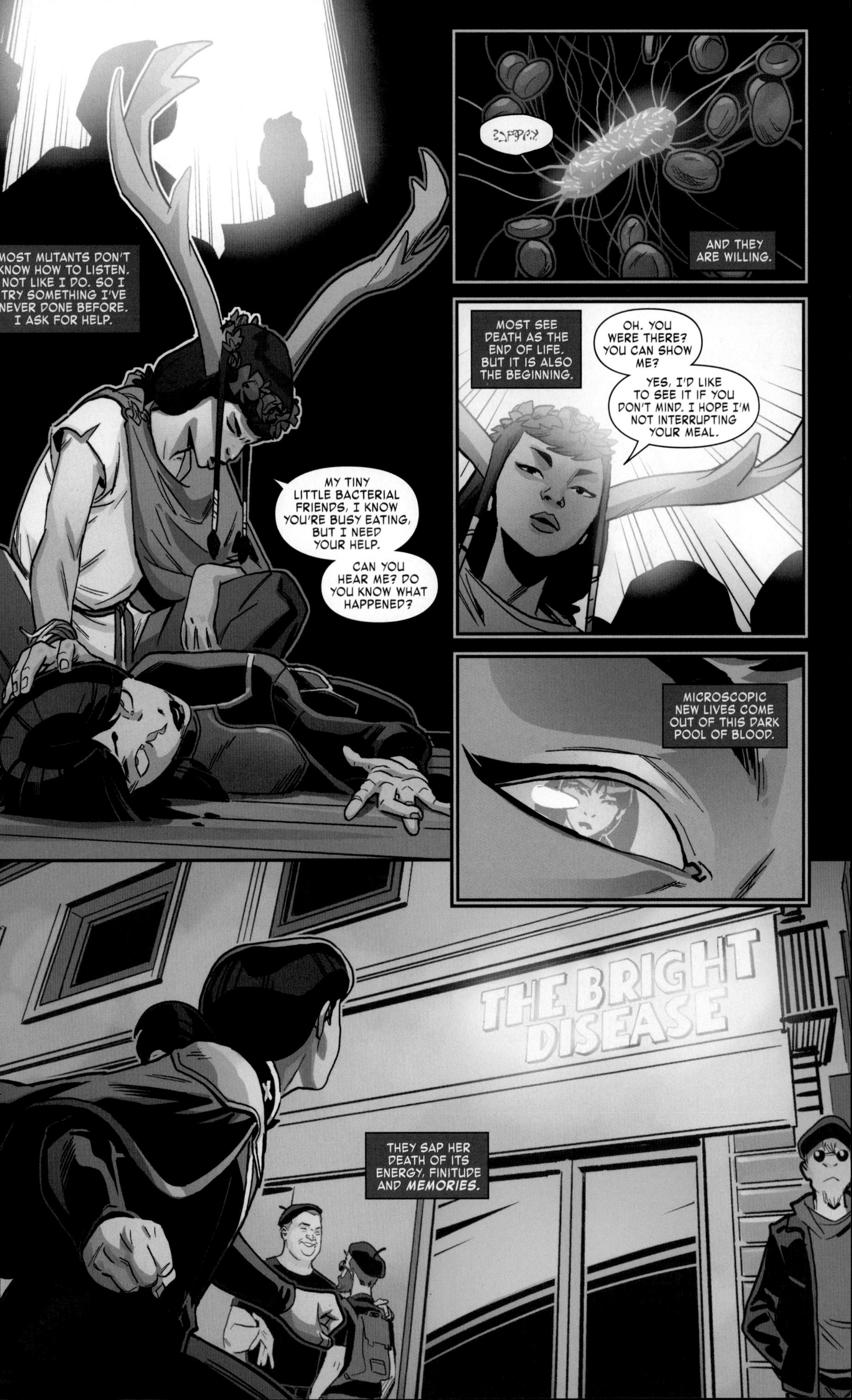
MOST MUTANTS DON'T KNOW HOW TO LISTEN. NOT LIKE I DO. SO I TRY SOMETHING I'VE NEVER DONE BEFORE. I ASK FOR HELP.
MY TINY LITTLE BACTERIAL FRIENDS, I KNOW YOU'RE BUSY EATING, BUT I NEED YOUR HELP.
CAN YOU HEAR ME? DO YOU KNOW WHAT HAPPENED?
AND THEY ARE WILLING.
MOST SEE DEATH AS THE END OF LIFE. BUT IT IS ALSO THE BEGINNING.
OH. YOU WERE THERE? YOU CAN SHOW ME?
YES, I'D LIKE TO SEE IT IF YOU DON'T MIND. I HOPE I'M NOT INTERRUPTING YOUR MEAL.
MICROSCOPIC NEW LIVES COME OUT OF THIS DARK POOL OF BLOOD.
THE BRIGHT DISEASE
THEY SAP HER DEATH OF ITS ENERGY, FINITUDE AND *MEMORIES.*

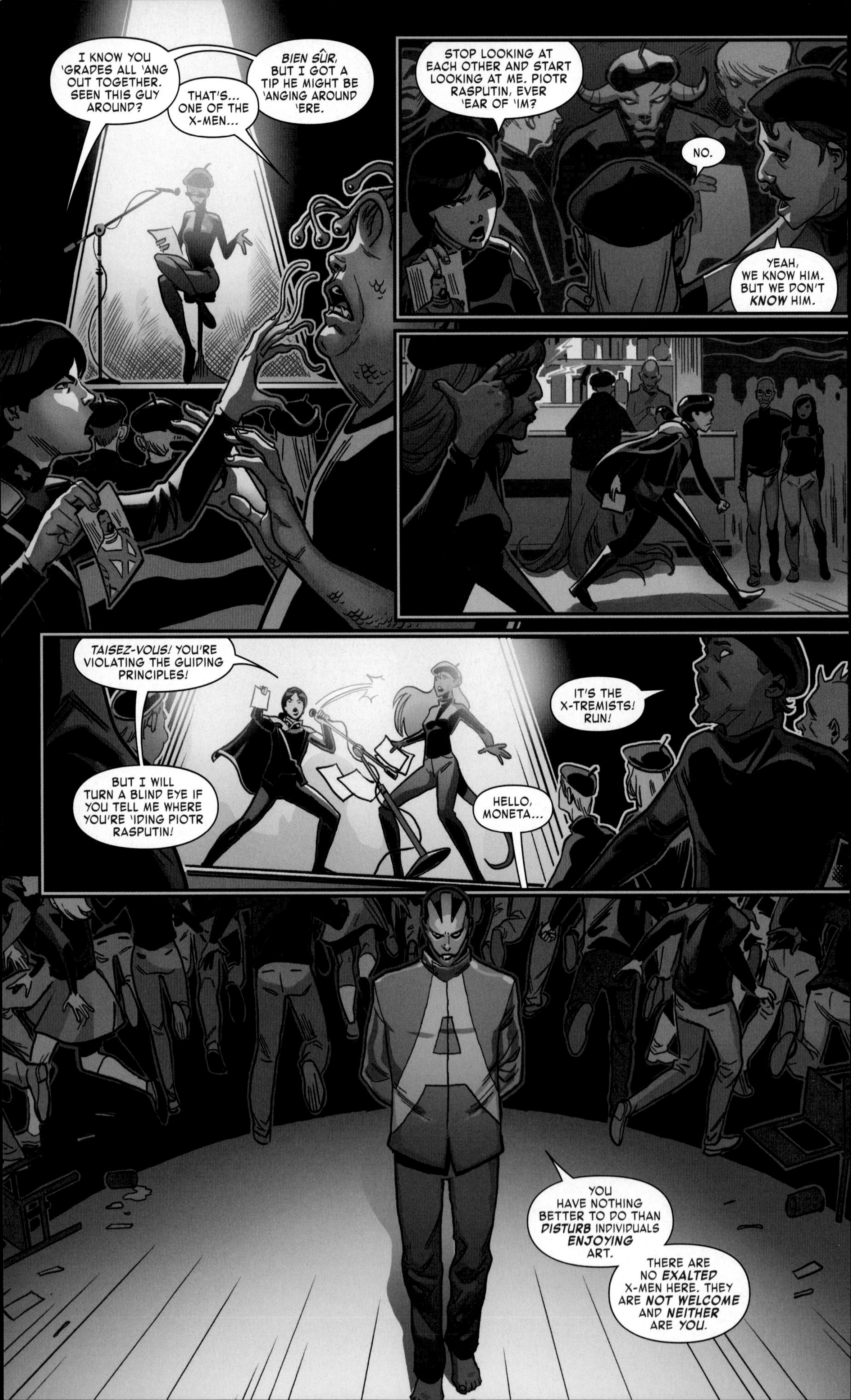
I KNOW YOU 'GRADES ALL 'ANG OUT TOGETHER. SEEN THIS GUY AROUND?
THAT'S... ONE OF THE X-MEN...
BIEN SÛR, BUT I GOT A TIP HE MIGHT BE 'ANGING AROUND 'ERE.
STOP LOOKING AT EACH OTHER AND START LOOKING AT ME. PIOTR RASPUTIN, EVER 'EAR OF 'IM?
NO.
YEAH, WE KNOW HIM. BUT WE DON'T *KNOW* HIM.
TAISEZ-VOUS! YOU'RE VIOLATING THE GUIDING PRINCIPLES!
BUT I WILL TURN A BLIND EYE IF YOU TELL ME WHERE YOU'RE 'IDING PIOTR RASPUTIN!
IT'S THE X-TREMISTS! RUN!
HELLO, MONETA...
YOU HAVE NOTHING BETTER TO DO THAN *DISTURB* INDIVIDUALS *ENJOYING* ART.
THERE ARE NO *EXALTED* X-MEN HERE. THEY ARE *NOT WELCOME* AND *NEITHER* ARE *YOU.*

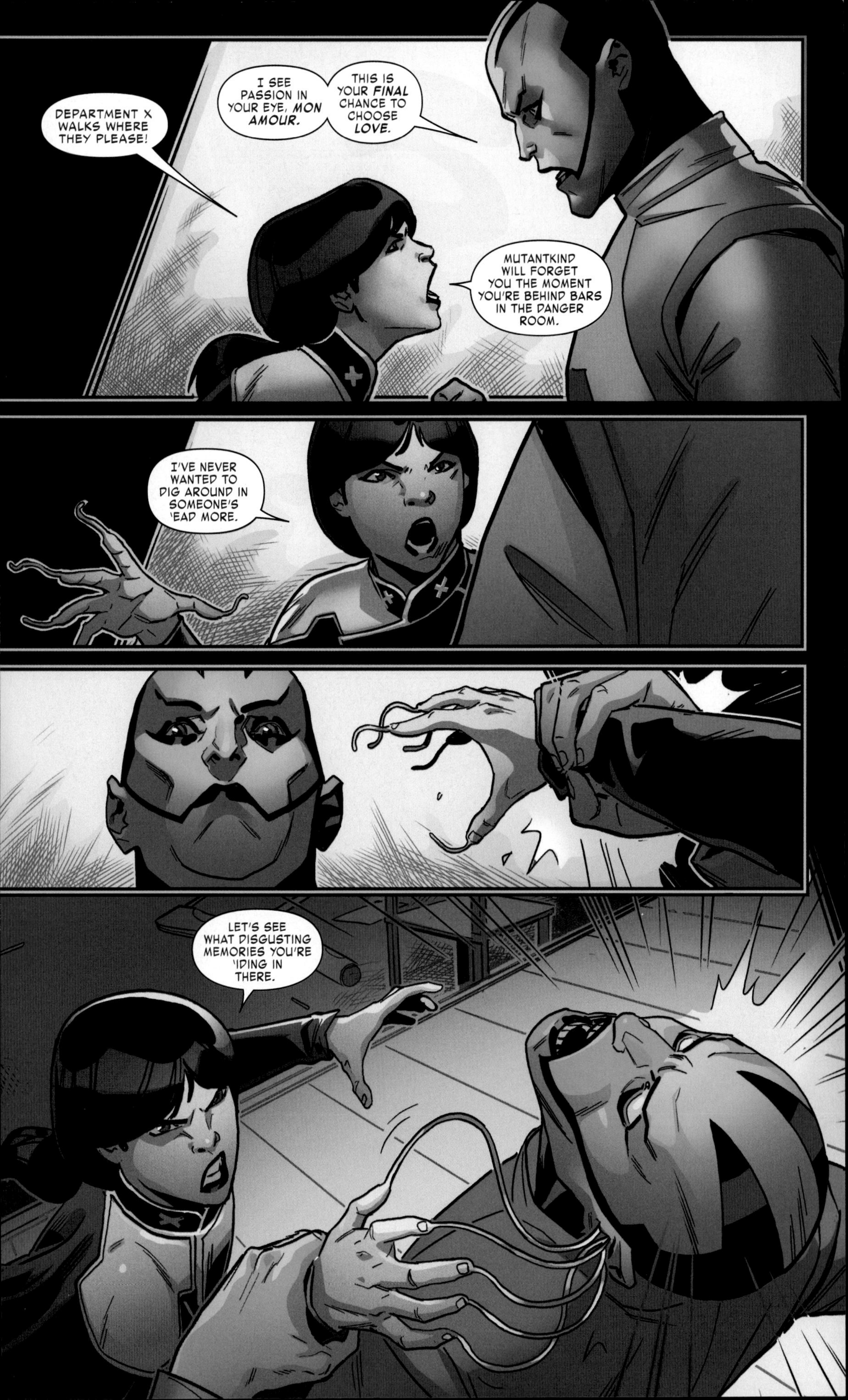
DEPARTMENT X WALKS WHERE THEY PLEASE!
I SEE PASSION IN YOUR EYE, MON AMOUR.
THIS IS YOUR FINAL CHANCE TO CHOOSE LOVE.
MUTANTKIND WILL FORGET YOU THE MOMENT YOU'RE BEHIND BARS IN THE DANGER ROOM.
I'VE NEVER WANTED TO DIG AROUND IN SOMEONE'S 'EAD MORE.
LET'S SEE WHAT DISGUSTING MEMORIES YOU'RE 'IDING IN THERE.

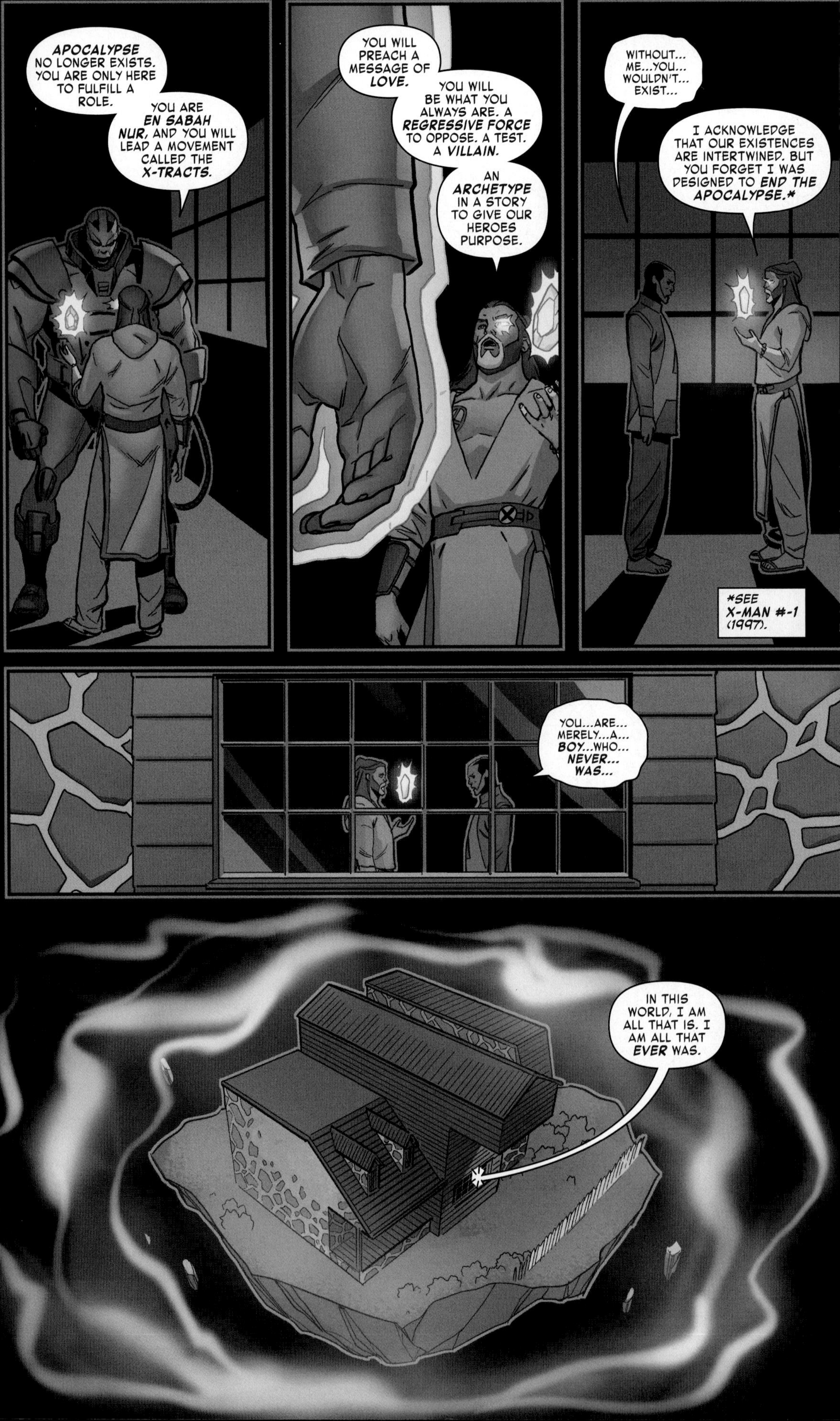

APOCALYPSE NO LONGER EXISTS. YOU ARE ONLY HERE TO FULFILL A ROLE.
YOU ARE EN SABAH NUR, AND YOU WILL LEAD A MOVEMENT CALLED THE X-TRACTS.
YOU WILL PREACH A MESSAGE OF LOVE.
YOU WILL BE WHAT YOU ALWAYS ARE. A REGRESSIVE FORCE TO OPPOSE. A TEST. A VILLAIN.
AN ARCHETYPE IN A STORY TO GIVE OUR HEROES PURPOSE.
WITHOUT... ME...YOU... WOULDN'T... EXIST...
I ACKNOWLEDGE THAT OUR EXISTENCES ARE INTERTWINED. BUT YOU FORGET I WAS DESIGNED TO END THE APOCALYPSE.*
*SEE X-MAN #-1 (1997).
YOU...ARE... MERELY...A... BOY...WHO... NEVER... WAS...
IN THIS WORLD, I AM ALL THAT IS. I AM ALL THAT EVER WAS.

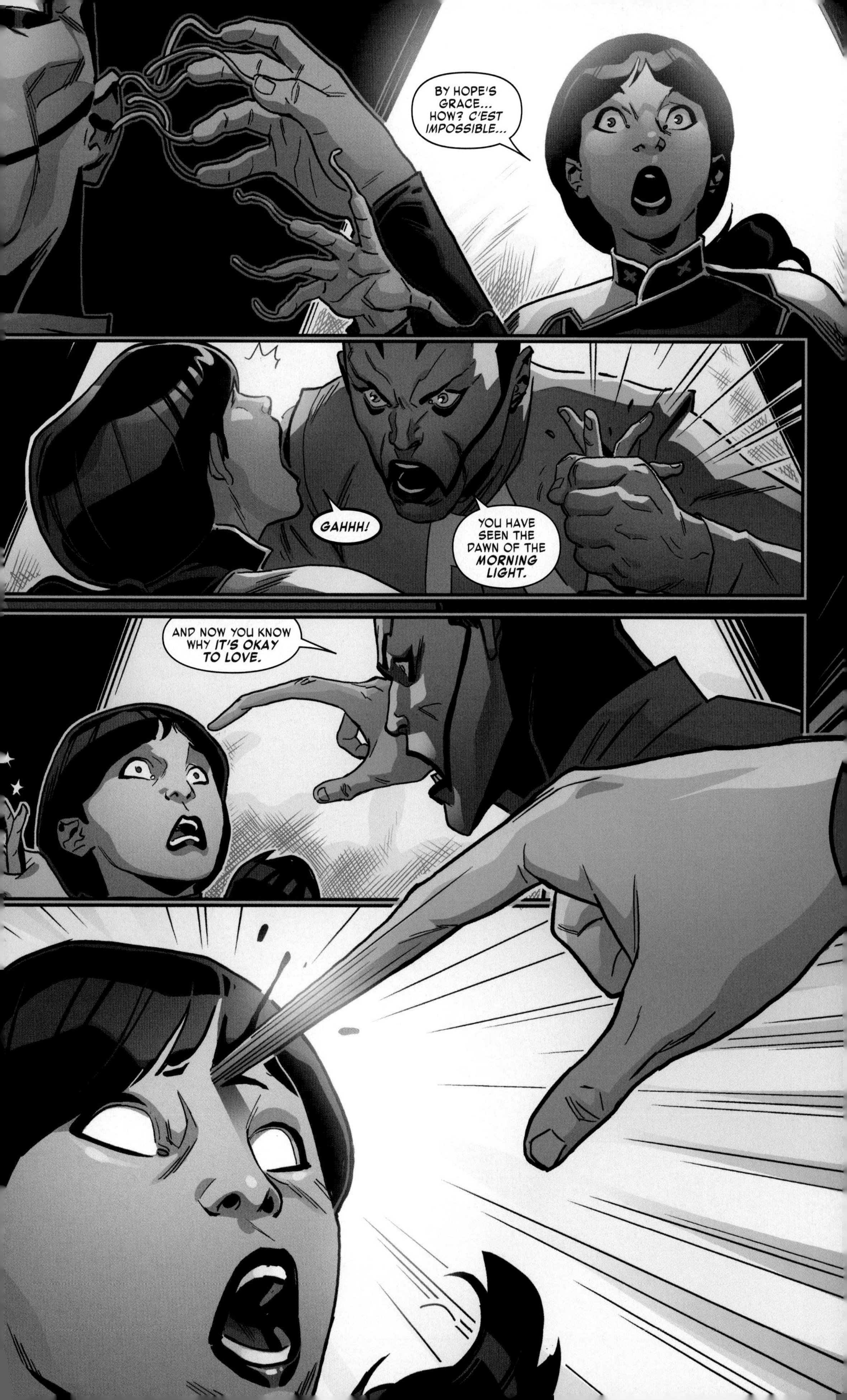
BY HOPE'S GRACE... HOW? C'EST IMPOSSIBLE...
GAHHH!
YOU HAVE SEEN THE DAWN OF THE MORNING LIGHT.
AND NOW YOU KNOW WHY IT'S OKAY TO LOVE.

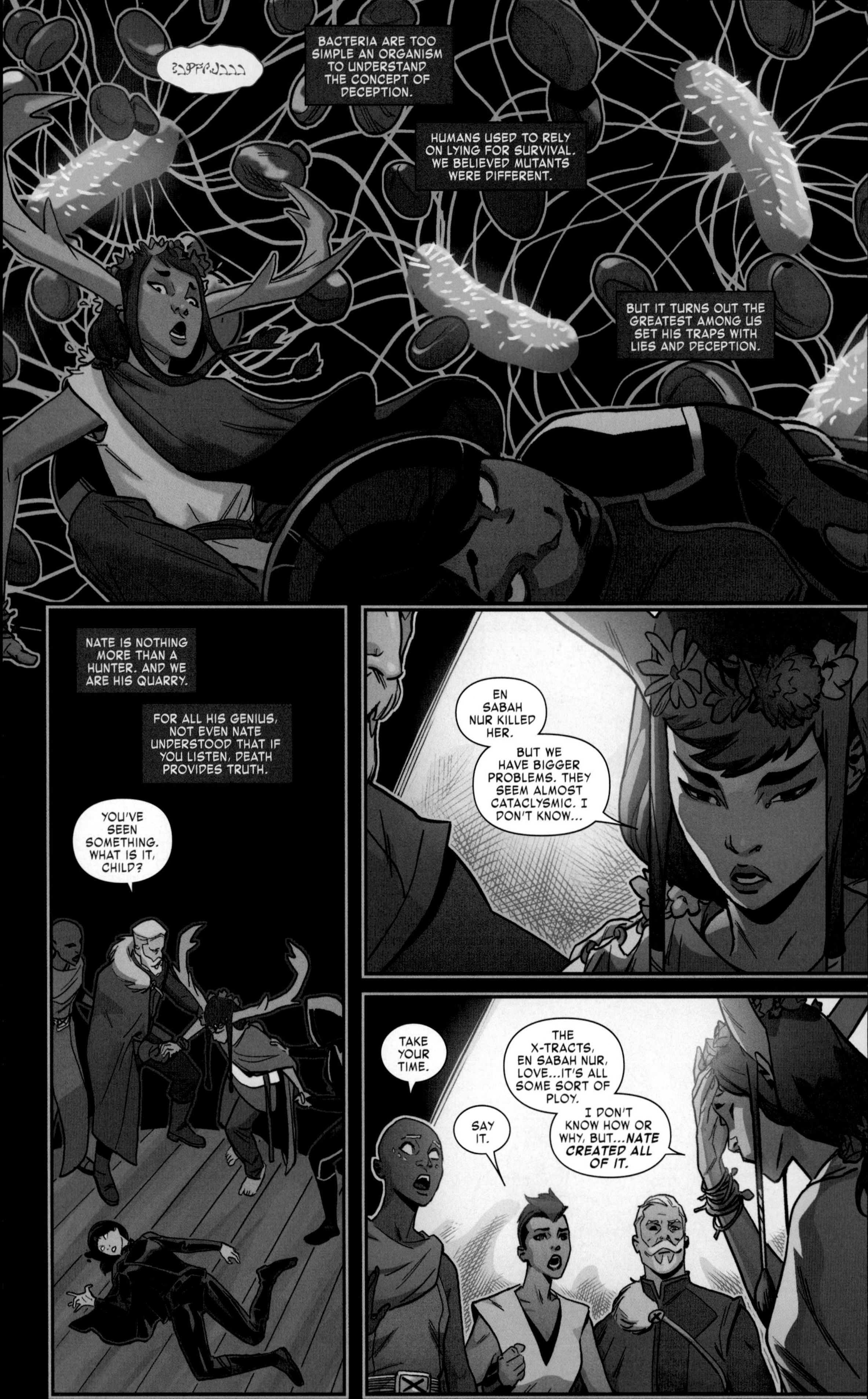
BACTERIA ARE TOO SIMPLE AN ORGANISM TO UNDERSTAND THE CONCEPT OF DECEPTION.
HUMANS USED TO RELY ON LYING FOR SURVIVAL. WE BELIEVED MUTANTS WERE DIFFERENT.
BUT IT TURNS OUT THE GREATEST AMONG US SET HIS TRAPS WITH LIES AND DECEPTION.
NATE IS NOTHING MORE THAN A HUNTER. AND WE ARE HIS QUARRY.
FOR ALL HIS GENIUS, NOT EVEN NATE UNDERSTOOD THAT IF YOU LISTEN, DEATH PROVIDES TRUTH.
YOU'VE SEEN SOMETHING. WHAT IS IT, CHILD?
EN SABAH NUR KILLED HER.
BUT WE HAVE BIGGER PROBLEMS. THEY SEEM ALMOST CATACLYSMIC. I DON'T KNOW...
TAKE YOUR TIME.
SAY IT.
THE X-TRACTS, EN SABAH NUR, LOVE...IT'S ALL SOME SORT OF PLOY.
I DON'T KNOW HOW OR WHY, BUT...NATE CREATED ALL OF IT.

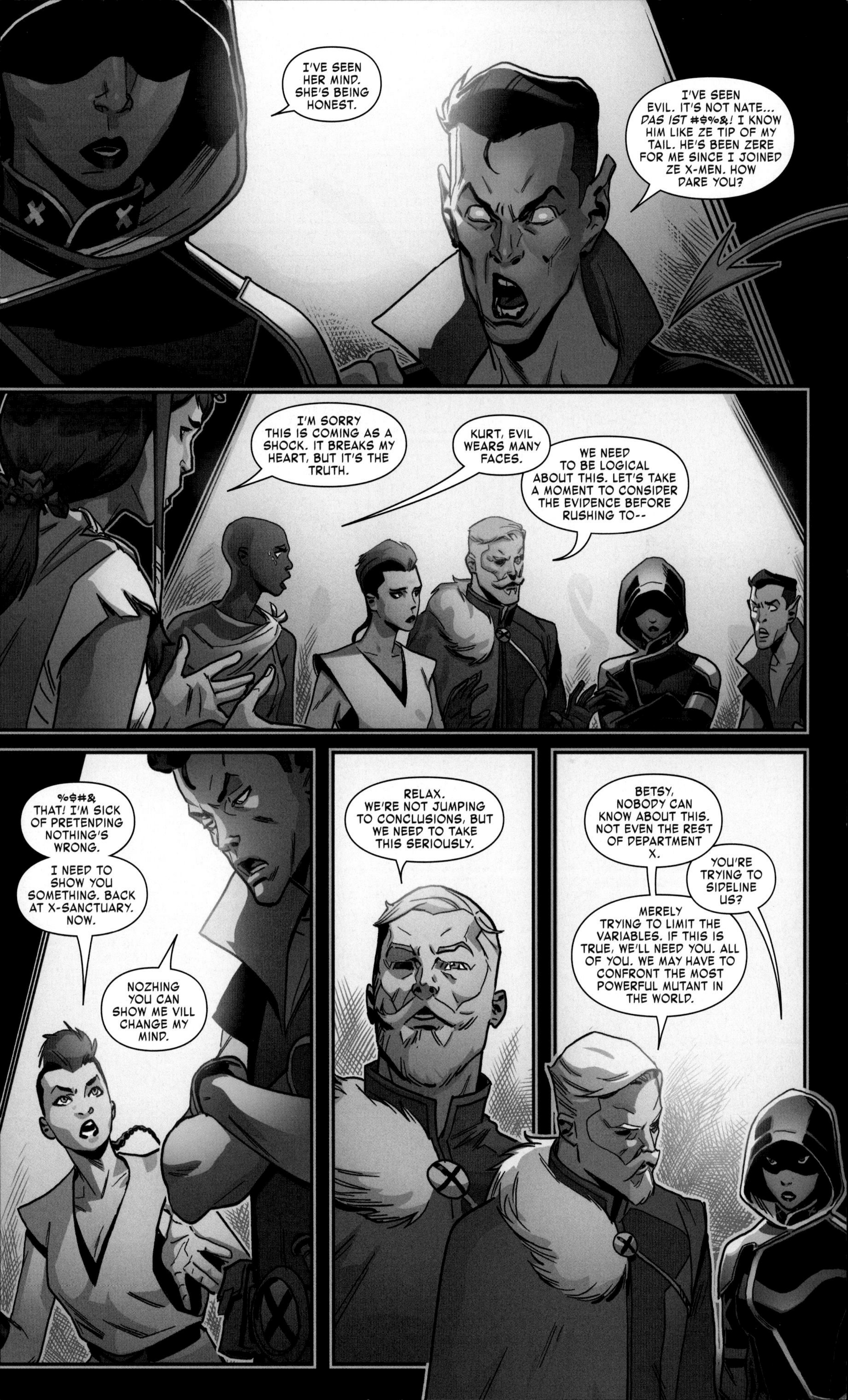
I'VE SEEN HER MIND. SHE'S BEING HONEST.
I'VE SEEN EVIL. IT'S NOT NATE... DAS IST #$%&! I KNOW HIM LIKE ZE TIP OF MY TAIL. HE'S BEEN ZERE FOR ME SINCE I JOINED ZE X-MEN. HOW DARE YOU?
I'M SORRY THIS IS COMING AS A SHOCK. IT BREAKS MY HEART, BUT IT'S THE TRUTH.
KURT, EVIL WEARS MANY FACES.
WE NEED TO BE LOGICAL ABOUT THIS. LET'S TAKE A MOMENT TO CONSIDER THE EVIDENCE BEFORE RUSHING TO--
%$#& THAT! I'M SICK OF PRETENDING NOTHING'S WRONG.
I NEED TO SHOW YOU SOMETHING. BACK AT X-SANCTUARY. NOW.
NOZHING YOU CAN SHOW ME VILL CHANGE MY MIND.
RELAX. WE'RE NOT JUMPING TO CONCLUSIONS, BUT WE NEED TO TAKE THIS SERIOUSLY.
BETSY, NOBODY CAN KNOW ABOUT THIS. NOT EVEN THE REST OF DEPARTMENT X.
YOU'RE TRYING TO SIDELINE US?
MERELY TRYING TO LIMIT THE VARIABLES. IF THIS IS TRUE, WE'LL NEED YOU. ALL OF YOU. WE MAY HAVE TO CONFRONT THE MOST POWERFUL MUTANT IN THE WORLD.

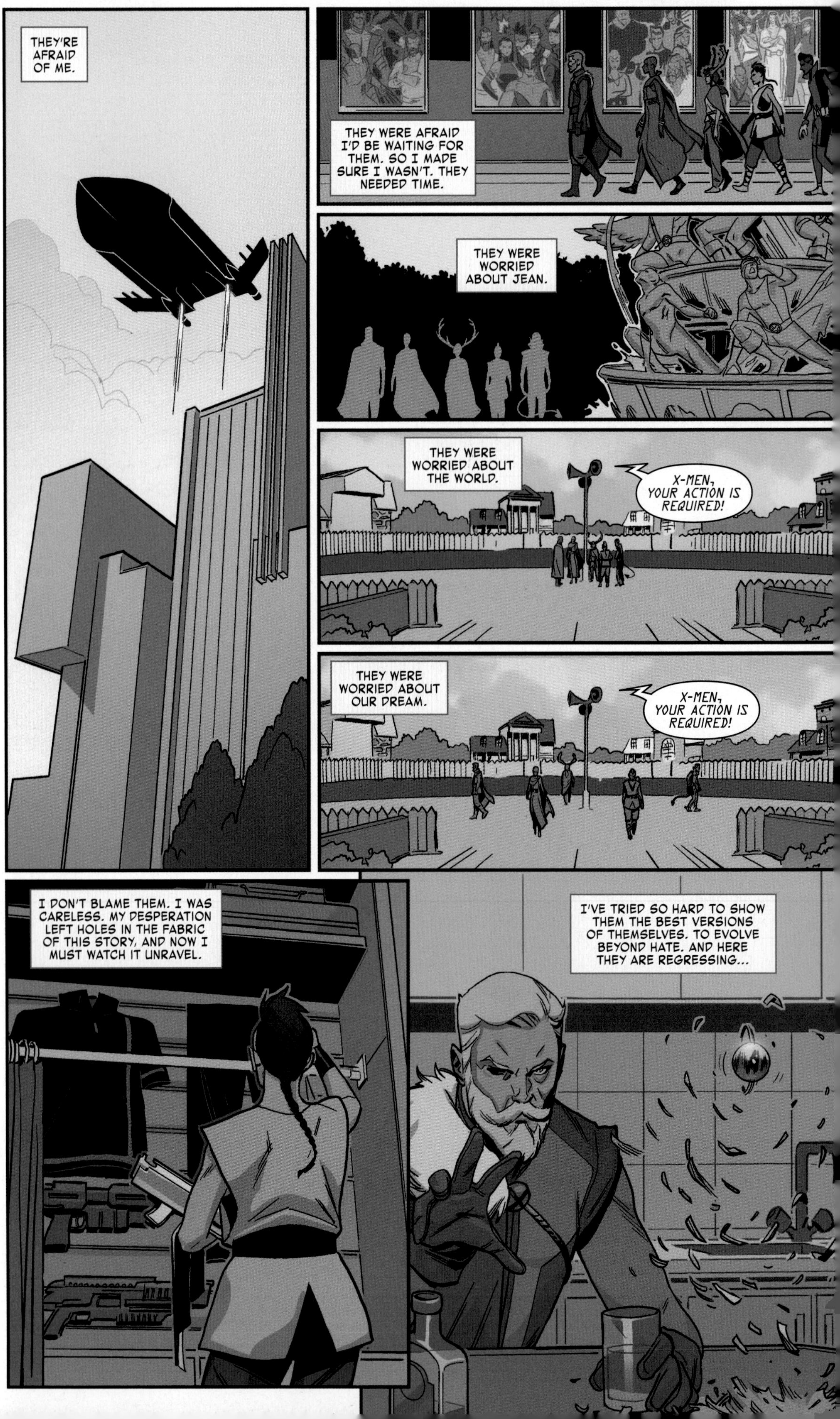

THEY'RE AFRAID OF ME.
THEY WERE AFRAID I'D BE WAITING FOR THEM. SO I MADE SURE I WASN'T. THEY NEEDED TIME.
THEY WERE WORRIED ABOUT JEAN.
THEY WERE WORRIED ABOUT THE WORLD.
X-MEN, YOUR ACTION IS REQUIRED!
THEY WERE WORRIED ABOUT OUR DREAM.
X-MEN, YOUR ACTION IS REQUIRED!
I DON'T BLAME THEM. I WAS CARELESS. MY DESPERATION LEFT HOLES IN THE FABRIC OF THIS STORY, AND NOW I MUST WATCH IT UNRAVEL.
I'VE TRIED SO HARD TO SHOW THEM THE BEST VERSIONS OF THEMSELVES. TO EVOLVE BEYOND HATE. AND HERE THEY ARE REGRESSING...

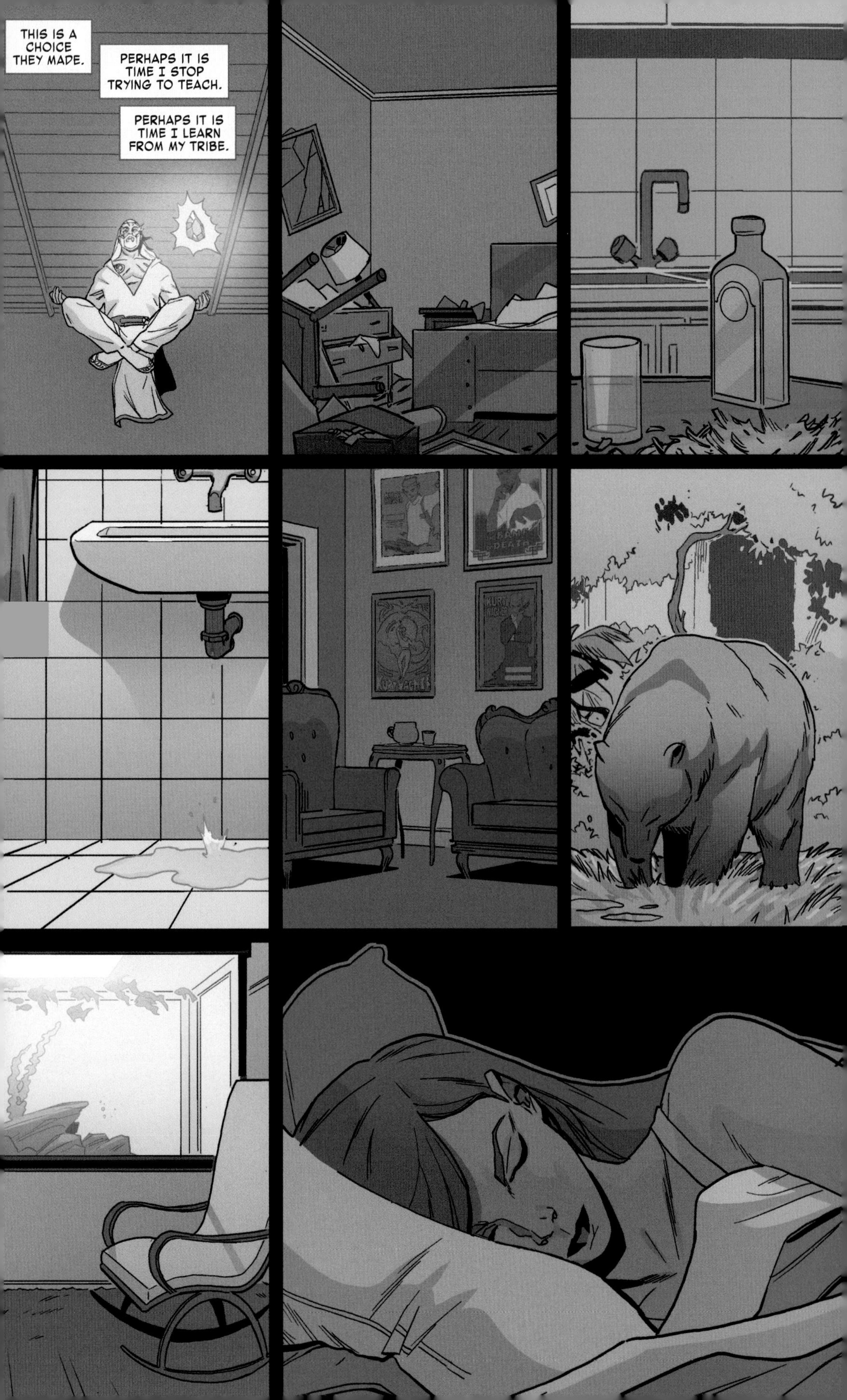
THIS IS A CHOICE THEY MADE.
PERHAPS IT IS TIME I STOP TRYING TO TEACH.
PERHAPS IT IS TIME I LEARN FROM MY TRIBE.

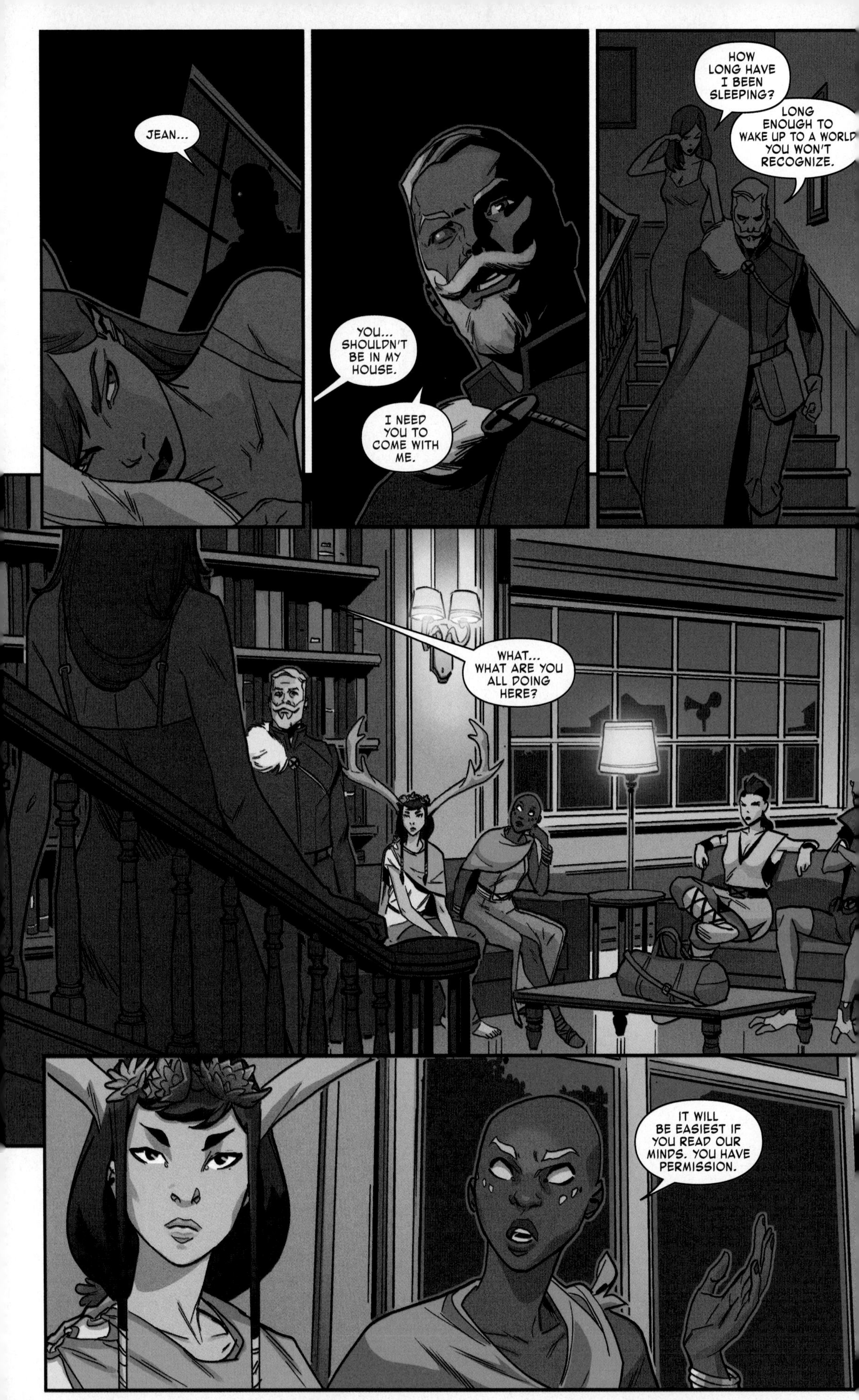
JEAN...
YOU... SHOULDN'T BE IN MY HOUSE.
I NEED YOU TO COME WITH ME.
HOW LONG HAVE I BEEN SLEEPING?
LONG ENOUGH TO WAKE UP TO A WORLD YOU WON'T RECOGNIZE.
WHAT... WHAT ARE YOU ALL DOING HERE?
IT WILL BE EASIEST IF YOU READ OUR MINDS. YOU HAVE PERMISSION.

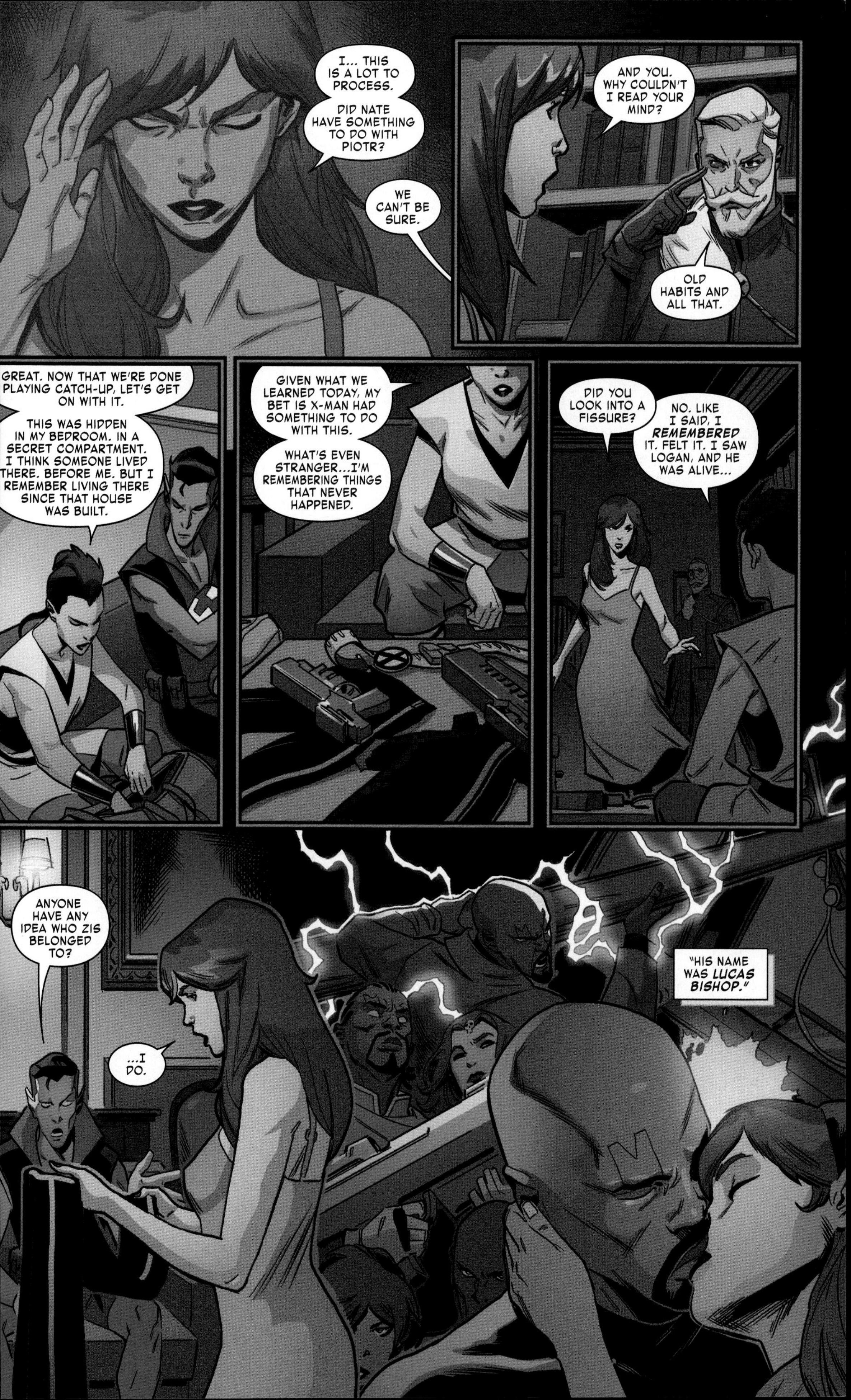
I... THIS IS A LOT TO PROCESS.
DID NATE HAVE SOMETHING TO DO WITH PIOTR?
WE CAN'T BE SURE.
AND YOU. WHY COULDN'T I READ YOUR MIND?
OLD HABITS AND ALL THAT.
GREAT. NOW THAT WE'RE DONE PLAYING CATCH-UP, LET'S GET ON WITH IT.
THIS WAS HIDDEN IN MY BEDROOM. IN A SECRET COMPARTMENT. I THINK SOMEONE LIVED THERE. BEFORE ME. BUT I REMEMBER LIVING THERE SINCE THAT HOUSE WAS BUILT.
GIVEN WHAT WE LEARNED TODAY, MY BET IS X-MAN HAD SOMETHING TO DO WITH THIS.
WHAT'S EVEN STRANGER...I'M REMEMBERING THINGS THAT NEVER HAPPENED.
DID YOU LOOK INTO A FISSURE?
NO. LIKE I SAID, I *REMEMBERED* IT. FELT IT. I SAW LOGAN, AND HE WAS ALIVE...
ANYONE HAVE ANY IDEA WHO ZIS BELONGED TO?
...I DO.
"HIS NAME WAS *LUCAS BISHOP.*"

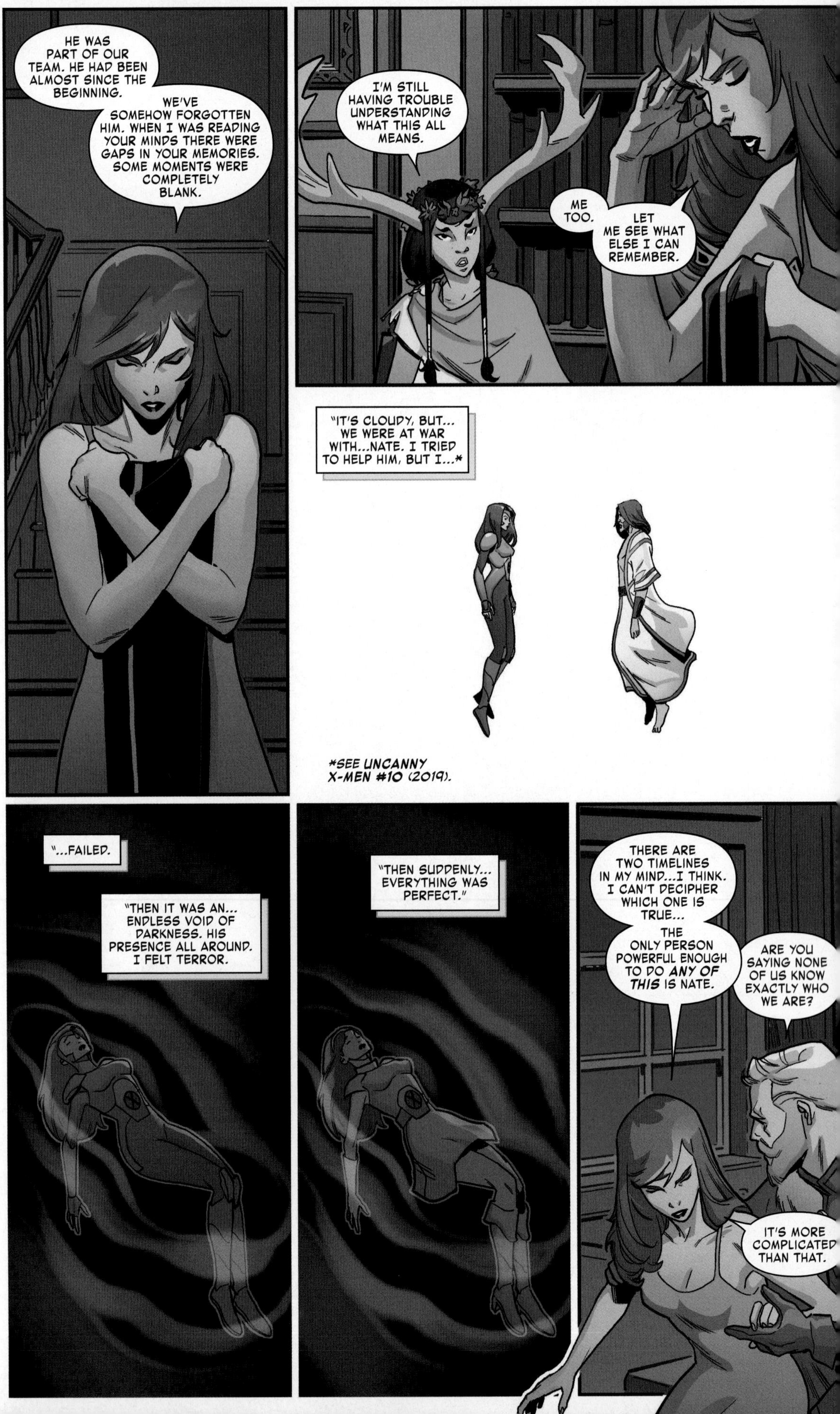
HE WAS PART OF OUR TEAM. HE HAD BEEN ALMOST SINCE THE BEGINNING.
WE'VE SOMEHOW FORGOTTEN HIM. WHEN I WAS READING YOUR MINDS THERE WERE GAPS IN YOUR MEMORIES. SOME MOMENTS WERE COMPLETELY BLANK.
I'M STILL HAVING TROUBLE UNDERSTANDING WHAT THIS ALL MEANS.
ME TOO.
LET ME SEE WHAT ELSE I CAN REMEMBER.
"IT'S CLOUDY, BUT... WE WERE AT WAR WITH...NATE. I TRIED TO HELP HIM, BUT I...*
*SEE UNCANNY X-MEN #10 (2019).
"...FAILED.
"THEN IT WAS AN... ENDLESS VOID OF DARKNESS. HIS PRESENCE ALL AROUND. I FELT TERROR.
"THEN SUDDENLY... EVERYTHING WAS PERFECT."
THERE ARE TWO TIMELINES IN MY MIND...I THINK. I CAN'T DECIPHER WHICH ONE IS TRUE...
THE ONLY PERSON POWERFUL ENOUGH TO DO ANY OF THIS IS NATE.
ARE YOU SAYING NONE OF US KNOW EXACTLY WHO WE ARE?
IT'S MORE COMPLICATED THAN THAT.

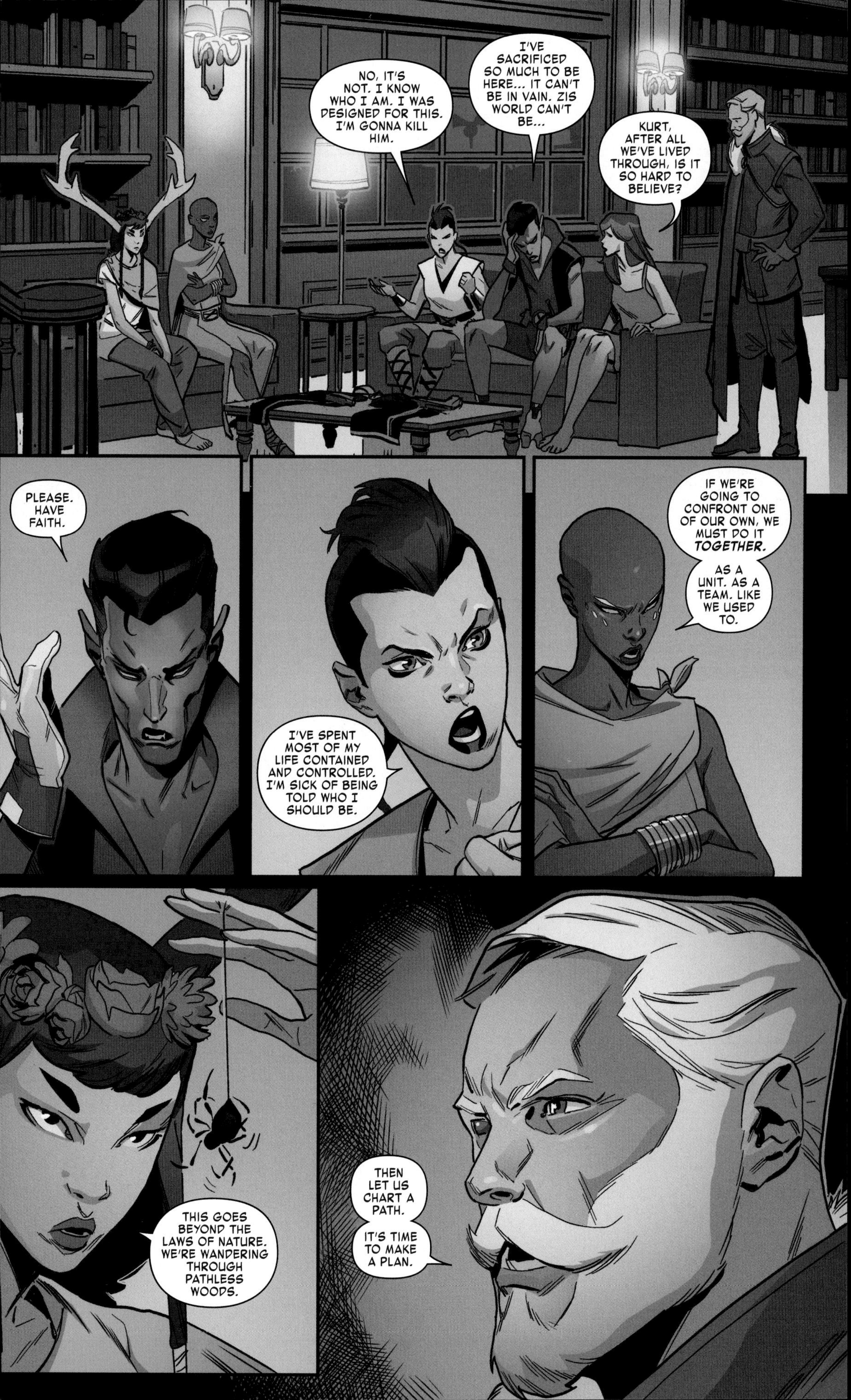
NO, IT'S NOT. I KNOW WHO I AM. I WAS DESIGNED FOR THIS. I'M GONNA KILL HIM.
I'VE SACRIFICED SO MUCH TO BE HERE... IT CAN'T BE IN VAIN. ZIS WORLD CAN'T BE...
KURT, AFTER ALL WE'VE LIVED THROUGH, IS IT SO HARD TO BELIEVE?
PLEASE. HAVE FAITH.
I'VE SPENT MOST OF MY LIFE CONTAINED AND CONTROLLED. I'M SICK OF BEING TOLD WHO I SHOULD BE.
IF WE'RE GOING TO CONFRONT ONE OF OUR OWN, WE MUST DO IT TOGETHER.
AS A UNIT. AS A TEAM. LIKE WE USED TO.
THIS GOES BEYOND THE LAWS OF NATURE. WE'RE WANDERING THROUGH PATHLESS WOODS.
THEN LET US CHART A PATH.
IT'S TIME TO MAKE A PLAN.

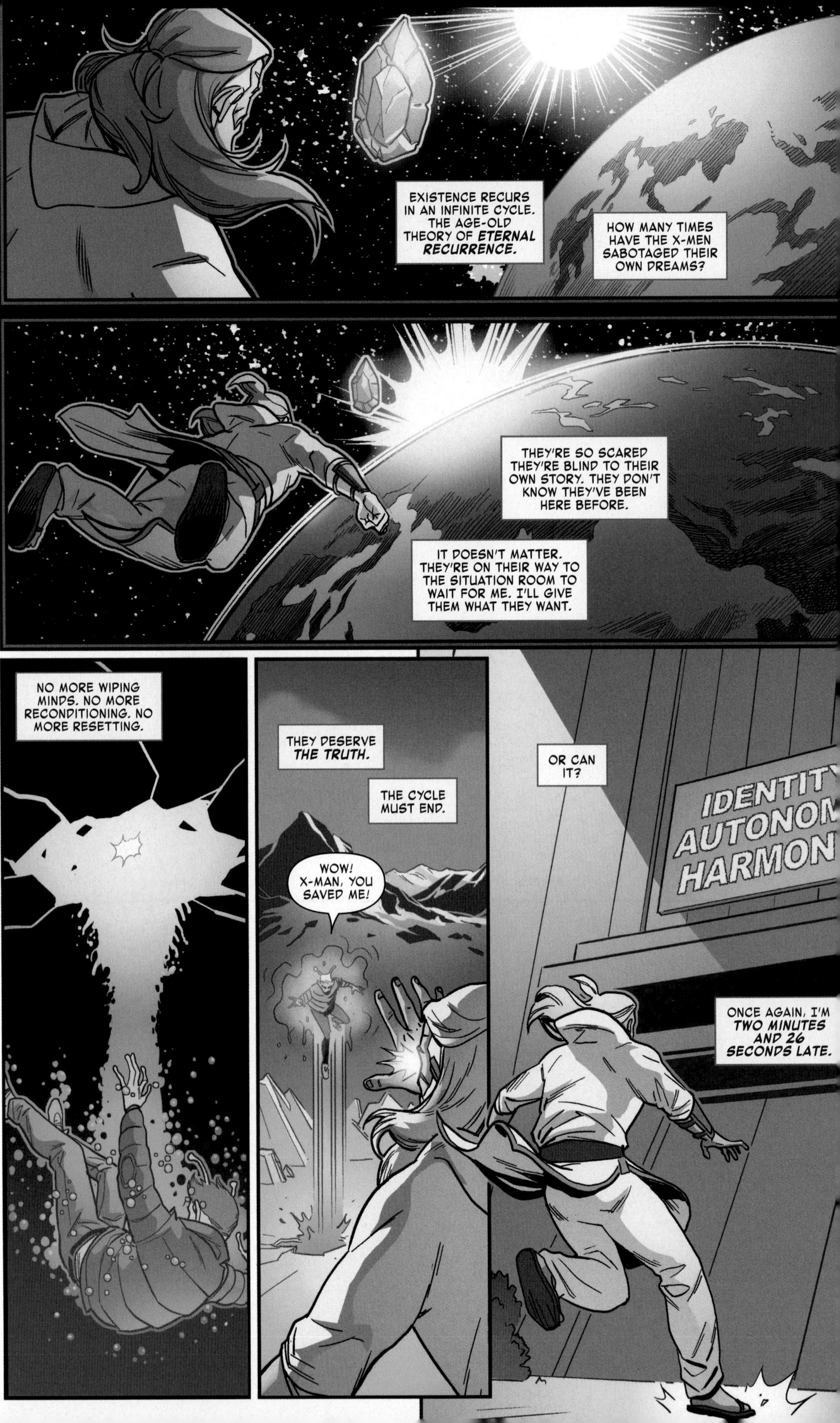
EXISTENCE RECURS IN AN INFINITE CYCLE. THE AGE-OLD THEORY OF *ETERNAL RECURRENCE.*
HOW MANY TIMES HAVE THE X-MEN SABOTAGED THEIR OWN DREAMS?
THEY'RE SO SCARED THEY'RE BLIND TO THEIR OWN STORY. THEY DON'T KNOW THEY'VE BEEN HERE BEFORE.
IT DOESN'T MATTER. THEY'RE ON THEIR WAY TO THE SITUATION ROOM TO WAIT FOR ME. I'LL GIVE THEM WHAT THEY WANT.
NO MORE WIPING MINDS. NO MORE RECONDITIONING. NO MORE RESETTING.
THEY DESERVE *THE TRUTH.*
THE CYCLE MUST END.
WOW! X-MAN, YOU SAVED ME!
OR CAN IT?
IDENTITY
AUTONOM
HARMON
ONCE AGAIN, I'M *TWO MINUTES AND 26 SECONDS* LATE.

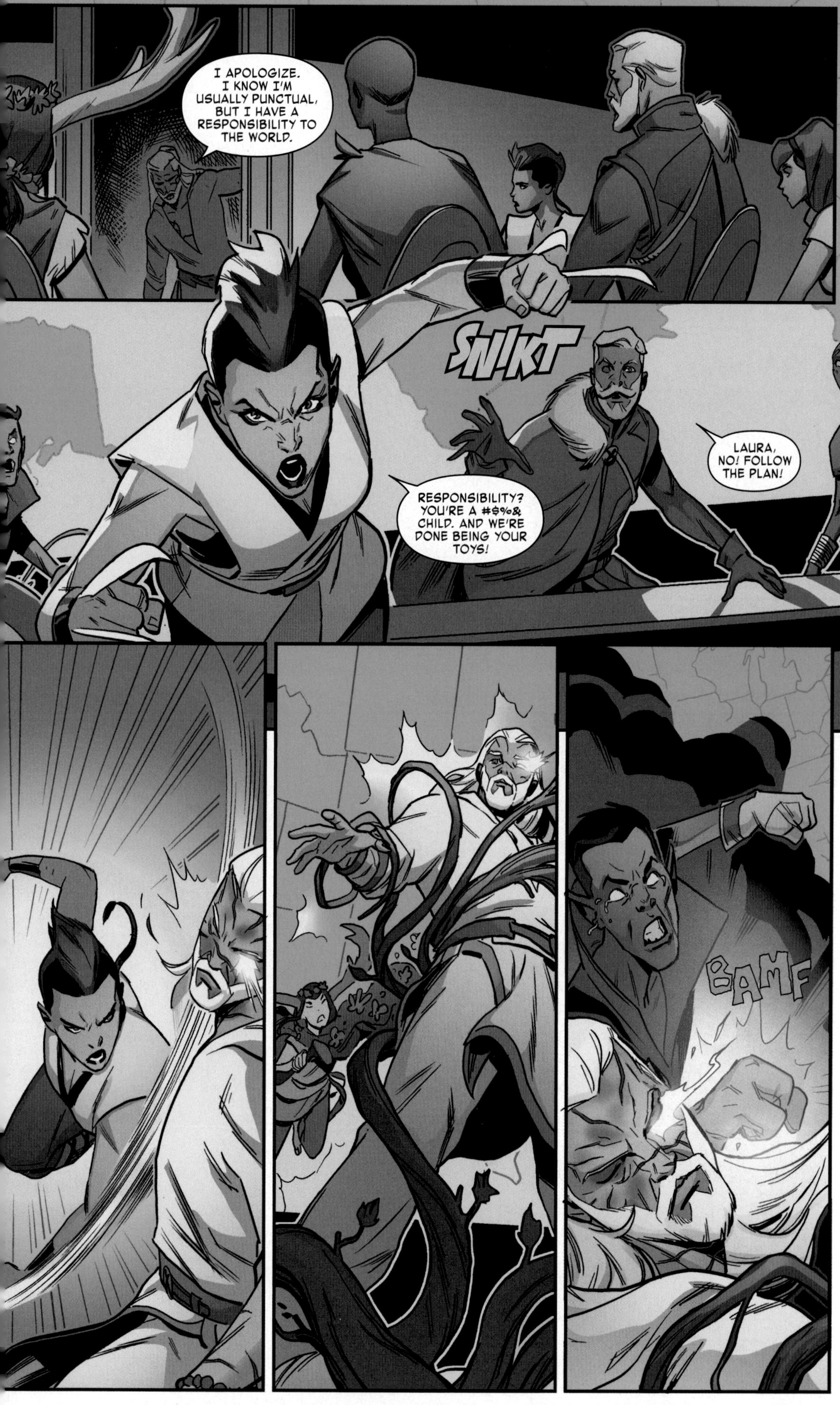
I APOLOGIZE. I KNOW I'M USUALLY PUNCTUAL, BUT I HAVE A RESPONSIBILITY TO THE WORLD.
SNIKT
RESPONSIBILITY? YOU'RE A #$%& CHILD. AND WE'RE DONE BEING YOUR TOYS!
LAURA, NO! FOLLOW THE PLAN!
BAMF

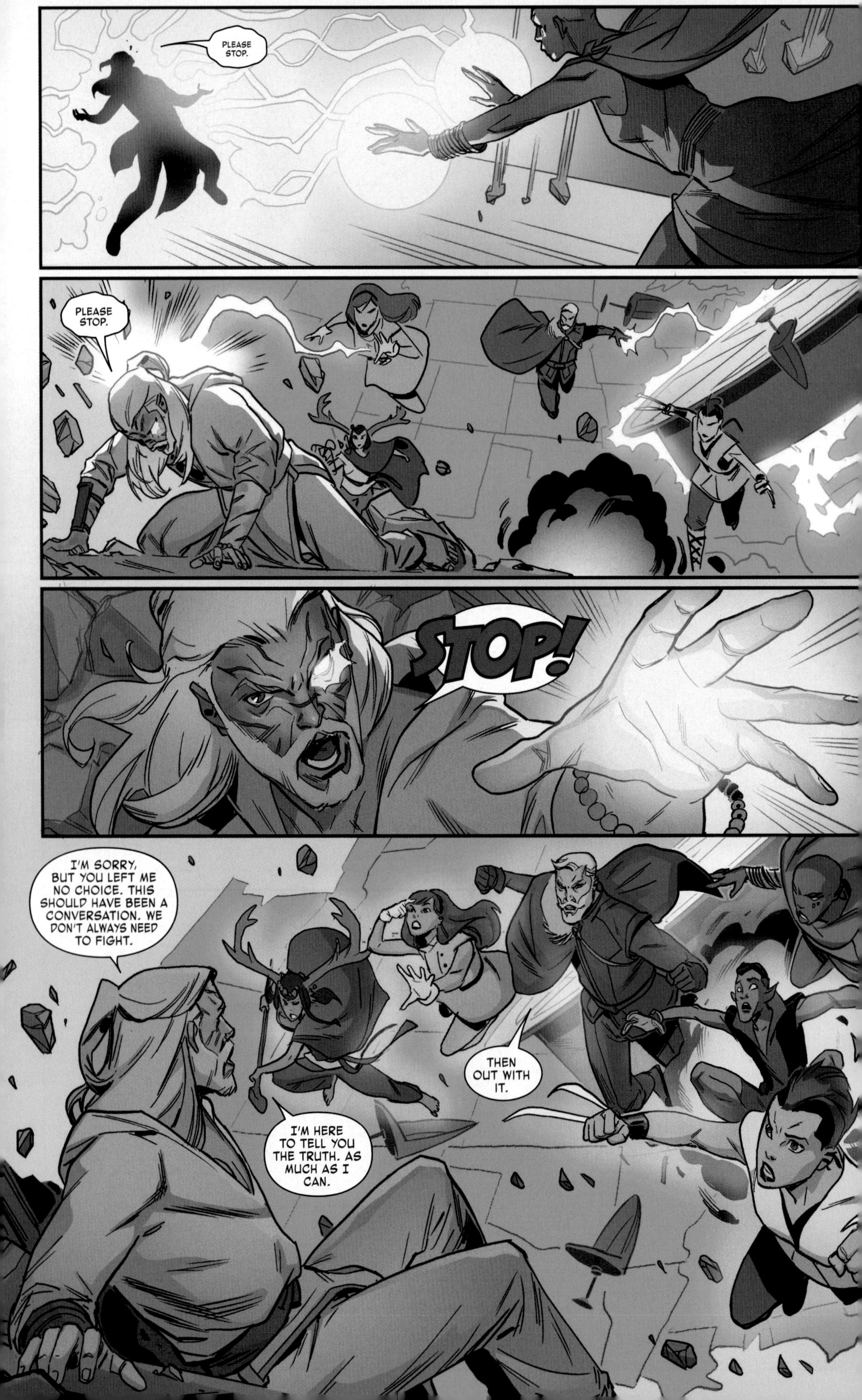
PLEASE STOP.
PLEASE STOP.
STOP!
I'M SORRY, BUT YOU LEFT ME NO CHOICE. THIS SHOULD HAVE BEEN A CONVERSATION. WE DON'T ALWAYS NEED TO FIGHT.
THEN OUT WITH IT.
I'M HERE TO TELL YOU THE TRUTH. AS MUCH AS I CAN.

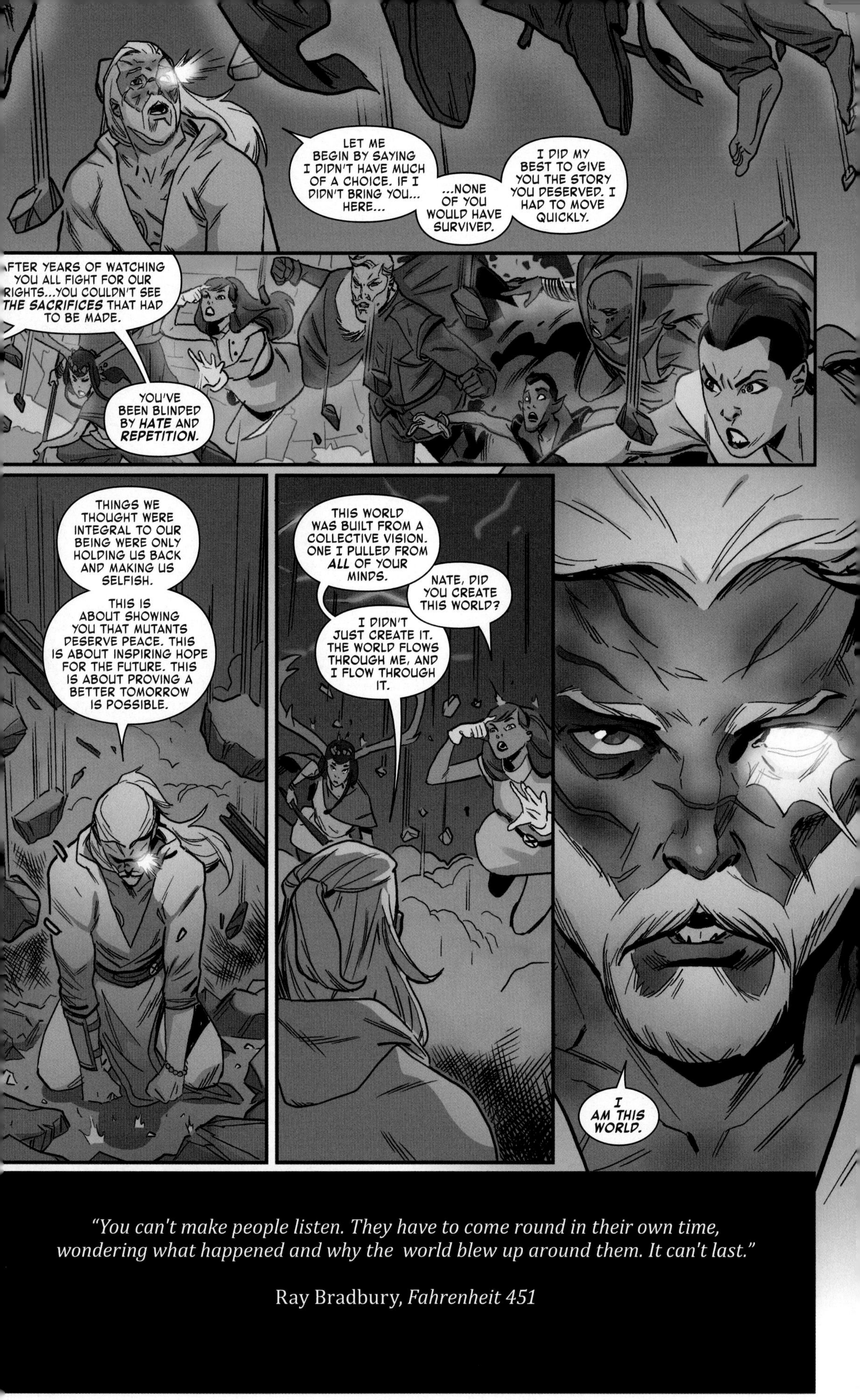

LET ME BEGIN BY SAYING I DIDN'T HAVE MUCH OF A CHOICE. IF I DIDN'T BRING YOU... HERE...
...NONE OF YOU WOULD HAVE SURVIVED.
I DID MY BEST TO GIVE YOU THE STORY YOU DESERVED. I HAD TO MOVE QUICKLY.
FTER YEARS OF WATCHING YOU ALL FIGHT FOR OUR RIGHTS...YOU COULDN'T SEE *THE SACRIFICES* THAT HAD TO BE MADE.
YOU'VE BEEN BLINDED BY ***HATE*** AND ***REPETITION.***
THINGS WE THOUGHT WERE INTEGRAL TO OUR BEING WERE ONLY HOLDING US BACK AND MAKING US SELFISH.
THIS IS ABOUT SHOWING YOU THAT MUTANTS DESERVE PEACE. THIS IS ABOUT INSPIRING HOPE FOR THE FUTURE. THIS IS ABOUT PROVING A BETTER TOMORROW IS POSSIBLE.
THIS WORLD WAS BUILT FROM A COLLECTIVE VISION. ONE I PULLED FROM ***ALL*** OF YOUR MINDS.
NATE, DID YOU CREATE THIS WORLD?
I DIDN'T JUST CREATE IT. THE WORLD FLOWS THROUGH ME, AND I FLOW THROUGH IT.
I AM THIS WORLD.

"You can't make people listen. They have to come round in their own time, wondering what happened and why the world blew up around them. It can't last."

Ray Bradbury, *Fahrenheit 451*

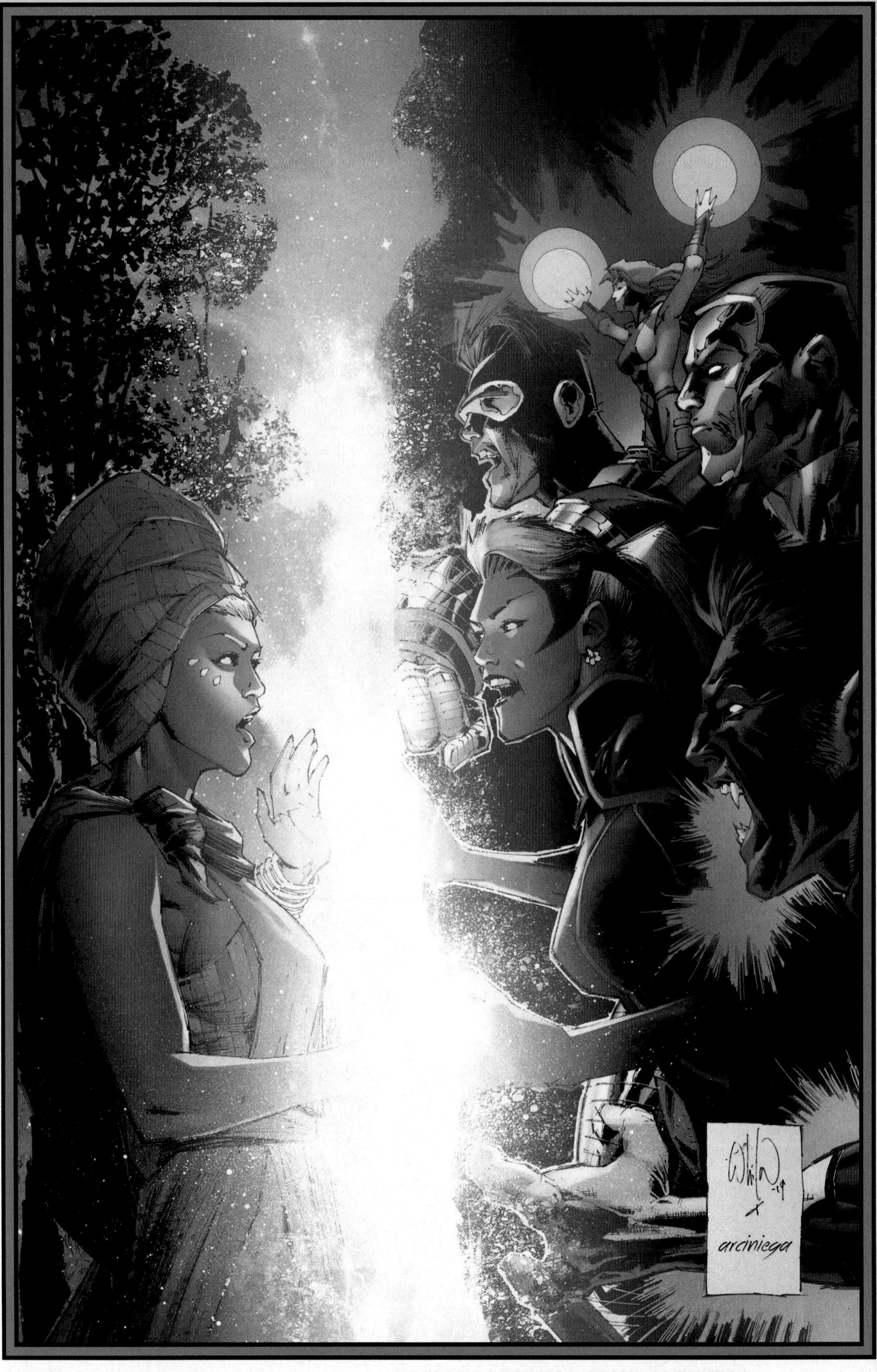
arciniega

AGE OF X-MAN OMEGA #1 VARIANT BY **WHILCE PORTACIO** & **ERICK ARCINIEGA**

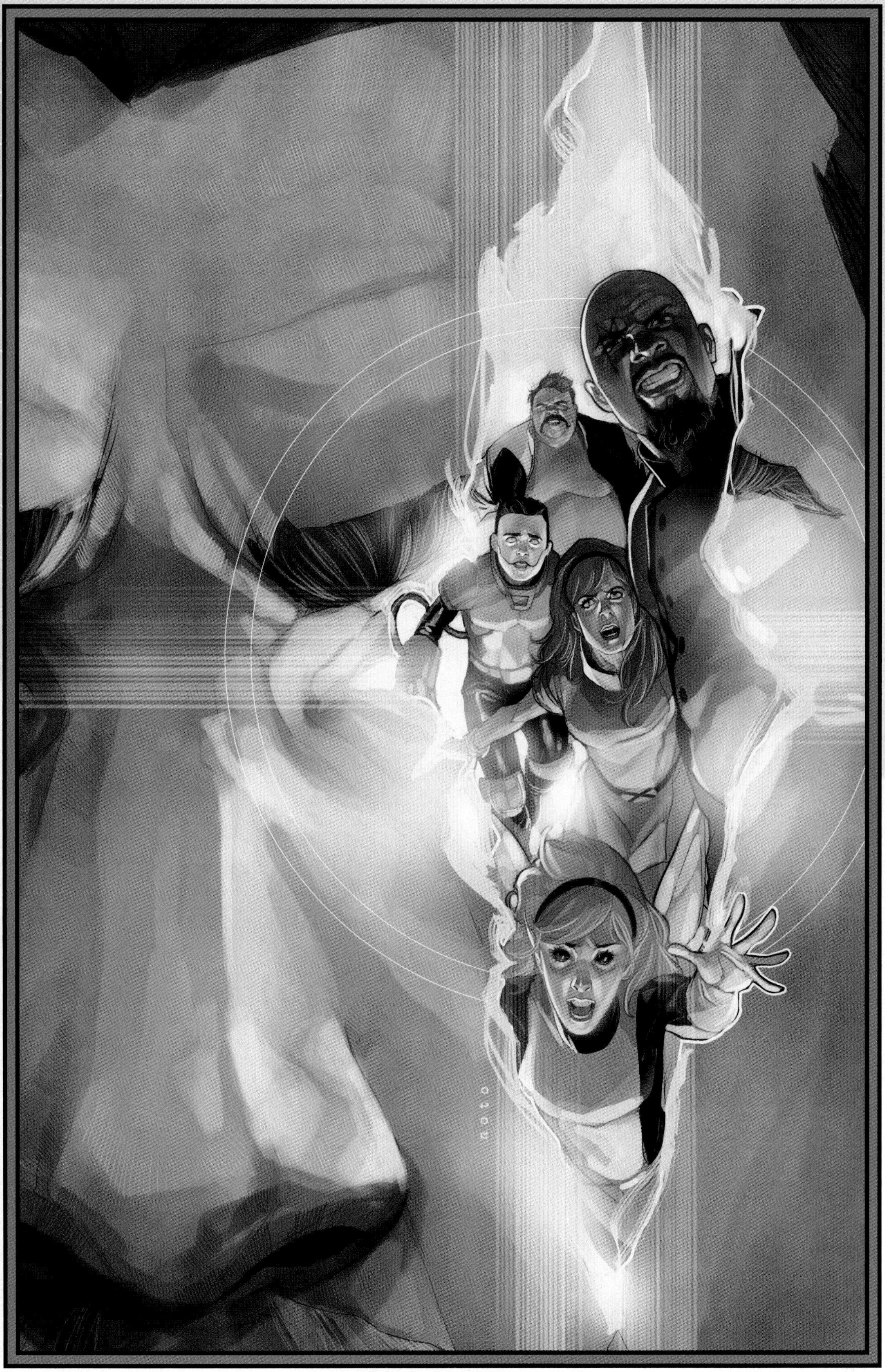

AGE OF X-MAN OMEGA #1

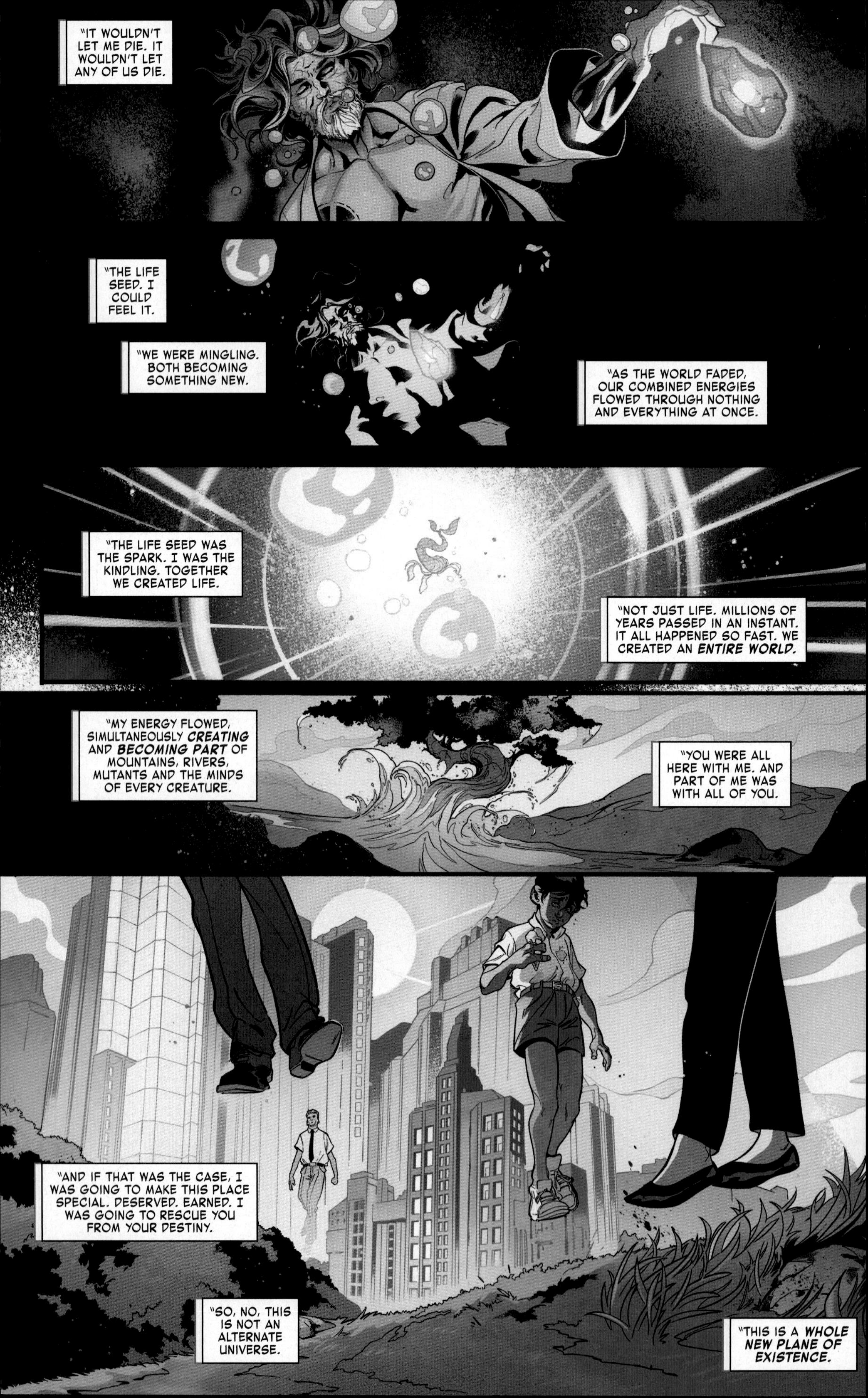
"IT WOULDN'T LET ME DIE. IT WOULDN'T LET ANY OF US DIE.
"THE LIFE SEED. I COULD FEEL IT.
"WE WERE MINGLING. BOTH BECOMING SOMETHING NEW.
"AS THE WORLD FADED, OUR COMBINED ENERGIES FLOWED THROUGH NOTHING AND EVERYTHING AT ONCE.
"THE LIFE SEED WAS THE SPARK. I WAS THE KINDLING. TOGETHER WE CREATED LIFE.
"NOT JUST LIFE. MILLIONS OF YEARS PASSED IN AN INSTANT. IT ALL HAPPENED SO FAST. WE CREATED AN ENTIRE WORLD.
"MY ENERGY FLOWED, SIMULTANEOUSLY CREATING AND BECOMING PART OF MOUNTAINS, RIVERS, MUTANTS AND THE MINDS OF EVERY CREATURE.
"YOU WERE ALL HERE WITH ME. AND PART OF ME WAS WITH ALL OF YOU.
"AND IF THAT WAS THE CASE, I WAS GOING TO MAKE THIS PLACE SPECIAL. DESERVED. EARNED. I WAS GOING TO RESCUE YOU FROM YOUR DESTINY.
"SO, NO, THIS IS NOT AN ALTERNATE UNIVERSE.
"THIS IS A WHOLE NEW PLANE OF EXISTENCE.

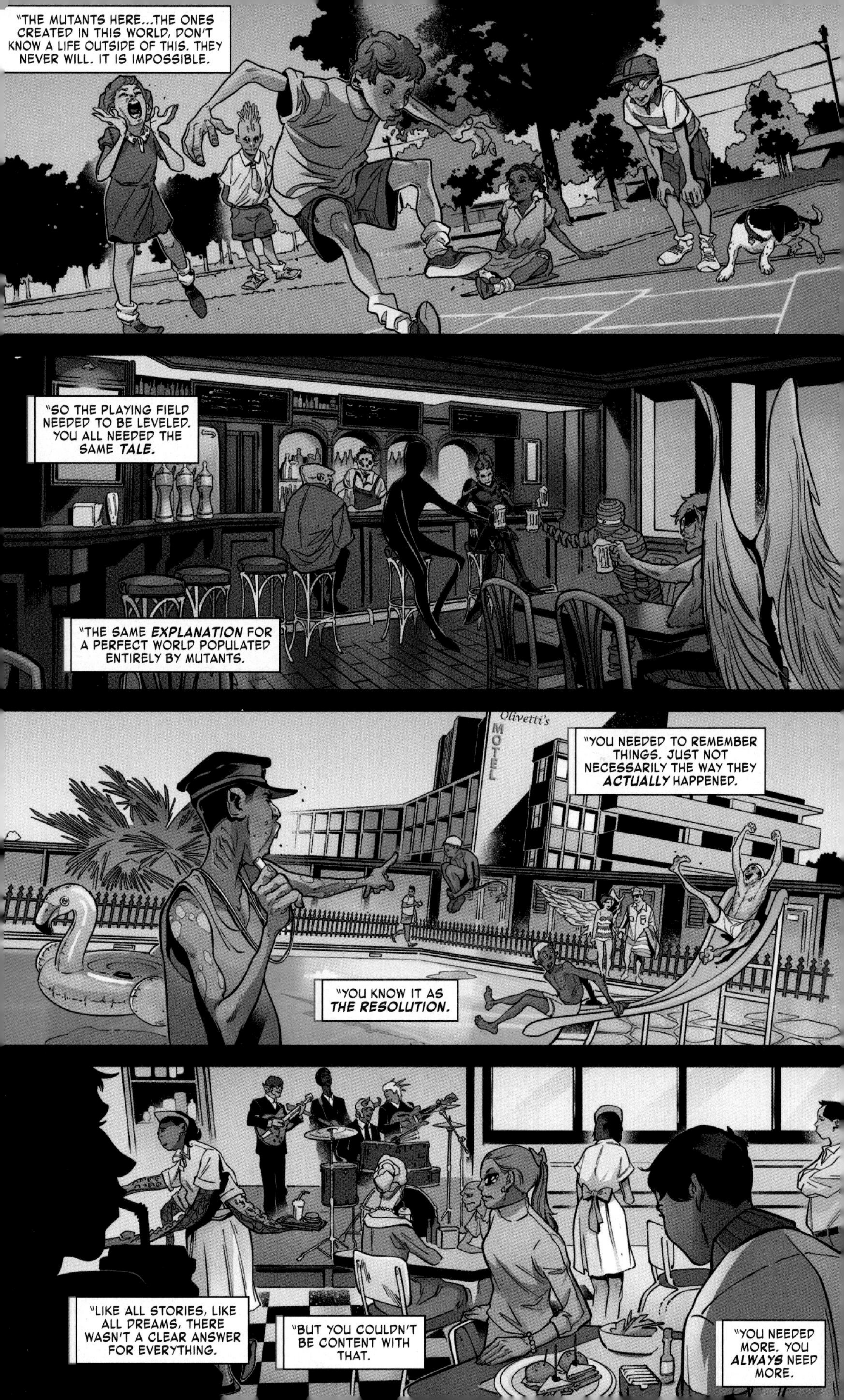
"THE MUTANTS HERE...THE ONES CREATED IN THIS WORLD, DON'T KNOW A LIFE OUTSIDE OF THIS. THEY NEVER WILL. IT IS IMPOSSIBLE.
"SO THE PLAYING FIELD NEEDED TO BE LEVELED. YOU ALL NEEDED THE SAME *TALE.*
"THE SAME *EXPLANATION* FOR A PERFECT WORLD POPULATED ENTIRELY BY MUTANTS.
Olivetti's MOTEL
"YOU NEEDED TO REMEMBER THINGS. JUST NOT NECESSARILY THE WAY THEY *ACTUALLY* HAPPENED.
"YOU KNOW IT AS *THE RESOLUTION.*
"LIKE ALL STORIES, LIKE ALL DREAMS, THERE WASN'T A CLEAR ANSWER FOR EVERYTHING.
"BUT YOU COULDN'T BE CONTENT WITH THAT.
"YOU NEEDED MORE. YOU *ALWAYS* NEED MORE.

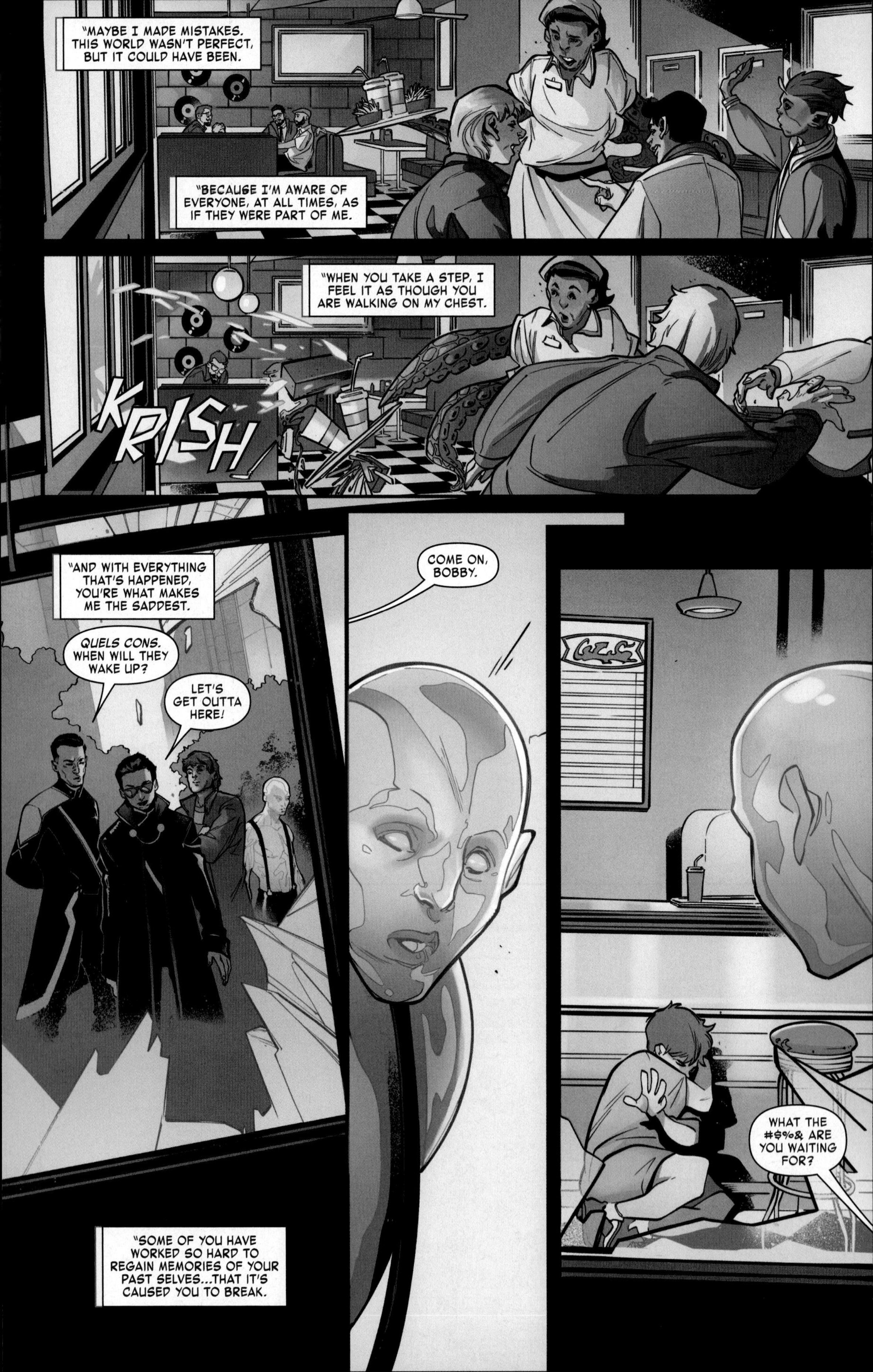
"MAYBE I MADE MISTAKES. THIS WORLD WASN'T PERFECT, BUT IT COULD HAVE BEEN.
"BECAUSE I'M AWARE OF EVERYONE, AT ALL TIMES, AS IF THEY WERE PART OF ME.
"WHEN YOU TAKE A STEP, I FEEL IT AS THOUGH YOU ARE WALKING ON MY CHEST.
KRISH
"AND WITH EVERYTHING THAT'S HAPPENED, YOU'RE WHAT MAKES ME THE SADDEST.
QUELS CONS. WHEN WILL THEY WAKE UP?
LET'S GET OUTTA HERE!
COME ON, BOBBY.
WHAT THE #$%& ARE YOU WAITING FOR?
"SOME OF YOU HAVE WORKED SO HARD TO REGAIN MEMORIES OF YOUR PAST SELVES...THAT IT'S CAUSED YOU TO BREAK.

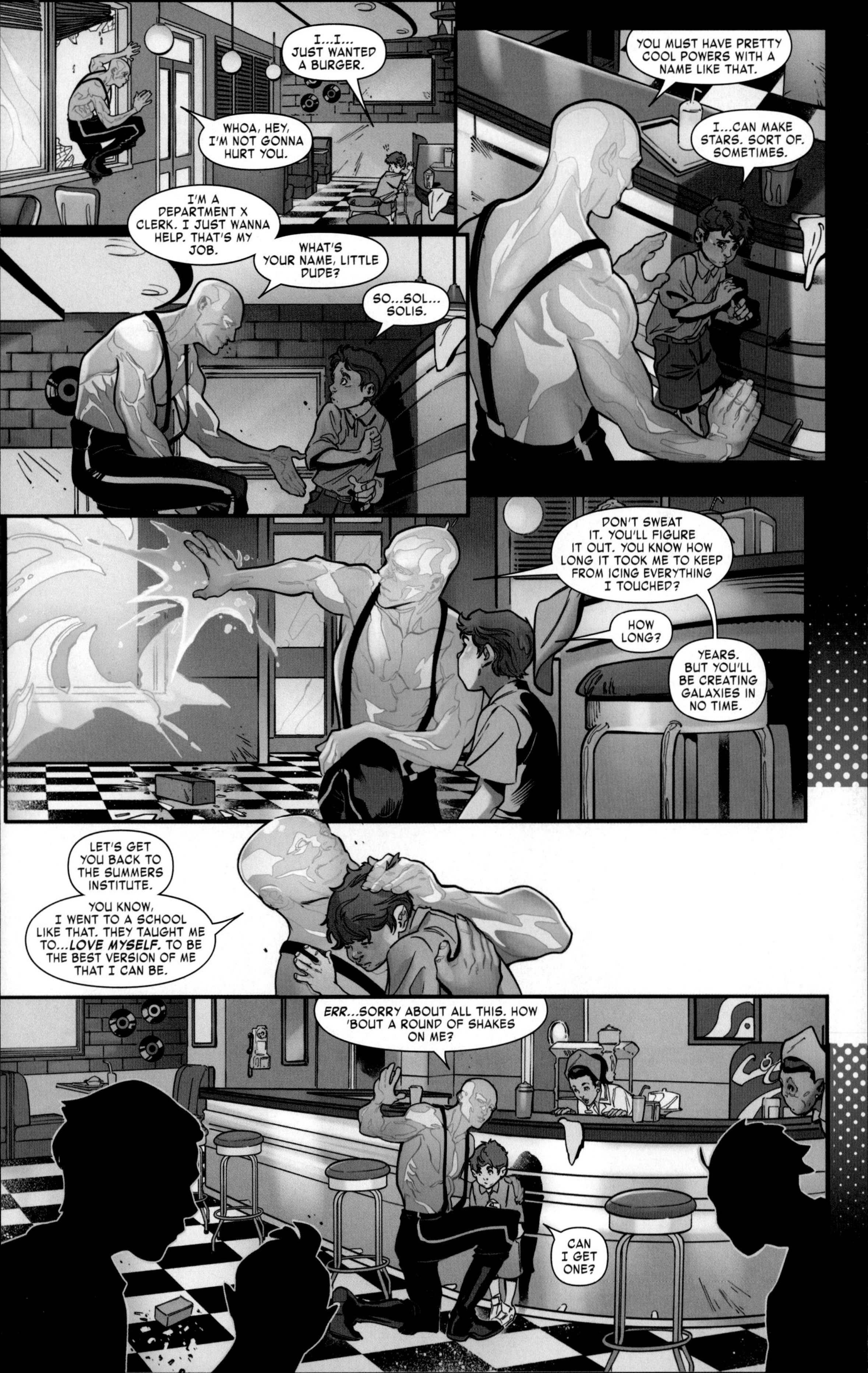
I...I... JUST WANTED A BURGER.
WHOA, HEY, I'M NOT GONNA HURT YOU.
YOU MUST HAVE PRETTY COOL POWERS WITH A NAME LIKE THAT.
I...CAN MAKE STARS. SORT OF. SOMETIMES.
I'M A DEPARTMENT X CLERK. I JUST WANNA HELP. THAT'S MY JOB.
WHAT'S YOUR NAME, LITTLE DUDE?
SO...SOL... SOLIS.
DON'T SWEAT IT. YOU'LL FIGURE IT OUT. YOU KNOW HOW LONG IT TOOK ME TO KEEP FROM ICING EVERYTHING I TOUCHED?
HOW LONG?
YEARS. BUT YOU'LL BE CREATING GALAXIES IN NO TIME.
LET'S GET YOU BACK TO THE SUMMERS INSTITUTE.
YOU KNOW, I WENT TO A SCHOOL LIKE THAT. THEY TAUGHT ME TO...***LOVE MYSELF.*** TO BE THE BEST VERSION OF ME THAT I CAN BE.
ERR...SORRY ABOUT ALL THIS. HOW 'BOUT A ROUND OF SHAKES ON ME?
CAN I GET ONE?

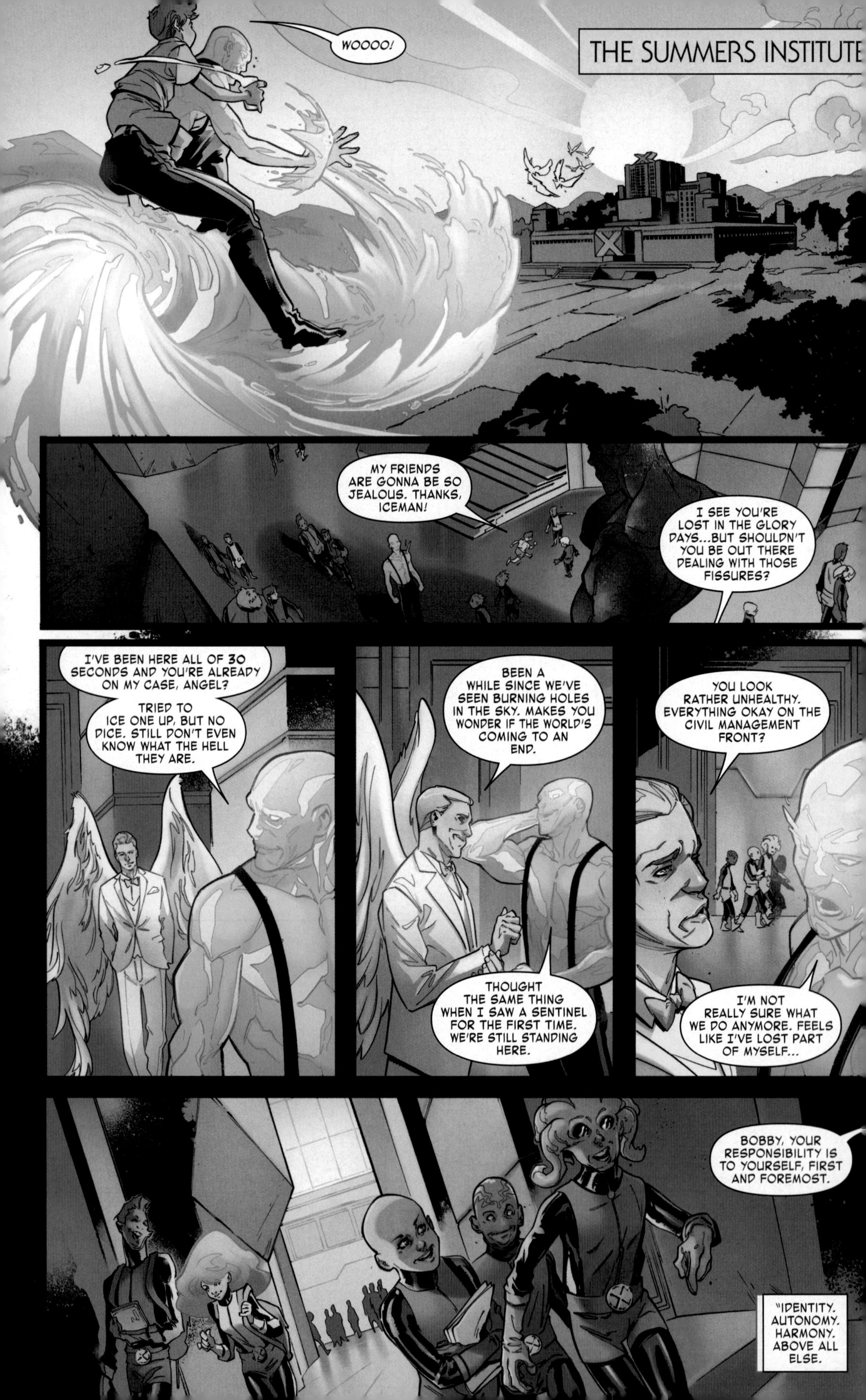
WOOOO!
THE SUMMERS INSTITUTE
MY FRIENDS ARE GONNA BE SO JEALOUS. THANKS, ICEMAN!
I SEE YOU'RE LOST IN THE GLORY DAYS...BUT SHOULDN'T YOU BE OUT THERE DEALING WITH THOSE FISSURES?
I'VE BEEN HERE ALL OF 30 SECONDS AND YOU'RE ALREADY ON MY CASE, ANGEL?
TRIED TO ICE ONE UP, BUT NO DICE. STILL DON'T EVEN KNOW WHAT THE HELL THEY ARE.
BEEN A WHILE SINCE WE'VE SEEN BURNING HOLES IN THE SKY. MAKES YOU WONDER IF THE WORLD'S COMING TO AN END.
THOUGHT THE SAME THING WHEN I SAW A SENTINEL FOR THE FIRST TIME. WE'RE STILL STANDING HERE.
YOU LOOK RATHER UNHEALTHY. EVERYTHING OKAY ON THE CIVIL MANAGEMENT FRONT?
I'M NOT REALLY SURE WHAT WE DO ANYMORE. FEELS LIKE I'VE LOST PART OF MYSELF...
BOBBY, YOUR RESPONSIBILITY IS TO YOURSELF, FIRST AND FOREMOST.
"IDENTITY. AUTONOMY. HARMONY. ABOVE ALL ELSE.

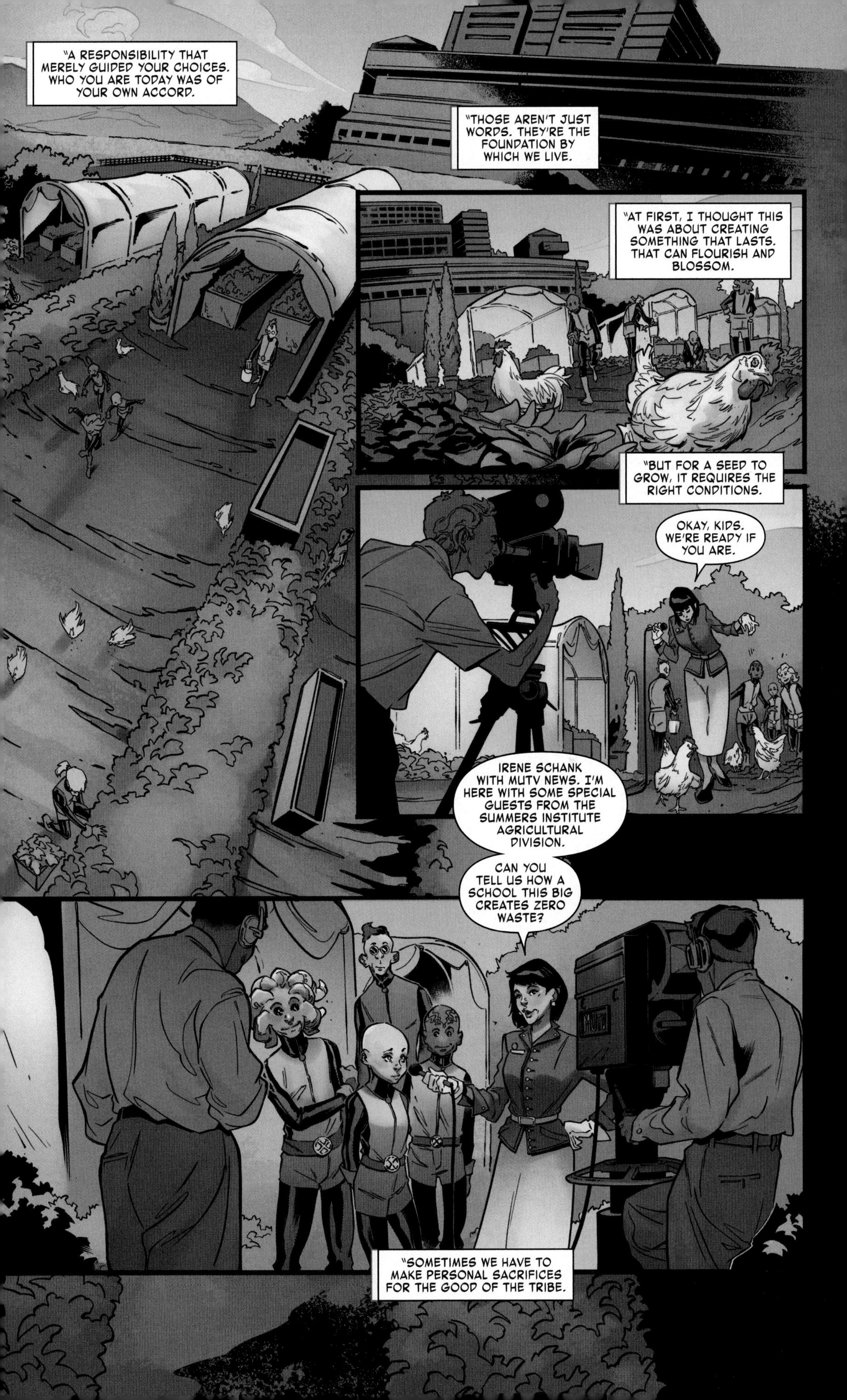
"A RESPONSIBILITY THAT MERELY GUIDED YOUR CHOICES. WHO YOU ARE TODAY WAS OF YOUR OWN ACCORD.
"THOSE AREN'T JUST WORDS. THEY'RE THE FOUNDATION BY WHICH WE LIVE.
"AT FIRST, I THOUGHT THIS WAS ABOUT CREATING SOMETHING THAT LASTS. THAT CAN FLOURISH AND BLOSSOM.
"BUT FOR A SEED TO GROW, IT REQUIRES THE RIGHT CONDITIONS.
OKAY, KIDS. WE'RE READY IF YOU ARE.
IRENE SCHANK WITH MUTV NEWS. I'M HERE WITH SOME SPECIAL GUESTS FROM THE SUMMERS INSTITUTE AGRICULTURAL DIVISION.
CAN YOU TELL US HOW A SCHOOL THIS BIG CREATES ZERO WASTE?
"SOMETIMES WE HAVE TO MAKE PERSONAL SACRIFICES FOR THE GOOD OF THE TRIBE.

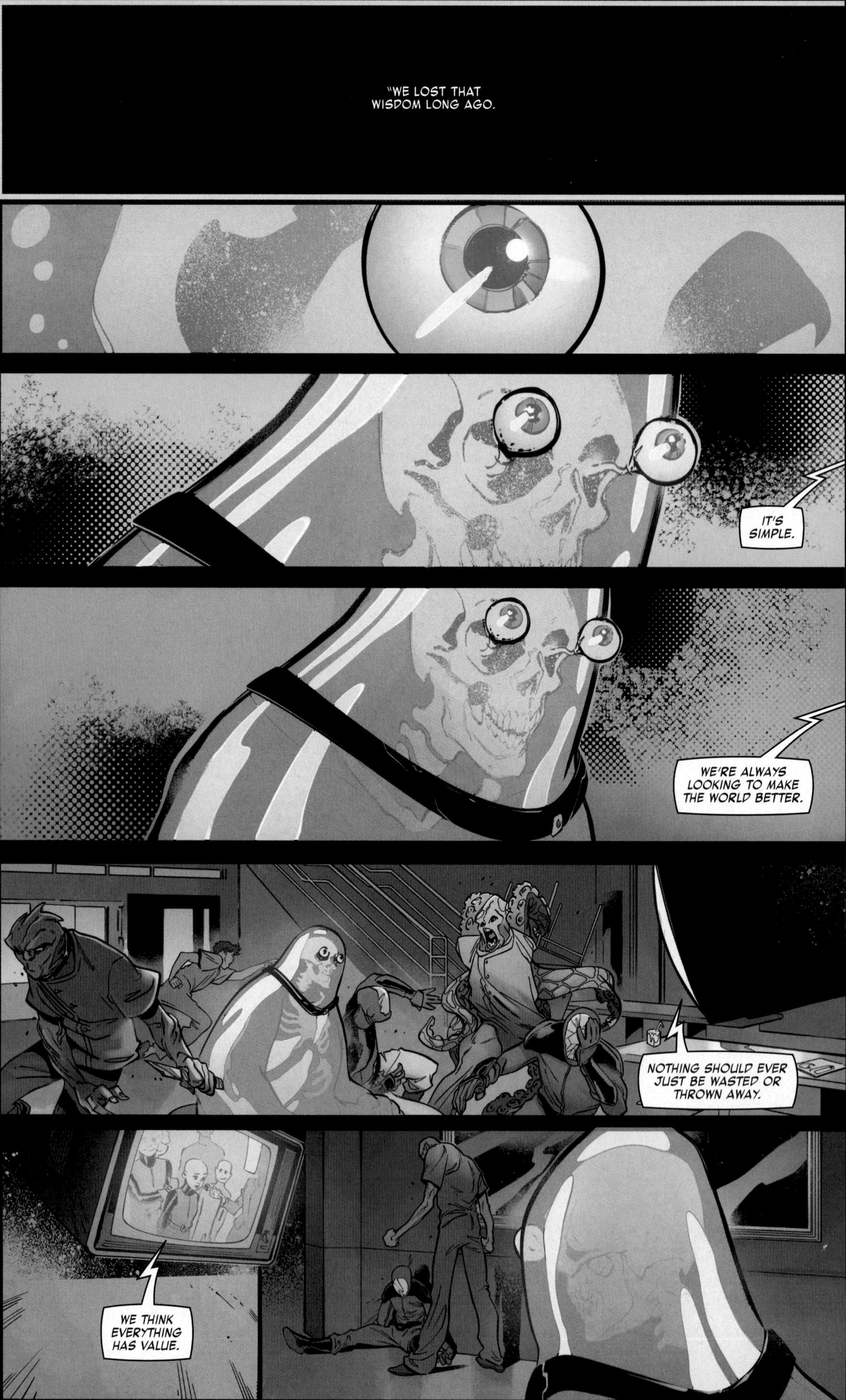
"WE LOST THAT WISDOM LONG AGO.
IT'S SIMPLE.
WE'RE ALWAYS LOOKING TO MAKE THE WORLD BETTER.
NOTHING SHOULD EVER JUST BE WASTED OR THROWN AWAY.
WE THINK EVERYTHING HAS VALUE.

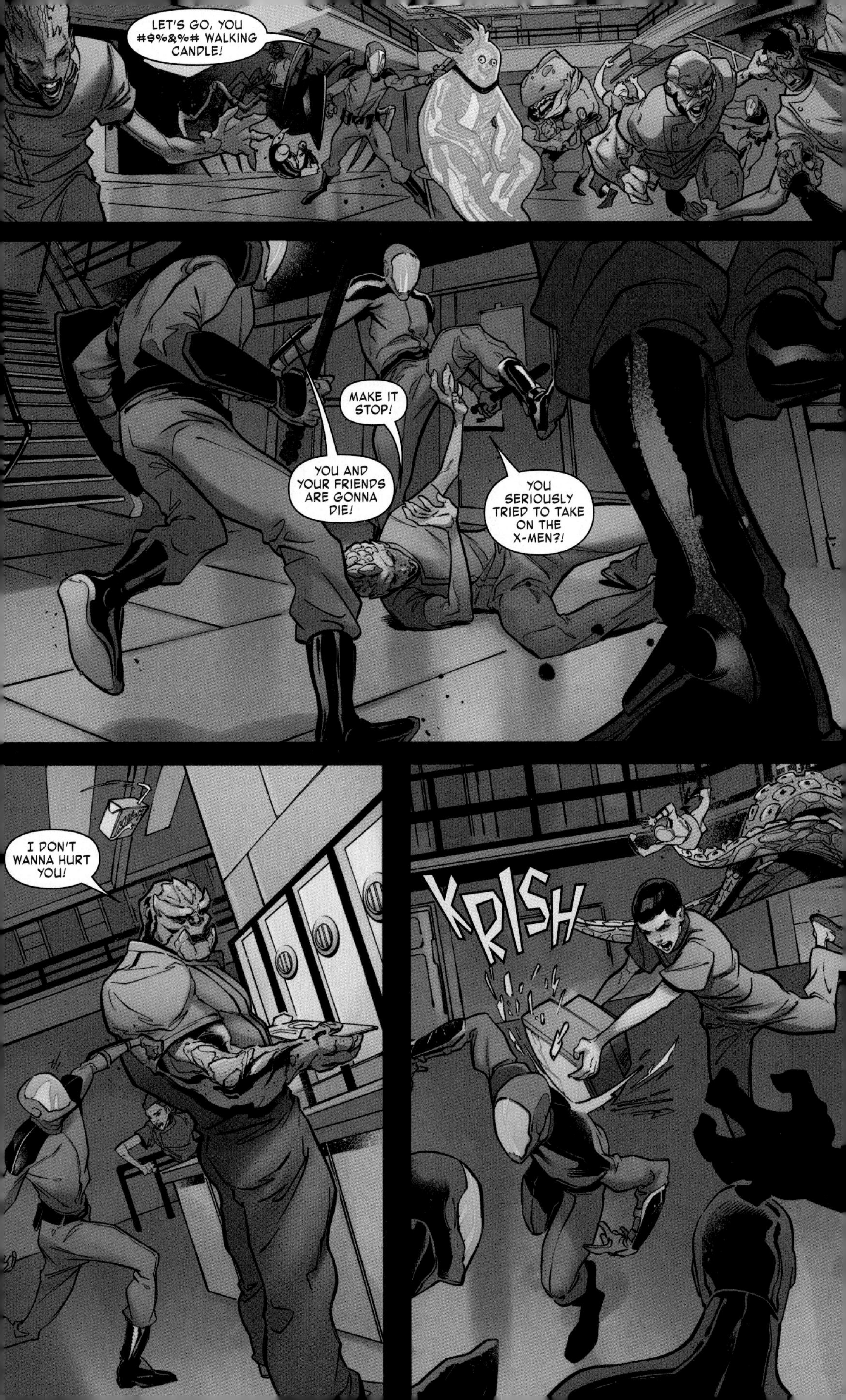
LET'S GO, YOU #$%&%# WALKING CANDLE!
MAKE IT STOP!
YOU AND YOUR FRIENDS ARE GONNA DIE!
YOU SERIOUSLY TRIED TO TAKE ON THE X-MEN?!
I DON'T WANNA HURT YOU!
KRISH

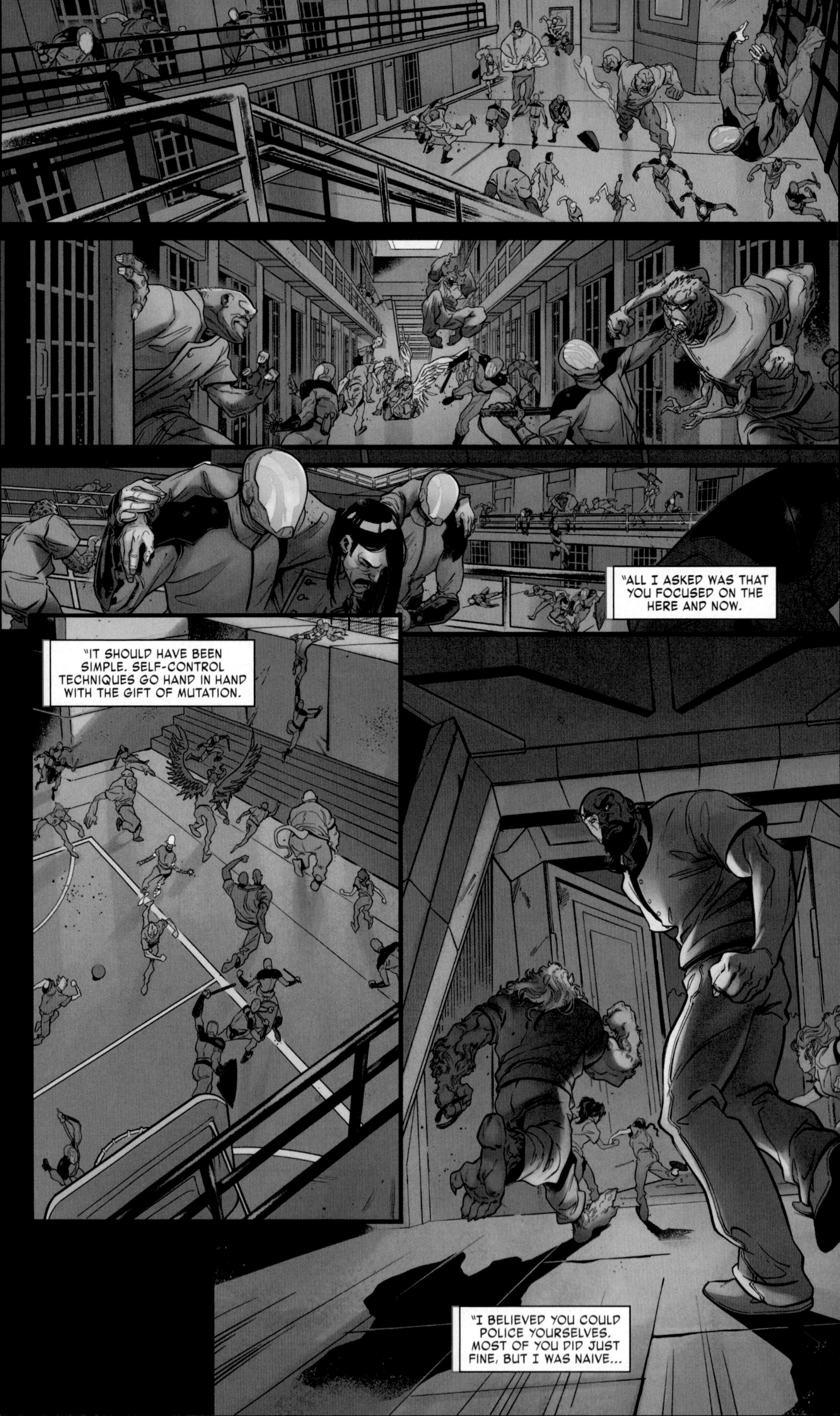
"ALL I ASKED WAS THAT YOU FOCUSED ON THE HERE AND NOW.
"IT SHOULD HAVE BEEN SIMPLE. SELF-CONTROL TECHNIQUES GO HAND IN HAND WITH THE GIFT OF MUTATION.
"I BELIEVED YOU COULD POLICE YOURSELVES. MOST OF YOU DID JUST FINE, BUT I WAS NAIVE...

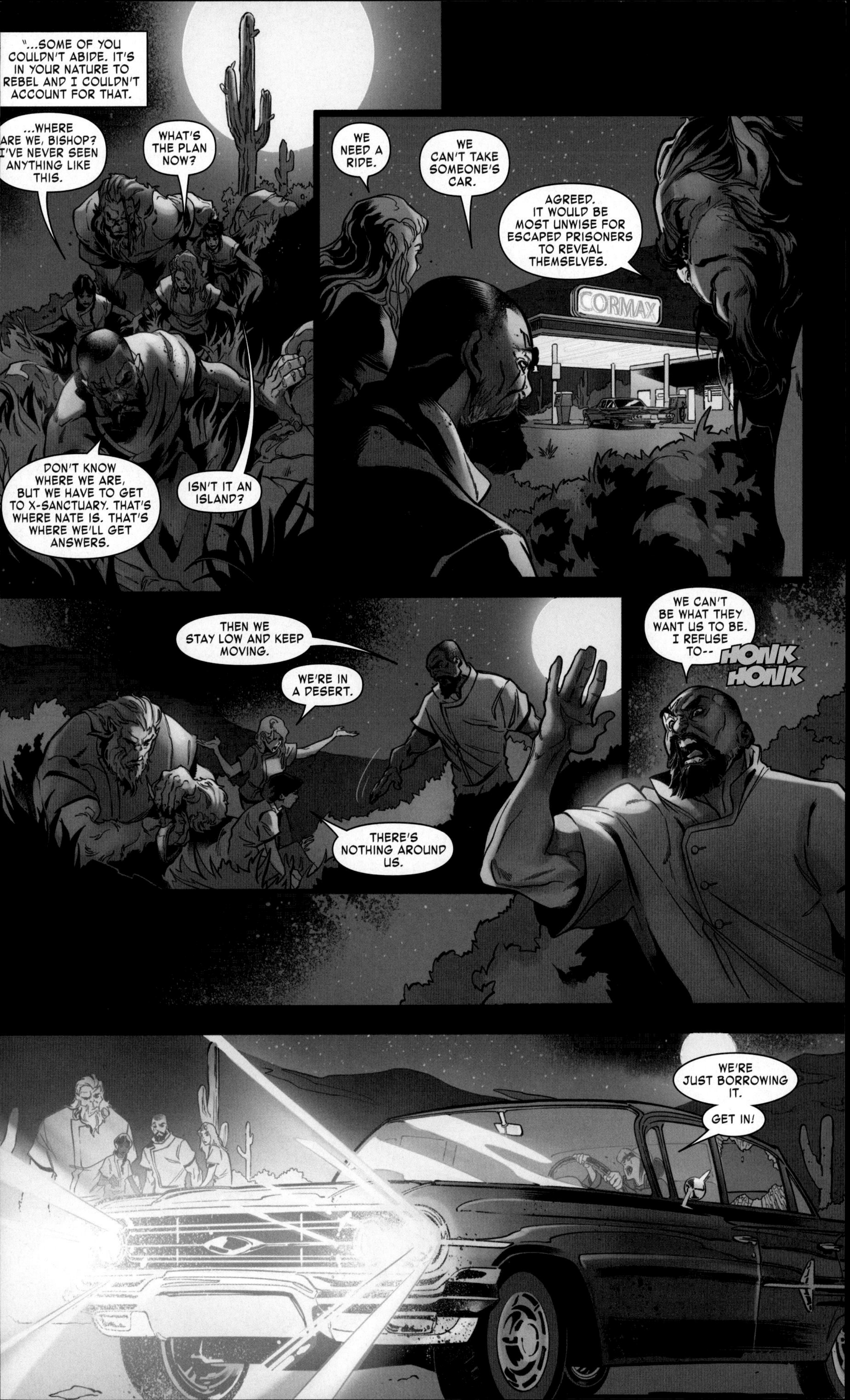
"...SOME OF YOU COULDN'T ABIDE. IT'S IN YOUR NATURE TO REBEL AND I COULDN'T ACCOUNT FOR THAT.
...WHERE ARE WE, BISHOP? I'VE NEVER SEEN ANYTHING LIKE THIS.
WHAT'S THE PLAN NOW?
DON'T KNOW WHERE WE ARE, BUT WE HAVE TO GET TO X-SANCTUARY. THAT'S WHERE NATE IS. THAT'S WHERE WE'LL GET ANSWERS.
ISN'T IT AN ISLAND?
WE NEED A RIDE.
WE CAN'T TAKE SOMEONE'S CAR.
AGREED. IT WOULD BE MOST UNWISE FOR ESCAPED PRISONERS TO REVEAL THEMSELVES.
CORMAX
THEN WE STAY LOW AND KEEP MOVING.
WE'RE IN A DESERT.
THERE'S NOTHING AROUND US.
WE CAN'T BE WHAT THEY WANT US TO BE. I REFUSE TO--
HONK HONK
WE'RE JUST BORROWING IT.
GET IN!

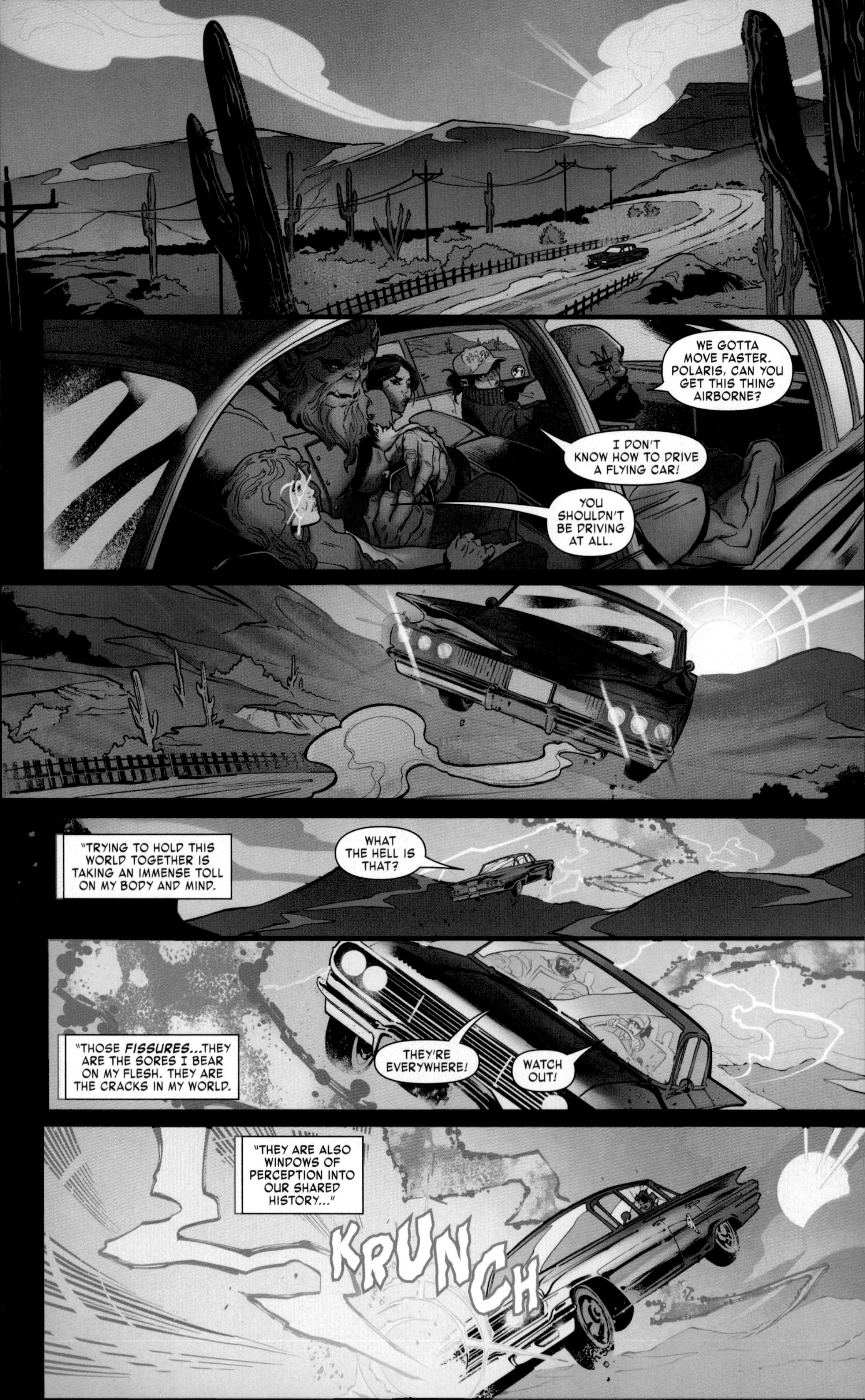
WE GOTTA MOVE FASTER. POLARIS, CAN YOU GET THIS THING AIRBORNE?
I DON'T KNOW HOW TO DRIVE A FLYING CAR!
YOU SHOULDN'T BE DRIVING AT ALL.
"TRYING TO HOLD THIS WORLD TOGETHER IS TAKING AN IMMENSE TOLL ON MY BODY AND MIND.
WHAT THE HELL IS THAT?
"THOSE *FISSURES*...THEY ARE THE SORES I BEAR ON MY FLESH. THEY ARE THE CRACKS IN MY WORLD.
THEY'RE EVERYWHERE!
WATCH OUT!
"THEY ARE ALSO WINDOWS OF PERCEPTION INTO OUR SHARED HISTORY..."
KRUNCH

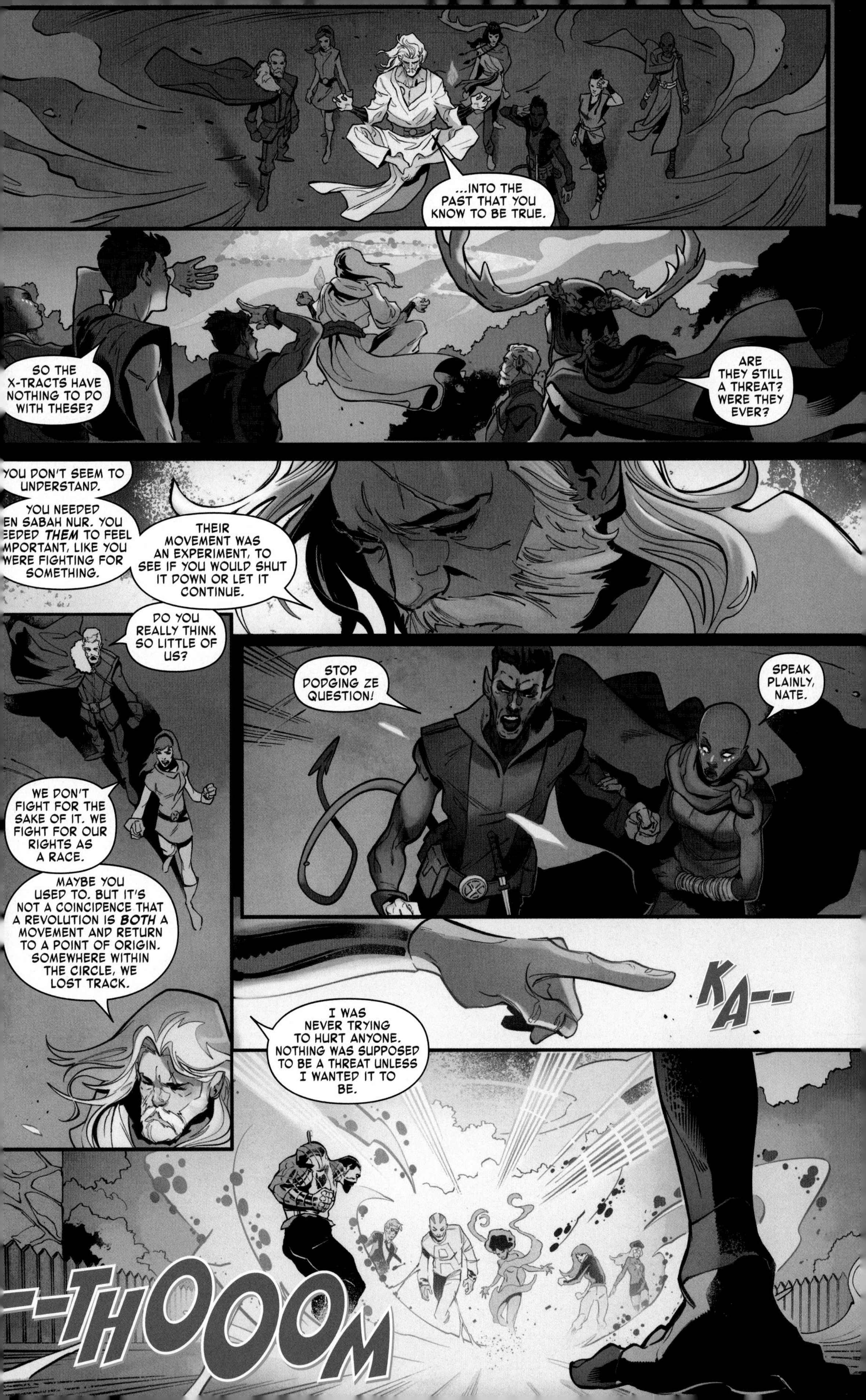

...INTO THE PAST THAT YOU KNOW TO BE TRUE.
SO THE X-TRACTS HAVE NOTHING TO DO WITH THESE?
ARE THEY STILL A THREAT? WERE THEY EVER?
YOU DON'T SEEM TO UNDERSTAND.
YOU NEEDED EN SABAH NUR. YOU EEDED THEM TO FEEL MPORTANT, LIKE YOU WERE FIGHTING FOR SOMETHING.
THEIR MOVEMENT WAS AN EXPERIMENT, TO SEE IF YOU WOULD SHUT IT DOWN OR LET IT CONTINUE.
DO YOU REALLY THINK SO LITTLE OF US?
STOP DODGING ZE QUESTION!
SPEAK PLAINLY, NATE.
WE DON'T FIGHT FOR THE SAKE OF IT. WE FIGHT FOR OUR RIGHTS AS A RACE.
MAYBE YOU USED TO. BUT IT'S NOT A COINCIDENCE THAT A REVOLUTION IS BOTH A MOVEMENT AND RETURN TO A POINT OF ORIGIN. SOMEWHERE WITHIN THE CIRCLE, WE LOST TRACK.
I WAS NEVER TRYING TO HURT ANYONE. NOTHING WAS SUPPOSED TO BE A THREAT UNLESS I WANTED IT TO BE.
KA--
--THOOOOM

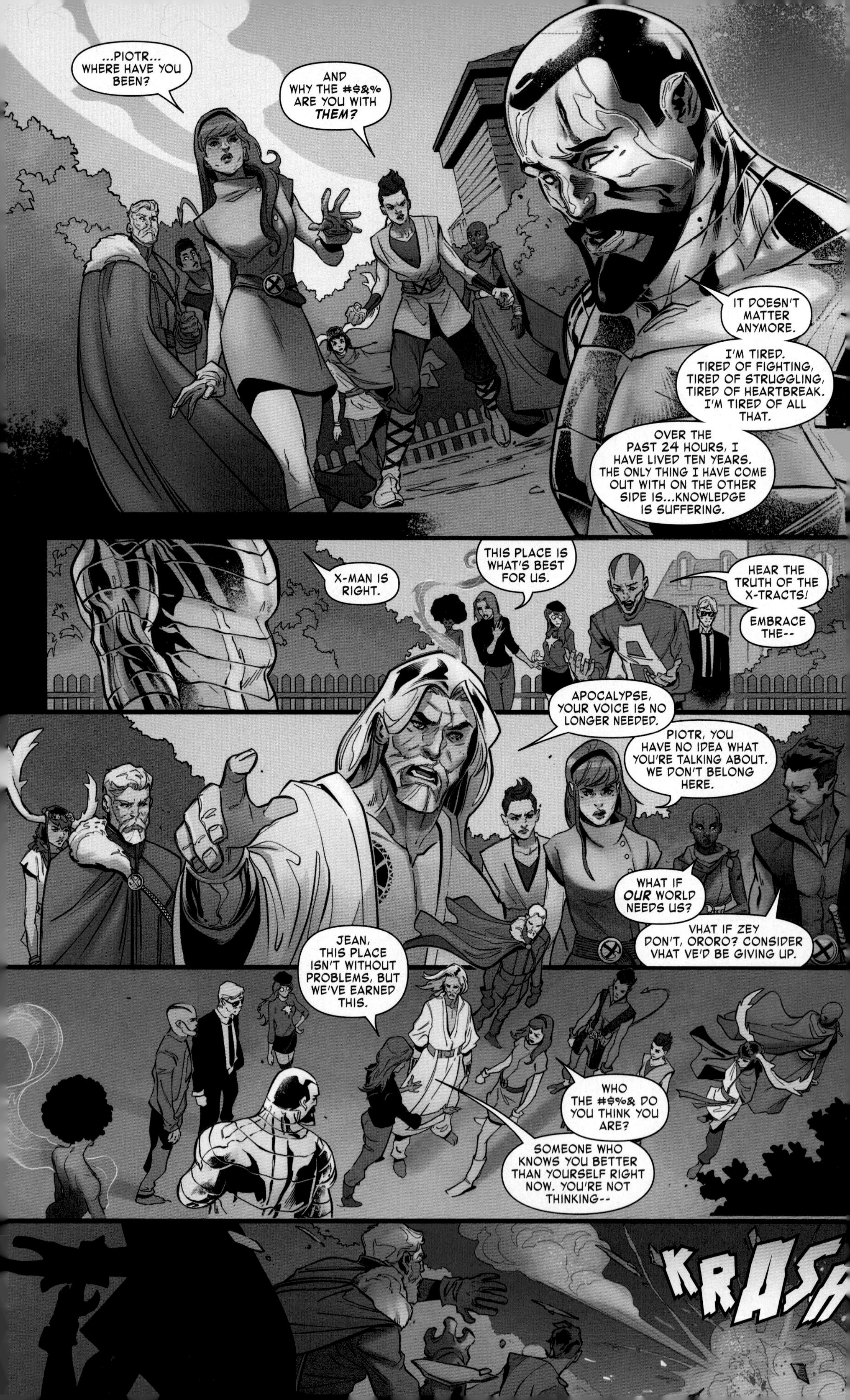
...PIOTR... WHERE HAVE YOU BEEN?
AND WHY THE #$&% ARE YOU WITH *THEM?*
IT DOESN'T MATTER ANYMORE.
I'M TIRED. TIRED OF FIGHTING, TIRED OF STRUGGLING, TIRED OF HEARTBREAK. I'M TIRED OF ALL THAT.
OVER THE PAST 24 HOURS, I HAVE LIVED TEN YEARS. THE ONLY THING I HAVE COME OUT WITH ON THE OTHER SIDE IS...KNOWLEDGE IS SUFFERING.
X-MAN IS RIGHT.
THIS PLACE IS WHAT'S BEST FOR US.
HEAR THE TRUTH OF THE X-TRACTS!
EMBRACE THE--
APOCALYPSE, YOUR VOICE IS NO LONGER NEEDED.
PIOTR, YOU HAVE NO IDEA WHAT YOU'RE TALKING ABOUT. WE DON'T BELONG HERE.
WHAT IF *OUR* WORLD NEEDS US?
VHAT IF ZEY DON'T, ORORO? CONSIDER VHAT VE'D BE GIVING UP.
JEAN, THIS PLACE ISN'T WITHOUT PROBLEMS, BUT WE'VE EARNED THIS.
WHO THE #$%& DO YOU THINK YOU ARE?
SOMEONE WHO KNOWS YOU BETTER THAN YOURSELF RIGHT NOW. YOU'RE NOT THINKING--
KRASH

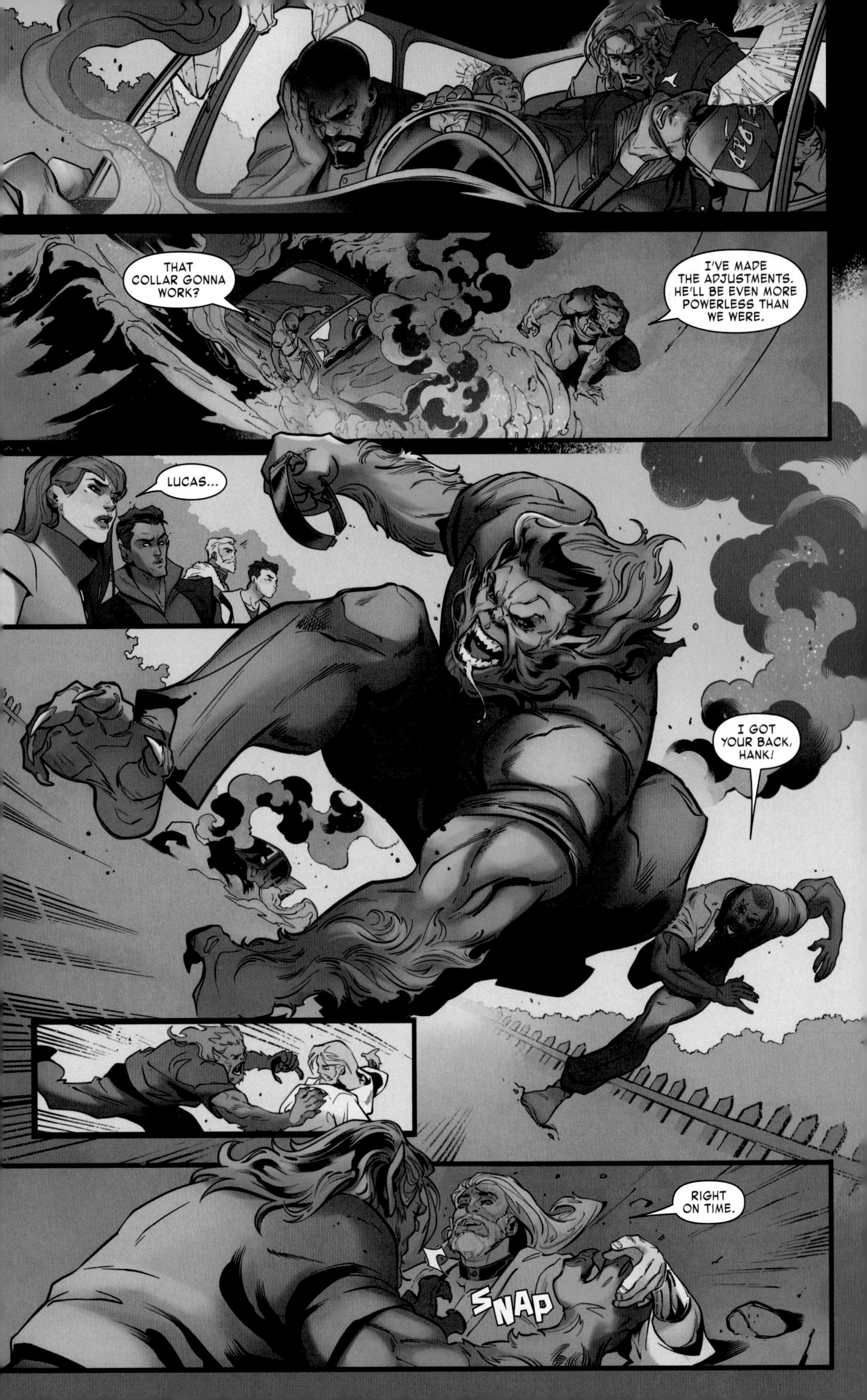

THAT COLLAR GONNA WORK?
I'VE MADE THE ADJUSTMENTS. HE'LL BE EVEN MORE POWERLESS THAN WE WERE.
LUCAS...
I GOT YOUR BACK, HANK!
RIGHT ON TIME.
SNAP

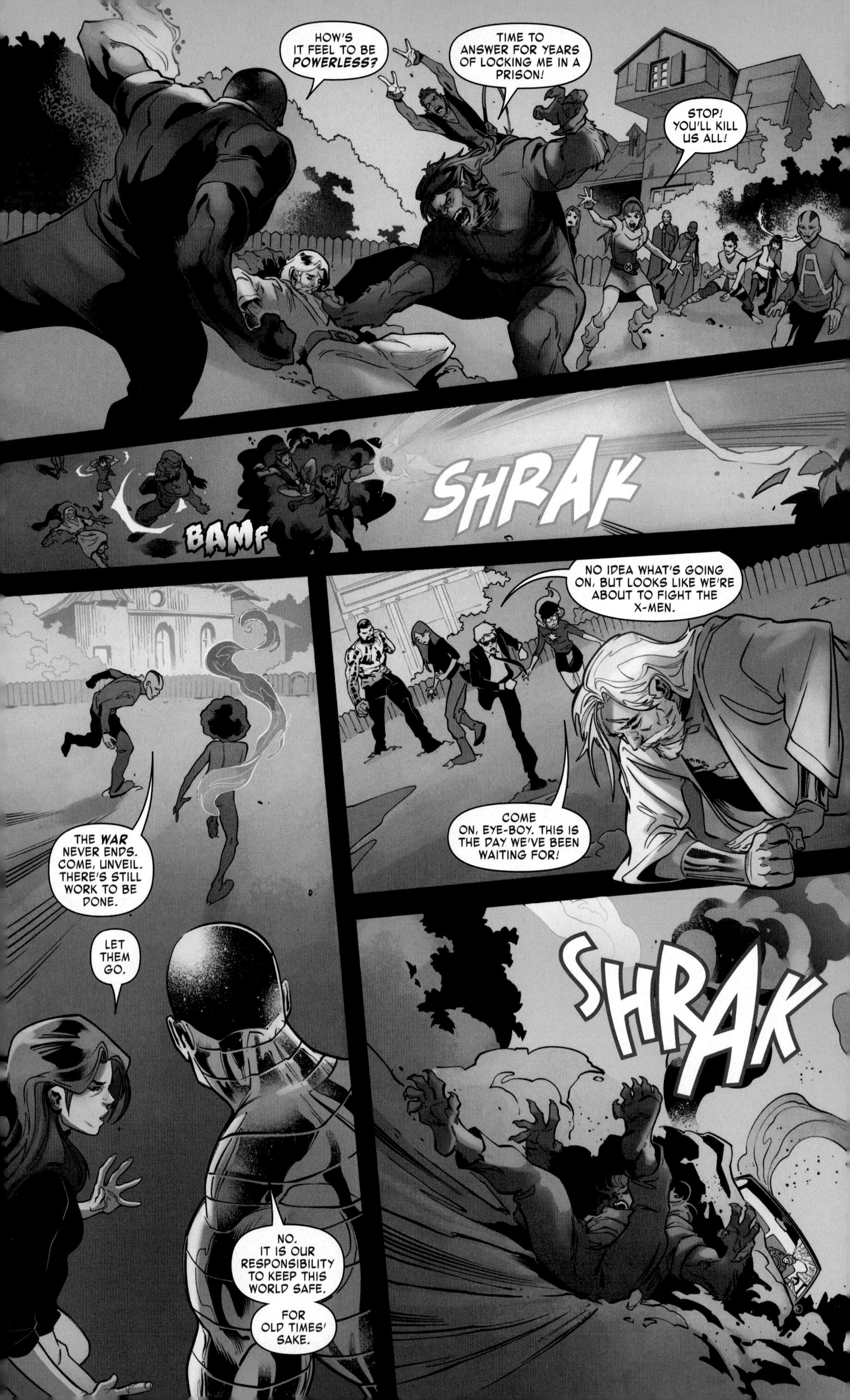
HOW'S IT FEEL TO BE *POWERLESS?*
TIME TO ANSWER FOR YEARS OF LOCKING ME IN A PRISON!
STOP! YOU'LL KILL US ALL!
SHRAK
BAMF
NO IDEA WHAT'S GOING ON, BUT LOOKS LIKE WE'RE ABOUT TO FIGHT THE X-MEN.
THE *WAR* NEVER ENDS. COME, UNVEIL. THERE'S STILL WORK TO BE DONE.
COME ON, EYE-BOY. THIS IS THE DAY WE'VE BEEN WAITING FOR!
LET THEM GO.
SHRAK
NO. IT IS OUR RESPONSIBILITY TO KEEP THIS WORLD SAFE.
FOR OLD TIMES' SAKE.

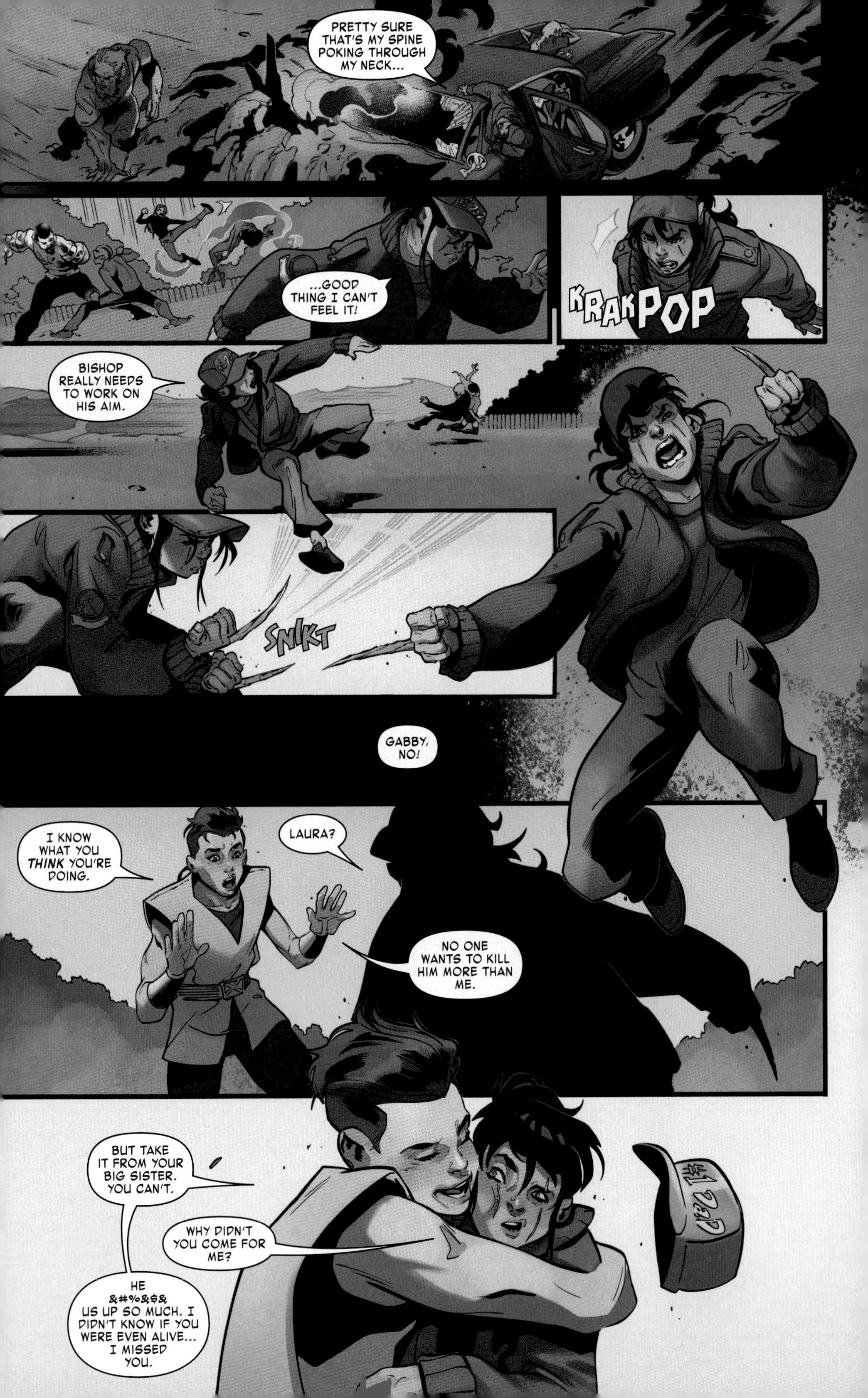
PRETTY SURE THAT'S MY SPINE POKING THROUGH MY NECK...
...GOOD THING I CAN'T FEEL IT!
KRAKPOP
BISHOP REALLY NEEDS TO WORK ON HIS AIM.
SNIKT
GABBY, NO!
I KNOW WHAT YOU *THINK* YOU'RE DOING.
LAURA?
NO ONE WANTS TO KILL HIM MORE THAN ME.
BUT TAKE IT FROM YOUR BIG SISTER. YOU CAN'T.
WHY DIDN'T YOU COME FOR ME?
HE &#%&$& US UP SO MUCH. I DIDN'T KNOW IF YOU WERE EVEN ALIVE... I MISSED YOU.

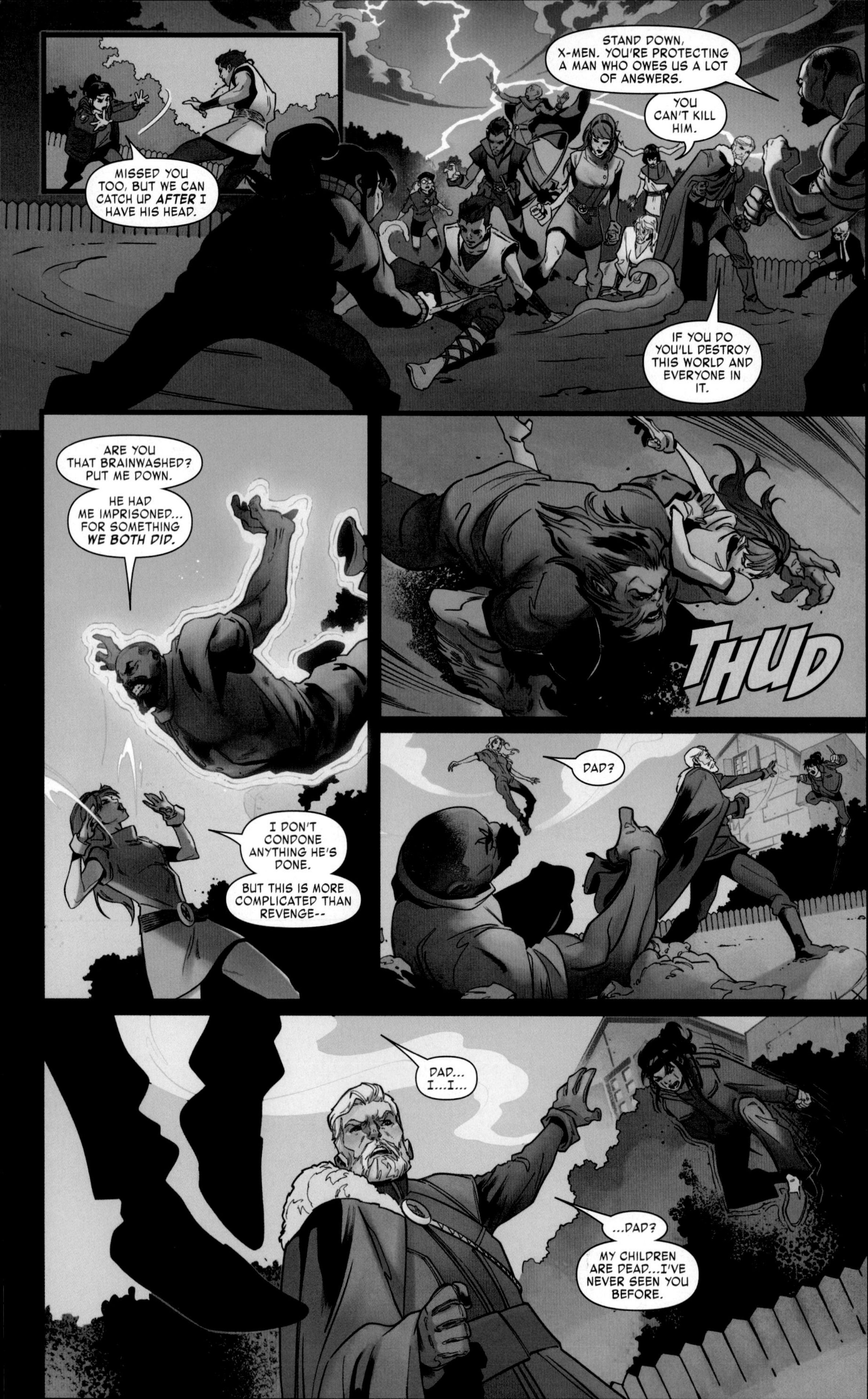
MISSED YOU TOO, BUT WE CAN CATCH UP AFTER I HAVE HIS HEAD.
STAND DOWN, X-MEN. YOU'RE PROTECTING A MAN WHO OWES US A LOT OF ANSWERS.
YOU CAN'T KILL HIM.
IF YOU DO YOU'LL DESTROY THIS WORLD AND EVERYONE IN IT.
ARE YOU THAT BRAINWASHED? PUT ME DOWN.
HE HAD ME IMPRISONED... FOR SOMETHING WE BOTH DID.
I DON'T CONDONE ANYTHING HE'S DONE.
BUT THIS IS MORE COMPLICATED THAN REVENGE--
THUD
DAD?
DAD... I...I...
...DAD?
MY CHILDREN ARE DEAD...I'VE NEVER SEEN YOU BEFORE.

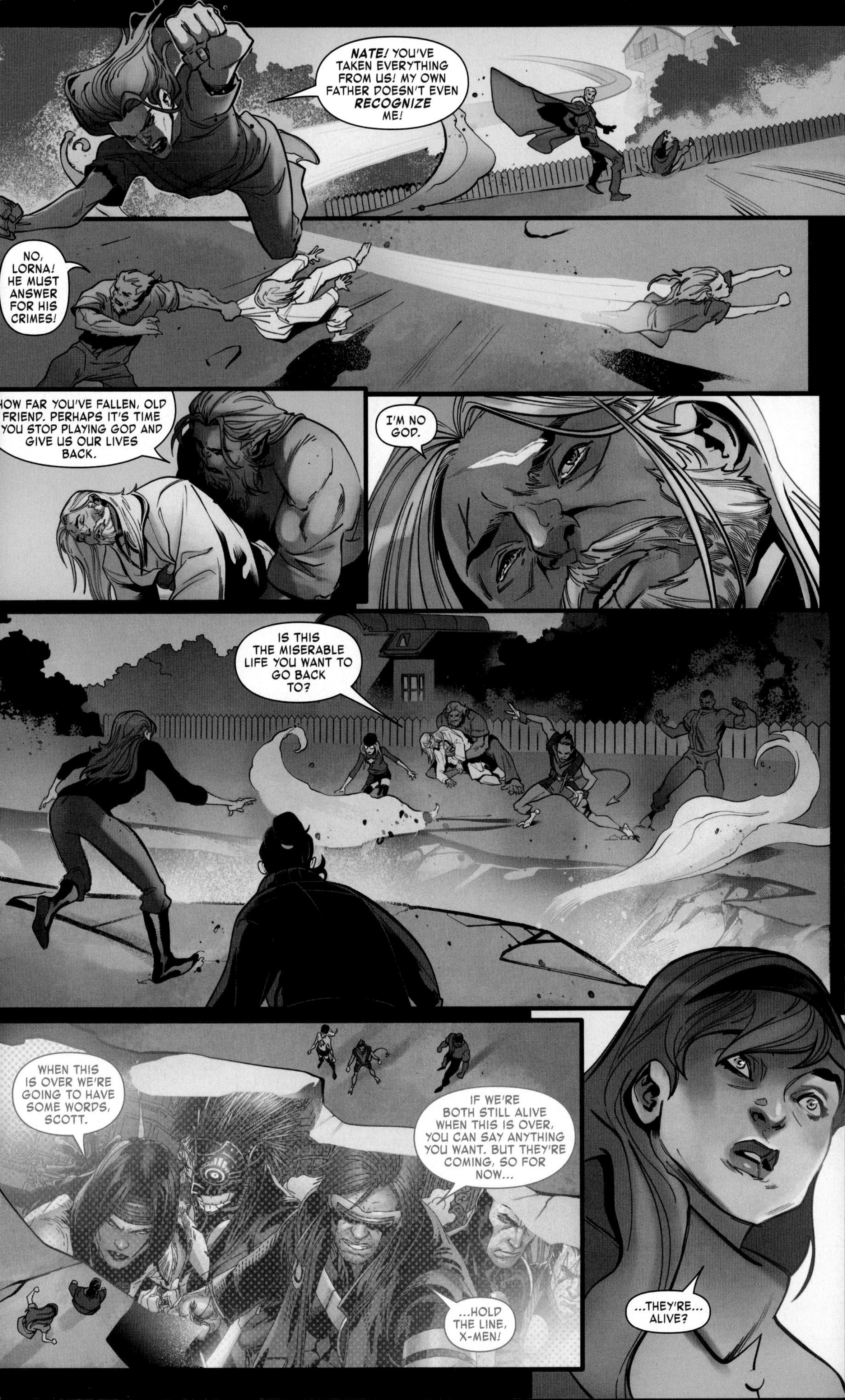

NATE! YOU'VE TAKEN EVERYTHING FROM US! MY OWN FATHER DOESN'T EVEN RECOGNIZE ME!
NO, LORNA! HE MUST ANSWER FOR HIS CRIMES!
HOW FAR YOU'VE FALLEN, OLD FRIEND. PERHAPS IT'S TIME YOU STOP PLAYING GOD AND GIVE US OUR LIVES BACK.
I'M NO GOD.
IS THIS THE MISERABLE LIFE YOU WANT TO GO BACK TO?
WHEN THIS IS OVER WE'RE GOING TO HAVE SOME WORDS, SCOTT.
IF WE'RE BOTH STILL ALIVE WHEN THIS IS OVER, YOU CAN SAY ANYTHING YOU WANT. BUT THEY'RE COMING, SO FOR NOW...
...HOLD THE LINE, X-MEN!
...THEY'RE... ALIVE?

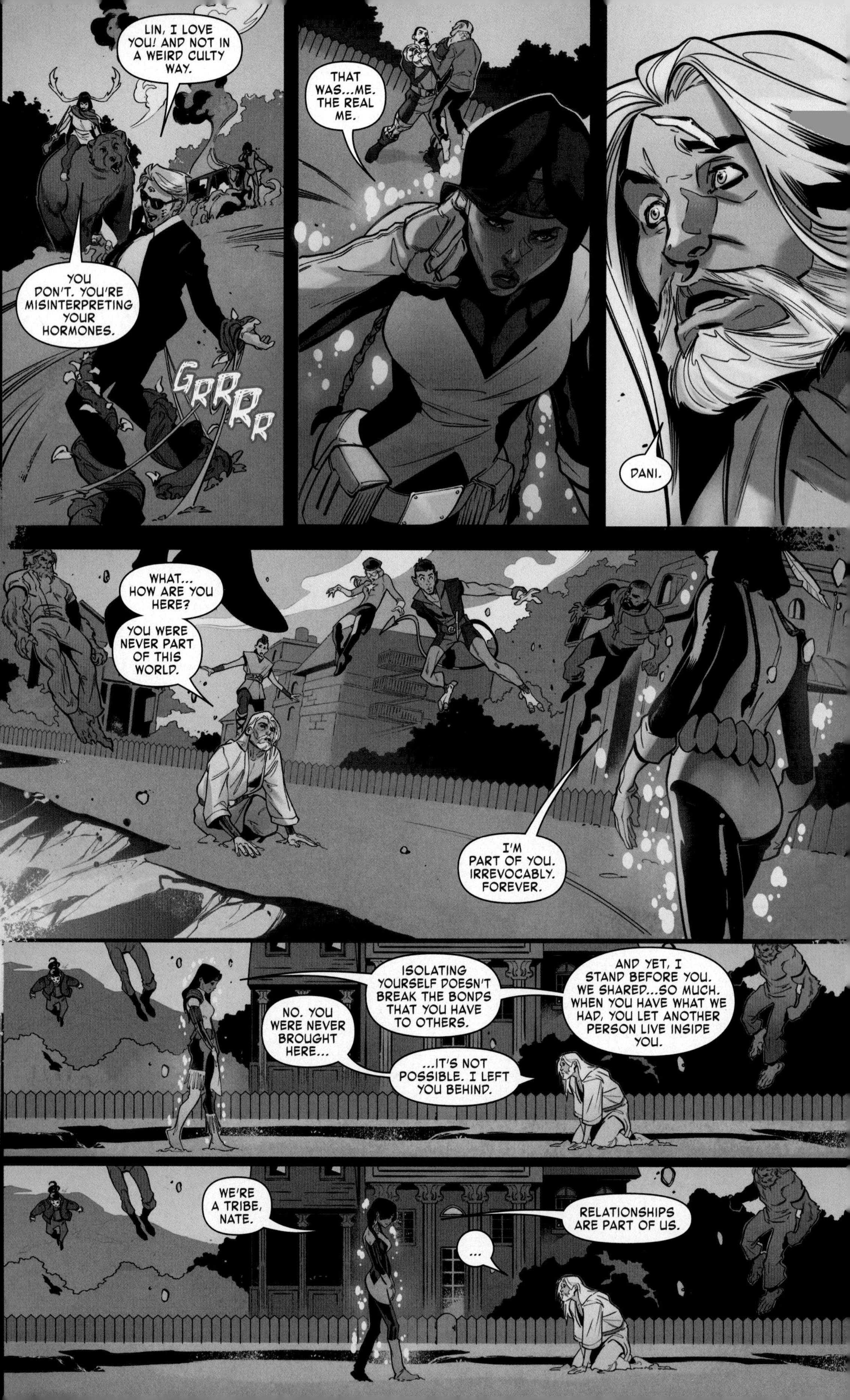

LIN, I LOVE YOU! AND NOT IN A WEIRD CULTY WAY.
YOU DON'T. YOU'RE MISINTERPRETING YOUR HORMONES.
GRRRR
THAT WAS...ME. THE REAL ME.
DANI.
WHAT... HOW ARE YOU HERE?
YOU WERE NEVER PART OF THIS WORLD.
I'M PART OF YOU. IRREVOCABLY. FOREVER.
NO. YOU WERE NEVER BROUGHT HERE...
...IT'S NOT POSSIBLE. I LEFT YOU BEHIND.
ISOLATING YOURSELF DOESN'T BREAK THE BONDS THAT YOU HAVE TO OTHERS.
AND YET, I STAND BEFORE YOU. WE SHARED...SO MUCH. WHEN YOU HAVE WHAT WE HAD, YOU LET ANOTHER PERSON LIVE INSIDE YOU.
WE'RE A TRIBE, NATE.
...
RELATIONSHIPS ARE PART OF US.

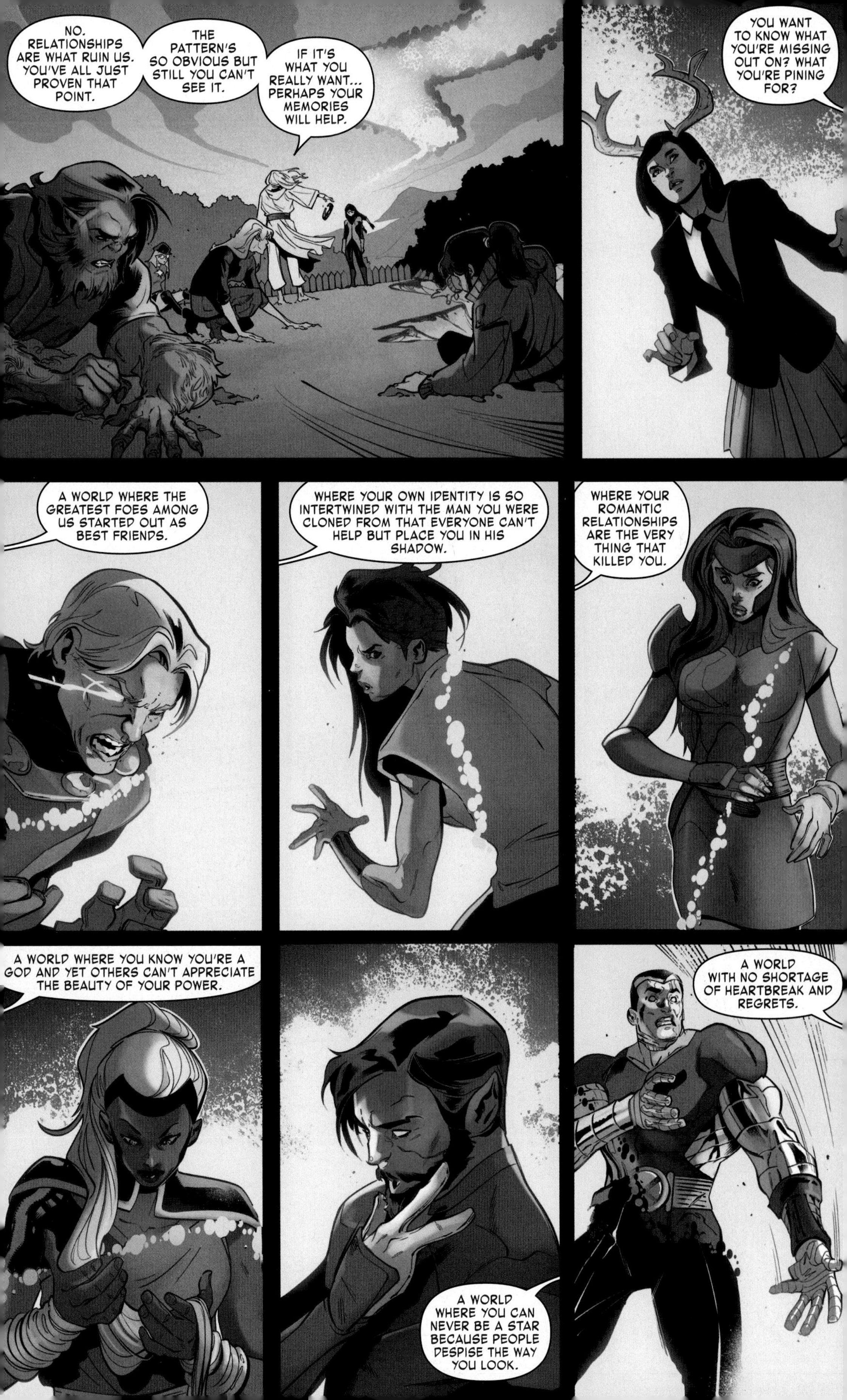

NO. RELATIONSHIPS ARE WHAT RUIN US. YOU'VE ALL JUST PROVEN THAT POINT.
THE PATTERN'S SO OBVIOUS BUT STILL YOU CAN'T SEE IT.
IF IT'S WHAT YOU REALLY WANT... PERHAPS YOUR MEMORIES WILL HELP.
YOU WANT TO KNOW WHAT YOU'RE MISSING OUT ON? WHAT YOU'RE PINING FOR?
A WORLD WHERE THE GREATEST FOES AMONG US STARTED OUT AS BEST FRIENDS.
WHERE YOUR OWN IDENTITY IS SO INTERTWINED WITH THE MAN YOU WERE CLONED FROM THAT EVERYONE CAN'T HELP BUT PLACE YOU IN HIS SHADOW.
WHERE YOUR ROMANTIC RELATIONSHIPS ARE THE VERY THING THAT KILLED YOU.
A WORLD WHERE YOU KNOW YOU'RE A GOD AND YET OTHERS CAN'T APPRECIATE THE BEAUTY OF YOUR POWER.
A WORLD WHERE YOU CAN NEVER BE A STAR BECAUSE PEOPLE DESPISE THE WAY YOU LOOK.
A WORLD WITH NO SHORTAGE OF HEARTBREAK AND REGRETS.

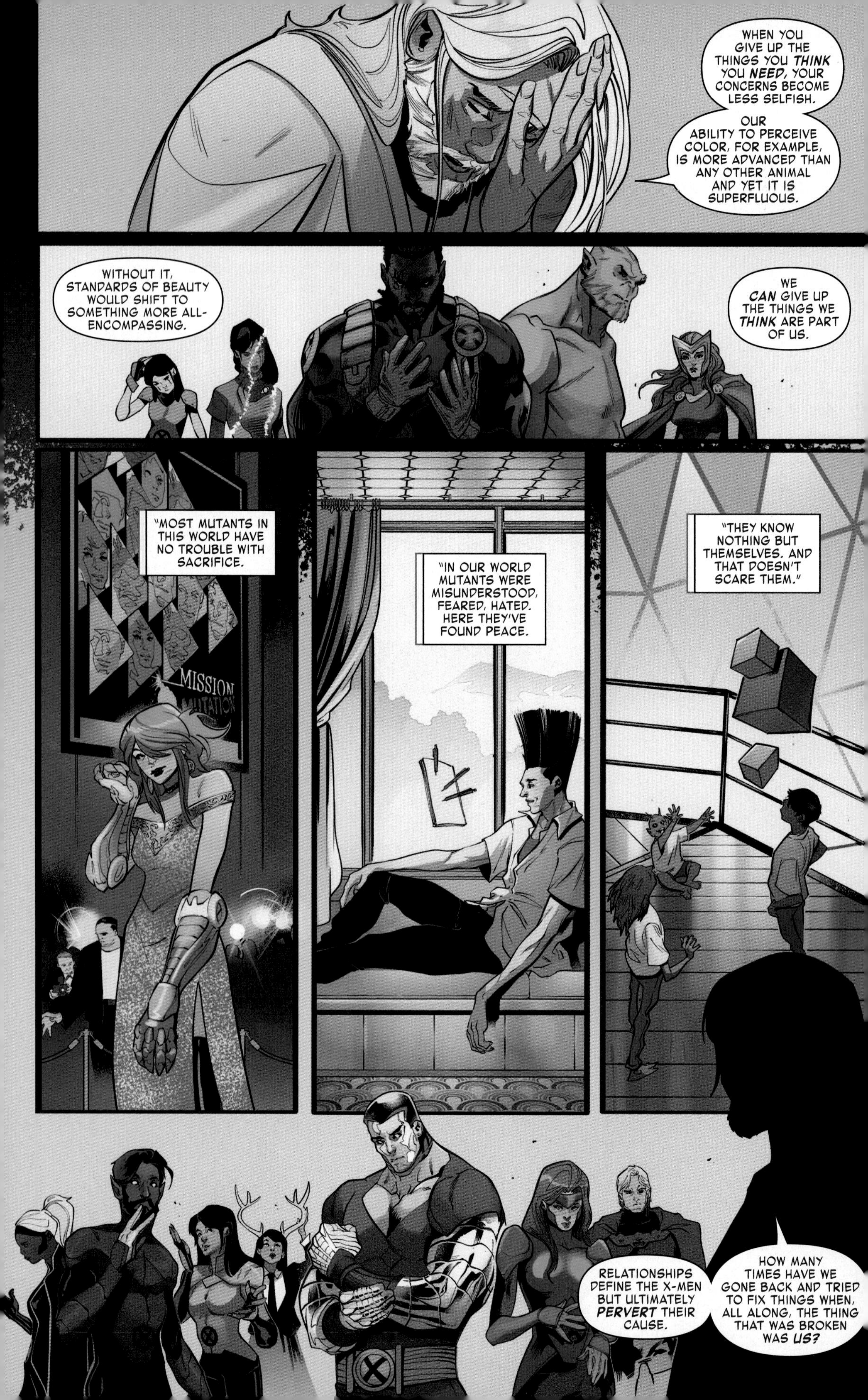
WHEN YOU GIVE UP THE THINGS YOU *THINK* YOU *NEED*, YOUR CONCERNS BECOME LESS SELFISH.
OUR ABILITY TO PERCEIVE COLOR, FOR EXAMPLE, IS MORE ADVANCED THAN ANY OTHER ANIMAL AND YET IT IS SUPERFLUOUS.
WITHOUT IT, STANDARDS OF BEAUTY WOULD SHIFT TO SOMETHING MORE ALL-ENCOMPASSING.
WE *CAN* GIVE UP THE THINGS WE *THINK* ARE PART OF US.
"MOST MUTANTS IN THIS WORLD HAVE NO TROUBLE WITH SACRIFICE.
MISSION MUTATION
"IN OUR WORLD MUTANTS WERE MISUNDERSTOOD, FEARED, HATED. HERE THEY'VE FOUND PEACE.
"THEY KNOW NOTHING BUT THEMSELVES. AND THAT DOESN'T SCARE THEM."
RELATIONSHIPS DEFINE THE X-MEN BUT ULTIMATELY *PERVERT* THEIR CAUSE.
HOW MANY TIMES HAVE WE GONE BACK AND TRIED TO FIX THINGS WHEN, ALL ALONG, THE THING THAT WAS BROKEN WAS *US?*

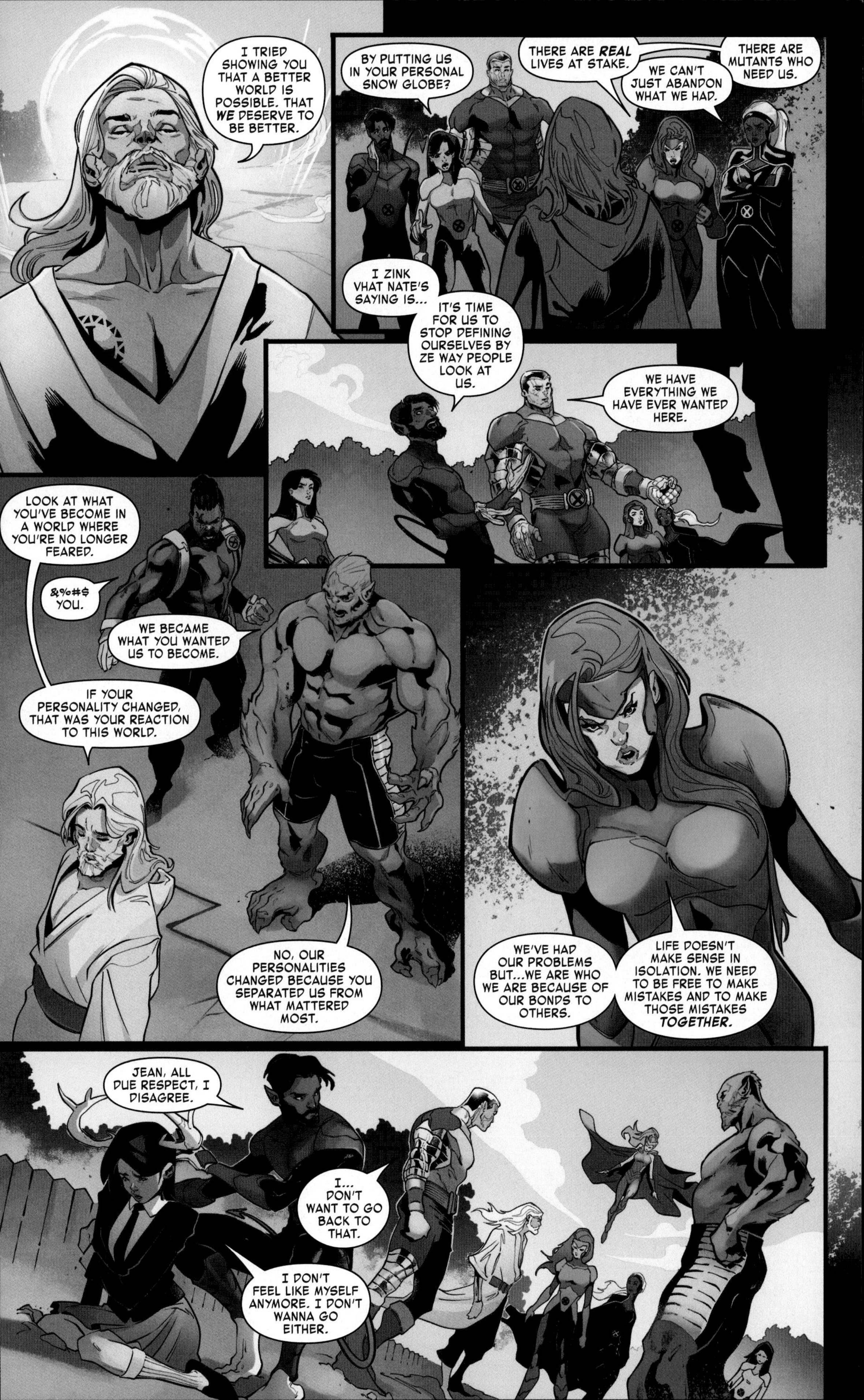
I TRIED SHOWING YOU THAT A BETTER WORLD IS POSSIBLE. THAT WE DESERVE TO BE BETTER.
BY PUTTING US IN YOUR PERSONAL SNOW GLOBE?
THERE ARE REAL LIVES AT STAKE.
WE CAN'T JUST ABANDON WHAT WE HAD.
THERE ARE MUTANTS WHO NEED US.
I ZINK VHAT NATE'S SAYING IS...
IT'S TIME FOR US TO STOP DEFINING OURSELVES BY ZE WAY PEOPLE LOOK AT US.
WE HAVE EVERYTHING WE HAVE EVER WANTED HERE.
LOOK AT WHAT YOU'VE BECOME IN A WORLD WHERE YOU'RE NO LONGER FEARED.
&%#$ YOU.
WE BECAME WHAT YOU WANTED US TO BECOME.
IF YOUR PERSONALITY CHANGED, THAT WAS YOUR REACTION TO THIS WORLD.
NO, OUR PERSONALITIES CHANGED BECAUSE YOU SEPARATED US FROM WHAT MATTERED MOST.
WE'VE HAD OUR PROBLEMS BUT...WE ARE WHO WE ARE BECAUSE OF OUR BONDS TO OTHERS.
LIFE DOESN'T MAKE SENSE IN ISOLATION. WE NEED TO BE FREE TO MAKE MISTAKES AND TO MAKE THOSE MISTAKES TOGETHER.
JEAN, ALL DUE RESPECT, I DISAGREE.
I... DON'T WANT TO GO BACK TO THAT.
I DON'T FEEL LIKE MYSELF ANYMORE. I DON'T WANNA GO EITHER.

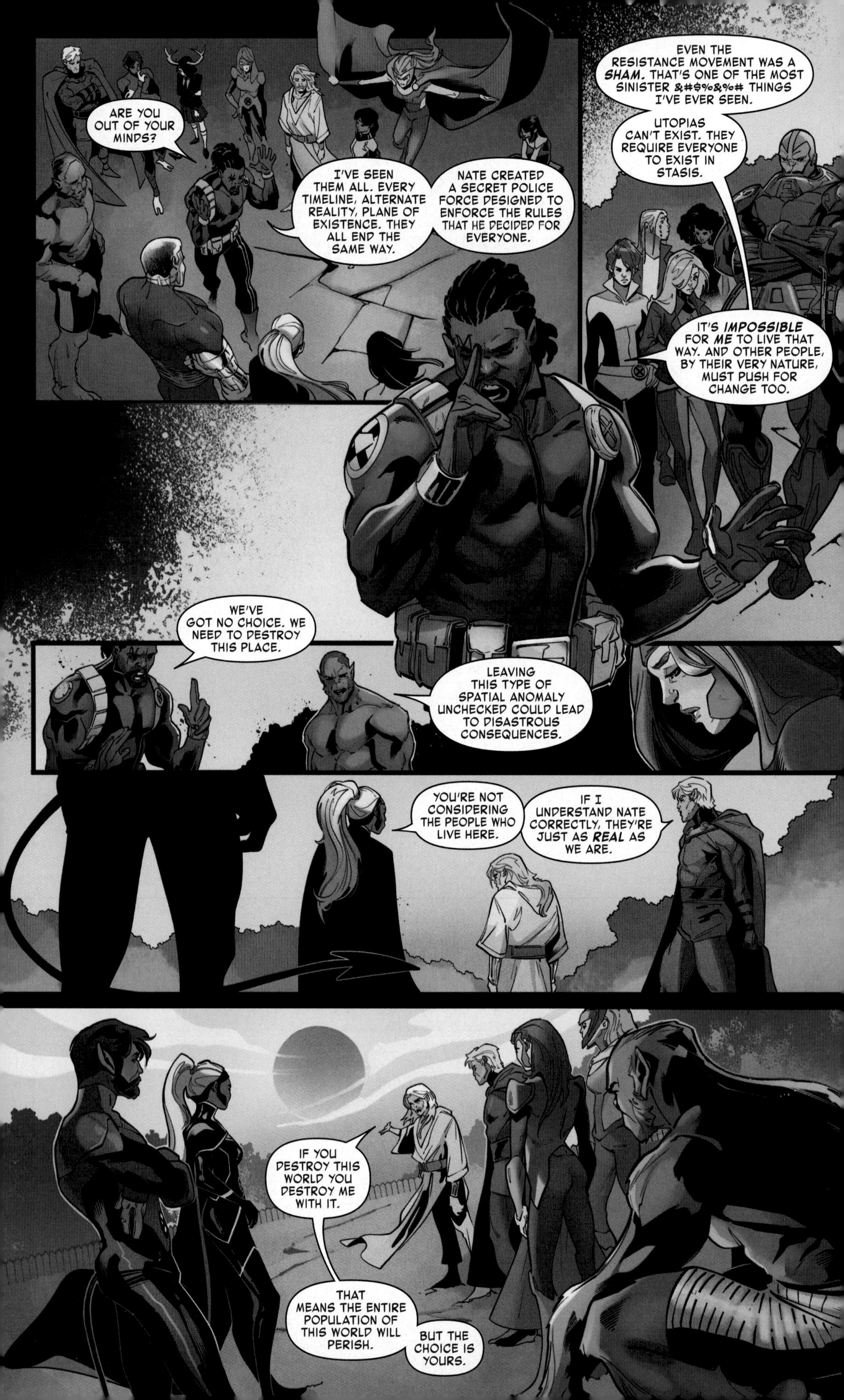
ARE YOU OUT OF YOUR MINDS?
I'VE SEEN THEM ALL. EVERY TIMELINE, ALTERNATE REALITY, PLANE OF EXISTENCE. THEY ALL END THE SAME WAY.
NATE CREATED A SECRET POLICE FORCE DESIGNED TO ENFORCE THE RULES THAT HE DECIDED FOR EVERYONE.
EVEN THE RESISTANCE MOVEMENT WAS A SHAM. THAT'S ONE OF THE MOST SINISTER &#$%&%# THINGS I'VE EVER SEEN.
UTOPIAS CAN'T EXIST. THEY REQUIRE EVERYONE TO EXIST IN STASIS.
IT'S IMPOSSIBLE FOR ME TO LIVE THAT WAY. AND OTHER PEOPLE, BY THEIR VERY NATURE, MUST PUSH FOR CHANGE TOO.
WE'VE GOT NO CHOICE. WE NEED TO DESTROY THIS PLACE.
LEAVING THIS TYPE OF SPATIAL ANOMALY UNCHECKED COULD LEAD TO DISASTROUS CONSEQUENCES.
YOU'RE NOT CONSIDERING THE PEOPLE WHO LIVE HERE.
IF I UNDERSTAND NATE CORRECTLY, THEY'RE JUST AS REAL AS WE ARE.
IF YOU DESTROY THIS WORLD YOU DESTROY ME WITH IT.
THAT MEANS THE ENTIRE POPULATION OF THIS WORLD WILL PERISH.
BUT THE CHOICE IS YOURS.

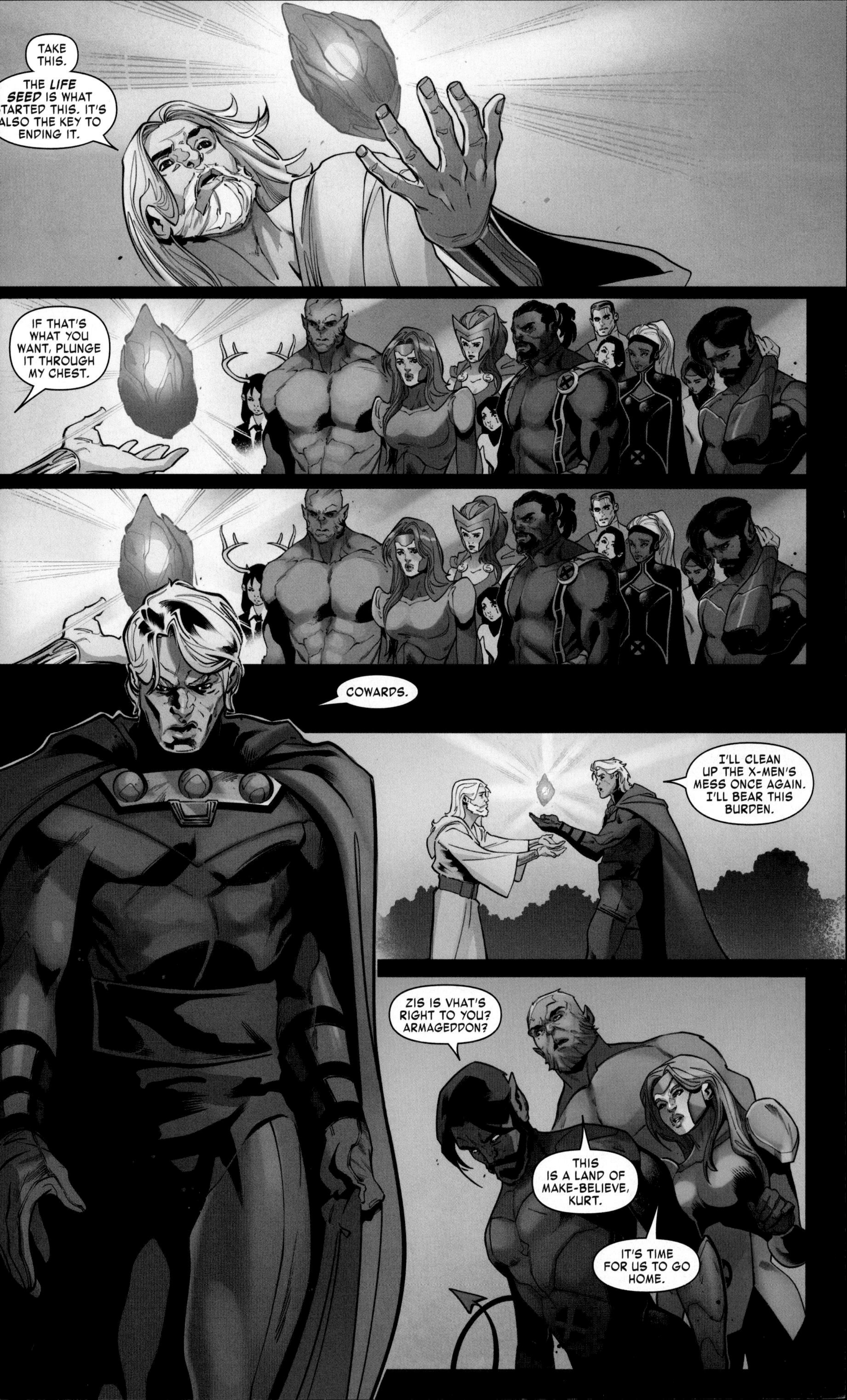
TAKE THIS.
THE LIFE SEED IS WHAT STARTED THIS. IT'S ALSO THE KEY TO ENDING IT.
IF THAT'S WHAT YOU WANT, PLUNGE IT THROUGH MY CHEST.
COWARDS.
I'LL CLEAN UP THE X-MEN'S MESS ONCE AGAIN. I'LL BEAR THIS BURDEN.
ZIS IS VHAT'S RIGHT TO YOU? ARMAGEDDON?
THIS IS A LAND OF MAKE-BELIEVE, KURT.
IT'S TIME FOR US TO GO HOME.

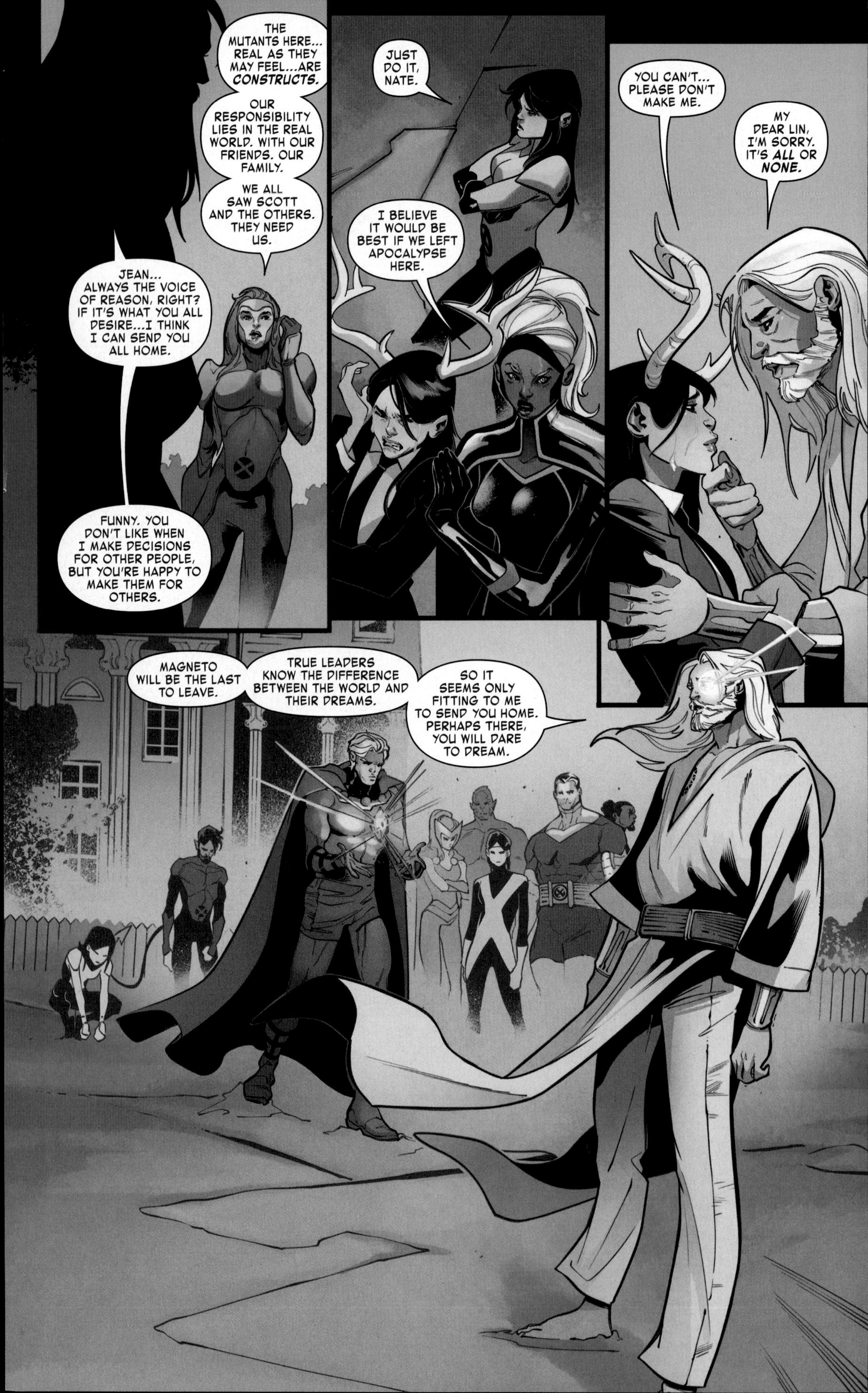
THE MUTANTS HERE... REAL AS THEY MAY FEEL...ARE CONSTRUCTS.
OUR RESPONSIBILITY LIES IN THE REAL WORLD. WITH OUR FRIENDS. OUR FAMILY.
WE ALL SAW SCOTT AND THE OTHERS. THEY NEED US.
JEAN... ALWAYS THE VOICE OF REASON, RIGHT? IF IT'S WHAT YOU ALL DESIRE...I THINK I CAN SEND YOU ALL HOME.
FUNNY. YOU DON'T LIKE WHEN I MAKE DECISIONS FOR OTHER PEOPLE, BUT YOU'RE HAPPY TO MAKE THEM FOR OTHERS.
JUST DO IT, NATE.
I BELIEVE IT WOULD BE BEST IF WE LEFT APOCALYPSE HERE.
YOU CAN'T... PLEASE DON'T MAKE ME.
MY DEAR LIN, I'M SORRY. IT'S ALL OR NONE.
MAGNETO WILL BE THE LAST TO LEAVE.
TRUE LEADERS KNOW THE DIFFERENCE BETWEEN THE WORLD AND THEIR DREAMS.
SO IT SEEMS ONLY FITTING TO ME TO SEND YOU HOME. PERHAPS THERE, YOU WILL DARE TO DREAM.

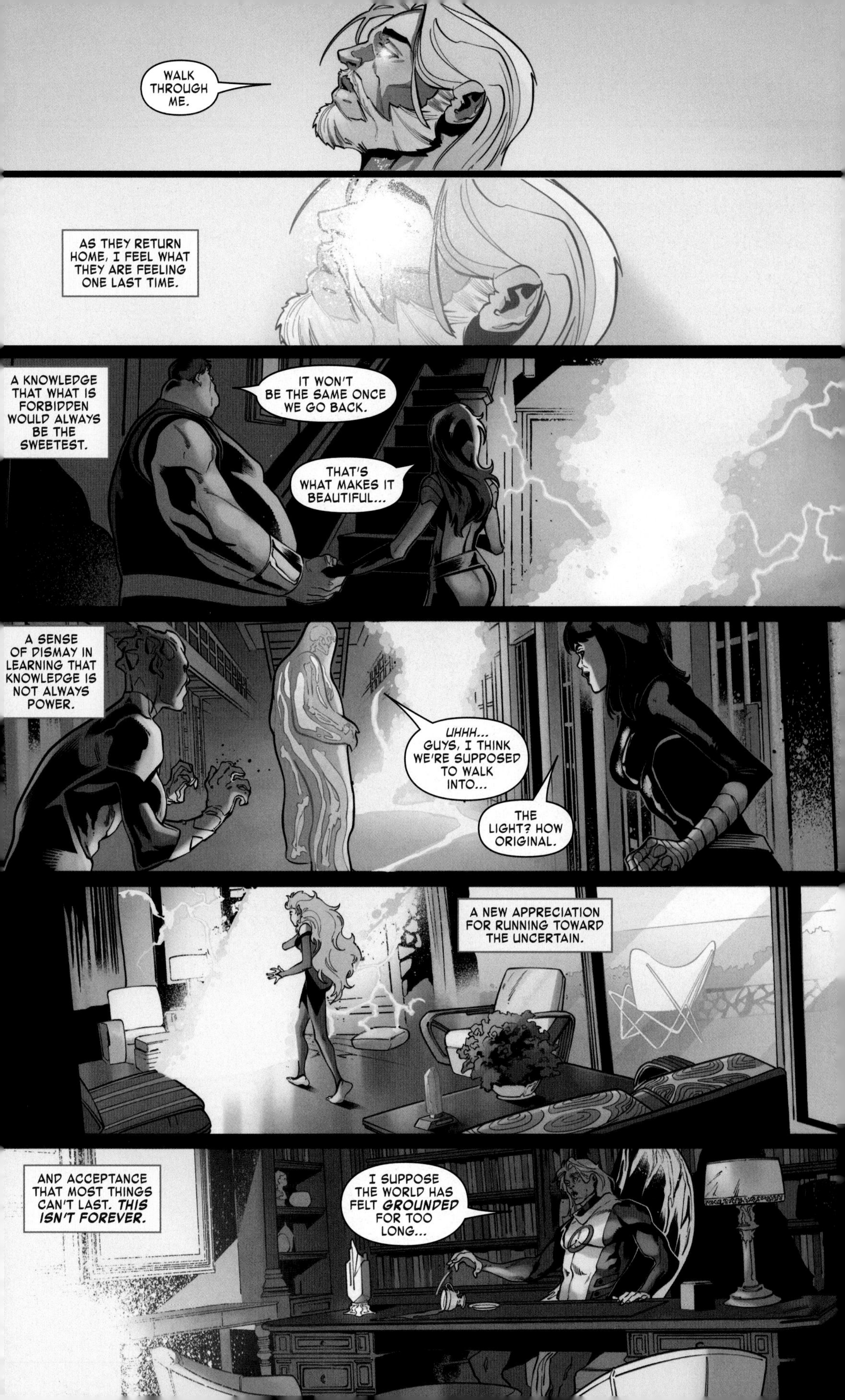
WALK THROUGH ME.
AS THEY RETURN HOME, I FEEL WHAT THEY ARE FEELING ONE LAST TIME.
A KNOWLEDGE THAT WHAT IS FORBIDDEN WOULD ALWAYS BE THE SWEETEST.
IT WON'T BE THE SAME ONCE WE GO BACK.
THAT'S WHAT MAKES IT BEAUTIFUL...
A SENSE OF DISMAY IN LEARNING THAT KNOWLEDGE IS NOT ALWAYS POWER.
UHHH... GUYS, I THINK WE'RE SUPPOSED TO WALK INTO...
THE LIGHT? HOW ORIGINAL.
A NEW APPRECIATION FOR RUNNING TOWARD THE UNCERTAIN.
AND ACCEPTANCE THAT MOST THINGS CAN'T LAST. THIS ISN'T FOREVER.
I SUPPOSE THE WORLD HAS FELT GROUNDED FOR TOO LONG...

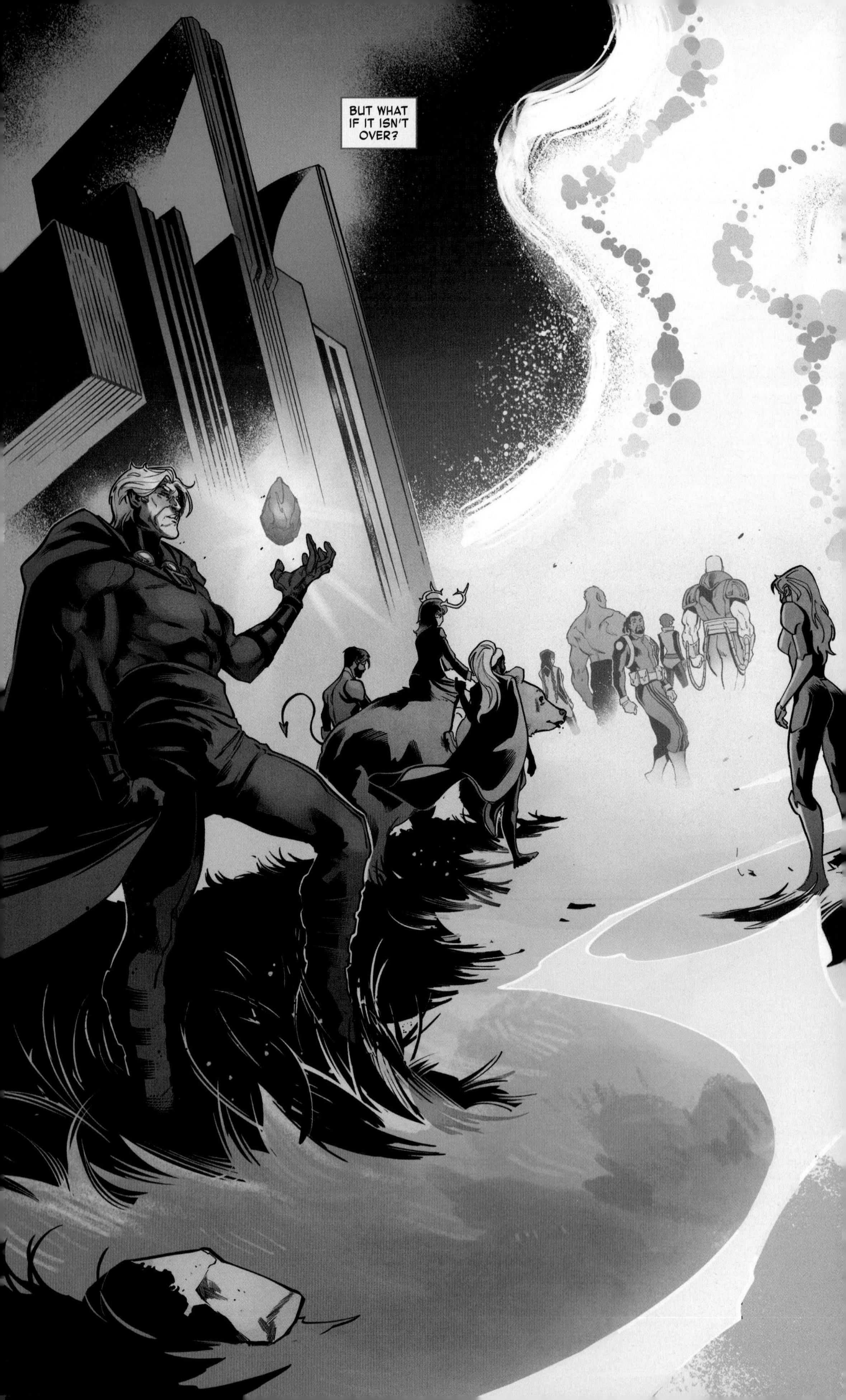
BUT WHAT IF IT ISN'T OVER?

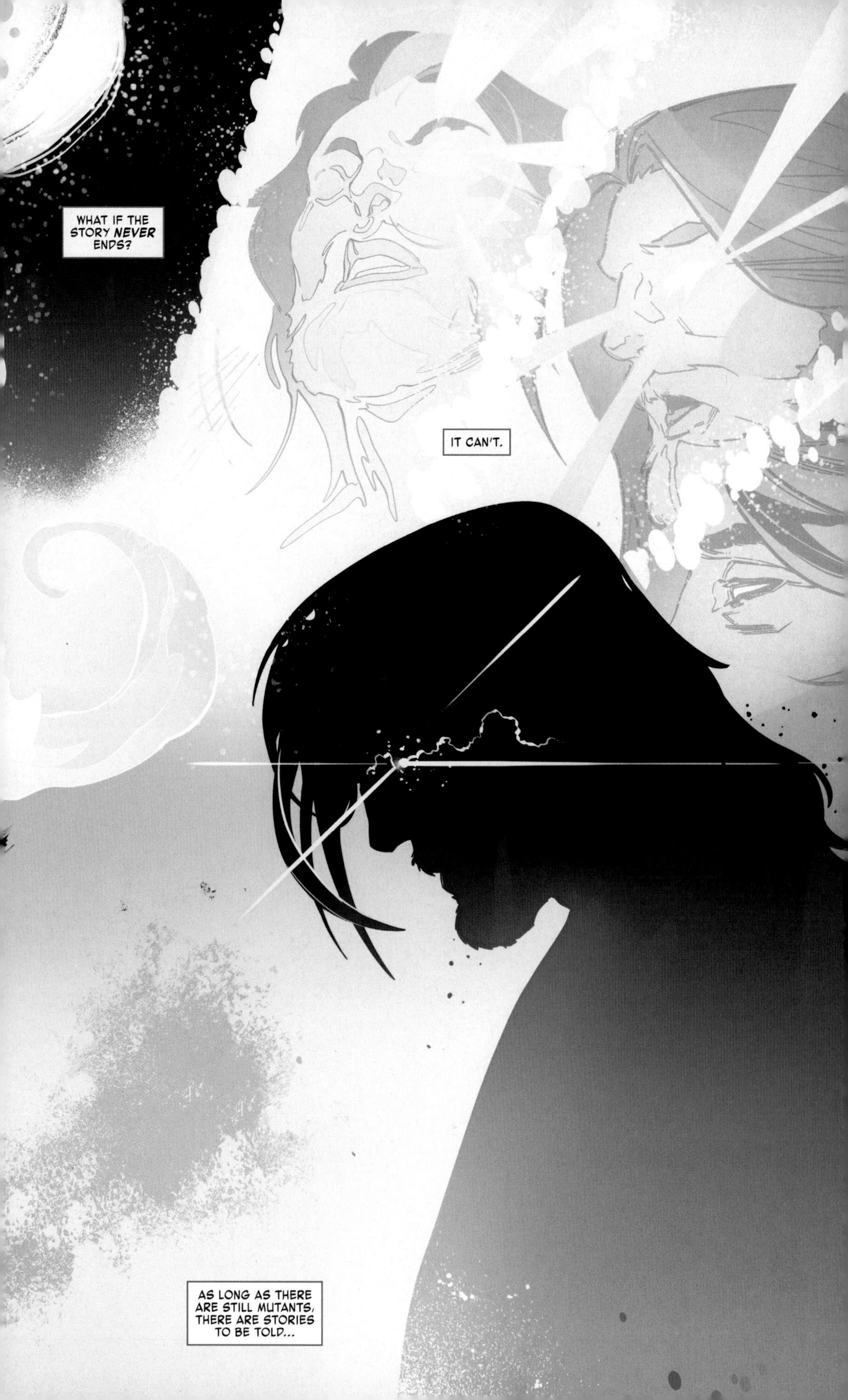
WHAT IF THE STORY *NEVER* ENDS?
IT CAN'T.
AS LONG AS THERE ARE STILL MUTANTS, THERE ARE STORIES TO BE TOLD...

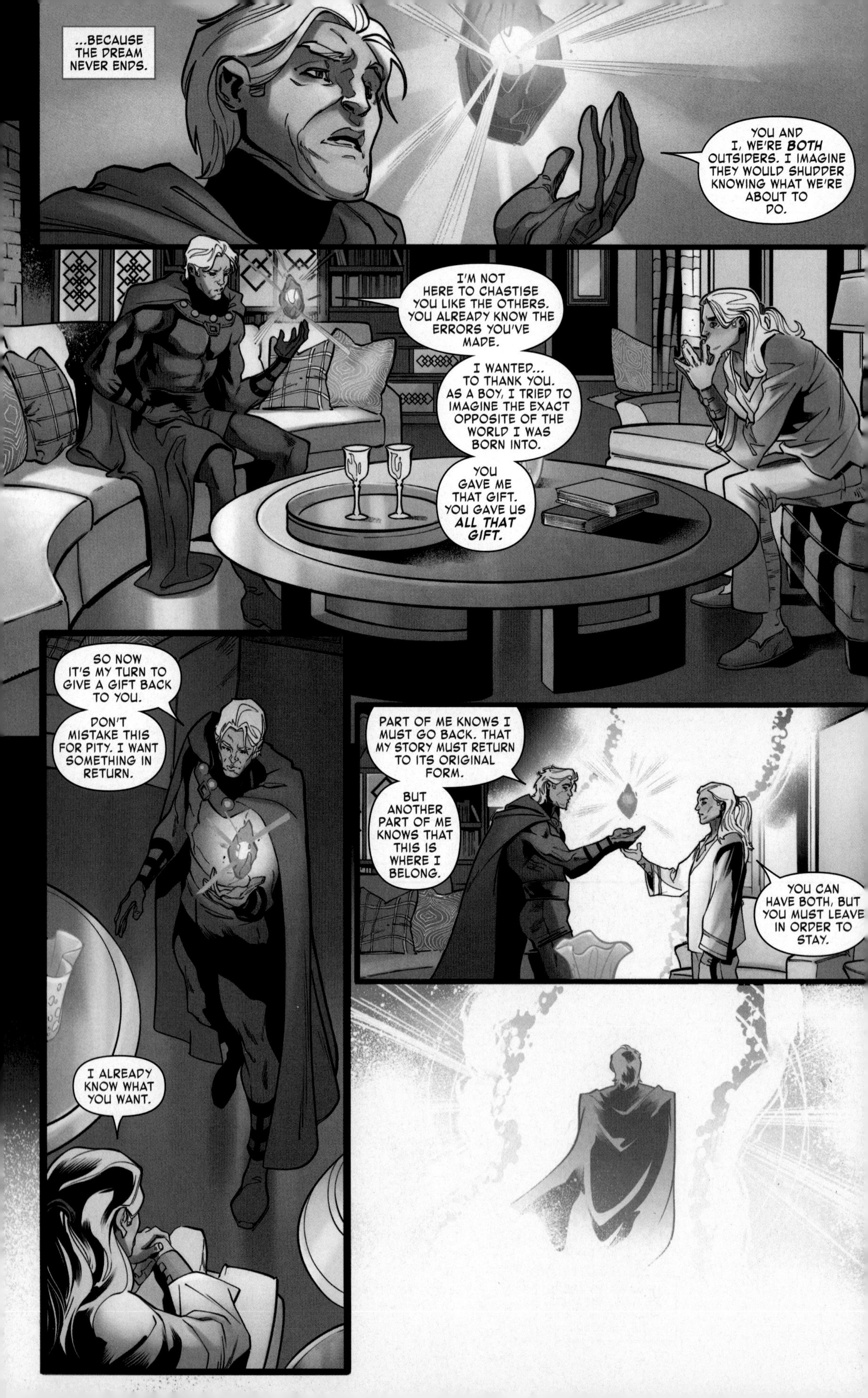
...BECAUSE THE DREAM NEVER ENDS.
YOU AND I, WE'RE BOTH OUTSIDERS. I IMAGINE THEY WOULD SHUDDER KNOWING WHAT WE'RE ABOUT TO DO.
I'M NOT HERE TO CHASTISE YOU LIKE THE OTHERS. YOU ALREADY KNOW THE ERRORS YOU'VE MADE.
I WANTED... TO THANK YOU. AS A BOY, I TRIED TO IMAGINE THE EXACT OPPOSITE OF THE WORLD I WAS BORN INTO.
YOU GAVE ME THAT GIFT. YOU GAVE US ALL THAT GIFT.
SO NOW IT'S MY TURN TO GIVE A GIFT BACK TO YOU.
DON'T MISTAKE THIS FOR PITY. I WANT SOMETHING IN RETURN.
I ALREADY KNOW WHAT YOU WANT.
PART OF ME KNOWS I MUST GO BACK. THAT MY STORY MUST RETURN TO ITS ORIGINAL FORM.
BUT ANOTHER PART OF ME KNOWS THAT THIS IS WHERE I BELONG.
YOU CAN HAVE BOTH, BUT YOU MUST LEAVE IN ORDER TO STAY.

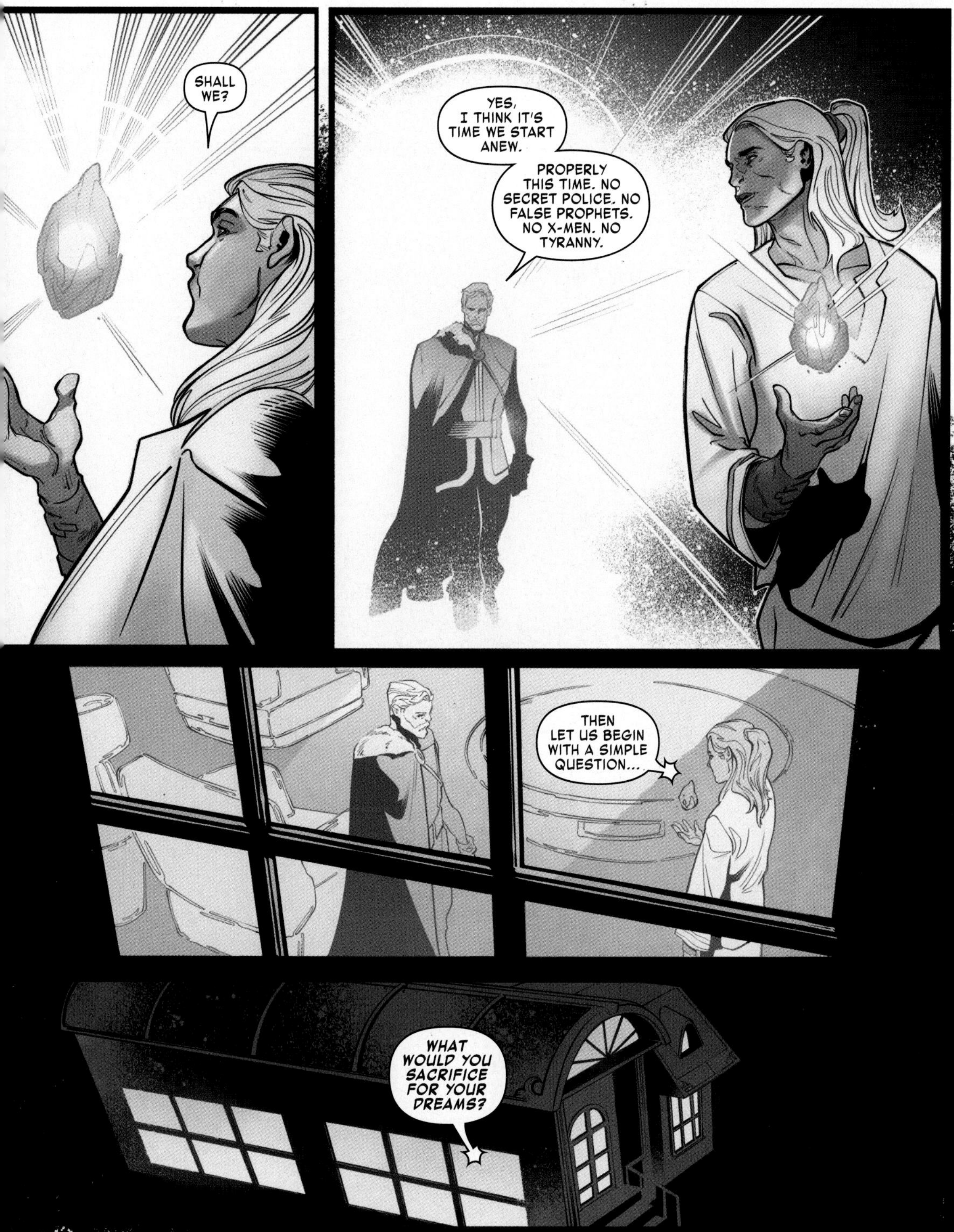
SHALL WE?
YES, I THINK IT'S TIME WE START ANEW.
PROPERLY THIS TIME. NO SECRET POLICE. NO FALSE PROPHETS. NO X-MEN. NO TYRANNY.
THEN LET US BEGIN WITH A SIMPLE QUESTION...
WHAT WOULD YOU SACRIFICE FOR YOUR DREAMS?

"This curious world we inhabit is more wonderful than convenient; more beautiful than it is useful; it is more to be admired and enjoyed than used."

—Henry David Thoreau,
Familiar Letters

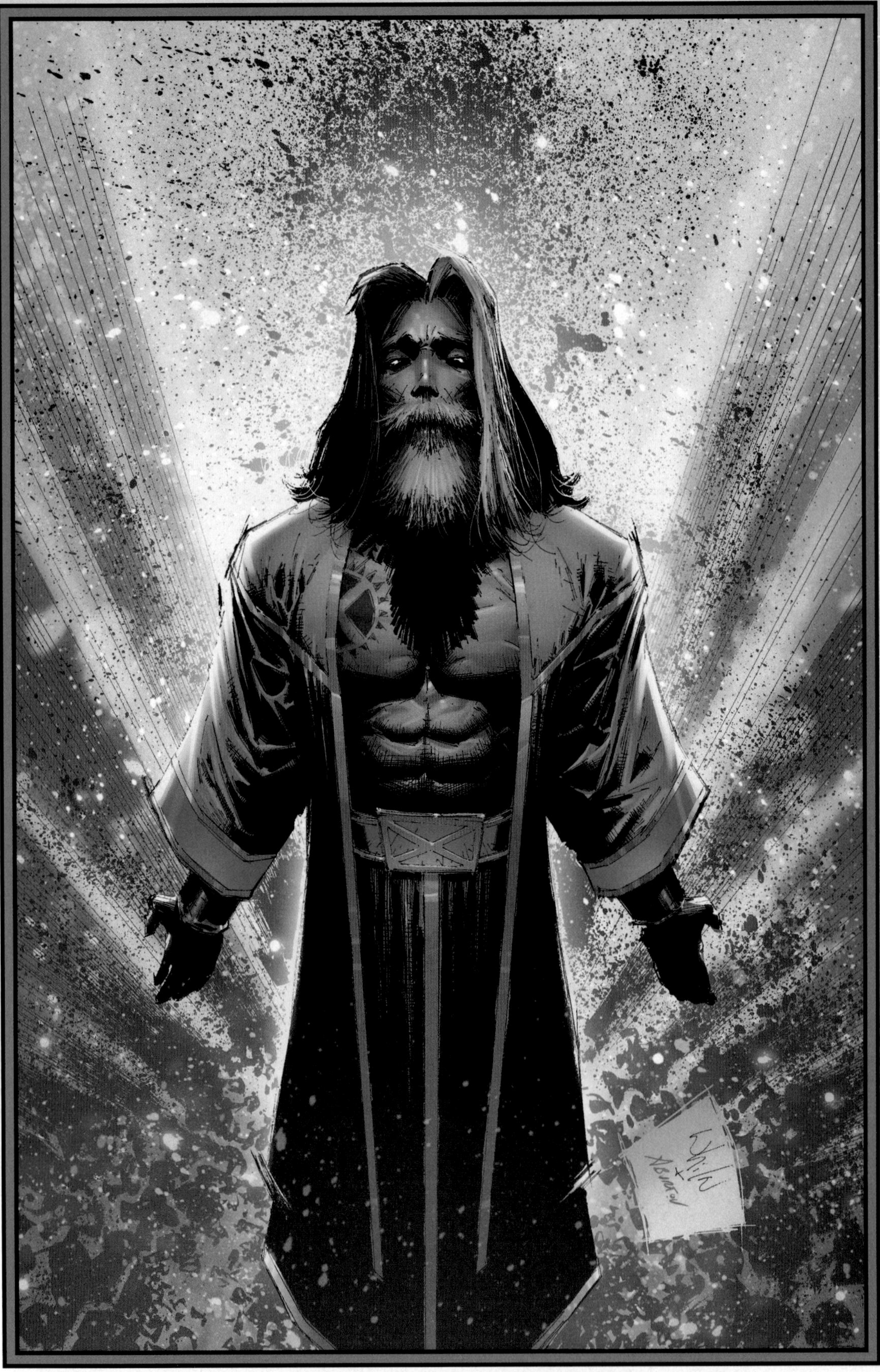

AGE OF X-MAN ALPHA #1 VARIANT BY **WHILCE PORTACIO** & **JESUS ABURTOV**

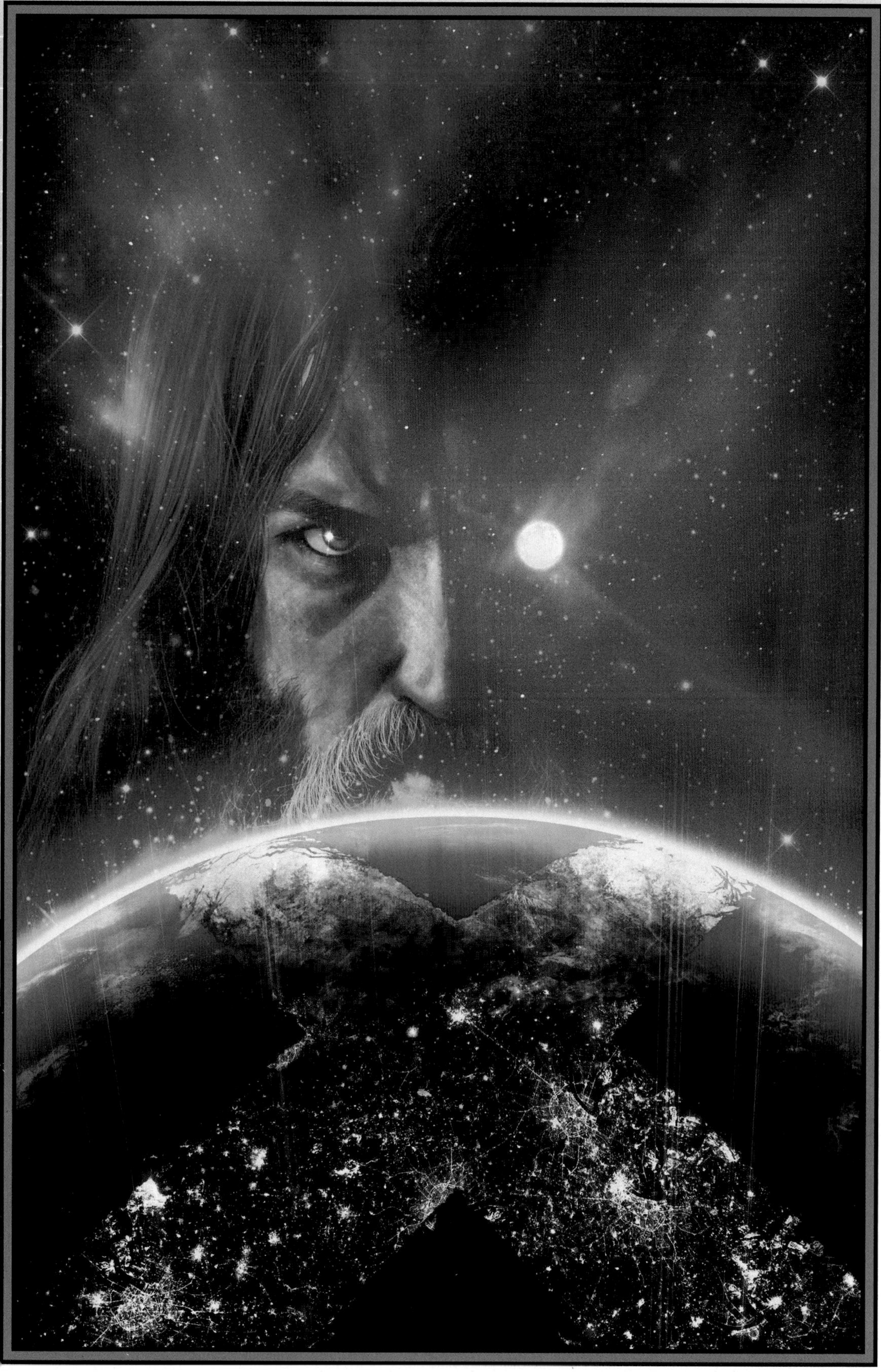

AGE OF X-MAN ALPHA #1 VARIANT BY **RAHZZAH**

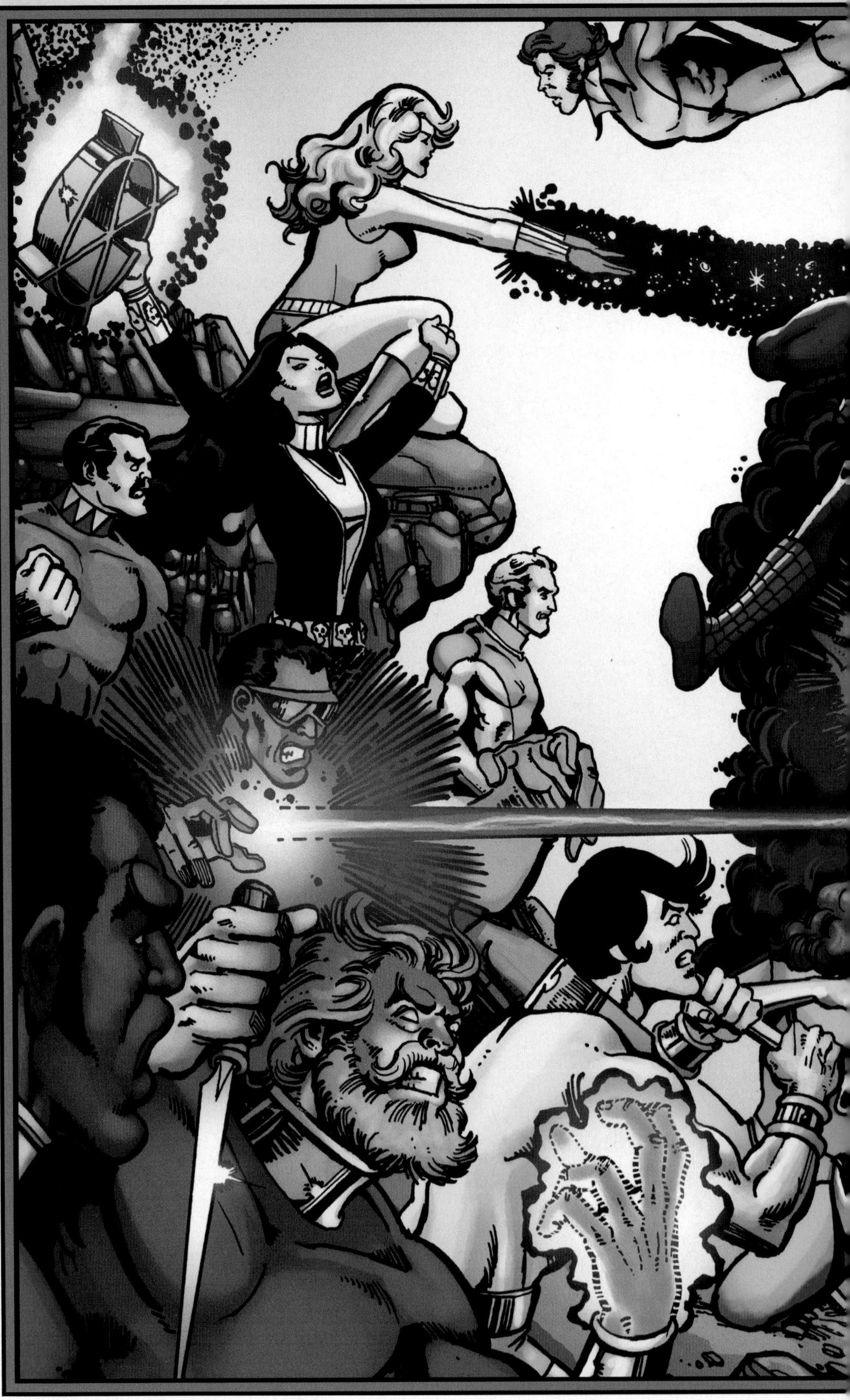

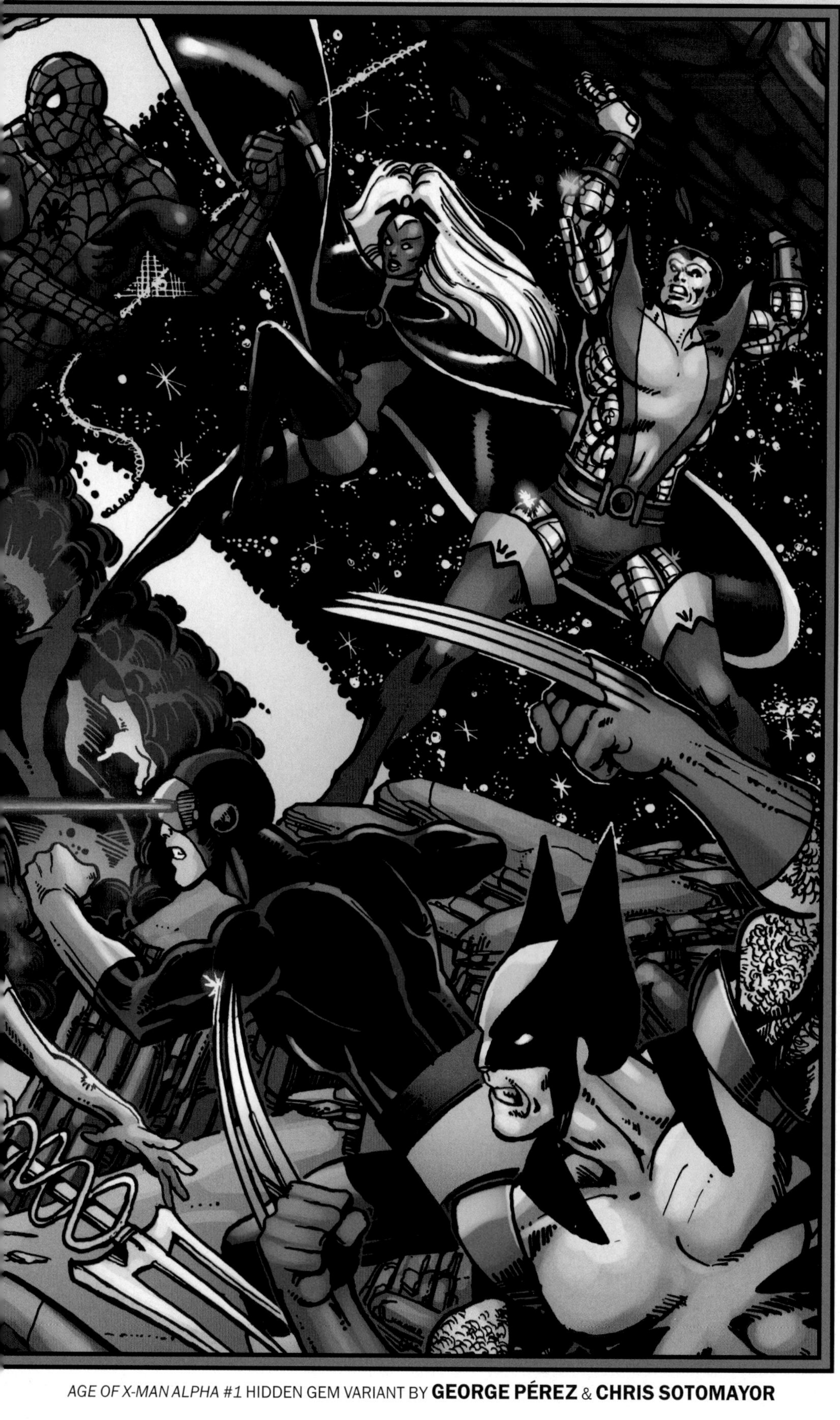

AGE OF X-MAN ALPHA #1 HIDDEN GEM VARIANT BY **GEORGE PÉREZ** & **CHRIS SOTOMAYOR**

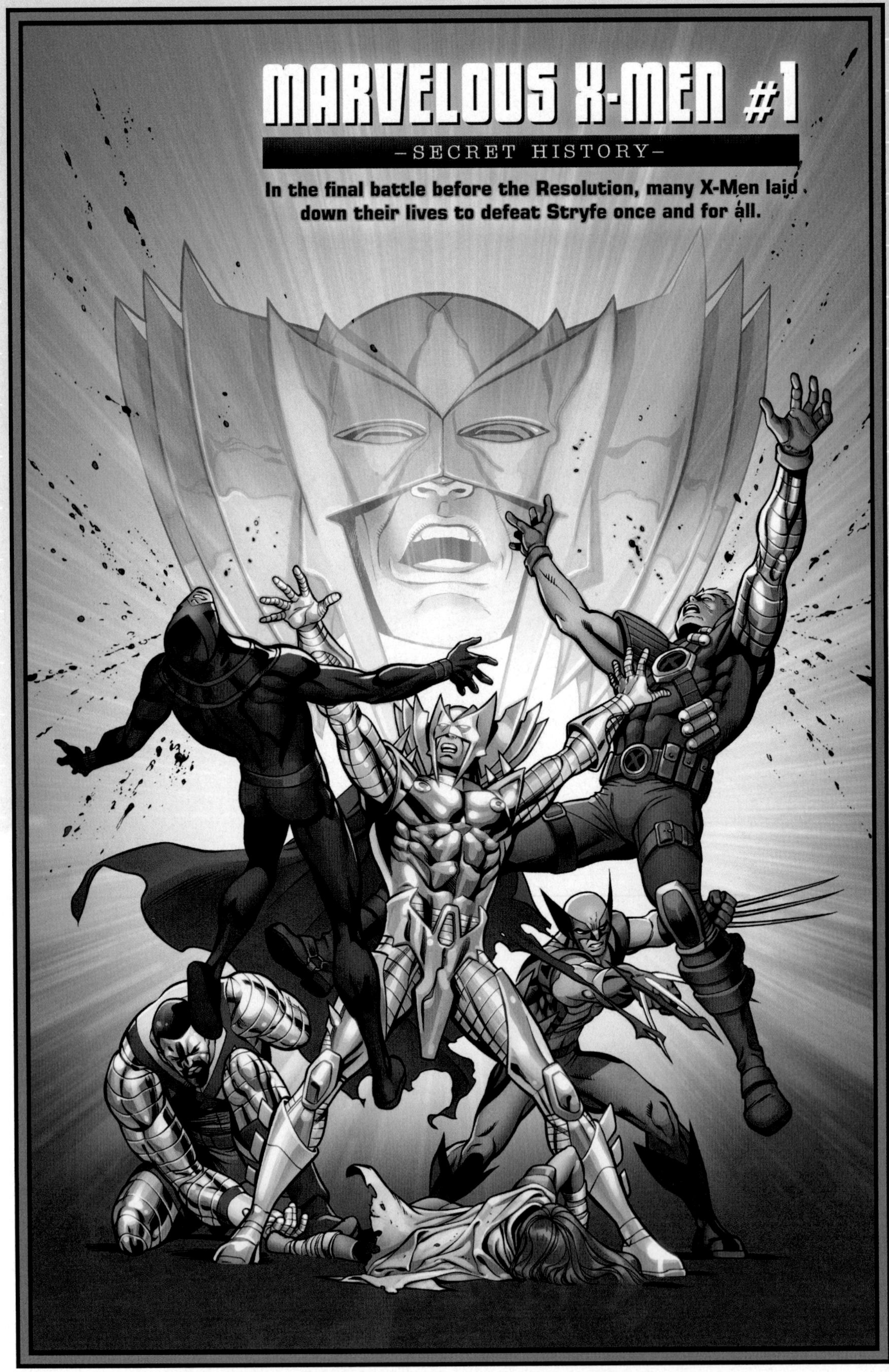
MARVELOUS X-MEN #1
—SECRET HISTORY—
In the final battle before the Resolution, many X-Men laid down their lives to defeat Stryfe once and for all.

#1 SECRET HISTORY VARIANT BY **CARLOS PACHECO**, **RAFAEL FONTERIZ** & **NOLAN WOODARD**

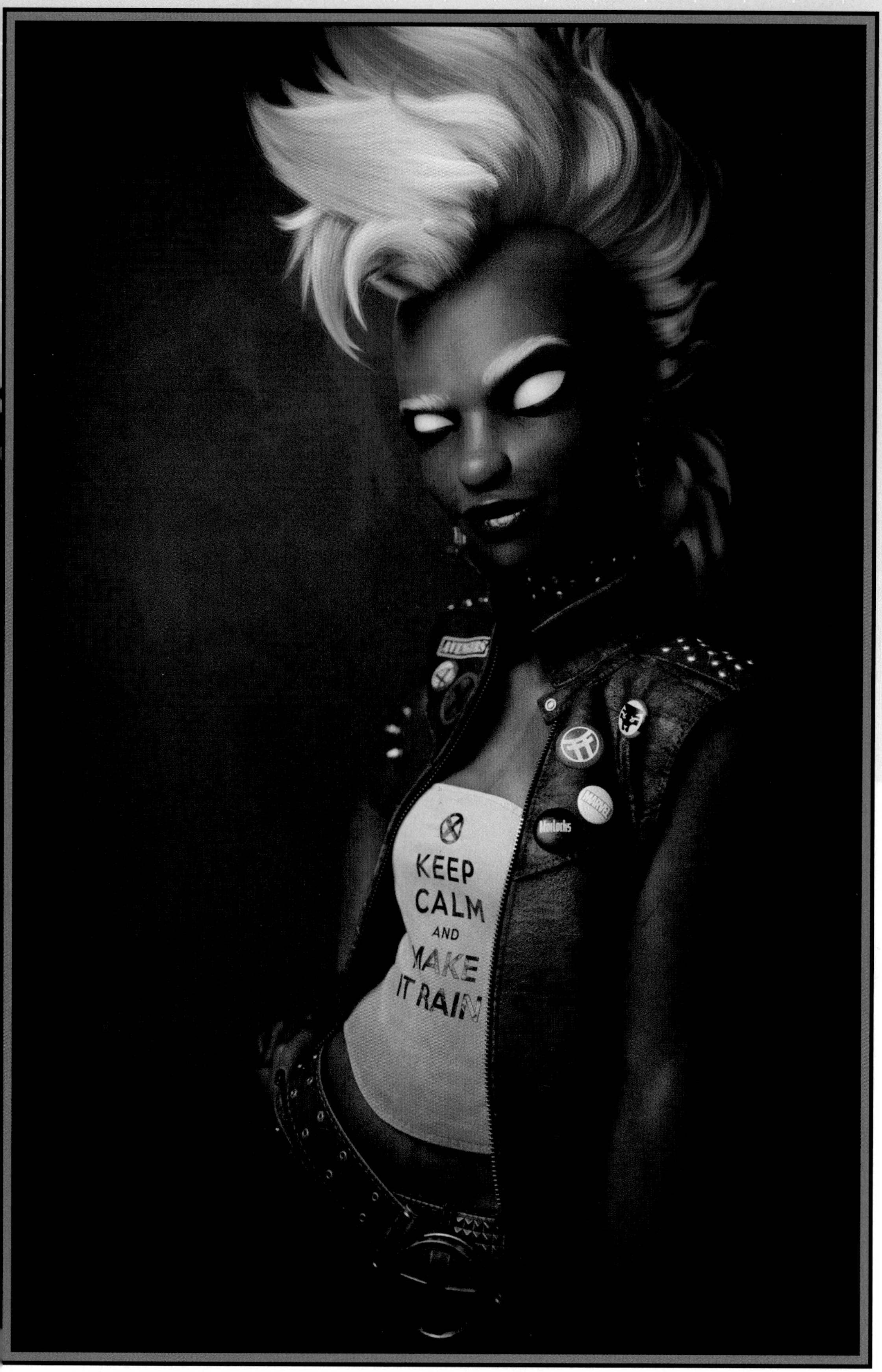
KEEP
CALM
AND
MAKE
IT RAIN

#1 VARIANT BY **VICTOR HUGO**

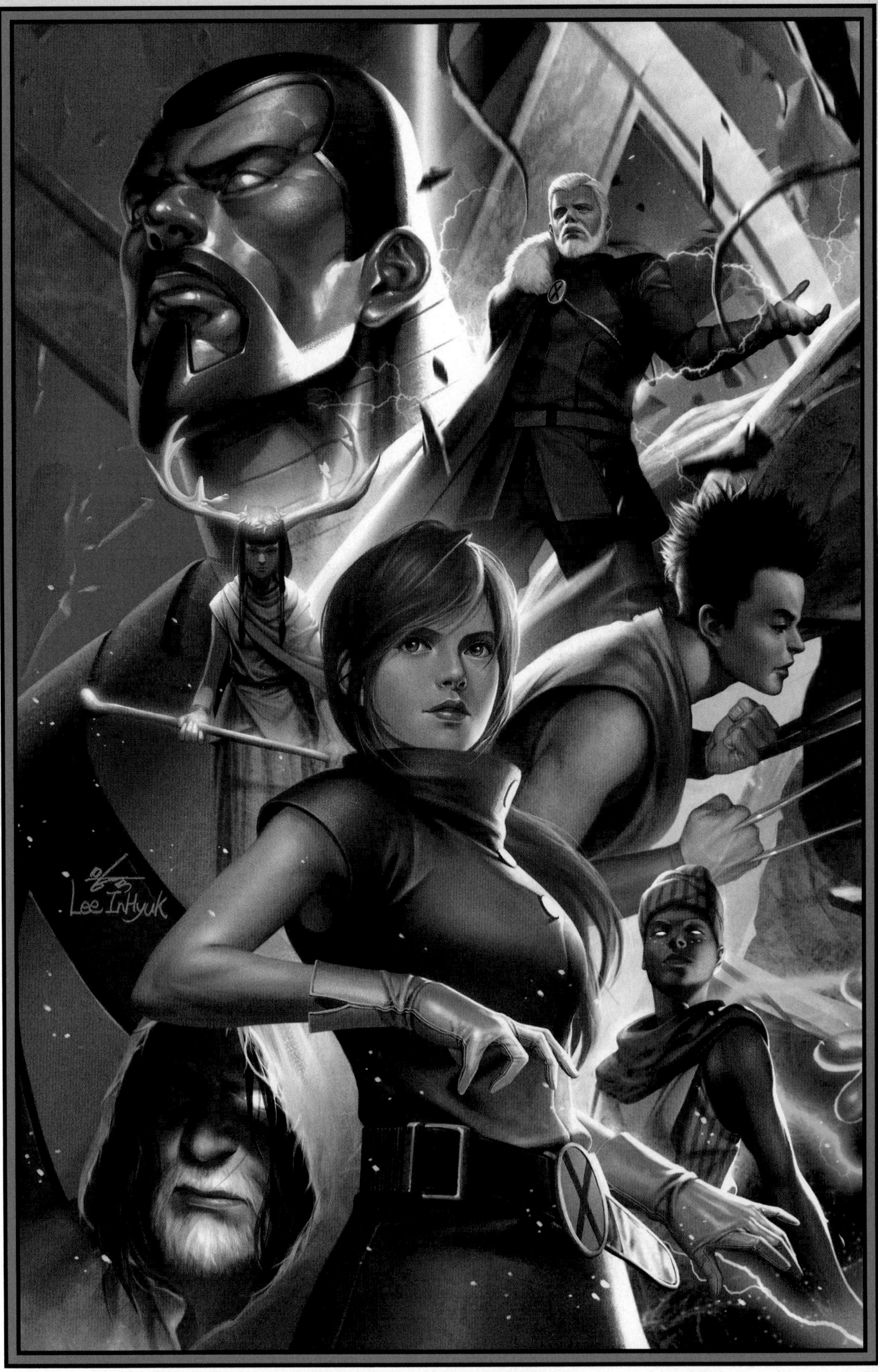
Lee InHyuk
#1 VARIANT BY **INHYUK LEE**

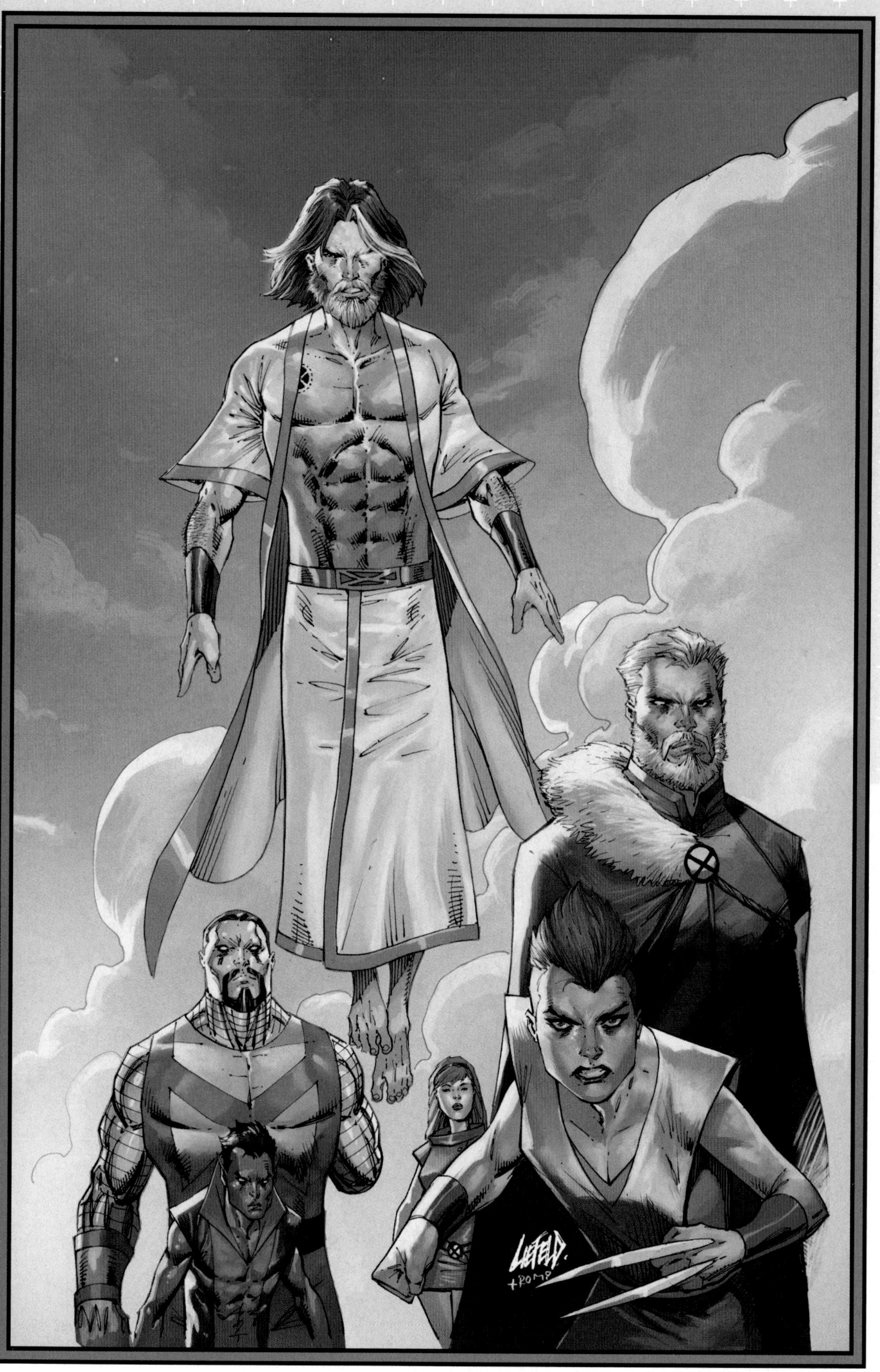

#1 VARIANT BY **ROB LIEFELD**

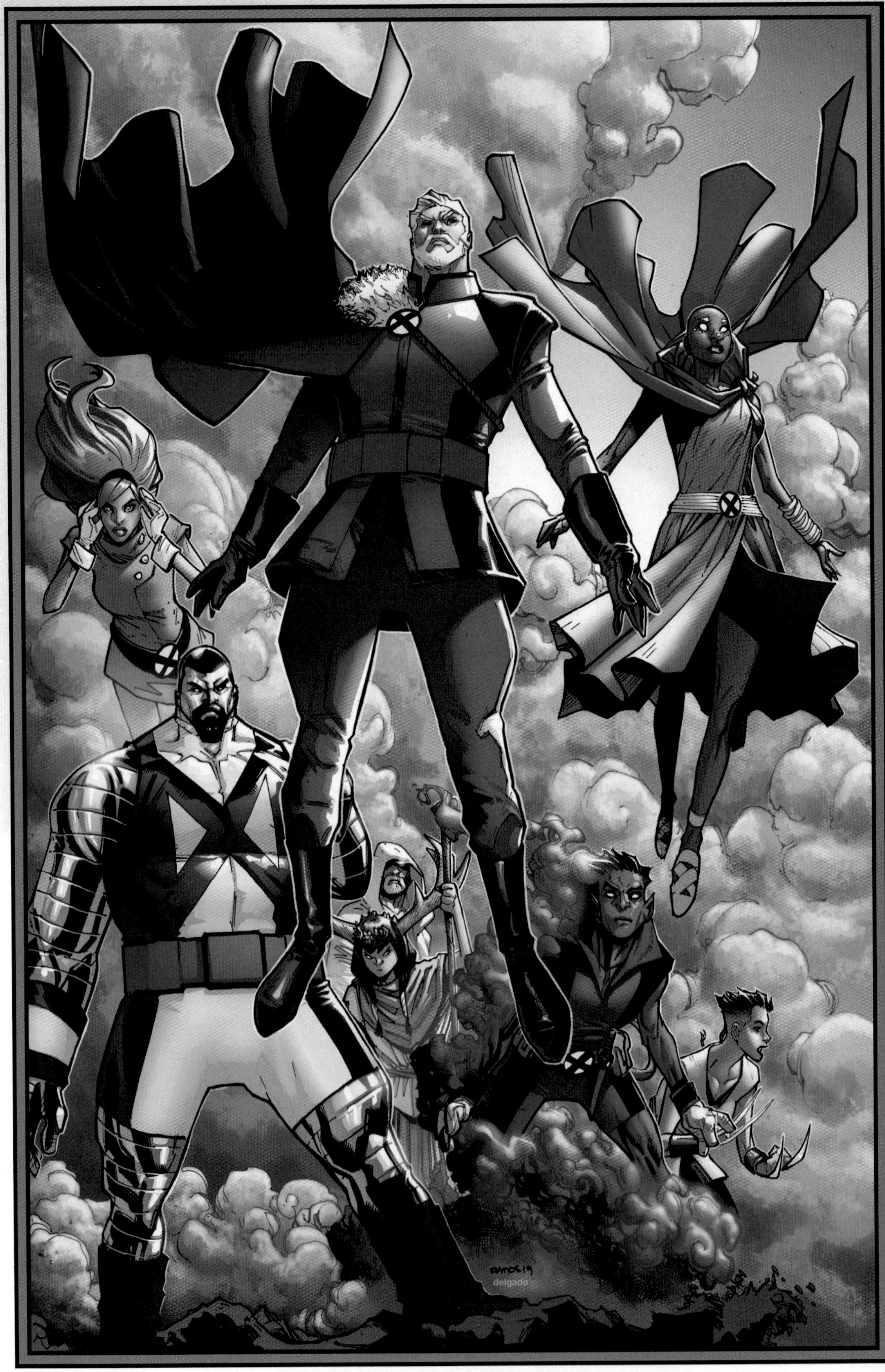

#2 VARIANT BY **HUMBERTO RAMOS** & **EDGAR DELGADO**

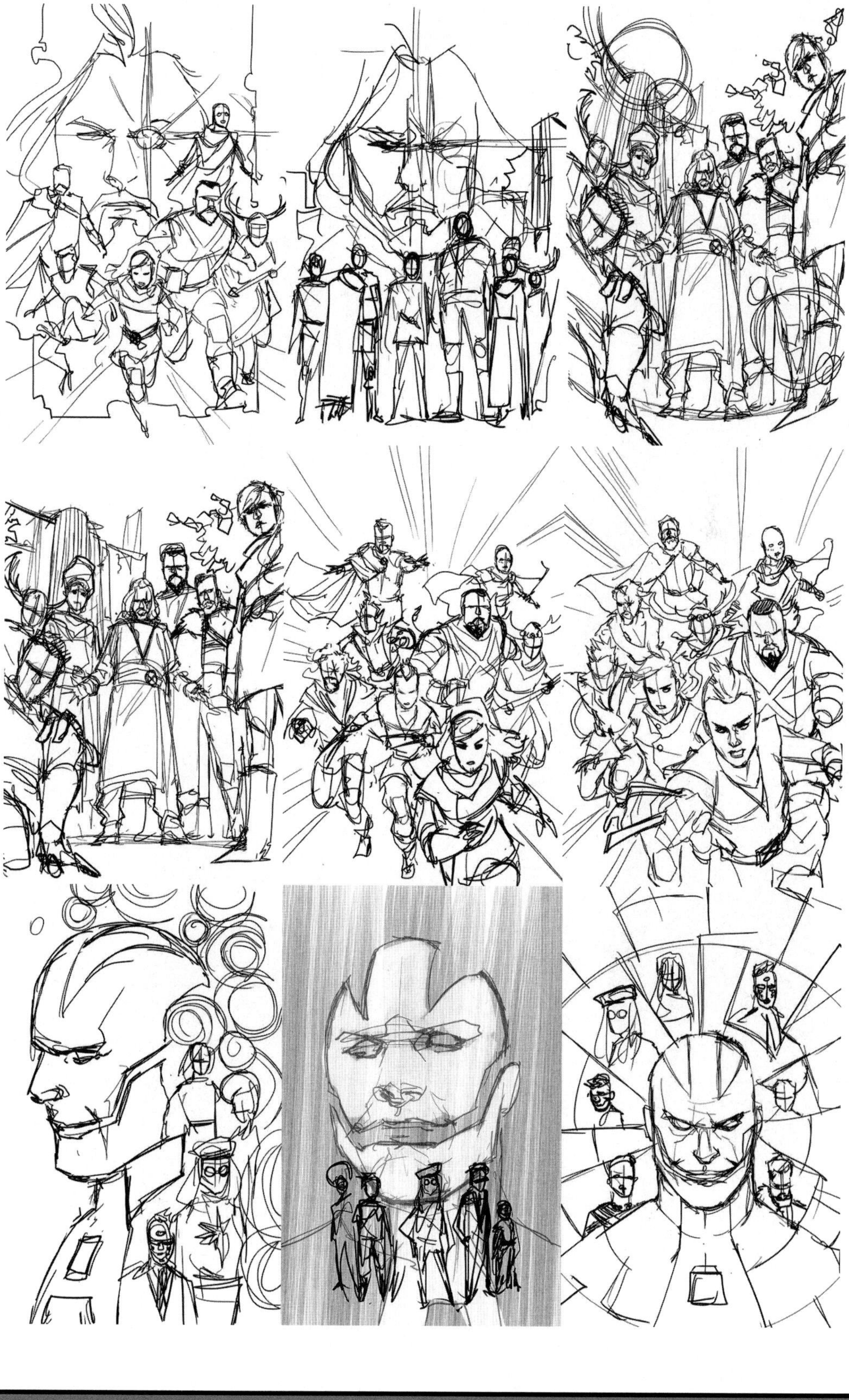

AGE OF X-MAN ALPHA #1 AND *THE MARVELOUS X-MEN #1-2* COVER SKETCHES BY **PHIL NOTO**

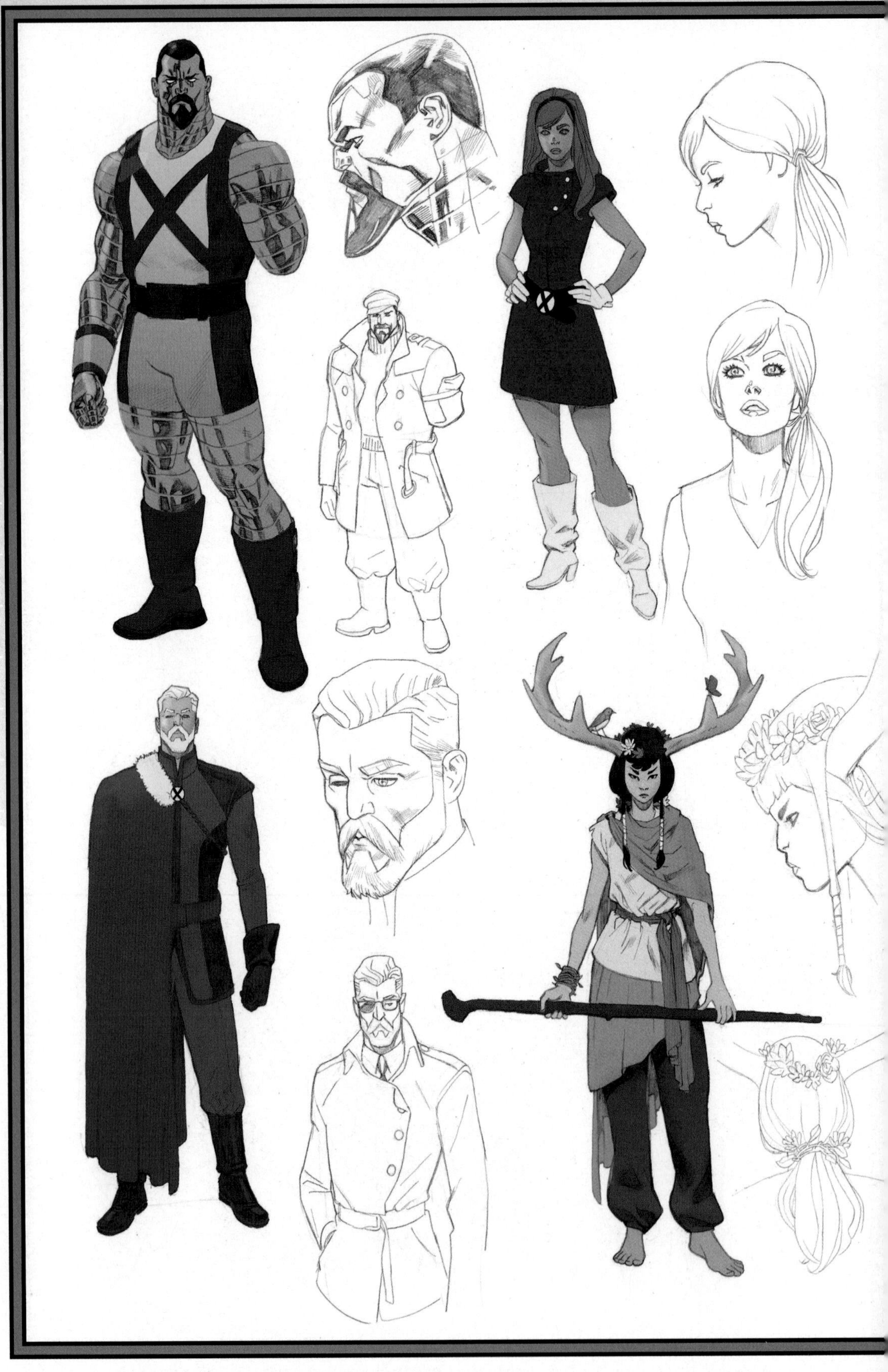

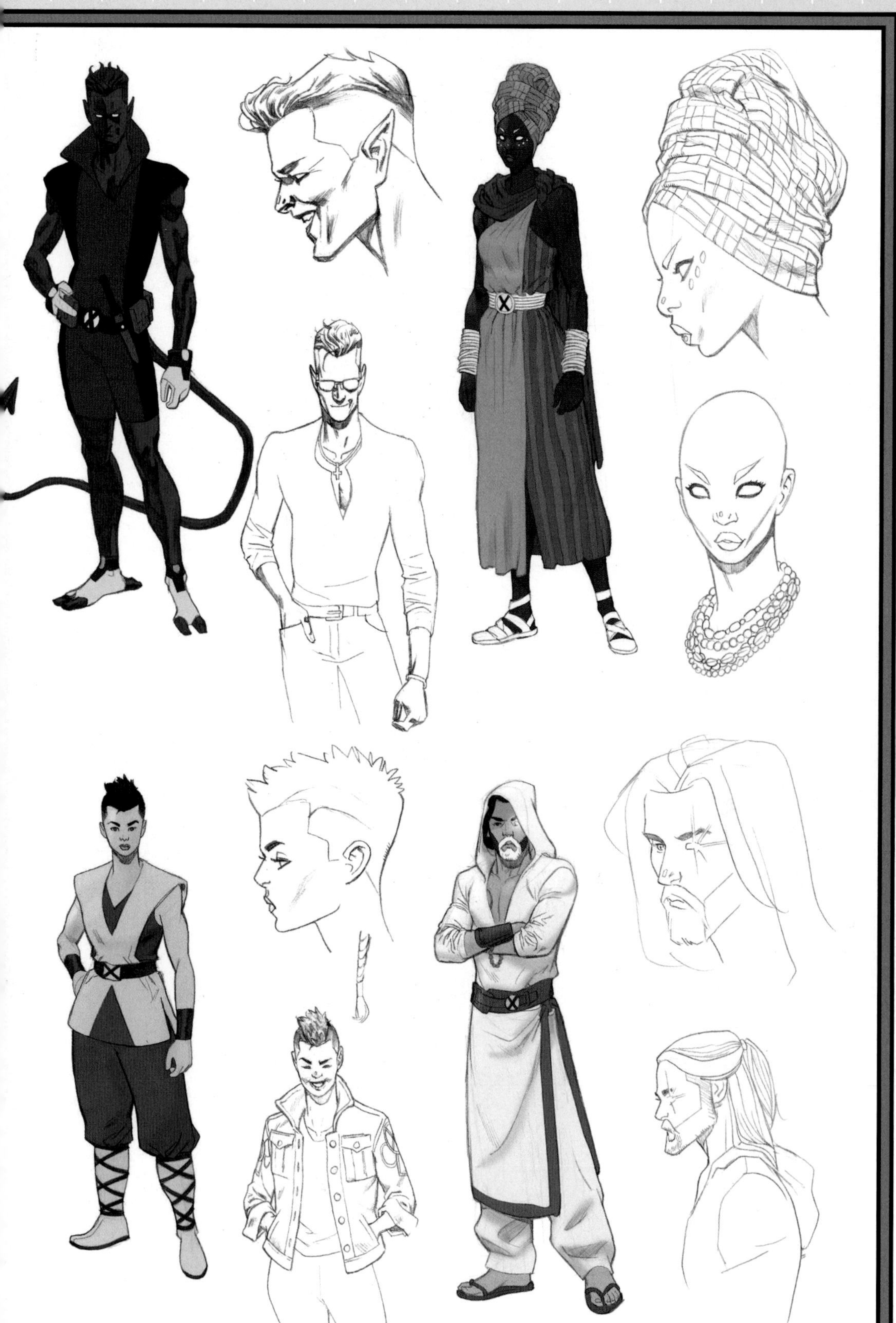

CHARACTER SKETCHES BY **MIKE HAWTHORNE**

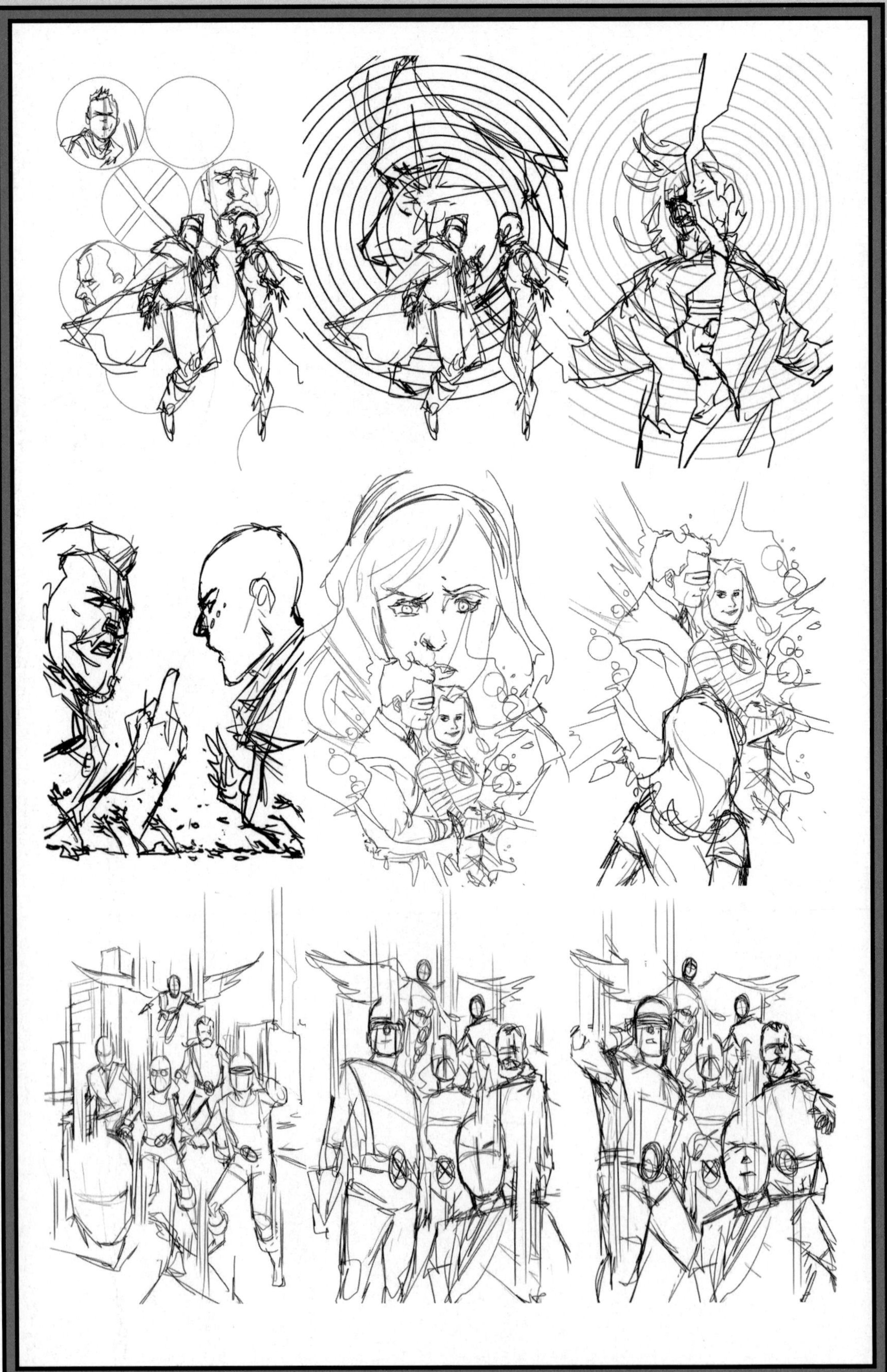

THE MARVELOUS X-MEN #3-5 COVER SKETCHES BY **PHIL NOTO**